C0-BSG-897

Windows 2000 Server: Planning and Migration

Sean Deuby

MACMILLAN
TECHNICAL
PUBLISHING
U·S·A

Windows 2000 Server: Planning and Migration

By Sean Deuby

Published by:
Macmillan Technical Publishing
201 West 103rd Street
Indianapolis, Indiana 46290 USA

FIRST EDITION

International Standard Book Number: 1-57870-023-x

Library of Congress Catalog Card Number: 97-81201

03 02 01 00 99   7 6 5 4 3 2 1

Interpretation of the printing code: The rightmost double-digit number is the year of the book's printing; the rightmost single-digit number is the number of the book's printing. For example, the printing code 99-1 shows that the first printing of the book occurred in 1999.

Composed in Quark and MCPdigital by Macmillan Computer Publishing

Printed in the United States of America

Trademark Acknowledgments

All terms mentioned in this book that are known to be trademarks or service marks have been appropriately capitalized. Macmillan Technical Publishing cannot attest to the accuracy of this information. Use of a term in this book should not be regarded as affecting the validity of any trademark or service mark.

Warning and Disclaimer

This book is designed to provide information about wide area networks. Every effort has been made to make this book as complete and as accurate as possible, but no warranty or fitness is implied.

The information is provided on an as-is basis. The authors and Macmillan Technical Publishing shall have neither liability nor responsibility to any person or entity with respect to any loss or damages arising from the information contained in this book or from the use of the disks or programs that may accompany it.

Feedback Information

At Macmillan Technical Publishing, our goal is to create in-depth technical books of the highest quality and value. Each book is crafted with care and precision, undergoing rigorous development that involves the unique expertise of members from the professional technical community.

Readers' feedback is a natural continuation of this process. If you have any comments regarding how we could improve the quality of this book or otherwise alter it to better suit your needs, you can contact us at networktech@mcp.com. Please make sure to include the book title and ISBN in your message.

We greatly appreciate your assistance.

Publisher
David Dwyer

Executive Editor
Linda Engelman

Managing Editor
Gina Brown

Acquisitions Editor
Karen Wachs

Development Editor
Kitty Wilson Jarrett

Copy Editor
Krista Hansing

Indexer
Cheryl Jackson

Acquisitions Coordinators
Jennifer Garrett
Amy Lewis

Manufacturing Coordinator
Brook Farling

Book Designer
Louisa Klucznik

Cover Designer
Aren Howell

Production Team Supervisor
Laurie Casey

Production
Wil Cruz
Amy Parker

Proofreader
Elise Walter

About the Author

Sean Deuby is a senior systems engineer with Intel Corporation, where he focuses on large-scale Windows 2000 and Windows NT Server issues. Before joining Intel, he was a technical lead in the Information Systems & Services NT Server Engineering Group of Texas Instruments (TI). In that role, he was a principal architect of TI's 17-country, 40,000-account enterprise Windows NT network. Sean has been a charter member of the Technical Review Board of *Windows NT Magazine*, has published several articles in the magazine, and is a contributing author to 21st Street Press's *Windows NT Administrator's Survival Guide*. He speaks on Windows NT Server and Windows 2000 topics at computer conferences around the world. His domain design white paper for TI, "MS Windows NT Server Domain Strategy," has been published monthly on the Microsoft TechNet CD since 1996. Sean has been a Microsoft Certified Systems Engineer since 1996 and a Certified Professional in Microsoft Windows NT Server and Windows NT Workstation since 1993. Away from the keyboard and monitor, he has practiced and taught Okinawan karate for 20 years and holds various degrees of black belts in three styles. He also has a patient wife and son.

About the Technical Reviewers

These reviewers contributed their considerable practical, hands-on expertise to the entire development process for *Windows 2000 Server: Planning and Migration*. As the book was being written, these folks reviewed all the material for technical content, organization, and flow. Their feedback was critical to ensuring that *Windows 2000 Server: Planning and Migration* fits our reader's need for the highest-quality technical information.

James Kelly is a Systems Engineer at Technology Partners International in Houston, Texas. TPI assists clients with the evaluation, negotiation, and management of outsourcing transactions. James received his B.A. in English in 1994 from the University of West Florida in Pensacola, Florida, and earned his B.S. in industrial engineering in 1996 from Florida State University in Tallahassee, Florida. He is currently a Microsoft Certified Systems Engineer and a Microsoft Certified Trainer.

Macmillan Technical Publishing would also like to offer our sincere thanks to Steven Hearn from Sydney, Australia, for his review of Systems Management issues.

Overview

Table of Contents

Dedication

To my wife, Sharon, for her patience during the long process of this book, and to my son, Connor. As a musician, Sharon likes to see her name on the program—so here you go, honey!

Acknowledgments

It isn't possible to write a book like this one in a vacuum. I'm used to working in a team environment, so receiving input from and bouncing ideas off a number of experienced Windows NT people has been invaluable. I'd like to thank my old group, the CSNT engineering team at Texas Instruments: Sam Blunk, David Ziemer, Keith Claiborne, Kal Mahesh, and Tim Lowrey. Mary Fleming Grant gave me insight into the problems that account operations must deal with. Rodney Brown gave me much practical information on server troubleshooting.

Steven Shultz provided invaluable insight on server hardware issues and futures. Terry Lemons lent his experience in enterprise storage management topics. My brother, Craig, an experienced IT professional in his own right, was a valuable sounding board for the clarity of my Windows 2000 descriptions. Mike Reed, Chris Jones, Steve Grobman, and John Dunlop helped me understand many of the complex issues surrounding domain architecture.

I've greatly valued my friends through *Windows NT Magazine*. Paula Sharick is a great confidant and good friend, and Mark Minasi has never hesitated (as is his manner) to recommend me to our colleagues. The magazine's staff has always been great to work with, both at its conferences and for my articles.

On the Macmillan side, Ann Trump Daniel as my original editor showed terrific patience (and good Japanese food) in the early phases of this project. Linda Engelman, Karen Wachs, and Jennifer Garrett carried it through to its conclusion.

And finally, I'd like to thank Scott Suhy. He not only taught me huge amounts about Windows NT, but he taught me how to look at the whole Windows NT enterprise in a logical, layered manner that has helped me analyze and dissect many problems and new technologies I'd otherwise be lost on. Without his mentoring (inadvertently or otherwise), this book wouldn't have been possible.

Introduction

One of my favorite cartoons of all time is a Dilbert cartoon strip named "Timeline," in which Dilbert's boss states that he has put together a timeline for his project, based on the assumption that anything he doesn't understand is easy to do. Therefore, he puts together a timeline for Dilbert to complete his project—designing a client/server architecture for their world-wide operations—in six minutes.

If you're looking at this book as a fellow Windows NT professional, you understand that there are times when we've all felt like Dilbert. Most people don't understand what's involved in a good Windows NT systems design—and frankly don't care. They care only when something breaks. This tends to give successful (that is, gainfully employed) Windows NT network designers a conservative outlook in their designs; if the Tacoma Narrows Bridge hadn't disintegrated and fallen into Puget Sound, we'd have never thought about the bridge engineers.

A good network design is usually invisible because most people don't work at that level. They're more concerned with their user account, password, and the availability of the document they spent three hours on yesterday. A few may even know what domain they log onto.

A flawed design, however, makes its presence known to everyone because the network can't handle what's asked of it and so the support costs sharply increase.

Remember this: The most expensive part of deploying and maintaining a Windows NT network isn't the hardware or software—*it's the support costs*. This book is about minimizing these costs as much as possible through implementing good network design, choosing the right server, and avoiding common support errors.

This book is written for you, the Windows NT professional, by a fellow professional that knows exactly what you go through in your job because I've been there myself. It's a result of my experience with planning and deploying Windows NT in large corporations since it was released in 1993, and working with Windows NT 5.0—uh, Windows 2000—since the first directory services previews in 1996. I make no claim of it being absolutely comprehensive; rather, I write what I know about and condense a *lot* of valuable tips, techniques, and learning about Windows 2000 and Windows NT 4 into these pages.

You should also be reading all the Windows 2000 documentation you can get your hands on to make better-informed decisions. Follow my example: When I last checked, I had more than 230MB of documents and presentations on Windows 2000 alone.

What This Book Is

This book is a guide to designing and deploying Windows 2000 networks. It contains this information:

- Clear explanations of Windows 2000 Advanced Server concepts.

- Windows 2000 design recommendations—what you should do, what you shouldn't do, and what you should start doing now to best position your existing Windows NT 4 network for Windows 2000.

- Hundreds of money-saving tips, based on experience designing and maintaining large Windows NT networks and extracted from discussions with Windows NT administrators around the world. Any one of this tips is worth the cost of this book.

- Recommendations for the support infrastructure needed for a Windows NT network of any version, and what it needs to keep the total cost of ownership down.

What This Book Isn't

This book isn't an encyclopedic volume on everything you ever wanted to know about Windows NT or about the physical aspects of network design—network topologies, routers, and TCP/IP subnet design. It won't tell you how to find Control Panel or where to change your virtual memory settings. It won't even give the Registry setting that will pop up a legal notice dialog on the console for every logon (though doing that remotely is a good trick to play on your friends that haven't tightened down their workstation security). It's designed to be relatively quick to read for the Windows NT professional who already has enough to do. It also takes a reasonably light tone; there are enough deadly serious technical books on the market. If you're looking for an all-encompassing work, I recommend that you also buy a larger "doorstop" reference work as a companion to this volume.

This book focuses on Windows NT Server and talks about the Windows NT client (either 4 Workstation or Windows 2000 Professional) only as it affects the server. The Windows NT client in a corporate environment deserves a book in itself, and indeed many are available.

This book also doesn't try to sell you on the advantages of a Windows 2000 network compared to other network operating systems. The Microsoft marking juggernauts have that job, and they've had *plenty* of time to prepare for it.

Who Should Read This Book

This book is for the following people:

- Anyone who is evaluating Windows 2000 and wondering how to get started. Part I contains clear explanations of Windows 2000 features and, more importantly, talks about whether they're important to you, the Windows NT professional focusing on Server.

- Anyone who's actively planning for Windows 2000. Part III discusses Windows 2000 design and migration and what you must do to prepare your network for this new version.

- The IT professional who's charged with increasing his or her company's Windows NT commitment. Part II discusses the various aspects of choosing, maintaining, and tuning a Windows NT server. Part IV discusses how to support a Windows NT network and talks about the places where the base product requires extra support consideration.

- Anyone who wants to learn how to performance-tune a Windows NT server. Chapter 5, "Building, Maintaining, and Tuning the Box," contains a thorough section on Windows NT performance.

- The IT manager who doesn't want to resemble Dilbert's pointy-haired boss. Even if you don't understand all of it, the book will look good on your bookshelf when you're interviewing employees, right?

Win2K, Y2K, and Microsoft

Windows 2000 is the most significant version since the product's initial release, and probably is its last significant version as well. The sweeping changes and updates to all aspects of the operating system bring it up-to-date with its competitors. Though it isn't possible to see into the future more than a few months in this business (remember the Web?), no gaping flaws in Windows NT's functionality are left that require revolutionary changes.

Windows 2000 is a big leap for Microsoft, however. It's by far the biggest project the company has ever undertaken, and Microsoft has stated publicly that it's "betting the company on it." With the Server version weighing in at a little under 30 million lines of code, this new release of

Windows NT contains more than 75% more code than Windows NT Server 4. That's a lot of code that hasn't been hardened by production use and inevitable Service Packs. It's not just more code, either; what's being added are extremely complicated subsystems such as Active Directory that other companies have taken several maintenance releases to get right. Microsoft's track record for reliability of new code is not stellar. Although they are taking steps such as wider distribution of betas, and a Rapid Deployment Program (RDP) and Joint Development Program (JDP) to get Windows 2000 into limited production at a few major companies as quickly as possible, it doesn't take a set of tarot cards to predict that the initial release will have its problems.

Compounding this problem is the timing of the released product. Windows 2000 has competition from an unusual front: the end of the century. The impact to Windows 2000, of course, is that any IT staff worth their paycheck will try to keep the current environment stable until all the effects of Y2K have settled down—and Windows 2000 in 1999 will not fall into the "stable" category.

Note

NT4 has a few Y2K bugs (date/time dialogs, for example), but maintenance beginning with Service Pack 4 and beyond makes it Year 2000–compliant. Windows NT 3.51, however, has no such fixes and will never be Year 2000–compliant. So if you're reading this and you have 3.51 systems in production, drop everything and upgrade to at least 4.0 Service Pack 4. ◆

Even at its release, Windows 2000 is far from a finished piece of work—it won't be until about the time when Service Pack 5 is released. However, though some of the inner workings are being adjusted by RDP/JDP customers feedback, the architecture, the concepts, and most of the details have been finalized.

Any computer technology today changes more quickly than a book, and Windows 2000 is no exception. Nevertheless, this product is so big and so different from its predecessor that it's important to understand as much as possible for your migration planning. Chapter 6, "Designing Your Windows 2000 Core Services"; Chapter 7, " Preparing a Windows NT 4 Network for Windows 2000"; and Chapter 8, "Migrating a Windows NT 4 Network to Windows 2000," explain many design, preparation, and migration principles, but equally as important I'll ask you questions to make you think about the issues you'll need to deal with. Right now there aren't any hard-and-fast, experienced answers for many design issues. The product is so new that experienced answers are very hard to come by—even if you're inside Microsoft. This is the truest sense of the EPA sticker on the side of every new car: "Your mileage may vary." Every company's situation is a little different, and unlike Windows NT 4, Windows 2000 is highly customizable to each situation.

No universal right or wrong answers exist in Windows 2000 design. You must use a combination of your product education, research into your company's needs, and awareness of the major Windows 2000 issues to arrive at an intelligent design for your enterprise.

What's in a Name?

The renaming of *Windows NT* to *Windows 2000* has made talking about the product a bit difficult. Here's the convention I'm following:

- Unless I specifically break out Windows NT 3.51, *Windows NT 4* includes both 4 and 3.51 versions of the operating system.

- Unless I specifically mention *Advanced Server* or *Datacenter Server*, you can assume that when I say *Windows 2000* (or perhaps *Windows 2000 Server*) that I'm talking about characteristics that are common across all three flavors of the server product.

- As you've already seen in this introduction, when I'm talking about the product as a whole (from its 3.1 Advanced Server roots to its current Windows 2000 incarnation), I just call it *Windows NT or NT*.

- Remember that *Windows 2000 Professional* is the (unhelpful; do they plan to release an amateur version as well?) name of the Windows 2000 client.

- I reserve the right to call the product *Windows NT 5.0* every once in a while, just because I'm annoyed at the new name. I think it's hilarious that the IT community (and Microsoft rank and file themselves), when faced with replacing the succinct *NT* moniker with the *Windows 2000* mouthful, came up with *Win2K* to informally name the product!

So Should You Upgrade to Windows 2000?

Since it was announced shortly after Windows NT 4, Windows 2000 has been so promised, so delayed, so praised, so vilified, so delayed, so expanded, so renamed... and so delayed that *everyone* in the business has an opinion about it, whether they truly understand it or not. Having spent a significant amount of time learning it, I'm quite convinced that the ratio of opinions to understanding is about 1,000:1.

The following table lists improvements in Windows 2000 over Windows NT 4:

Windows 2000	Windows NT 4
Directory Services	
Delegation of administrative rights	Domain-wide rights only
Directory trees	Two-level master/resource domains
OUs	—
Extensible Active Directory schema	Fixed schema
Centralized interesting object storage in Active Directory	Objects stored many places
LDAP-compatible for complex queries through ADSI	Win32 API to enumerate SAM contents; cannot be queried
DNS primary naming service	WINS primary naming service
Sites	—
Group Policy	System Policy Editor
Single account database in the Active Directory	Account database in every domain
Global catalog	—
Multiple master replication	Master–slave replication
IntelliMirror caching of user data	—
Windows Installer	—
Advanced System Recovery	Last-known good only
Improved automation	—
Management/administration:	—
MMC	Individual tools
Hardware	
Notebook-friendly	—
Plug and Play	—
1394 support	—
USB support	—
I_2O support	—
Improved SMP support	—
Very large memory support	4GT support in Enterprise Edition
Security	
Transitive trusts	Non-transitive trusts
NTLM trusts	NTLM trusts
Mutual authentication through Kerberos	One-way authentication through NTLM
Public Key Infrastructure	—

continues ▶

Windows 2000	Windows NT 4
NTLM authentication	NTLM authentication
Encrypting File System	—
Distributed File System	Distributed File System (no fault tolerance)
IPSec	—
Network	
Dynamic DNS	Static DNS
DHCP-DNS integration	—
Directory-enabled networks	—
Quality of Service	—
Storage	
Volume management	Disk Administrator
Hierarchical storage management	—
Disk defragmentation	Third-party
Quotas	Third-party
Media management	—
Removable storage management	Basic management built in
Reparse points	—
Integrated indexing service	—
NTFS support	NTFS support
FAT support	FAT support
FAT32 support	—
CDFS support	CDFS support
UDF support	—
Distributed link tracking	—
Sparse file support	—
Volume mount points	—
NTFS directory junctions	—

To be truly candid, you don't have to understand all of it to make intelligent basic choices on what to do with Windows 2000. You do, however, have to understand its main features at enough of a level that you can figure out if and how these features will benefit your company, and then explain them to the management that will fund this project.

Remember, the bottom line is that Windows 2000 is supposed to benefit your company; no one will go through the pain involved in a migration like this without significant benefit at the far end. Windows 2000 will eventually lower the total cost of ownership—but getting there won't be pretty. So back to the question: Should you upgrade? If you have an existing Microsoft network, it isn't so much a question of *if* you upgrade as *when* you upgrade. As with all previous versions, support for Windows NT 4 will eventually end—although it will be several years away.

First, no IT department in its right mind should consider deploying Windows 2000 before that magic millennium mark is reached. Questions of the operating system's reliability aside, there are too many things that could go wrong (in and out of your control) at the end of the century to be messing with your infrastructure.

To help define when you should consider deployment of Windows 2000, let's classify potential customers into several categories. (These time frames assume that Windows 2000 product research and planning begin in the company at least six to eight months before deployment):

- Bleeding edge—GA (general availability)+ 0 to GA+2 months, OR Base Product to Service Pack 1
- Early adopters—GA+2 months to GA+6 months, OR Service Pack 1 to Service Pack 2
- Mainstream—GA+6 months to GA+18 months, OR Service Pack 2 to Service Pack 4
- Conservative—GA+2 years OR Service Pack 4+

Bleeding edge users would be small to medium companies that must have the technology as an advantage over their competitors. Deploying Windows 2000 on a smaller network is less risky than on a larger one. IT product engineers should take the position of assuming nothing about the product's capabilities but what they've tested.

Early adopters may also want Windows 2000's competitive advantages, but they're unwilling to take the product straight out of the starting gate. They may also be the ones with a dire need for one or more new features to correct existing Windows NT 4 infrastructure problems.

Mainstream users have been evaluating the product for a while, watching the released product's reliability from the sidelines, and know what they want to do with it. Their infrastructure works pretty well right now, however, or at least it it's holding together well enough to allow them to wait until many of the bugs have been shaken out. Remember, the first truly stable maintenance level for Windows NT 4 was Service Pack 3.

Conservative users have a reliable infrastructure and reasonably high availability, and they need to keep it that way. Motivation for their migration is the development of migration knowledge from all the previous groups, the eventual stability of the product and its features, and the imminent end of support of Windows NT 4.

This will be a big project for your company, so start *now,* and keep in mind the following:

- Everything you know is wrong—well, almost. Just about everything in Windows 2000 is either changed completely or significantly upgraded.

- The administrative model for Windows 2000 can be very different from that in Windows NT 4. To make it work well and not impact your users, you must do a lot of up-front work with your organizations and processes.

- Experience tells me that I should be more pessimistic, but this is also a chance to look down the road and get your corporate petty infighting straightened out. Use delegated administration to get everyone satisfied. Think of it as streamlining the 8th OSI layer—politics—as well as layers 5 through 7.

- Windows 2000 will have a major impact on the enterprise's DNS architecture. Your DNS team must learn about Windows 2000 to understand all its ramifications. Otherwise, you (the Microsoft bigot to them) must teach them (the UNIX stalwarts). Big fun, eh? And this is a critical path item; you can't get very far on your domain design before bottoming out on the DNS design.

- You need to think about domain restructuring. Should you do it before, during, or after migration? Or should you do it at all? Each has its advantages.

- Windows 2000 will impose big hardware requirements on your existing domain controllers, and that's something you must forecast for.

- And, of course, you have a host of new features to decide upon and architect.

Stephen Covey says the most productive type of work we get done is in Quadrant III, which is work that is important but not urgent. Windows 2000 topics are just this—but because there's so much work to do, they're becoming more urgent by the day. Buying this book is a good start, but I don't pretend to have all the answers. It'll be quite a while before anyone does, including Microsoft. Windows 2000 is so highly configurable, you must take your learnings and apply them yourself to your company's situation. Now get to work!

Part I

Windows 2000: NT Meets the Enterprise

Base Services in Windows 2000

The best way to describe all the major and minor changes incorporated in Windows 2000 is to divide this huge product into the general categories Microsoft itself uses: base services, storage services, and distributed services. The changes made to Windows NT's base services—its hardware support and scalability—are a good warm-up for the many differences between Windows NT 4 and Windows 2000.

Windows 2000's hardware support has grown considerably from its predecessor. The new release is consciously embracing the latest technology from hardware manufacturers like Intel in a twofold effort. The first, described in the section "Hardware Support," is an attempt to grow the Windows 2000 client into areas dominated by Windows 9x because of its broad hardware support. The second drive, described in the section "Scalability," is to climb into the enterprise mission-critical application arena that has eluded it so far because Windows NT hasn't scaled well to the size these applications require.

The renaming of Windows NT to Windows 2000 has made talking about the product a bit difficult. Just remember that Windows 2000 is still Windows NT, no matter what they rename it to. If it looks like a duck....

Hardware Support

Windows 2000 has greatly improved hardware support; in particular, it is more compatible with Windows 9x than is Windows NT 4. In fact, Windows 2000 and Windows 98 are both supposed to support the same hardware. This is a nice feature, but it really doesn't affect the server market as much as it does the workstation market. This is because Windows 98 is targeted to a fundamentally different audience than the Windows NT server crowd. As a result, only a few of the new features, including Hot Plug and Play and the Windows Driver Model, really affect the Windows NT system architect or administrator. The following sections describe the most important hardware support enhancements in Windows 2000.

(Hot) Plug and Play

The more peripherals you add to a server, the more difficult the server is to configure because you must avoid resource conflicts. Plug and Play, a specification developed by Microsoft in cooperation with Intel and many other manufacturers, was created to solve the problem of configuring the myriad of different add-in cards on the market. Better known as "Plug 'n Pray" for the first year after its introduction, the technology has matured, and a large percentage of peripherals are now Plug and Play-compatible.

Plug and Play in Windows 2000 will have its biggest server impact as part of the Hot Plug PCI feature to increase availability. You can add and remove Hot Plug PCI components from a "live" server without crashing the server or requiring a reboot.

Microsoft's Plug and Play Web site is `http://www.microsoft.com/hwdev/plugnplay/default.htm`.

Power Management

Power management isn't a big concern for servers. About the only power management concern you have is that the box keeps getting power no matter what, not that it saves a few watts when a device isn't being used. A server's first priority is being available to service its users; its second is to service them as fast as possible. Easing up on the utility bill is pretty far down the list. That said, the new power management specification, combined with the OnNow specification (which is described later in this chapter), has far-reaching consequences and is worth knowing about.

Advanced power management (APM), the original power management specification, has run out of steam in today's systems. Whenever you look at an old specification, it's important to remember the time in which it was created. When APM was finalized, the Intel x386 and x486 and compatibles were standard on notebooks. There was never more than one processor available, and notebook add-in boards such as sound cards and multimedia cards were still on the horizon. The limits of the specification have now been reached, though, and manufacturers have come up with creative ways to achieve greater power management. Unfortunately, this comes at a cost: Each solution is becoming less standardized and more proprietary. This is where Advanced Configuration and Power Interface (ACPI) comes in.

ACPI is the next generation of PC power management. It's an open industry specification co-developed by Intel, Microsoft, and Toshiba. Essentially, ACPI integrates power management and device configuration into the operating system instead of the system's BIOS. This offers a number of advantages and at least one significant disadvantage.

The first advantage is that finally Windows NT will recognize a power management scheme, opening the system up to the mobile user market. Lack of power management has been the biggest factor keeping the Windows NT operating system out of notebooks, closely followed by its tougher hardware requirements. It's important to note that ACPI isn't only for Windows NT; it's designed to be OS-independent. Device drivers are being developed for a number of popular operating systems, the most prominent being Windows 98, Windows 2000, and UNIX.

The second advantage is that power management can finally be standard-ized across the whole industry. Because the current standard, the APM specification, is in the BIOS, each BIOS manufacturer has a slightly different approach. As a result, what works with one manufacturer might not work with another.

Unlike APM, ACPI can manage add-in cards and motherboard devices. For example, if an internal modem on a notebook isn't being used, ACPI will power off the modem. Network cards can be power managed as well because ACPI has the capability to turn on a device or the PC remotely.

ACPI supports a hibernate mode in which the system state is stored to disk for a deeper power savings than the existing APM suspend mode offers. The OS also can have Power and Sleep buttons that enable system power-off and sleep modes right from the operating system's user interface.

With ACPI, OnNow, and IEEE 1394 (also known as "Firewire"— described later in the chapter), you'll eventually be able to do nifty home automation gymnastics such as using your PC to control your home theater system. The PC will sleep until you put a DVD in your DVD player; then it will wake up, turn on your television and A/V receiver, and set the appro-priate home theater settings. (As long as we're dreaming up this scenario, we can say that if you insert an audio CD into the same player, it'll only turn on the A/V receiver and choose a different setting. As you can see, unfortunately, this will require upgrading all your A/V components to 1394-aware pieces—which don't yet exist.)

Because ACPI is integrated into the Windows NT operating system, policies could be set up that dictate power management for different classes of desktops. These policies could be set and stored in the Active Directory.

Warning

The most significant disadvantage of ACPI is compatibility, or lack thereof. Support for the ACPI specification must be built into the BIOS and chipset of the PC, so the multitude of notebooks and PCs already on the market can't use it. Corporations that are waiting to deploy Windows 2000 Professional (i.e., the workstation client) on their notebooks for its power management capabilities should be aware that their entire existing inventory can't use it. However, the BIOS-level utilities currently in use on today's non–ACPI-compliant systems will continue to provide the same limited functionality on Windows 2000 as they do on Windows NT 4. This is because ACPI operates closer to the hardware than the operating system does. In addition, because Windows 2000 has been delayed so much, ACPI compliance has become a standard notebook feature. ◆

OnNow

OnNow is Microsoft's design initiative to comprehensively handle system and device power management. It's based on the ACPI hardware specification, but it goes beyond that to encompass the operating system, I/O specifications such as Universal Serial Bus, IEEE 1394 (that is, Firewire), and the PCI bus. The overall goal is to control system power intelligently and in a manner that's deeply integrated into the hardware and software. The user of an OnNow-enabled system simply must push a GUI button to shut down the system, or must move the mouse to bring it instantly back on. This feature will be of limited use in the enterprise server environment where power savings falls significantly behind throughput and reliability in terms of priority. However, in small offices and home environments, OnNow opens up a whole new class of uses for the PC or server.

The OnNow PC or server doesn't just respond to user commands. It also responds to interrupts generated by peripherals such as network cards, modems, and fax boards. For example, a fax, phone call, or network request coming into a small office or home can wake up a hibernating OnNow-compliant server that's used to monitoring its systems. The server will wake up, handle the request, and then go back to sleep again. Speaking as someone who has several computers up and running most of the day (what a nerd, eh?), I look forward to OnNow systems just to silence the constant background fan noise.

OnNow has three main states: working, sleeping, and off. The working state is a full-on condition with power conservation dictated by the system policy. Is it a notebook? Then power management will be dynamically balanced with computing demands. Is it a desktop? Then perhaps only the monitor will go inactive and the hard drives will spin down after a short inactivity period. Is it a server? The monitor and remote monitoring dialup card will become inactive while all other systems remain at full power. The working state corresponds to ACPI state 0.

A home system will likely spend most of its time in the sleeping state. Sort of an "undead" state, the sleeping state causes the system to appear to be off—the processor is stopped and the peripheral devices are off. If some kind of interrupt comes in, however—whether it's from an important incoming fax or your 4-year-old whacking the keyboard—the system immediately wakes up and responds to the interrupt. Only the subsystems that are needed to service the interrupt will be turned on; for example, the video subsystem won't be turned on to receive a fax. The server can also wake up in a timed manner, say, to begin system backups. Servers in 24x7 shops will never be in the sleeping state; the sleeping state corresponds to ACPI states 1 to 4, depending on how you've set the system power management policy.

The off state is close to but not quite the same as an off system before ACPI. The operating system is shut down and the system power is off. Most devices will have to be reinitialized, but some will retain knowledge of their state.

To get to this utopian situation, however, a lot has to happen. The system must comply with the ACPI specification, the devices must comply with new Bus and Class Power specifications, the operating system must follow the OnNow initiative, and the applications must be OnNow-compliant. Unfortunately, there's still a little work to be done before we see true OnNow systems.

Win32 Driver Model (WDM)

Printers, scanners, video, disks, tape drives—every hardware component needs a device driver to communicate with the Windows NT operating system. Now take this requirement and add to it the need of updating a driver whenever the device (or Windows NT itself) is upgraded or when bugs are fixed in the released driver. The independent hardware vendor is tied up in a never-ending cycle of writing and fixing its drivers from the ground up, and the end user must have the skills of a professional change manager to keep track of and stay updated on everyone's driver sets.

Microsoft created the Win32 Driver Model (WDM) to make the job of writing device drivers for Windows 98 and Windows 2000 a simpler task. It's also supposed to make it easier for the end user to keep drivers up to date. The model is common to both these operating systems, so the independent hardware vendor supposedly has to write only one WDM-compliant driver for both.

Well, maybe that's not so simple. Microsoft has recently indicated that users will have to recompile Windows 98 drivers before they will work under Windows 2000. How many users do you know that have the capability of compiling device drivers? This will most likely mean that you or your users will have to download new Windows 2000 device drivers from the vendor.

WDM has three layers, the first two of which are provided by Microsoft:

- WDM core services—These services are a subset of Windows NT kernel services, new Plug and Play services, and power management services. The WDM core services are documented in a Windows 2000 device driver kit (`http://www.microsoft.com/hwdev/onnow.htm`).

- Class driver—The class driver provides support for a generic type of device, such as a USB device or a DVD. This driver has a standard set of interfaces; for example, all DVD devices require the same type of input, output, and control interfaces. The standard device classes that will be supported in Windows 2000 include USB, the 1394 driver stack, digital audio; human interface devices such as keyboards, mice, joysticks, and gamepads; imaging (still image and video capture); and DVD decoder support. Key support for many devices relies on the WDM Streaming class driver, which optimizes data flow in the operating system kernel. The streaming class driver is essential for high-speed media and is used for audio devices, video devices, and decoders for DVD movies.

- Minidriver—The minidriver is the part that the independent hardware vendor must write. The minidriver can be very small, and its purpose is to extend the generic characteristics of the class driver to the specific requirements of a particular piece of hardware. For example, a new digital camera on the market comes with a nifty feature—say, a button that immediately saves the picture to the computer. The camera manufacturer would write a new minidriver that maps that feature into the generic imaging class driver, and voila—it's in place.

For Windows NT Server users, the WDM coupled with Plug and Play will make life a little bit easier for Windows NT system administrators installing new hardware on their systems.

If you've ever had a burning desire to learn more about or write device drivers, you can find more information on WDM at `http://www.microsoft.com/hwdev/desinit/WDMview.htm`. Another title to consider is *Windows NT Device Driver Development*, by Viscarola and Mason (Macmillan Technical Publishing, 1999).

Accelerated Graphics Port (AGP)

Windows 2000 Server and Professional will support Accelerated Graphics Port (AGP) technology. AGP is the solution to a bandwidth problem on the motherboard caused by the dramatic increase in 3D graphics. Not long ago, only computer-aided design (CAD) professionals needed to quickly and accurately render 3D texture maps. Now 3D is very big in the consumer market thanks to extremely popular first-person "you are there" games such as *Quake II* and *Duke Nukem*.

The problem is that texture maps use a lot of memory, up to 20MB for a single map. This is built up in main memory and then must be output to the video adapter for display. Graphics controller cards, however, have relatively limited onboard memory, so a display of large maps takes a while as the controller memory is loaded, displayed, reloaded, and so on. More importantly, this large amount of data causes congestion on the PCI bus, which affects the rest of the I/O system.

AGP sidesteps this problem by providing its own high-speed bus between main memory and the graphics controller. This bus, capable of speeds up to 533MBps peak as compared to PCI's peak speed of 132MBps, can supply frames to the graphics controller up to 12.5 frames per second faster than the local video memory solution.

> ### Note
>
> *Note that this book uses the a MBps for megabytes per second and the abbreviation Mbps for megabits per second.* ◆

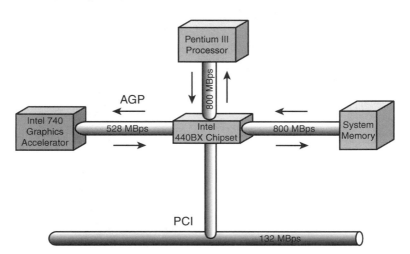

Figure 1.1 *Accelerated Graphics Port structure*

Even though AGP will have a significant effect on PCs and workstations, it will have little or no effect on servers because the console is used only for basic administration needs. Indeed, most servers ship with only rudimentary graphics adapters—the kind that were popular about five years ago.

Universal Serial Bus (USB)

As with Plug and Play, the Universal Serial Bus (USB) specification was developed to make connecting peripherals to a computer as painless as possible. In fact, USB is part of the Plug and Play specification and requires Plug and Play to work. Though it has limited application in the server world where devices are all SCSI or Fibre Channel, USB represents a huge leap beyond serial and parallel I/O ports. Some of USB's features are listed here:

- USB is faster than legacy I/O ports, with data rates of 12Mbps or 1.5Mbps for low-speed devices such as game controllers.

- The physical connector is the same for all USB-compatible devices. That means no more PS/2, 9-pin serial, 24-pin serial, Centronics parallel, and so on.

- USB devices can be smaller and simpler because they don't require their own power supply. Power is supplied through the USB cable. For larger peripherals such as printers, or when so many devices are on the USB that auxiliary power will be required, most peripherals will come with the capability of having auxiliary power supplies added.

- USB has "hot" insertion and removal devices. For example, I keep a small USB scanner disconnected in a drawer. When I need to scan a photo, I just pull it out and plug it into an unused USB port on my Windows 2000 system. Plug and Play in Windows 2000 Professional (or Windows 95 OSR2, Windows 98, or Windows 2000 Server) recognizes and loads the scanner's driver, and I can immediately scan without rebooting. When I'm done, I simply unplug the scanner and put it away. (It's worth noting though, that just like devices today, many of these drivers won't be on the operating system's distributed media. This means that you'll have to run the setup program that comes with each peripheral to load its USB driver.)

While normally only one peripheral can be connected to a standard I/O port (or a few more with special switches or sharing devices), USB devices are connected in a tiered star topology much like that of Ethernet. A USB hub can be connected to the computer, and other USB devices (up to 127, including other hubs) are plugged into the hub. Thus, there's only one USB cable attached to the computer instead of a tangle of serial and parallel cables. These USB hubs don't have to be separate devices; in fact, most hubs will be incorporated into USB peripherals such as monitors or keyboards.

Intel's Universal Serial Bus Web site is at http://developer.intel.com/design/usb/.

IEEE 1394

IEEE 1394 is the decidedly unsexy name for a high-speed serial bus standard that was developed to support demanding peripherals that require a large amount of I/O bandwidth. (I personally prefer its "Firewire" moniker; if you're in Dallas, it's pronounced "Fahrwahr." IEEE 1394 was co-developed by Texas Instruments and Apple.) The legacy serial/parallel port architecture used in PCs is unfriendly and inadequate to the job; the 1394 standard corrects all these problems and more.

To explain what 1394 can do, let's compare it with USB. Why have both 1394 and USB? It's important to understand that USB and 1394 are complimentary technologies for slightly different applications. Though they have a lot in common (most notably, they both support hot-plugging devices onto and off of their buses), they shine in different areas.

1394 is a high-performance serial bus. P1394a supports speeds from 100 to 400Mbps, and the second version, 1394b, will eventually support up to 3200Mbps. (For comparison, the PCI bus speed of 133MBps is equal to 1064Mbps.) USB offers speeds ranging from 1Mbps to 12Mbps.

1394 is designed for bandwidth-hungry devices such as DVD players, mass storage devices, and digital video cameras. USB, on the other hand, is best suited for low- and medium-bandwidth devices such as keyboards, joysticks, scanners, mice, and digital still cameras.

The 1394 standard is also isochronous, which means that it delivers data at a guaranteed rate. This is mandatory for applications such as video. If you can't guarantee the rate, the video will become jerky or will drop out.

1394 and USB have different topologies. 1394 has a tree topology, supports up to a maximum of 64 devices, and is peer-to-peer between the devices. This means, for instance, that the server doesn't need to get in the way when two 1394 disk storage arrays must mirror data. USB supports up to 128 devices and is a tiered star topology with the server or PC acting as the host. If the host is down, the devices are dead.

1394 is being designed into consumer electronics as a standard interface to personal computers. Finally, a standardized, high-speed interface will exist to integrate PCs with A/V systems, camcorders, VCRs, DVD players, HDTV, and home automation systems.

As a final note, 1394 is much more expensive than USB. USB adds only about $1 to a peripheral's cost in OEM quantities, but 1394 costs about $15. Because of the impact this has on the computer manufacturer's already thin hardware profit margins, Intel doesn't plan to support 1394 until the end of 1999. Because Intel manufactures the majority of PC chipsets, widespread adoption will be unlikely before then.

Though faster than USB, 1394 will still find its greatest use in the PC rather than the server. SCSI in all its incarnations still rules supreme as the server I/O architecture of choice, but Fibre Channel is beginning to dominate on higher-end servers for several manufacturers.

Scalability

As Microsoft continues to push Windows NT deeper into the enterprise, it must improve this system's scalability. *Scalability* is a term often bandied about but rarely defined. My definition of scalability is the capability to grow a Windows NT platform to support very large applications, large databases, and high throughput rates without being held back by operating system limitations. UNIX is the king of scalability, and Windows NT has some catching up to do. In all fairness though, Windows NT is a relatively young operating system (born in August 1993, a few months before my son—and he's scaling quite well) and has grown terrifically—some would say bloated—since then.

Scalability for an operating system breaks up (I hate to use the term "breaks down" when talking about servers) into the four areas you examine when looking at an operating system's performance: memory, processor, the I/O subsystem, and network I/O. Windows 2000 specifically has enhancements to the first three.

Very Large Memory (VLM) Support

One of Windows 2000's features, available only in the Advanced Server version, is Very Large Memory (VLM) support. *Very Large Memory* is too succinct and clear a term, so of course it has been renamed to the more vague and buzzword-intensive *Enterprise Memory Architecture* (EMA).

Remember that Windows NT is currently a 32-bit operating system and remains so in Windows 2000. A 64-bit Windows NT is being released "at a later date," so you know where to put *that* in your calendar. Before Windows 2000, the operating system could address memory up to 4GB, 2GB of which is reserved for the operating system. ("4 Gigabyte Memory Tuning" in Windows NT 4 Enterprise Edition sacrificed 1GB normally reserved for the operating system kernel and gave it to applications, increasing usable memory from 2GB to 3GB.) EMA will raise the upper bar on memory from 4GB to 64GB, depending on the implementation and the supporting chipsets used.

One of the biggest benefits of EMA is that it can load very large multigigabyte databases such as SAP, Oracle, and SQL Server into memory to minimize paging out to disk. Because memory I/O is approximately 100 times faster than disk I/O, this makes a huge difference in performance. (See Chapter 5, "Building, Maintaining, and Tuning the Box," for more details on demand-paged virtual memory operating systems.) Alpha's 64-bit architecture is already being used with VLM UNIX operating systems and will support the Windows 2000 EMA model. Intel Page Size Extension 36-bit microprocessors (PSE36)—including the Intel Pentium II Xeon using the Intel 450NX chipset—will also support this model.

Symmetric Multiprocessing (SMP) Optimizations

From its inception, Windows NT has included SMP (symmetric multiprocessing) support. Though you could buy Windows NT out of the box with four-processor support, historically it has never really taken best advantage of more than two processors. You'd still get performance improvement with up to four processors (and customized HALs from OEMs for more than that), but the "bang per processor" curve tapered off noticeably after two and dramatically after four.

Windows NT Server 4, Enterprise Edition, increased the out-of-box support from four to eight processors. It's an open question whether anything but the support level changed in that flavor, but things get better in the new release. Windows 2000 Advanced Server supports the same processor maximum of eight, but kernel optimizations have been made that supposedly make the performance improvements beyond two and four more linear.

I_2O Support

One justifiable criticism mainframe fans have about Intel-based server architecture is that its I/O design has been primitive compared to their favorite piece of Big Iron. Mainframe designers have long realized that to maximize the movement of data through a computer, you must keep the very slow tedium of I/O away from the central processor so that it can do its job much more quickly. In a nutshell, Intelligent Input/Output (I_2O) is the evolution of PC architecture to mainframe I/O processing standards.

Big Iron is mainframers' term for their computer systems. ◆

Remember that I/O processing is a very slow business compared to micro-processor speeds. The average access time for a fast modern hard drive is 8–10 milliseconds. A single clock cycle in a 450MHz microprocessor, which may contain several instructions, takes only 1/450,000,000 seconds, or about 2 nanoseconds. Now imagine living in the speed of a microprocessor. You're merrily running along, adding and subtracting, and then you realize that you have to ask for some data on a hard drive. If you think of one clock cycle as 1 second, it would be 42 days before you received the data from the hard drive. Until I_2O came along, the processor was intimately involved in processing I/O requests, which took it away from its more important duty of serving up networked Quake II death matches.

Remember that one of the basic tenets of performance tuning is that there's always a bottleneck somewhere; it just moves around the system as each subsystem's performance improves. As the server platform has improved, the bottleneck has moved from the microprocessor to the network interface, and now to the I/O subsystem. The PCI bus, with its high bandwidth and sophisticated features, was widely adopted in late 1993 and provided the foundation to remove the I/O bottleneck.

I_2O takes the work involved in I/O processing away from the micro-processor and gives it to a special input/output processor (IOP—the Intel i960 family) on the motherboard. This IOP has a small, very fast real-time operating system that's specifically designed to process I_2O transactions. That's only part of the story, however. For I_2O to work, everything in the I/O path must be I_2O-compliant—motherboard, operating system, and peripheral hardware and software.

For Windows 2000 to understand I_2O, it must have an *operating system module* (OSM—everything in this business must be made into an acronym) that interfaces with the I_2O communications layer. In other words, instead of telling various peripherals what to do directly with a customized driver for each, the operating system communicates with an I_2O interface. The interface then reformats and passes the information on to the I_2O-compliant peripherals. The OSM is unique for each operating system.

The peripherals don't communicate directly with the I_2O communications layer, either. They must have a *hardware device module* (HDM) that, as with the OSM for the operating system, serves as the go-between for the standardized I_2O communications layer and the unique properties of each peripheral. Also similar to the operating system, the HDM is unique for each peripheral.

This sounds confusing, but just picture many different hardware and software systems communicating with each other through a standard interface. This isn't so different from the concept of the HAL, Windows NT's hardware abstraction layer. The HAL is the middle layer that allows many different kinds of hardware to communicate with a standard Windows NT operating system interface. The interface between Windows NT and the HAL is standardized, but the HAL can be unique for every hardware manufacturer.

So what happens under the covers in an I_2O subsystem? When a user application needs data in an I_2O system, Windows 2000 creates a read request from disk and routes it through its OSM. The OSM sends the I_2O message across the PCI bus to the IOP subsystem. The real-time operating system in the I/O processor passes the message to the appropriate disk-subsystem HDM. The HDM converts it to a device-specific request to pass it to a disk controller installed on a separate PCI bus used for I/O adapters.

The device gets the requested data and notifies the IOP, and the IOP tells the CPU that the data is ready and where it is located in memory. Only a single I/O interrupt is generated; the CPU collects its data from the I_2O subsystem and moves on.

Certainly this improves system performance, but I_2O also boosts performance in the business area. If driver manufacturers only have to write drivers for an I_2O interface instead of a number of different platforms, their time to market with new hardware will be that much faster.

Unlike USB and AGP, then, I_2O technology will definitely have a powerful impact in the Windows NT server world. Keep this technology in mind for your upcoming servers, but remember that all your peripherals must be I_2O-compliant to reap its full benefits.

Information about the I_2O initiative can be found at `http://www.i2osig.org/`.

Summary

Microsoft has two goals for Windows 2000 hardware support. The first is that Windows 9x and Windows 2000 support the same hardware. This will make life easier for independent hardware and software vendors, and it will create a simpler migration path to Windows 2000 from the enormous installed base of Windows 9x customers.

The second goal is to remove the limitations the operating system has historically had in its SMP performance and memory utilization. Hitting both SMP and memory improvement targets are a critical piece of the company's drive into the large enterprise applications market now dominated by UNIX.

Microsoft isn't counting on these improvements alone to shoulder Windows 2000 into enterprise applications; a single machine scales only so far. Instead, Microsoft is combining this increased power on a single system with clustering—grouping multiple computer systems together that function as a single whole computer (discussed in Chapter 4, "Choosing the Box")—as their key to the largest uses in the enterprise.

2

Storage Services in Windows 2000

The storage services Microsoft put in Windows NT Advanced Server 3.1 were by far the most comprehensive the company had ever done, and these services handled storage requirements quite well for the first release of an operating system. But, like everyone else, Microsoft couldn't have anticipated the huge boom in storage. Remember that when the operating system was released in 1993, all Windows applications were 16-bit, and a 1GB SCSI-2 hard disk was the standard bearer for mass storage. The predominant backup medium was 8mm, and the tapes held 2GB. Now six years later, all Windows applications are 32-bit, the standard server hard drive is more than nine times larger, the processor power has increased exponentially, and digital linear tapes hold up to 70GB each.

In short, the need to manage large amounts of different types of storage has been an important goal for Windows 2000. Microsoft has added a lot of functionality to storage system components, but only a few are intended to be used directly by the end user (the Windows NT administrator or the Windows 2000 client). The rest are for the independent software developer. The components are intended to enable the software developer to come up with new and innovative ways to handle large amounts of diverse storage. Indeed, at the 1996 Professional Developer's Conference, Microsoft took great pains to point out potential applications that could be built from its new storage features. The message was clear: "Come and get it, guys!"

Of the new features that are intended to be used immediately, several (volume management, quota management, hierarchical storage management [HSM], and defragmentation) are basic implementations. It's kind of like the NTBACKUP analogy. The NTBACKUP backup program, included with the OS, gets the data backed up quite nicely. If you want any kind of large-scale storage management of your server data however, you must buy a product that expands on NTBACKUP's basic functionality. These new storage features can get the job done, but if you need to use them on any kind of scale, you must purchase a more fully featured product that uses the same new file system hooks as the basic versions.

Volume Management

Managing change in a system's physical disk configuration is an area in which Windows NT 4 falls short of the high-availability goals Microsoft is seeking. In an enterprise-class server, disks come and go, and configurations change on a regular, if not frequent, basis. The most common scenario is growing an array by adding disks, or adding a new array entirely, to keep up with the ever-increasing need for disk storage. Configurations change with the times. What used to seem like a gigantic boot partition with tons of free space shrinks with fatter operating systems, 100MB service packs, and larger utilities.

To make any of these disk changes effective in Windows NT 4, a reboot is required. For example, if you hot-plug a disk into a RAID array that supports a large C: logical drive, you can run a utility from the server OEM to dynamically extend the hardware RAID set. When this is complete, however, Windows NT still won't be capable of using the extra space. What you end up with is a logical drive (C:) of the same size you had before (but restriped across all disks) and a *new* logical drive (D:) of a size equivalent to the new drive(s) you added. This isn't very useful because generally the reason you add disks to an array is to increase the contiguous free space of a partition, not to create more partitions.

Disk management in Windows 2000 now has the capability to bring dynamic disk reconfiguration up into the operating system. Microsoft has teamed up with Veritas Corporation to provide a version of the Volume Manager product as a driver that sits below the file system. Called the Windows NT Logical Disk Manager, it works with the Microsoft Management Console (MMC) Disk Management snap-in to provide remotely usable and more scalable disk management. You plug in a new disk or two, incorporate them into an existing RAID array, restripe the array with an OEM utility, and then use the Disk Management snap-in to extend a logical disk to encompass the new free space.

To incorporate dynamic disks into the storage framework, Microsoft divides the disk world into two camps: basic and dynamic. The definition of a *basic disk* is very simple: It's any disk that has been initialized with a utility from a previous version of Windows 2000, such as FDISK. The storage structure a basic disk supports is that little number we all know and love: the *partition*. Every Microsoft-related disk we're familiar with (until now) uses partitions and falls into the *basic* category.

In contrast, a dynamic disk supports the *volume* structure. The volume concept is easy; it's like a partition except for these features:

- There are no "primary" and "extended" volumes as in partitions. These are all "simple" volumes.

- No logical disks exist, just simple volumes.

- Volume sets (which aren't recommended in servers; instead just size the free space correctly to begin with) are called *spanned volumes*.

- Stripe sets, mirror sets, and stripe sets with parity are called stripe volumes, mirror volumes, and RAID-5 volumes. (See the section "RAID" in Chapter 4, "Choosing the Box," for a discussion about fault-tolerant disk configurations, specifically RAID.)

- Volumes can be *extended*, which means that you can grow them as disks are added.

There's a catch, of course. You can't extend a partition as it exists today; you must either initialize it as a dynamic disk or upgrade it from a basic disk. This requires two reboots before the upgraded volume is ready.

When you upgrade the partition to a dynamic volume, no other operating system will recognize it. This isn't a big deal on most servers because they run only one operating system, but you should be aware of the limitation. This also means that if you should have to back out of Windows 2000 and install Windows NT 4, you'll have to wipe the entire logical disk and start over.

Disk management isn't affected by how you format a volume. You can create a dynamic volume and format it for FAT16, FAT32, NTFS Version 4, or NTFS Version 5. You can also mix basic and dynamic storage on a disk system in most cases. You do have to stick to one type on the same disk, however. Again, for most recommended server configurations this doesn't matter because a volume will typically span many disks in a hardware RAID array. However, the Disk Manager snap-in doesn't handle hardware RAID itself yet. Because many different disk controller types exist, you must still use a RAID configurator provided by the hardware manufacturer. Microsoft and Veritas are working on this problem and hope to incorporate hardware RAID configuring and reporting in the next release of Disk Manager.

Volume Management Recommendations

My recommendations for volume management are listed here:

- Unless you have a dire need for dynamic disk capabilities, don't implement this feature right away. It's relatively new, you can't easily go back after you upgrade, and frankly there are enough new features and unknowns a-plenty in a new Windows 2000 network. Volumes are useful but definitely must be thought out if you're going to run anything but Windows 2000 on a system.

- Don't implement striping, mirroring, and RAID-5 volumes in software if you don't have to. Instead, do this in hardware. (And certainly don't do it in *both* hardware and software.) Just make the volume or partition as large as your application, data, or backup requirement and let the hardware handle the fault tolerance. There are advantages to software fault tolerance in certain configurations, but economies of standardization across your servers greatly outweigh the benefits.

NTFS 5

Most of us Windows NT professionals don't really appreciate everything the Windows NT File System (NTFS) does for us. We know that it lets us stop worrying about how large a partition we can create, that it assigns security to every directory and file, and that it compresses files on a file or directory basis. It also allows us to create fault-tolerant volumes (disk mirroring and striping with parity) on hardware that doesn't understand fault tolerance.

Under the covers, however, NTFS has a number of well-planned features we should at least be aware of. I'll give a quick overview of some the aspects of NTFS you may not be acquainted with, and I'll explain how they play a role in protecting your data. These revolve around two concepts you may be familiar with: object orientation and database transaction processing.

Objects in the File System

A quick refresher on object-oriented technology is needed here. An *object* is a thing, a self-contained creation that can be manipulated as a whole. For example, an apple is an object. This apple object also has *attributes*. It has a color attribute that's equal to red, a shape attribute that's round, and so on. A lemon is also an object that has many of the same attributes, but many of the values are different (as anyone who has bitten into a lemon instead of an apple will immediately discern).

Because NTFS is integrated into the Windows NT Object Model, the files and directories are treated like objects. In fact, they're called file objects and directory objects. Everything else associated with the file—its name, size, archive bits, and compression—is an attribute of the object. Even the file's data is another attribute of the object. The implications of this will become clear later in this chapter, after we talk about the transactional model in NTFS.

A Relational Database Hidden in the File System

While we're doing technology refreshers, let's talk about the transactional database model. This is used by most relational databases and guarantees integrity of the changes made to the database, no matter what happens. (Note that I said integrity of the *changes*, not of the database itself.)

When a change is being made to a relational database, it's tracked so that the entire change either works completely or doesn't happen at all. The series of steps that occur to make a change, and what must be rolled back to undo the changes entirely, make up a *transaction*. A good example of a transaction is a transfer of money from your checking to your savings account. (In fact, bank tellers call them *transactions* for this very reason.) To perform this transaction, the bank must first withdraw the money from your checking account and then deposit it into your savings account. If the bank's computers crash after your withdrawal but before your deposit, you don't want your money disappearing in a cloud of electrons. When the computers come back up, a *transaction log* checks to see what transactions were in progress and then rolls back the transactions that didn't complete successfully.

What does this have to do with NTFS? NTFS uses a transaction model for its file system recovery feature. At the heart of the Windows NT file system is the *Master File Table* (MFT), a relational database table whose rows correspond to files and directories on the disk, and whose columns correspond to file or directory attributes. (A directory looks like a file in the MFT; it just uses some different attributes. For example, the Data attribute for a directory is null because a directory doesn't have any data.)

Figure 2.1 is an extremely simplified MFT for an NTFS boot volume with Windows NT installed on it.

You can see that winnt, a directory, uses many of the same attributes as boot.ini and ntdetect.com. Instead of a data attribute, however, this director has index root, index allocation, and bitmap attributes that are used to index file name attributes.

Standard Information	File Name	Security Descriptor	Data			Extended Attributes
boot.ini						
ntdetect.com						
ndldr						
			Index Root	Index Allocation	Bitmap	
winnt						

Figure 2.1 *An example of the master file table.*

How does NTFS use the MFT? An NTFS transaction is defined as any operation that alters the volume structure or file system data (for example, creating or deleting a file or directory). These operations are logged before they occur to the structure. If something happens to interrupt the transaction before it's complete, the system will rolled back the transaction after it restarts when an application attempts to access the volume.

As we well know, this elegant recoverability model covers only file system data, not user data. The NTFS data model makes it possible to extend the transaction concept to user data, but this hasn't been done. I imagine the overhead would be enormous; vastly more file data changes exist than file creates/deletes on a large NTFS user volume. Anyway, tape backup and RAID configurations are much more efficient ways to ensure recoverability.

Note that this file system recovery I've described is *not* CHKDSK. CHKDSK, the Windows NT disk-checking program, is automatically invoked for disk I/O errors such as bad disk sectors or program file errors. You can also run it from a command prompt. Incidentally, the boot sequence has been enhanced so that you have the opportunity to skip CHKDSK if you must. To deter all but the most determined, Microsoft issues dire warnings during the boot on the consequences of skipping CHKDSK.

One useful aspect of this relational database model is that it's easy to add new attributes by simply adding more columns to the MFT. This is what Microsoft has done for NTFS Version 5.

New Features in NTFS Version 5

The NTFS format has changed for Windows 2000. Now that people have actually started to pay attention to it, versions of NTFS before Windows 2000 are referred to as Version 4; Windows 2000's is—surprise—Version 5.

Of the changes to NTFS for Version 5, only a few are immediately useful to the administrator or the end user. Most of the extensions are hooks that developers need to create truly large-scale storage management applications. I'll cover the immediately useful extensions in some detail and will briefly describe some of the other improvements.

A format change for something as fundamental as a file system is a decision not made lightly. It's done because of serious flaws or because it has become apparent that the existing file system structure won't be capable of keeping up with where the operating system is headed. FAT32 is an example of a file system format change to keep up with storage trends. (More will be covered on that in the section "FAT and FAT32" later in the chapter.)

In the case of NTFS, extensions were required for the storage management hooks we're talking about here, as were Active Directory and IntelliMirror features. As you've seen, NTFS was designed to be easily extensible.

Warning

Limited compatibility exists between NTFS Version 5 and NTFS Version 4. The fundamental guidelines are listed here:

- *Of downlevel operating systems, only Windows NT 4 will recognize NTFS Version 5, and it must have Service Pack 4 installed. Windows NT 3.51 will not recognize it, and no updated NTFS drivers are planned. Therefore, a Windows 2000 NTFS-formatted system can coexist only with a Windows NT 4 Service Pack 4 system. Note that this compatibility issue is only for a dual boot on one system; network drives are readable from all Windows versions as they've always been. This shouldn't be a problem for production systems because they are rarely dual boot. If you decide to implement the backup OS technique described elsewhere in the book, however, make sure you upgrade it to at least Windows NT 4 Service Pack 4, and preferably to Windows 2000. What's a little more disk space, anyway?*

- *A logical follow-up to the previous warning is that you can't install Windows NT 4 on a system that's running Windows 2000 and that has its boot partition (usually C:) formatted as NTFS. Windows 2000 will automatically install or upgrade an NTFS volume to Version 5, so Windows NT 4's WINNT / WINNT32 installation program won't recognize the file system. Even if your C: partition is formatted as FAT, you must use the latest version of WINNT and WINNT32 available in Service Packs to guarantee success.*

- *NTFS Version 5 functions (including disk quotas and encrypting file system) aren't accessible from Windows NT 4. Some functions will return "Access Denied;" others will simply not be recognized. If it wasn't in Windows NT 4, don't try messing with it. ◆*

Defragmentation

File fragmentation and free space fragmentation does happen in NTFS, and depending on the server, it can seriously affect system performance. Windows 2000 finally includes a defragmenter, but it's not really new. This is the latest in a series of defragmenters from one company.

Executive Software created DisKeeper—the first Windows NT defragmenter—in 1995 and has been the market leader ever since. The company holds such a dominant position in this niche that only Symantec has even tried to come up with a competing product. To my knowledge, DisKeeper still holds the dominant position and certainly is the best-known defragmenter ("Defrag? Oh, you mean DisKeeper") to all Windows NT administrators.

One of the principal tenets of Windows NT works under this principle: "You there, Mr. Program! You *cannot* directly touch my hardware like you used to before I came along. You must ask me to touch the hardware for you, and if what you ask is reasonable, I'll do it and tell you what happened. If you try to talk to the hardware anyway, I will *shut you down*." To defragment a disk, the program and the microkernel (or kernel, for short) must share the right words, never before used by the kernel, so that the kernel can tell the hard disk what to do. In other words, the operating system must have application programming interfaces (APIs) for defragmenting.

The Windows NT 3.1 to 3.51 kernel had no defragmentation APIs, so this couldn't be done before. Executive Software took the risky position of working with Microsoft to provide an independent replacement kernel that did include defragmentation interfaces. I suppose it was risky in the sense that Microsoft has a history of eating up small, innovative companies. What I really mean, however, is that it was risky for the company and for Windows NT administrators because to defragment your server you had to replace the Windows NT kernel—the heart of your operating system—with an altered (albeit slightly altered) version. Not only did you have to run an altered version, but you also had to replace it with a new version from Executive Software whenever a Service Pack came out. Of course, this meant that you couldn't apply much-needed service to all your servers until this small company in California provided you with its modifications.

Despite these restrictions, DisKeeper was a successful product. The defragmentation APIs finally appeared in Windows NT 4, and predictably, the product's popularity took off. Executive Software took the innovative approach of providing a free defragger, DisKeeper Lite, for Windows NT 4 that is fully functional. The catch is that it's manual; you can't schedule it to run automatically on a regular basis on servers across your enterprise.

This brings us up to Windows 2000. Because I was windy about Windows NT defragmentation's history, I can summarize defragmentation support in this new release with three words: *DisKeeper Lite 5.0*. This product does the job, but it's manual. As a result, it's a reactive trouble-shooting tool; if you have a sizable network, the task of manually defragging your servers will be too time-consuming. Unless you put together a way to schedule it from another scheduler, you'll probably use it only to defragment volumes when server problems bring it to your attention. To really implement defragmentation on a proactive basis for your company, you must buy DisKeeper 5.

Figure 2.2 shows the defragmenter snap-in. As with everything else that uses the MMC, you can access the defragmenter by pressing Start, Run; entering MMC; and then selecting Console, Add/Remove Snap-in. If you're familiar with DisKeeper, you'll see that the program operation is the same: You select a volume and ask it to analyze or defragment. If you choose to analyze, you'll get both a report (which can be informative—it's amazing to see how many fragments some files can have) and a recommendation of what to do.

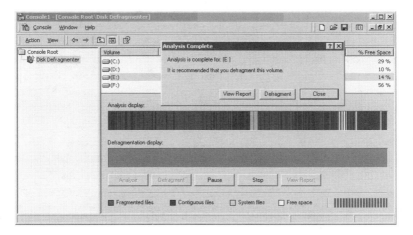

Figure 2.2   *A defragmentation analysis.*

If you choose to defragment the volume (see Figure 2.3), the service will re-analyze the volume and then attempt to defragment it. Two graphic displays, one from the analysis and the other from the defragmentation, present an easy before-and-after comparison but don't really tell you the details. To find those, you must choose the View Report button before and after the defragmentation.

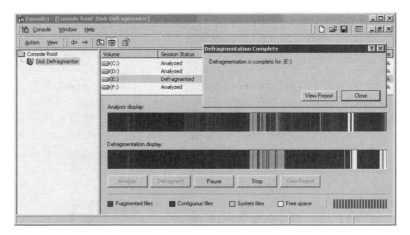

Figure 2.3   *Completed defragmentation from the MMC console.*

Defragmentation in Windows NT has always been dynamic—that is, you don't need to restrict access to the server or otherwise take the volume offline. Even though the server stays fully functional, however, manual defragmentation will noticeably affect the server's performance because the priority level of the DisKeeper NTFS service (DKNTFS.EXE) is pretty high. In the full product, it runs at a much lower priority, is therefore less noticeable, but takes much longer to complete a defragmentation run.

If you *really* want the internals on disk defragmentation, check out http://www.sysinternals.com/defrag.htm for Mark Russinovitch's excellent essay on the topic.

Quota Management

Take any Windows NT system administrator out to lunch, ask him what his top 10 complaints as an administrator are, and I can guarantee that managing disk space use will be one of them. There's just something about a user seeing the words "27GB free" on the network file server drive that causes him to think "Man, that's a lot of space!" and "It's free. It says so, right there at the bottom of Explorer." Who wouldn't want to copy their C: drive up there for safekeeping?

Obviously, this leads to thousands of copies of Microsoft Office and archived Dilbert cartoons on a file server. When's the last time you heard of disk space usage going *down* on a file server? Keeping disk space in check is high on an administrator's list of priorities.

Windows 2000 includes basic quota management built into the operating system. This is managed on a per-user and per-volume basis, and a user's quota is totaled by his ownership of files. As with other storage management features in Windows 2000, quota management is very basic. To manage quotas on a large scale, you'll have to buy a full-featured quota management system from the likes of New Technology Partners or Argent Software. I suspect that they will release Windows 2000-compatible versions of their products that will use the new quota APIs to make them more useful.

Figure 2.4 shows how quota management is enabled. This is a property sheet of volume properties, reached by right-clicking an NTFS volume. It's disabled by default, so you must check the Enable Quota Management checkbox. After you've done that, you can set the quota limit for new users on a volume with a spin control. You can't fault Microsoft for thinking small here—this allows you to restrict disk usage up to 5 exabytes (5 million terabytes)!

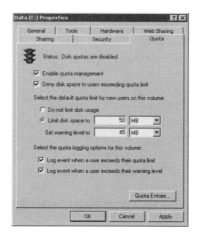

Figure 2.4 *Enabling disk quotas.*

How do you set quotas on existing users (certainly where most of the quota work is to be done)? You must use quota entries. Choose the Quota Entries button at the bottom of the Quota property sheet to launch the Quota Entries window. Figure 2.5 shows the default entry of Administrators and its columns.

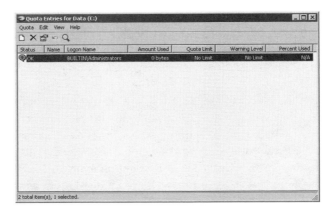

Figure 2.5   *A quota entry.*

To add existing users, click the New icon at the left of the toolbar, or choose Quota, New Quota Entry. You can add a single user—unlikely unless you feel like persecuting someone—or you can select a range of users with standard mouse and keyboard techniques (Shift-click, Ctrl-click). Note that there's no way to add groups for quota management, so this must be done by individual users. Talk about tedious!

For our example, the user singled out for quota is one Ima Hogg, member of the PackRat group, whose members are known for backing up their PCs by copying their C: drives to the local file server. (There really was an Ima Hogg. She was the daughter of Texas governor James Hogg, who liked to keep ostriches at the governor's mansion. Seriously.) Figure 2.6 shows how Ima is selected for quota management.

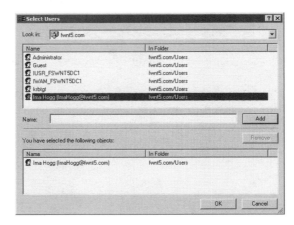

Figure 2.6   *Selecting Ima Hogg to be limited.*

Now you must choose what kind of quota to give Ima. As with the New User setting, this is a simple control (see Figure 2.7).

Figure 2.7   *Selecting Ima's quota limit and warning threshold.*

If Ima uses up her quota, she gets the pop-up message shown in Figure 2.8.

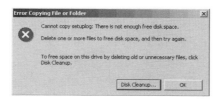

Figure 2.8   *Quota limit notification.*

The only way Ima can save her file is to delete some existing files on the C: volume.

You can use the Quota Entries dialog box to check quota usage for a volume, but it's not really designed to handle very large amounts of users without a lot of administrative overhead.

Quota Management Recommendations

You must have good answers to a lot of questions before you should even consider enabling quotas:

- Disk quota must be set on every volume, regardless of how many physical disks it covers. Jim Bob may have only a 25MB quota on D:, but if he has access to E: and his quota isn't set, he can two-step you. You must set quota manually on many servers.

- File ownership determines a user's quota, so if Jim Bob updates your build document (which you own) with lots of screen shots to make it more readable, *your* quota will be exceeded, not his. There's nothing you can do about this. Audit your user's file shares. Do their directories all say Administrator or Acct Svcs because your Accounting Services group set them up?

- Quota is set individually for users. You can't set quota for a group. You can select multiple users and give them all the same quota, but setting quotas for thousands of users will be *extremely* tedious and error-prone. If you choose to migrate to a new, unpopulated Windows 2000 environment instead of upgrading in place, you can set up quota management before new accounts are created. You won't have to do it on a one-by-one basis as you create the accounts; they'll automatically pick it up.

- File errors due to exceeded quotas can be very cryptic. The user will get a popup message, and perhaps any quota-savvy applications (when there are any) will clearly say why they can't save the file. The vast majority of applications, however, will say "Unknown File Error."

- How will your Help Desk going to handle this last problem? Quota management could be a huge drain on Help Desk resources. All users will hit their quota, and when someone has an open file with work from the last few hours hanging in the breeze, someone had better get the problem resolved quickly.

- The standard user workstation being deployed now has about 4GB of disk space, 75% of which is unused. If a user is denied access, why wouldn't they naturally save it to their local drive instead of sitting in the Help Desk queue, twiddling their thumbs and enduring smooth jazz favorites? Do you back up your clients? Sure, they intend to copy back to the network drive once they clean out some space (whenever that is). By enabling quota management, you can be subverting your network-centric file storage model.

- Who is willing to take the responsibility to say, "Keeping storage size down is more important than the user data itself"? Not I! Imagine design-run data lost due to a system crash, because an impending deadline meant more runs, which created a higher than normal amount of data, which caused quota to be exceeded. Disk storage is cheap compared to potential lost data.

Windows 2000 also has HSM. For the company's own inscrutable reasons, Microsoft has again added to the acronym feast by calling it Remote Storage Service (RSS). My recommendation is that system administrators should use RSS to manage disk space by moving least recently used data to offline storage instead of squashing a user's current storage. This is a policy many mainframe shops have followed for years: Make the disk space appear unlimited to users by backing it up with large tape storage.

Remote Storage Service (RSS)

RSS is the HSM for Windows 2000. HSM isn't a new concept—it's just new to Windows NT. HSM has been in use on mainframe and UNIX systems for years. The basic idea behind it is that administrators define several classes of storage, usually in order of cost or access time. Where a user's data resides in this hierarchy of storage is also defined by administrators. The most common criterion is how frequently the data is accessed, weighted perhaps by the size of the file; larger files will be migrated faster than smaller files. If you don't use it, the data is moved to slower and cheaper storage. In a good HSM system, just about every criterion is definable by administrators (though it's wise to take the defaults until you understand it well). Figure 2.9 shows how a typical HSM system might define its classes.

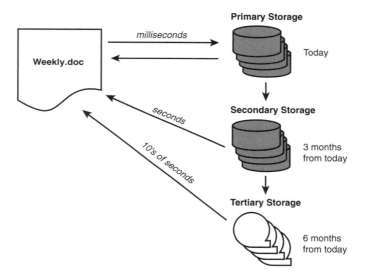

Figure 2.9   *A three-class HSM system.*

This example has three classes of storage: primary, secondary, and tertiary. These classes are also sometimes described as online, near-line, and offline storage.

Primary storage is the disk storage that we use today. Secondary storage could consist of an optical storage system, or perhaps older and slower (and depreciated) disk arrays. Tertiary storage would be tape storage, usually an automated tape library or silo that can automatically fulfill a mount request without waiting for an operator.

A possible fourth class of storage would be created by moving the offline tapes to a cold storage site. This would obviously be *very* offline, but it still fits the model in that the user could attempt to access the file and it would (eventually) show up.

In this example, a user has written her weekly progress report, named Weekly.doc. When she saves the document, it's stored in primary storage on the local file server. If no one has accessed the file in three months, the data is moved to secondary storage at, say, a disk farm at a central location. Note that getting "last accessed" information wasn't possible in NTFS Version 4; NTFS Version 5 provides this capability.

If no one looks at Weekly.doc for another three months, it's moved from the disk farm to a DLT tape library. At year end, however, the user wants to review all her weeklies so she can remember what she has done all year for her annual performance review. She simply tries to access Weekly.doc, and the tape library retrieves it from storage. If no changes are made, nothing else is done. If the file data is changed, however, the process starts over again. The file is saved to primary storage and the file on tape is marked for deletion. This example doesn't involve multiple versions of a file because the system is supposed to be transparent to the user; a user saves a file to a location, accesses it, and deletes it. All this migration to different storage classes happens under the covers.

RSS in Windows 2000 is another example of enhancements to the Windows NT operating system in which Microsoft provides a basic product and, more importantly, also the storage management APIs to allow software developers to hook in fully featured HSM systems. RSS was co-developed by Microsoft and Eastman Software's Storage Management Group. Thanks to the musical chairs of mergers and acquisitions in the software business, it's now owned by Seagate Software (of Backup Exec storage management software fame). As a result, you can count on Seagate Software to immediately offer products well-integrated into Windows 2000 storage management.

RSS offers two tiers of storage: local and remote. These translate to disk or optical storage and tape. When a file's last access exceeds the time set by the system's administrators, the data in the file is moved to tape, the file size is set to zero, and the file icon shows a tiny clock next to it. This is a nice touch; users can tell at a glance if the file they want to access has been migrated to remote storage.

RSS Recommendations

My recommendations for remote storage management are listed here:

- Tapes are cheaper than lost data. You already spend thousands of dollars on tapes and tape drives that rarely restore user data, don't you? Hierarchical storage management products should be an essential part of any Windows NT storage management system. A well-designed HSM system, or network of systems, can provide users with enough storage at a moderate price to make space restrictions for most conditions a thing of the past.

- A hierarchical storage management system isn't a substitute for backups.

- Whether you stick with Microsoft's free software or purchase a more complete system from a software developer, the software cost for an HSM system is only part of the price. You must have some kind of a tape library as well. A small office could use a simple DLT changer that supports a few tapes, while large corporations need libraries that can hold terabytes of data. Estimating the size library you need is part of any HSM evaluation, but I'm sure that HSM vendors will have methods to calculate what you need. Just keep in mind that their estimates may be a bit optimistic: Their job is to sell their software, so they want to minimize the scare of sobering hardware costs.

- RSS is Microsoft's first step into hierarchical storage management for Windows NT. I haven't been able to extensively test its features, but I believe that it can satisfy the small company looking for better ways to manage its existing storage. For a more complete HSM system, you'll have to look to software developers such as Seagate Software.

Encrypting File System (EFS)

Secure though NTFS is, a file you want protected on NTFS can still be read under the right circumstances. If you lock down a file so that only your own account has full control and everyone else has no access, it still can be read by several methods:

- The system the file resides on is booted to DOS, either from a floppy or on the disk itself, and NTFSDOS is loaded. NTFSDOS reads the NTFS structures but pays no attention to the security. This is what might happen if your notebook computer were stolen.

- The file or directory gets copied from one server to another for load-balancing purposes with a regular copy or xcopy command. These programs don't copy access control lists (ACLs) along with the files, and they're wide open in their new directories.

- Someone with Administrator rights (and we all know there are way too many of these people) takes control of the file, despite its locked-down status. You'll know it's been tampered with, but you probably won't be able to backtrack to who owns—or took—the account.

The Encrypting File System (EFS) is a new attribute of NTFS Version 5 that adds encryption to a file or directory (see Figure 2.10). It's done at the file-system level; encryption and decryption are performed during file operations. In the same way that NTFS compression is "invisible," the user isn't aware of anything different when accessing an EFS file. If this user isn't the user that originally encrypted the file, he will get an "Access Denied" message. This illustrates a key point of EFS: One and only one user—the one who encrypted the file—can access an EFS-encrypted file without getting into administrative file recovery procedures.

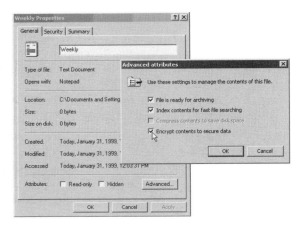

Figure 2.10   *Setting the EFS attribute.*

EFS is based on public-key encryption (see Chapter 3, "Distributed Services in Windows 2000"), in which each file is encrypted with a randomly generated key and in which each file's encryption key is unique. Key uniqueness means that you can move an EFS-encrypted file around on the same volume (changing its fully qualified pathname) without affecting its encryption. If users want to use their encrypted files on a computer other that the one on which the files were encrypted, however, either the files must be set up by an administrator with a roaming profile, or the user must manually move the keys himself with the Certificate Manager snap-in.

There's a problem with the effectiveness of EFS, and it has to do with downlevel file systems. A number of circumstances exist in which encrypted files can be seen in clear text, and almost all are related to file systems that don't understand EFS. In other words, an EFS-encrypted file can be seen in clear text on every file system except NTFS Version 5:

- If an encrypted file or directory is copied to a FAT (either FAT16 or FAT32) partition, the file will be in clear text.

- If an encrypted file or directory is copied to a Windows NT 4 or 3.51 system, or even to some old 386 running Windows 3.1, the file will be in clear text.

There's one other circumstance in which your file will be clear-text flappin' in the breeze. If you copy the file to a computer on which EFS is disabled, encryption disappears and only ACLs (perhaps) protect it.

Let's be clear on what's required to copy an EFS-encrypted file. The only user who can copy it is the one who originally encrypted it. For example, a malicious user can't make a copy of the file and examine it on a Windows NT 4 system at her leisure. Microsoft recommends that you examine the advanced file properties after you copy an encrypted file or directory to see if it's still encrypted. While this is workable for the occasional single file, it's clearly impractical for copying a directory.

It's worth pointing out that NTFSDOS, the (in)famous read-only NTFS file system driver from Mark Russinovich and Bryce Cogswell (http://www.sysinternals.com), can't read or copy an EFS-encrypted file either. This is because the file or directory is in its encrypted state when it resides on an NTFS V5.0 volume; it's unencrypted only during the file open operation.

What if Jim Bob leaves the company before revealing his chili recipe (stored in an EFS-encrypted file of course) that took first place in the company picnic? EFS provides built-in data recovery support. In fact, Windows 2000 won't enable EFS unless the system is configured with one or more recovery keys.

EFS Recommendations
Viewed through the narrow lens of a Windows NT system architect or administrator, the features of EFS are more suited to the client than the server. However, as an administrator (especially as a security administrator), you definitely need to know how to perform data recovery if a user leaves the company or loses encryption keys:

- Consider disabling EFS by setting an empty recovery policy for a domain or organizational unit (OU). To do this, you must define a group policy object (GPO) with an *empty* (as opposed to *no*) recovery policy. This disables EFS because it won't work without recovery certificates.

- If you don't disable EFS, your help desk and security administrators must be prepared for some mayhem as users discover EFS and then try to move it to another computer.

- EFS can be a very powerful security tool for notebook users, but be prepared for a good deal of education for the security staff and some basic training for the users. Otherwise, the resulting trouble calls will be difficult for the help desk to resolve (yet another feature to train the support staff on!).

Compression on the Wire

NTFS directory and file compression became available beginning with Windows NT 3.51. This was a welcome feature for administrators because it immediately gave them breathing room on their most heavily loaded servers. (It was also nice for Executive Software because compressing a nearly full disk immediately fragmented it.) However, whenever a compressed file was accessed, the server had to decompress it before sending the data to the client. This chewed some processor cycles on the server and didn't save any network traffic. Windows 2000 has "compression on the wire," which is a slick way of saying that compressed Windows 2000 server data, when requested by a Windows 2000 client, remains in compressed format until it's expanded at the client. This accomplishes two nice things: It distributes the processor cycles required to decompress the data out among the clients, and it reduces network traffic by the amount the data is compressed.

If benchmarks prove that compressed file access times to Windows 2000 clients are as speedy as uncompressed times to Windows NT 4 clients, compressed files on data volumes in a full Windows 2000 network should become the standard rather than the exception. The power available on today's standard corporate desktop is certainly up to the task of decompressing network files, and the network performance improvement will help significantly.

Reparse Points

Reparse points, another new feature of NTFS 5.0, allow new storage system applications (written by Microsoft or software developers) to slip into the regular flow of directory and file operations. This tremendously extends the storage subsystem's future capabilities. A reparse point is a system-controlled attribute that can be associated with any directory or file.

During a file or directory I/O operation, the NTFS driver sees that a file has the reparse point attribute set and then passes it up the driver stack. In this I/O stack, the tag associated with the reparse point is examined to see what vendor it belongs to. The owner of the tag intercepts the call and routes it into its own application. This finally gets application developers where they've never been able to get before: directly into the "file" open path.

The important concept to remember about reparse points isn't that they're directly useful to the administrator—they aren't—but that they are the basis of features you *will* find useful, including directory junctions, mount points, RSS, and EFS.

Microsoft Indexing Service

The newest version of Microsoft's indexing engine has been expanded from its Internet Information Server roots to all of a system's volumes. NTFS itself does indexing, but only on file names. Microsoft Indexing Service (I won't confuse us all with *this* acronym) gathers enough information on directories and files in a volume for a user or application to do full text and property searches, or even to view the file on a volume sorted by size. This capability isn't enabled by default; you must go to the Computer Management snap-in and expand the Server Applications and Services object. You don't perform searches on the Indexing Service catalogs by using the Find application, either. You work in the same Index Server container you accessed to start the service in the first place. Figure 2.11 shows the Indexing Service query dialog and its location in the Computer Management snap-in.

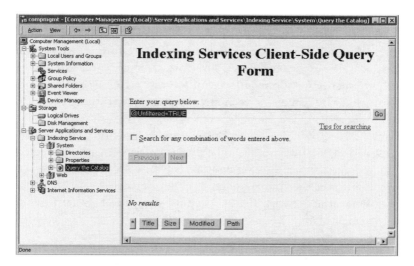

Figure 2.11   *The Indexing Service query dialog.*

Volume Mount Points

Volume mount points are a way of grafting a disk volume, either local or remote, onto an empty directory. When you move around in the directory structure, by simply descending into the directory you move to the mounted volume. If the volume happens to be on a Windows 2000 server halfway around the world, the only way a user will notice a difference is from the network delay. Volume mount points can mount only the root of the volume, which means that you can't mount a directory somewhere on the volume to another directory. There's another way to do that as well. A very useful application for volume mount points would be to expand storage on a server share.

For example, a Windows 2000 server named \\SOFTSUPP has the share called Software. This server is out of space, but much more software needs to be loaded into the Software share. An administrator could add a volume mount point to the Software directory, name it OS, and mount a 4GB volume from \\SOFTSUPP2. The administrator now moves all the operating system source files from their original directory in Software to the new one named OS. The files are moved to the roomier SOFTSUPP2, space is freed on SOFTSUPP, and the only change the users see is that the name of the directory holding the OS files has changed.

NTFS Directory Junctions

An overview of NTFS directory junctions is an excellent warm-up for discussing the Distributed File System (Dfs), which we'll get to in just a minute. Directory junctions take the concept of grafting a remote volume onto a local namespace (such as a directory structure) and extends it. Directory junctions not only allow you to graft a volume root onto a local directory, but you can also attach any directory structure from another server.

Figure 2.12 shows a common Windows NT network configuration: Users store personal data on a home directory (let's say it's connected as H:) and shared department data on another network drive (S:). To get to his personal data, the user must launch Explorer and scroll past the local hard drive down to the network shares. He must switch to another drive to reach the department data.

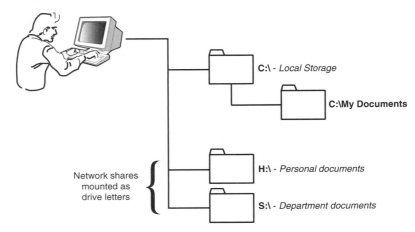

Figure 2.12 *A typical corporate client network-centric data access model.*

NTFS directory junctions can simplify this considerably in two operations:

1. Mount the network share currently accessed as H: into C:\my documents\personal. (There's a New button to help you create the \ personal directory during the process.)

2. Mount the network share currently accessed as S: into C:\my documents\shared.

Figure 2.13 shows the results. The user can access all his local and network documents within the My Documents directory structure instead of inconveniently jumping back and forth between the C:, H:, and S: drives. Applications don't have to be tricked into setting network drives as their default document locations, and file searches can all be based from My Documents instead of three separate searches from C:, H:, and S:.

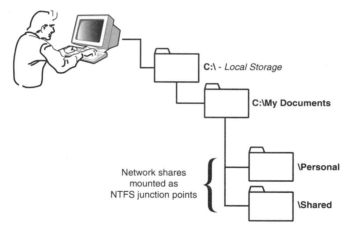

Figure 2.13   *Two network drives grafted onto C:\My Documents with NTFS directory junctions.*

NTFS directory junctions are the next step up from volume mount points, but they don't have all the functionality of Dfs. In particular, directory junctions are designed to attach other shares to local storage only, while Dfs can build a namespace out of many network shares. Another limitation (or, rather, yet another reason to format with NTFS) is that NTFS directory junctions work only with—you guessed it—NTFS. A final important limitation is that directory junctions aren't aware of the Active Directory, so they can't take advantage of the knowledge stored within.

Other Nifty Storage Features

Windows 2000 storage has added a number of other nice features, but they're of more interest to the developer than the administrator. The administrator will appreciate them when the developer makes a useful product based on them.

- Distributed link tracking—This is a service used in the OS to heal broken shortcuts. It uses object IDs, which are systemwide indexed identifiers to uniquely identify a file.

- Sparse file support—Sparse files are large files that are pre-allocated but mostly empty, like a database device. Before NTFS Version 5, the file used up its whole allocation just as if it were full. In NTFS Version 5, however, a sparse file is allocated on demand—it only takes up as much room on disk as is truly being used within the file.

Other File Systems

NTFS is the only file system Microsoft is enhancing for Windows 2000. The other file systems it will support—including FAT and CDFS/UDF—are good examples of an upgrade providing a change in format.

FAT and FAT32

When Microsoft created the FAT (File Allocation Table) file system, magnetic hard drives for PCs didn't even exist. Today you can pick up an IDE hard drive for under 2 cents a megabyte, but ancient FAT is still the most widely used file system in PCs. FAT32 is a recent upgrade to the FAT file system to improve efficiency and handle these cheap disks. Specifically, FAT32 offers these capabilities:

- Supports volumes up to 2TB
- Has smaller allocation units and cluster size
- Has better stability through an expanded boot record

Windows 2000 includes support for FAT32, but you probably won't ever use it on a server. Even though it can support up to 2TB, for server use it's inferior to NTFS in almost every way. FAT32 lacks robust recovery, security, and all the features required to implement the new storage features described in this chapter.

CDFS and UDF

Compact Disc File System (CDFS) is the legacy file system that enables Windows NT to read from CD-ROM drives, and Windows 2000 will continue to support it. Universal Disk Format (UDF) is the successor to CDFS. It still supports CD-ROM, but it's the primary format for DVD. UDF will support features such as access control lists, read/write capability (though not in base Windows 2000), and bootability. And, yes, you will be able to play your DVD movies on Windows 2000; it will use the same DirectShow drivers as Windows 98, which provides standardized support for DVD-Video and MPEG-2 playback[1].

> ### Note
>
> *I don't think anyone knows what DVD stands for anymore. It started out as digital video disc, then digital versatile disk. The last I heard, the consortium that controls DVD had dropped even the pretense of it standing for anything. See what we've come to? Acronyms that don't represent anything. What does NT still stand for? It's no longer New Technology.* ◆

Distributed File System (Dfs)

The Distributed File System (Dfs—note the lowercase; it's a legal thing) is a new way of looking at the data you already have on your Windows NT network. This isn't really a new file system; it's a way to organize what you have into a more logical structure.

Dfs adds a layer of abstraction to the \\server\share view of Windows NT resources we're all familiar with. Figure 2.14 demonstrates what we've all been through—trying to remember the location of a file we looked at six months ago.

The directory lookup in this case is your brain, which is trying to remember the name of the server and share where the research proposal was stored. Add in the facts that server names rarely have anything whatsoever to do with the data that's stored on them and that shares are notoriously spelling-challenged, and this has become a real chore.

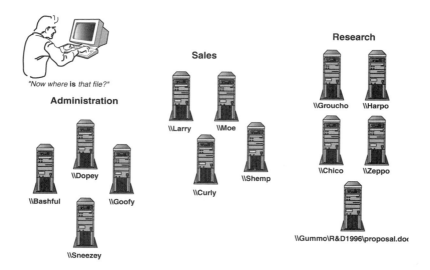

Figure 2.14   *Digging up a file in the \\server\share namespace.*

Why not look at this same quagmire of naming conventions as a logical hierarchy of directories? (See Figure 2.15 for an illustration.)

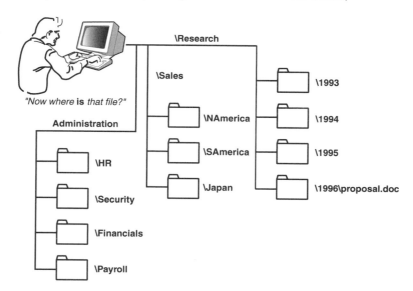

Figure 2.15   *A possible Dfs namespace of the same resources.*

This is what Dfs does. It creates a hierarchical, logical, searchable directory tree, the contents of which are the various shares already scattered throughout your Windows NT network. The existing shares aren't altered in any way; you can think of Dfs as a layer above the traditional UNC (universal naming convention—well, it's universal within Microsoft networks) \\server\share metaphor.

Dfs does a number of cool things:

- The administrator can construct a well-planned, logical hierarchy of data on the network instead of being stuck with the legacy of servers and shares created over time.

- A logical hierarchy can be independent of location. An administrator could construct a Dfs tree called RESEARCH that encompasses only research server shares from the company's research locations around the world. The Dfs user has no idea what servers they're moving to and from.

- Dfs directories can be constructed with replicas to increase data availability and fault tolerance.

- Dfs incorporates knowledge of sites to intelligently select the lowest-cost replica when it's available.

- Dfs is interoperable with other file systems such as HPFS, NetWare, and NFS.

- Backups can use the tree, spanning many volumes across the network. (Of course, your network infrastructure must be left up to the demands of networked backups.)

- Virus detection can use the tree or perhaps its own tree specially organized to scan common department shares.

- Search engines can index the tree for fast searches.

- Because Dfs directories hide the real UNC name, administrators can transparently add storage to the tree.

- A well-organized Dfs namespace incorporates many network shares, so a client's network-connected drives can be reduced down to one or two.

Let's back up a bit and describe some basic Dfs concepts and terminology.

Dfs Concepts and Terms

The key concept to understand Dfs is this: When a user drills down into a subdirectory in a Dfs tree, it looks to the user just like he's going down into any old subdirectory. But under the covers, the user may be jumping (*junctioning*) across the network to one server share, and then perhaps another as he continues down. Dfs adds a layer of a logical tree structure in which the user moves around. This hierarchy is glued to the existing network shares, and when the user touches files, it's through the same sharepoints that he has always accessed.

As I've said, Dfs uses the tree metaphor to describe its namespace. Actually, it's more of an upside-down tree:

- The *Dfs root* is the top of the Dfs hierarchy.

- A *child node* is any directory or folder added underneath the Dfs root. A child node can be either a branch node or a leaf node.

- A *branch node* is a directory that has other child nodes underneath it (like a real branch, though upside-down). It can also reference other Dfs trees, but the child node must be a Windows 2000 server also running Dfs.

- A *leaf node* is a directory that has no subdirectories; it's a terminus of the Dfs tree.

- A *replica* is a network share that contains duplicate data from another share. In the Dfs context, the original and duplicates (up to 128 of them) are branch nodes in a Dfs tree.

- A *junction point* is a logical bridge between two nodes in the network. This is what glues a Dfs tree together. When a user traverses a Dfs tree and drills down into what looks like a subdirectory, this is really a share on another server; the junction point is that subdirectory.

You can expand a Dfs tree by adding child nodes to an existing tree with the Dfs management snap-in (DFSGUI.MSC). These child nodes can be directories, entire volumes, or other Dfs trees. If you want, you can link together Dfs trees to put all your network shares into one gigantic logical tree structure.

Dfs doesn't add any security; it just uses existing Windows NT security in share permissions and directory/file ACLs. This keeps administration simpler, but it's added incentive to keep your permissions policy clear and straightforward. If users have trouble accessing a Dfs directory or file, they have no clue what share they're contacting because it's hidden from them.

Active Directory Integration

Dfs exists as an add-on for Windows NT 4 (http://www.microsoft.com/ntserver/nts/downloads/winfeatures/NTSDistrFile/default.asp), and to the client it functions identically. The difference between Dfs 4.1 and Dfs 5.0 is on the back end, in Dfs 5's integration with the Active Directory.

In Dfs 4.1, the topology (how Dfs directories map to server shares) is stored in the Partition Knowledge Table (PKT) on the Dfs root server. If you create a standalone Dfs root, you'll still use a descendant of the PKT, but 99% of the time you'll want to create a fault-tolerant Dfs root. The difference between a standalone root and a fault-tolerant root is that the latter is published into the Active Directory as a Volume object. This means that the Dfs topology isn't a single point of failure anymore because it's published in the Active Directory, and Active Directory objects are replicated to all domain controllers in the domain. This also means that all servers in the domain running the Dfs service are aware of all the Dfs topologies of all the other Dfs servers.

A Windows 2000 client accesses a fault-tolerant Dfs root differently than a Windows NT 4 client. In Dfs 4.1, and with Windows NT 4 clients, the syntax for accessing an object in the Dfs tree is as follows:

```
\\Dfs-root-server\root-name\directory\file.ext
```

The syntax for accessing a Windows 2000 fault-tolerant root with a Windows 2000 client is shown here:

```
\\Domain-name\root-name\directory\file.ext
```

For example, a possible fault-tolerant Dfs UNC would be this:

```
\\research.bigcompany.com\ResRoot1\OpsReviews\1stQuarter.doc
```

Note, however, that until your clients have upgraded to Windows 2000 they must still access Dfs from a particular server, as in the first example.

The Referral Process—Dfs Under the Covers

When a Windows 2000 Dfs client touches a junction point while traversing the Dfs tree, the Dfs server sends an error message back to the client (SMB error code (599)STATUS_PATH_NTDFS) that essentially says, "This isn't a real directory; it's a Dfs junction point to a network share." The client then queries the Active Directory on his authenticating domain controller for the UNC name of the network share. The domain controller returns the UNC name, and the client sets up a session to the network share just as though the user was typing in a net use command.

Figure 2.16 shows how a referral works between a Windows 2000 workstation, appropriately named \\WORKSTATION, and a Dfs server \\NTDFS servicing the fault-tolerant Dfs tree named \\hr.bigco.com\DFSroot. When the client hits the \Benefit Info child node (step 1), NTDFS returns the 599 STATUS_PATH_NTDFS error (step 2). The client queries the Active Directory on its authenticating domain controller (such as., the domain controller that performed the client's original Kerberos authentication) (step 3). The domain controller returns the rather unfriendly UNC name (step 4), and the client performs a session setup with the CORPSRV3 server to access the HR$BENE share.

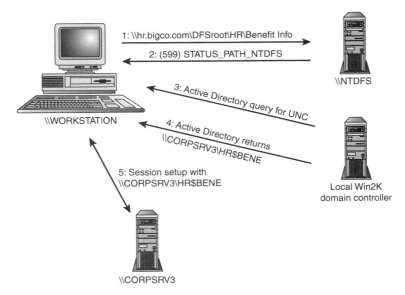

Figure 2.16 *Dfs 5 referral with a Windows 2000 client.*

This looks ugly and complicated, but it's really quite fast (and not nearly as complicated as the original Kerberos logon authentication—see Chapter 3 for more information). You should get two important points out of this example:

- At the end of the referral process, the client simply does a net use command to the resource it's accessing.

- The Dfs server isn't required for the actual session setup, and all I/O traffic with the Dfs child node Benefit Info goes through CORPSRV3, not NTDFS. This is important because it means you don't need to have a monster Dfs server to funnel all a tree's traffic through. The Dfs server just does the referrals.

> **Note**
>
> *As you examine all these new features and analyze the new operating system's characteristics, always keep in mind that you must deal with two states. The first is the end state everyone talks about, where both servers and clients are running Windows 2000. The second state, but the one that occurs first, is the transitional state, where the server infrastructure is upgraded to Windows 2000 but the clients are still at some previous level (hopefully Windows NT 4). In a large company with tens of thousands of PC clients, a year in this transitional state is optimistic.*
>
> *I can't overemphasize the importance of performing two sets of analyses—pure Windows 2000 and Windows 2000 server/downlevel clients—at every step. These*

two environments can have very different and very significant impacts on your Windows NT network and the underlying physical network. You won't see your elegant end-state Windows 2000 network design if you lose your job due to transitional mayhem! ◆

Creating a Dfs Tree

Creating a Dfs tree is a straightforward procedure. You can find the Dfs Manager from within Administrative Tools. After launching it, you must create a new root volume (see Figure 2.17).

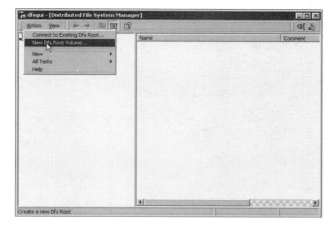

Figure 2.17   *Creating a Dfs root volume.*

Doing so launches the Create New Dfs Root Wizard, shown in Figure 2.18. (These wizards are getting pretty specialized, aren't they?) Following our own recommendations, let's choose the fault-tolerant root.

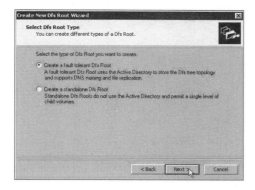

Figure 2.18   *Creating the fault-tolerant root.*

Figure 2.19 shows the new root, named \\win2kdomteam.com\DfsRoot.
Note that the start of this UNC name is the domain in which the Dfs tree
exists, not the particular server. Because the Dfs tree topology is stored in
the Active Directory, a Dfs client doesn't depend on any single server's
availability to determine what Dfs child node maps to what network share.
The client queries the Active Directory of the domain, not the server. This
figure also shows all the tasks you can perform against a Dfs root, brought
up as the context menu by right-clicking the root.

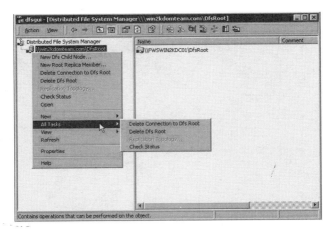

Figure 2.19   *The new Dfs root and its context menu.*

A root isn't very useful without somewhere to go inside it, so let's add a
child node (see Figure 2.20). This network share is a software repository
named \\VEGA\PUBLIC; inside the tree we give it the more descriptive name,
\Software.

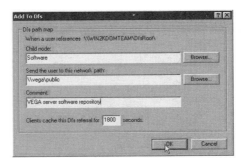

Figure 2.20   *Adding a child node.*

Note the icons in the top-right of the MMC console in Figure 2.21. These are context icons, similar to items in the context menu that vary depending on the characteristics of the object on which you've right-clicked. These icons also vary according to the object and, in this case, perform tasks such as creating or deleting a new child node, creating a new replica, or checking the health of the tree.

Figure 2.21 shows the end result of a Dfs root and two child nodes. (\Department was also added.)

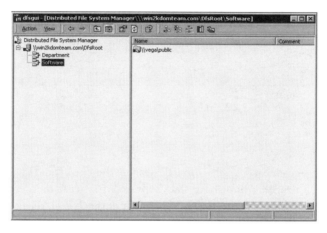

Figure 2.21   *A Dfs root with two child nodes.*

When connected to the Dfs root, the client sees a standard network connection (see Figure 2.22). The subdirectories under this network drive are actually junction points to the network shares \\FWSCOMMON001\FWIT and \\VEGA\PUBLIC, respectively. Note that this is a Windows NT 4 client; it's connected to a specific machine (FWSWIN2KDC01) instead of the system's domain.

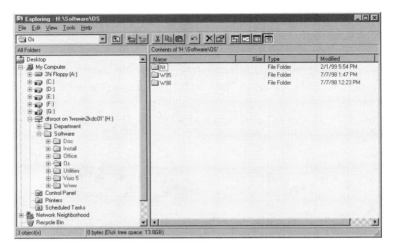

Figure 2.22   *The client's view of the Dfs tree.*

Replicas

As I mentioned before when I first described the cool things that Dfs can do, a replica is a network share that contains duplicate data from another share. A good non-Dfs example of a replica is the NETLOGON share on Windows NT 4 domain controllers. These shares contain identical data that is (usually) replicated via the Replicator service.

When a Windows 2000 Dfs client touches a junction point while traversing the Dfs tree, and when this junction point maps to a set of replicas, the client queries the Active Directory for a list of the replicas. The client keeps this replica list in its local cache. Because a Windows 2000 client is aware of network costs through the site concept (see Chapter 3 for more information), it chooses the lowest-cost replica. (Specifically, the Windows 2000 client tries to choose a replica at his own site. For details on how a client chooses site-specific services, see Chapter 6, "Designing Your Windows 2000 Core Services.") If more than one replica exists in the lowest-cost site, the client chooses one randomly. At this point, the client performs a session setup and continues as with a regular referral. If one of these replicas should die, the client chooses another out of its cache.

A Windows NT 4 Dfs client isn't aware of sites and so simply chooses a replica at random. This has unfortunate consequences if your replicas are spread out across a large enterprise.

The two most common reasons to use replicas are for load distribution and fault tolerance. Replicas distribute the load because clients access a number of network shares instead of just one. Because the replicas must be kept in synchronization, and because it's only done in a loosely coupled manner by the File Replication Service (FRS), replicas work best in a read-only situation such as a software repository.

Replicas are fault-tolerant because if one fails, the client simply chooses another one and continues. This fault tolerance is still tempered by the replica's "read mostly, write occasionally" limitation. A good use of replicas would integrate Dfs with a popular Web site. The Web server or round-robin list of servers, as Dfs clients, would simply see a directory containing a popular or important section of its Web site, but underneath many replicas would support the high traffic to its pages.

To be a replica, data must have been replicated from somewhere. With Dfs 4.1, the administrator had to scare up some replication scheme of his own with Robocopy from the *Windows NT Resource Kit* or some other utility. Dfs 5 uses the FRS, yet another service (and acronym) that comes with the product.

Dfs Recommendations

Dfs is a great thing. It lifts the user up a layer from the plumbing of the network so that she can focus on the data itself and not where it's physically distributed on the network. The degree to which you deploy Dfs depends on your administration model. Your support team must answer a few questions:

- To what level should the right to administer Dfs trees be delegated? Users can't modify Dfs tree structures themselves.

- How should the enterprise Dfs topology be designed? Should trees be scattered throughout the enterprise, or should they all be linked into one overarching Dfs tree?

- What will the access rights be once the tree has been put together? A consequence of putting together a well-laid-out, logical tree is that more people will tend to traverse it. If your share permissions are lax, you have some underlying permission cleanup to do depending on obscurity of UNC names to keep people from poking around.

- What state is your physical network in? Though it won't be large, more people traversing a large, diverse Dfs topology will increase WAN traffic.

- Just because you *can* backup, search, and virus-scan a Dfs tree doesn't mean that you *should*. These operations will have significant impact on network utilization, and you should consider carefully how much of an enterprise Dfs topology Joe User has the ability to search when he's looking for Weekly.doc.

It's worth mentioning again that you won't see the benefits of Dfs's integration with the Active Directory (in particular, fault tolerance and intelligent replica selection) until its clients have upgraded to Windows 2000. Therefore, Dfs should be deployed only on a limited basis until the client upgrade is complete. A good interim solution would be to sponsor several Dfs pilots around the company to familiarize some users—but more importantly, the administrators and help desk—with the concepts of Dfs.

Summary

Windows NT's file system has been an excellent design from its inception, but it lacked the extensions needed to support enterprise-scale applications and manage large user populations. Microsoft has added those extensions in Windows 2000 for software developers to create storage products that haven't been possible in previous versions of Windows NT. Microsoft also has partnered with several software companies to provide basic functionality for management tools such as defragmentation, HSM, volume management, and quota management. It's up to us as administrators and architects, though, to sift through this array of new features and decide whether a feature is usable "out of the box," whether the full product must be purchased, or whether to simply leave it alone. Just because it's offered doesn't mean it's wise—or manageable—to use it.

---

[1]*Official DVD FAQ,*
`http://www.videodiscovery.com/vdyweb/DVD/dvdfaq.html`

3

Distributed Services in Windows 2000

The distributed services of Windows 2000 are the subsystems whose components are spread throughout the network. The most important of these services are the Active Directory, security, management, and network services such as Domain Name System (DNS). In addition to being the most important components of Windows 2000, they're also highly dependent on one another. In this chapter, you'll learn about these services, and you'll be able to make a more informed decision about whether you need to upgrade to Windows 2000.

The Active Directory

"Information through a firehose." That's a common description for the problem so many of us deal with every day: how to organize the information we decide to keep from the ocean that washes over us. Names, addresses (business/home/email/IP), three or four phone numbers for each contact, personal Web sites, appointments, due dates, birthdays, anniversaries... the list is endless. We all have a friend who uses sticky-note pads as a data store ("Wait! I know it's here somewhere..."). My personal information manager is my dumping ground for any piece of information I may need in the future. Once I enter it into this central information database (replicated across three computers for safety!), I know that a simple query will instantly retrieve it.

Windows NT suffers from the same problem. Information in a Windows NT 4 network can be stored in many places, and there's no master card catalog to help you find a piece of data. The Security Accounts Manager (SAM) database on Windows NT Server is shared among domain controllers, but it contains only security information such as accounts, groups, and policies, and you can't add any other type of information to it. If something isn't in the SAM, applications must put it in the registry or must create their own reference file.

The Active Directory is designed to be the mother of all directory services. Every service in Windows 2000 (and there are a lot of them!) that requires a directory store now uses—or can use—Active Directory. It's designed to be the centralized information store for a Windows NT network of any scale you can imagine.

In a computer network, a *directory service* is a service used to locate all network services and information. This simple definition covers a lot of ground. Do you need to know what subnets make up the site XYZ? It's in there. What's user Jim Bob's phone number? It's in there (if the administrators loaded it in to begin with). What users are authorized to distribute software to workstations? It's in the Active Directory.

The Active Directory is designed to hold all the network information that's relatively static. This means that it holds printer information but not print jobs, email-related information but not email. Because all network information that's useful and relatively static is in the Active Directory, it's available to be used by a wide variety of services and applications.

Some of the most prominent features of the Active Directory follow:

- It's designed to be capable of growing to a size so large that no enterprise will ever run out of capacity. Each data store (that is, domain) is designed to hold up to 10 million objects. In Beta 1, the Active Directory scaled to 1.1 million objects; as of Beta 3, it has been tested to 32 million objects—enough to support even the most growth-oriented companies for a while (see Part II, "Choosing Hardware for Windows 2000," for more on the hardware costs of such scalability).

- Administrative rights to create and manage user or group accounts can be delegated to the level of organizational units (OUs). Access rights can be granted to individual properties on user objects to allow, for example, the Help Desk to have the right only to reset passwords, but not to modify other account information.

- It's designed to open standards, being X.500-compatible without being X.500-*compliant* (few directory services put in all the overhead necessary for full compliance). The Active Directory uses Lightweight Directory Access Protocol (LDAP) as its main communication protocol. Because it uses standard Internet protocols, the Active Directory can talk to other directories that use these protocols.

- It supports Windows NT 3.51 and 4, to which it appears to be another Windows NT 4 domain controller.

- It uses DNS, the naming service of the Internet, to perform name resolution (finding a system's IP address from its name) instead of Windows Internet Naming Service (WINS), a proprietary Microsoft product. *Windows 2000 and Active Directory depend on DNS.*

- It's *partitioned* into domains, which means that the Active Directory objects aren't all in one place. The directory store in a domain contains only the objects that are part of that domain. If you query domain1.com for a user who is part of domain2.com, you'll come up empty. This keeps the size of the Active Directory data store down because no single data store in the whole network contains *every* object and *every* attribute. How do you get information about an object in another domain? The Global Catalog contains the Active Directory index.

- It's *replicated*, which means that information shared among the domain controllers of a domain—and also between the Global Catalog servers—is passed around so that everyone updates everyone else.

- It's designed to be pretty flexible. Many reconfiguration tasks that were very time-consuming or practically impossible can now be performed much more easily, most without rebooting. Also, the Active Directory comes pre-populated with all kinds of objects that a network might need. If you determine that its default objects aren't enough, you can add objects and attributes to it.

There are many components to Active Directory's namespace structure, and very few are familiar to the Windows NT 4 professional. Some are familiar concepts done in a new way, and others are brand-new to the Windows NT environment.

> **Note**
>
> *I'll explain the concepts and any new terms we come across in the process. Unfortunately, these are all interrelated, so I'm occasionally guilty of using a term I haven't yet described to define a new term!*

Namespace Architecture and Concepts

A term that soon gets lobbed around in Active Directory discussions is *namespace*. This is one of those terms that spreads quickly because it sounds kind of neat and you think you kinda know what it means—maybe. Well, a namespace is the naming structure, the framework in which a name can be resolved. For example, a namespace we're all familiar with is POTS—plain old telephone system. Name resolution in this namespace means resolving a phone number from a name in the phone book—or, if you're lazy like I am, calling Information. (For a fee, many POTS name resolvers will automatically establish a point-to-point session as well—they'll connect you to your caller.) The WINS namespace is the collection of all NetBIOS names registered in the WINS server architecture. The Windows NT 4 namespace is the domain because it's the framework in which a name—the user's account—can be resolved.

As with WINS, the Windows NT 4 domain is a *flat namespace*; this means there's only one level of name resolution. Only one spdeuby account can exist in a Windows NT 4 domain. There's no structure to support something such as GodlikeAdmins\spdeuby and LowlyUsers\spdeuby as separate, valid accounts in the same domain. Because the directory store is part of the Windows NT registry, it's also limited in how large it can be manageably scaled. The limit most often mentioned is a SAM of 60MB; I know of several examples much larger than that, but no one would ever say they're easy to manage.

In contrast, the DNS namespace is hierarchical, built on domain names (DNS domains, not Windows NT domains). In a DNS name, these are added from right to left, which means that the *root domain* is at the top of the naming scheme. Because DNS is the naming service of the Internet, anyone who has ever surfed the Web has used DNS names. A simple example is well-known: www.yahoo.com. Parsing the name from right to left, we have these components:

- com—Originally reserved for commercial enterprises (for-profit businesses)
- yahoo—The domain name (which in most cases is the company name)
- www—The Web services of Yahoo!

This is important as we begin talking about Windows 2000 domains.

As if the average Windows NT administrator doesn't have enough to learn about Windows 2000, he must also learn some of the basic concepts of object-oriented programming.

This is because the Active Directory is based on an object model; everything in a Windows 2000 domain—users, groups, machine accounts, printers, published disk volumes—is an object. (And, I think, another reason is because it's written by a bunch of folks who live and breathe this stuff, so why shouldn't you, too? See the introduction to Appendix D, "Glossary," for a little more information on this.) So, let's cover a few object-oriented concepts, moving from smallest to largest, before we delve into Active Directory architecture any further.

An *attribute* is a characteristic of something. For example, one attribute or characteristic of an apple is that it has a skin. The value of this particular skin attribute is (for a Macintosh) "red." Attributes are also referred to as *properties*.

An *object* is a collection of attributes or characteristics that represent something. Objects are a pretty easy concept because they're all around us: pencil objects, tree objects, Oscar Mayer Wienermobile objects. All these have a distinct set of attributes that make one object different from another. In Active Directory, the user object is a good example. It has a name, a description, an employee number, an email address, and so on that collectively make it different than a printer.

An *object class,* or just *class,* is a grouping or categorization of objects. Apples, oranges, and lemons may have different color attributes, but they all belong to the object class "fruit." An important attribute of classes is *inheritance*, the capability of one class of objects to inherit properties from a higher class. Because an orange is an object from the class fruit, it inherits all the properties of that class, such as having a skin.

A *container* is an object that can contain other objects. The most obvious example of a container is that little manila folder icon we see every day on our screens: the directory. A file directory is a container than can contain other directories (containers) and documents. In the Active Directory, for example, the Computer container holds both server and workstation objects (machine accounts).

Figure 3.1 shows the composition of a container that holds fruit and Oscar Mayer Wienermobile classes.

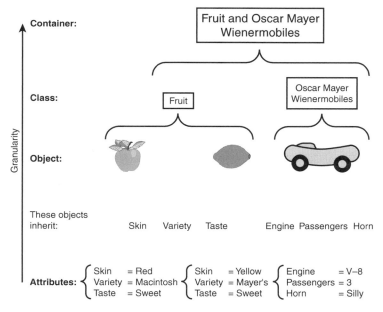

Figure 3.1   *Object-oriented programming constructs.*

Domains

The domain is one of several concepts in the Active Directory namespace architecture that carries over from Windows NT 4. The Active Directory is broken into pieces and spread out across the enterprise. This *partitioning*, as Microsoft likes to describe it, takes advantage of a well-known principle: Most of us do most of our work close to home, most of the time. As the well-known statistic tells us, "Most accidents occur within 25 miles of home" because that's where we spend most of our time. When we go shopping, it's usually nearby. If we need to buy that special gadget and can't find it locally, we probably have to make some inquiries to find a place that carries it. That's okay; most of the time we can find what we need without having to do extended searches.

For the Active Directory, "within 25 miles of home" means a domain. I'm not necessarily talking about *physically* close together, but in terms of what you as a Windows NT client reference. A domain is the unit of partitioning for the Active Directory. Every directory object contained in your domain—user names, user security credentials, phone numbers, email addresses, printer locations, and so on—can be accessed directly from your friendly neighborhood domain controller. In a well-designed domain architecture, this is usually also where most of your local resources are located. This way, everyone does most of their work locally, with local computing resources.

A domain is also the unit of replication for the Active Directory. Inside a domain (that is, intradomain) the entire contents of that domain's objects are replicated among all the domain controllers, with no one domain controller owning the master copy. I go into more detail on this in the section "Server Security Roles" later in this chapter. Outside the domain, only some of this information is replicated, to servers called Global Catalog servers.

Domain Structure

An often-overlooked change in the domain paradigm is how you're supposed to *draw* them. Windows NT 3.x/4 domains were always drawn as ovals; Windows 2000 domains seem to always be drawn as triangles. Perhaps they've changed because it's easier to draw Windows 2000 security relationships with triangles—or because the marketing wizards want to distinguish Windows 2000 from its predecessors. Figure 3.2 shows a default Windows 2000 domain, which includes the following components:

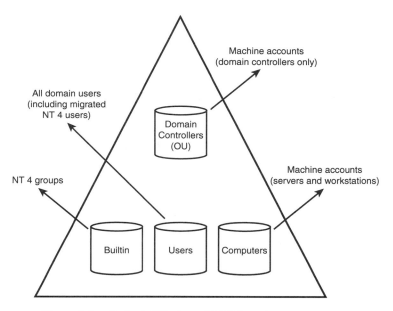

Figure 3.2 *Default Windows 2000 domain structure.*

- A built-in container holds group objects from Windows NT 4.
- The Computers container holds computer accounts in the domain. This includes servers, workstations, and migrated Windows NT 4 computer accounts.
- The Users container holds all user accounts, including migrated Windows NT 4 accounts and Windows 2000 groups.
- Domain Controllers is a special kind of container—an OU—that holds domain controllers for the domain, including downlevel Windows NT 3.5x and 4 domain controllers.

Figure 3.3 shows a domain's default containers, as well as sample user and printer objects. Note that there's no printer container; a domain that contains printers and that has been upgraded will have a printer container. A domain that has been constructed from scratch won't have a printer container unless one of the domain controllers had print services installed before it was promoted.

You can create a number of new objects in the Windows 2000 domain. Just a few examples are:

- Computers—Member servers and Windows NT 4/Windows 2000 clients.
- Contacts—For example, an Outlook contact, a reference to a person that holds personal information.

- Groups—See the "Groups" section later in the chapter.
- OUs—See "OUs and Distributed Administration" later in this chapter.
- Printers—Printing resources, with location, model, and management information.
- Users—Information about each user, from account name to fax number. Literally hundreds of attributes are associated with the User object.
- Shared folders—Used when a network share is published to the domain rather than a server alone. Most often used with the Distributed File System.

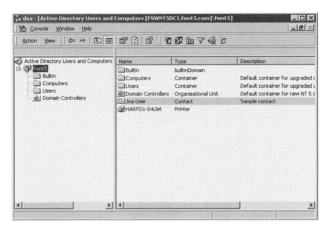

Figure 3.3 *Default Windows 2000 domain (viewed from the MMC) with sample Contact and Printer objects.*

Domain Schema

In addition to data, all relational databases contain *metadata*, which means data about the data. The metadata we're concerned with now is the *schema,* which is the definition of all the object types that can be stored in the Active Directory. In other words, it describes how the contents of the Active Directory are structured. There's a class definition for each type of object and an attribute definition for each attribute. For example, the Active Directory schema has a class definition for User and an attribute definition for AccountExpires.

Figure 3.4 shows the Classes and Attributes containers, viewed in the Active Directory Schema Manager.

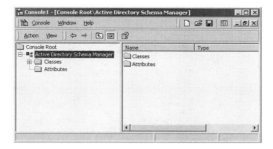

Figure 3.4 *Classes and Attributes containers in the Active Directory schema.*

Figure 3.5 shows a small sampling of all the object definitions (Classes) in the schema.

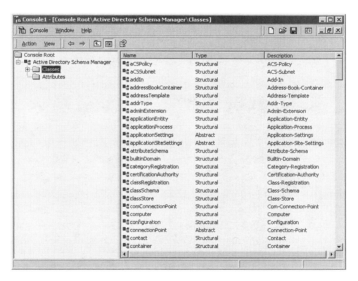

Figure 3.5 *Some of the Classes in the Active Directory schema.*

Figure 3.6 is a small sampling of the attributes predefined for the User object. More than 300 attributes are defined for the User object alone, so you're likely to find an appropriate attribute already in place for your use.

As you can tell from the preceding figures, the schema is itself defined in the Active Directory. (It's sort of a chicken-and-egg thing.) The practical upshot of this feature is that if the existing schema classes won't do what you need, you can extend the schema by adding classes and attributes.

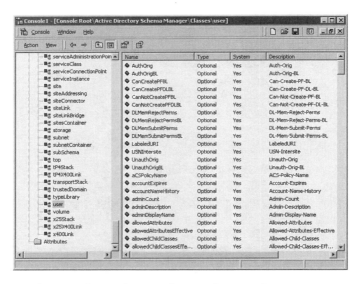

Figure 3.6   *The User class and some of its attributes in the Active Directory schema*

Warning

Just because you can do something doesn't mean that you should. Schema extension is a serious business. You thought hacking the Registry was serious? This can be many times more dangerous. Changing a server's Registry only affects that server; schema changes are permanent, are enterprisewide, and cannot be undone. After you add a class, it can be disabled but never deleted from the schema. If you do create a new class, you must also provide a globally unique X.500 object ID (OID). OIDs are issued by a national registration authority, which in the United States is American National Standards Institute (ANSI) at `http://web.ansi.org./public/services/reg_org.html`*. Think very carefully— and then think again—before you modify the schema. A corollary to this is that no one should by default have access to the Schema Administrators group. The rights should be locked away and be accessible only after a review board has approved an application to modify the schema.*

OUs and Distributed Administration

OUs are part of the logical structure of the Active Directory. As a container that holds other objects (such as users, groups, printers, and even other OUs), the main purpose of an OU is to create a security boundary within a domain that allows administrative rights to be delegated. Good examples of OUs are divisions, departments, and workgroups—it all depends on how far down into the organization you want to distribute administration. The OU wraps a boundary around a group of people that can be managed together. This is different than a group of people with similar security requirements; security groups handle that task.

For example, in Figure 3.7 the domain research.mycompany.com has an OU named Res-ProgMgrs for the corporate program managers. The global group PMAdmins contains ordinary users in the domain, but these users have administrative rights over only the objects in the Res-ProgMgrs OU. This is an example of *delegation*—the ability of a higher administrative authority to grant specific rights to groups and individuals. There's another OU in this figure: It's called PM-Assistants (note the DNS-friendly hyphen instead of a space or underscore), and the arrow from the Res-ProgMgrs OU to it indicates that it's in the Res-ProgMgrs OU container. This means that by default PM-Assistants *inherits* security entries from its parent container, the Res-ProgMgrs OU. In other words, the PMAdmins group can also administer PM-Assistants. Delegation and inheritance are two features that can easily control administrative rights in an entire domain tree. There's also a Delegation Wizard to help you through the commons steps for delegating administration responsibility.

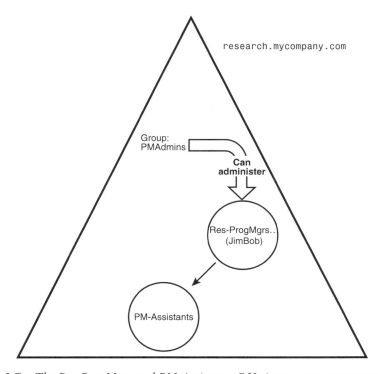

Figure 3.7   *The Res-ProgMgrs and PM-Assistants OUs in* research.mycompany.com.

One more important point about OUs: Just as with the unwritten law that says domains should be drawn as triangles, OUs should be drawn as circles.

Names and GUIDs

Naming domains and their objects in Windows 2000 can be confusing because an object can be accessed several ways. The following sections describe the naming systems.

DNS Names

Domains are usually referred to by their *DNS names*. In fact, Windows 2000 domain names *are* DNS names. A Windows NT 4 account domain named RESEARCH that's upgraded to Windows 2000 becomes research .mycompany.com. Because domain names are DNS names, you can tell exactly where a Windows 2000 domain fits into the company hierarchy by dissecting its name. We'll look at this in more detail later in the chapter, in the section "Trusts and Domain Trees."

Windows 2000 domains also have a NetBIOS name so that downlevel Windows NT systems can reference them. You choose the downlevel name during the domain controller upgrade process; a name is suggested by the DCPROMO wizard and is usually a good choice.

UPNs

User principal names (UPN) are also called RFC 822 names. Most of us (fortunately) don't recognize RFC numbers for the standards they represent, though, so this is better known as a UPN or "friendly" name in a format we all recognize: JimRobert@mycompany.com. Mr. Robert (Jim Bob, to his friends) can use this exact name to log in to a Windows 2000 workstation. See the Windows 2000 domain name of mycompany.com in the address? This means that one name is used as both the user's email address and the domain location in MyCompany Corporation's Windows NT network.

X.500 Distinguished Names

The distinguished name (from RFC 1779) is really unfriendly, and most of us won't have cause to use it; it's meant to be used by directory protocols such as LDAP. The structure is designed to be capable of linking directory services together in sort of a planetary white pages directory—literally billions of objects. A consequence is that there are no shortcuts; everything must be specified every time. A typical X.500 name used by LDAP to reach Jim Bob might be this one:

```
CN=James Robert, OU= Res-ProgMgr, OU=Research, O= mycompany,C=US
```

In this name, working from left to right, you have Jim Bob's components:

- User name. (CN = common name)
- Organizational unit of his department. (OU = organizational unit name)
- Research domain. Note that X.500 OUs aren't identical to Active Directory OUs; this Windows 2000 domain is described as an OU in an X.500 distinguished name.
- Company name. (O = Organization)
- Company's country. (C = Country)

As you can see, this name locates an object anywhere on the planet, but it's major overkill for the average user. If you want to know more about X.500, check out *X.500 Directory Services* by Sara Radicati (published by Van Nostrand Reinhold), which is a clear and concise reference on the topic.

HTTP URL Names
You can reach domain objects via HTTP, although it isn't really any friendlier than the X.500 name:
```
http://www.mycompany.com/User.ASP?path=/OU=Research
➥/OU= Res-ProgMgrs /CN=JimBobUser
```

UNC Names
Universal naming convention (UNC) names (for Microsoft networking, \\server\share\path-to-file) are used to refer to shared volumes, printers, and files published in the Active Directory.

GUIDs
Even though any object in the Active Directory can be referred to by any of the names mentioned in the preceding sections, underneath the covers there's one attribute that does not change: the globally unique identifier (GUID, pronounced "gwid"). You can think of GUID as the Son of SID (security identifier). As with a Windows NT 4 SID, a GUID is supposed to be a unique security identifier. I say "supposed to be" because the SID was also supposed to be unique until the technique of cloning systems (and therefore their SIDs) became popular. A GUID is a 128-bit integer, guaranteed to be unique, that an application can use to reference an Active Directory object, no matter what it has been named or renamed.

Trusts and Domain Trees

A maxim of the Windows NT 4 architect or administrator is "NTLM trusts are non-transitive." (The *LM* stands for LAN Manager, Microsoft's original networking product.) For those of us who have forgotten our high school math theory, this means that if Domain A trusts Domain B, and if Domain B trusts Domain C, then Domain A *doesn't* trust Domain C. For the two domains to pass account information back and forth, explicit one- or two-way trusts must be set up between them.

This limitation of the NTLM trust model determines the entire Windows NT 4 series of domain models: single, master, full trust, and multiple master. (Independent domains also exist, which is what you get if you don't use trusts at all.) To break free of this limitation, Windows 2000 uses the Kerberos authentication protocol. Kerberos is a very powerful, recognized security protocol used around the world. For the purposes of this discussion, let's just say that Kerberos enables Windows 2000 to have transitive trusts: Domain A can now trust Domain C.

This enables Windows 2000 to build *domain trees*, which are domains linked together by Kerberos transitive trusts in much the same manner as a directory structure (see Figure 3.8). The domains have DNS names, so the naming structure logically follows the tree structure. This domain tree forms a contiguous namespace, because the DNS names can all be traced back to the root domain mycompany.com. The domain tree also shares a common Global Catalog.

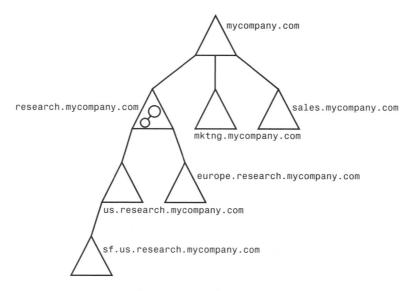

Figure 3.8   *A domain tree and its member domain names.*

The trusts in a domain tree are automatic; you don't have to explicitly set up any trusts in this example to get full connectivity around the tree. The only action the administrator takes is choosing where in the tree the domain should join (i.e., "Do you want your domain under `research.mycompany.com` or `sales.mycompany.com`?" A user in `sf.us.research.mycompany.com` can then grant a user in `sales.mycompany.com` access to his presentation.).

You can follow the path of a Kerberos referral by simply traversing up the domains along the trust path as far as you need to reach the topmost domain that contains both "legs," and then traversing through the "downward leg" that contains the target domain. Figure 3.9 shows the referral path from `sf.us.research.mycompany.com` to `sales.mycompany.com`.

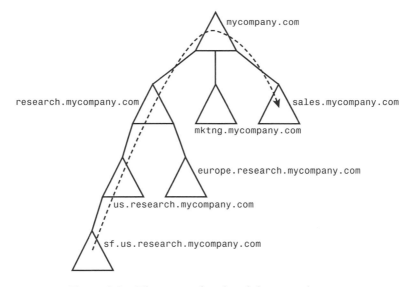

Figure 3.9 *The trust referral path between domains.*

The logical representation of a hierarchical directory database is an X.500 concept, where it's called a *directory information tree* (DIT). This is actually what Microsoft called this construct until the marketing people got Active-ly involved (sorry).

There's another kind of trust in a Windows 2000 domain tree: the explicit trust. This is an NTLM one-way trust, just as with Windows NT 4. It's used to link downlevel Windows NT domains to the domain tree and to establish links between domain trees. The domains linked with these trusts establish their relationship only with each other; they're not transitive. This trust could be used to grant access to a single domain in a company's domain tree for a joint venture.

A special case exists for referrals with downlevel trusts. As I've said, a Windows NT 3.5x/4 server or domain that establishes a trust with a Windows 2000 server trusts only the Windows 2000 server's domain, not the entire domain tree or forest. However, a downlevel Windows NT 3.5x/4 workstation that is part of a Windows 2000 domain (usually from an upgrade to Windows 2000), which automatically has an implicit NTLM trust to a Windows 2000 domain controller, *can* access other objects in the domain tree. This property can be turned off from the Trusts property sheet in the domain properties of the Active Directory Tree Manager.

Forests

A forest takes the tree analogy a bit further: It's simply two or more domain trees that share a common schema and a Global Catalog. The signature characteristic of a forest is that, unlike a domain tree, a forest doesn't have a contiguous namespace. All trees in a forest (and therefore, domains) trust each other via transitive trusts even though they aren't explicitly shown in tree diagrams.

Forests could be used when an enterprise has several autonomous business units that don't need to communicate extensively with one another. Figure 3.10 is a very recognizable example of a forest.

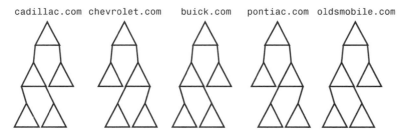

cadillac.com chevrolet.com   buick.com   pontiac.com oldsmobile.com

Figure 3.10   *A possible forest.*

The Global Catalog

Because the Active Directory is partitioned off into domains—each of which contains its own objects but no others—how do you discover resources and objects in other domains? That's where the Global Catalog comes in.

The Global Catalog is an index that contains every object in the Active Directory—that is, every object in every domain in the forest of directory trees. Even though it contains every object, to keep its size manageable the Global Catalog holds only a few select attributes of each object. The attributes it keeps are the ones you're most likely to search for, such as user names, email addresses, and printer locations.

If your Windows 2000 client issues a local query (i.e., in your domain) for an object and it's not found, it will query the nearest Global Catalog server for it. If the attribute you're searching for is in the Global Catalog (for example, Jim Bob's email address), the server will return the attribute value. If the object is in the Global Catalog but the attribute isn't, it will return the domain that contains the object so that you can be referred there via Kerberos trusts. If the object isn't in the Global Catalog, it doesn't exist in the forest.

With the Global Catalog, you have an address book that you can query without having to chase information all over the enterprise. In its default implementation, you don't have to do anything; Global Catalogs will be created on the appropriate servers. However, if you're implementing Windows 2000 in an enterprise of any size—especially when your company is spread across a wide area network, and *especially* if you use Microsoft Exchange—you need to pay careful attention to Global Catalog server placement.

Groups

The best explanation I've heard for why you should use groups is also the simplest: crowd control. Groups allow the administrator to manipulate large numbers of users at one time. Windows NT has been around long enough that everyone has figured out how to use global groups and local groups, so the rules have changed. Generally, this is for the better, but naturally it's another example of a basic shift in one's Windows NT-think. Let's list the biggest changes to groups in Windows 2000:

- Group types—Windows NT 4 has two group types: global and local. Windows 2000 has three types of groups: universal, global, and domain local.

- Nesting—Windows NT 4 has two layers of nesting groups, and then only local groups can be in global groups. Windows 2000 groups can be nested in one another (with some limitations), theoretically without limit.

- Distribution lists—Windows NT 4 has no provision for using groups as mail distribution lists. Microsoft Exchange 6.0 can use Windows 2000 groups as distribution lists. Fallout from this also means that you can create groups with the security features disabled so that they act as simple lists.

Universal Groups

Universal groups are truly that—and they're pretty straightforward. Universal groups can contain members from anywhere in the forest and can go in any access control list (ACL) on any object in the forest. That's about as far-reaching as anything in the Active Directory gets. Universal groups can contain other universal groups, global groups, and individual users. They contain administrative security groups such as Enterprise Administrators. Universal groups are published only in Global Catalog servers because they're the only universal Active Directory security principal.

Global Groups

Global groups are a lot like they used to be in Windows NT 4, but with some differences in nesting. Global groups can go into any ACL anywhere in the forest, but they contain only members from the group's domain. Unlike Windows NT 4, however, they can't contain domain local groups; they can contain only other global groups and individual users. Global groups aren't published in the Global Catalog.

Domain Local Groups

As you might guess from the name, domain local groups are the Windows 2000 equivalent of Windows NT 4 local groups that reside in the domain, not on a member server. Windows NT 4 domains that upgrade to Windows 2000 will have their local groups converted to domain local groups. (Member server's local groups aren't part of the Active Directory, so they remain unchanged from Windows NT 4. Hey, we found one thing that hasn't changed!) Domain local groups can contain universal groups, global groups, and individual users, but their scope is only in their own domain. They can be used on any ACL only in their own domain. Local groups also aren't published in the Global Catalog.

Another small difference between the two operating system releases is that you see Windows 2000 groups explicitly referred to as *security groups*. This is because you can now disable security in a group if you want to make it just a distribution list. For clarity, call them security groups or distribution groups. All groups can be nested together in limited combinations, not just to simplify management as in Windows NT 4, but also to minimize replication of changes around the Active Directory. Chapter 6, "Designing your Windows 2000 Core Services," discusses how to use these groups to minimize replication.

Server Security Roles

The security roles a server can play in Windows 2000 have changed a lot, both in the broad sense and in the details. Here's a quick rundown of the changes:

- The roles of primary domain controller and backup domain controller have gone away. They've been replaced with the concept of *multi-master replication*, where no single server owns the master copy of domain security principals. (See the section "Replication" later in this chapter for more details.) If a server participates in domain authentication, it's just called a *domain controller*.

- The role of domain controller is no longer set in stone. Until Windows 2000, a domain controller was determined when the operating system was installed. The only way to change the role of a server was to completely rebuild it, losing all settings in the process. Windows 2000 simplifies the process considerably with the DCPROMO Wizard. Not found anywhere in the Windows 2000 user interface, DCPROMO changes the role of a Windows 2000 server. Running DCPROMO on a member server promotes it to a domain controller, and running it on a domain controller demotes it to a member server. (These actions still require a server reboot.)

- Many services can now run on a Windows 2000 server. You can install up to 22 services when first building a Windows 2000 member server; for example, in the Advanced Server configuration, Clustering Service and IIS are automatically installed. Promoting a member server to a domain controller adds more services, including Kerberos Key Distribution Center, Global Catalog, File Replication Service, and, of course, the directory service. These services don't even show in the Services management application.

- Member servers are architecturally mostly the same as their Windows NT 4 ancestors. They still use a SAM for their local accounts, but they query the Active Directory for domain accounts. They rely on domain controllers for initial authentication of a client, but because they're running the Kerberos server service as the primary authentication mechanism, they use tickets instead of implicit trusts to the friendly neighborhood domain controller. They can be moved from domain to domain with relative ease. Member server is still the backbone configuration for 90% of production servers.

Sites

The sites concept is very straightforward and long overdue in Windows NT; it finally brings knowledge of the physical topology of the network into the operating system. A site is a collection of domain controllers that have high-speed connections to optimize replication and logon traffic. They're defined in Active Directory as well-connected subnets. Figure 3.11 illustrates two sites, Site_1 and Site_2. Each has its own collection of subnets that describes the site's boundaries.

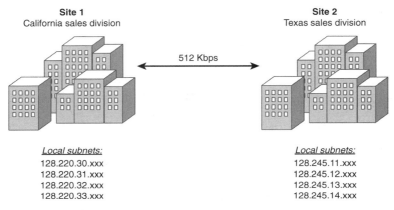

Site 1
California sales division

512 Kbps

Site 2
Texas sales division

Local subnets:
128.220.30.xxx
128.220.31.xxx
128.220.32.xxx
128.220.33.xxx

Local subnets:
128.245.11.xxx
128.245.12.xxx
128.245.13.xxx
128.245.14.xxx

Figure 3.11   *Two sites separated by a WAN link.*

Sites are used throughout Windows 2000, specifically to control replication and to aid logon authentication. How sites influence replication is described in the following section. In logon authentication, sites are used to solve that perennial problem: How to ensure that the client gets authenticated by a local domain controller instead of by \\TIMBUKTU-DC1. For details on the client startup and logon authentication process, see Chapter 6.

Replication

It's really not accurate to say that the Active Directory uses multimaster replication. What the Active Directory really has is a multimaster update *model*; replication is the process of passing the updates between the domain controllers.

The Update Model

The multimaster update model says that there is no primary domain controller, no single keeper of the read/write master copy of the security database. Instead, every domain controller in a domain has an updateable copy of the domain's objects (multiple masters).

Because updates can be made to any domain controller, there must be a way to keep them all in synchronization. How tightly should they be kept in sync? Too tight a synchronization introduces all kinds of problems—high processor utilization, high bandwidth utilization, poor tolerance to network, or topology faults. Too loose a synchronization schedule increases consistency problems—the chance that changes will conflict with one another.

The compromise Microsoft reached is a loosely consistent replication model, with some special cases. "Loosely consistent" means that changes are not so tightly synchronized that it is possible (but generally unlikely) that the same change will be made someplace else, on another domain controller. In contrast, a well-known example of a tightly consistent replication model is a database transaction processor. Multiple reads can be made from any given element in a database, but only one process can update an element. The concept of a transaction means that any query or update of a database will always have the up-to-date data. A loosely consistent model, however, depends on the empirical fact that directory service databases are "read mostly, write occasionally." Most services query information in the Active Directory—such as user accounts, email addresses, DNS records, security keys such as hashed passwords, and so on—but don't update them. This means that updates are the exception rather than the norm, so the probability of an update conflict is low enough that the high-power rules of a transaction processor aren't required. There's a fairly high overhead associated with updates to the Active Directory because of replication, contention for resources, and possible conflict resolution.

This is where sites tie into replication. The Active Directory takes sites into account when determining replication frequency to its various domain controllers. Replication between domain controllers within a site (that is, intrasite) happens much more frequently than replication between sites. Updates between sites (that is, intersite) can be scheduled and the data is compressed. Intrasite updates can't be scheduled and the data is uncompressed.

Because a loosely consistent replication model makes its updates on a regular basis but doesn't lock out the element being updated, it introduces the problem of *replicative latency*. It's a great nerd phrase, but it means that it takes time for the change to work its way across the network. If you change your email address and someone at another site queries your email address from the Active Directory a minute later, this person will get the old email address.

This isn't a big deal for objects such as email addresses, but what about passwords or account lockouts? If someone is attempting to crack your network using a user account, you want your lockout of that account to happen immediately across the network, not as the replication scheme sees fit. *Urgent replication* was created for this reason. Urgent replication is used for certain Active Directory updates, such as password changes and account lockouts. These changes are replicated across all domain controllers and Global Catalog servers immediately instead of waiting for the normal update schedule.

How does Active Directory keep track of what needs to be replicated among the domain controllers within a site? The conventional way is with a timestamp: Every change to an object property that occurred after time X should be replicated to the target domain controller. The problem with using timestamps is that time synchronization in a distributed system can be very tricky. It's difficult to get a lot of servers in exact time synch, and it's easy to unintentionally change the system time. The mechanism that something as important as directory replication relies upon shouldn't be accessible by a user or an application.

Instead, the Active Directory uses *update sequence numbers* (USNs) for synchronization. USN synchronization doesn't require that domain controllers march in lockstep with the master server. It does, however, require that they're tightly coupled to the changes made to object properties on a given domain controller. At this level, this is like transaction processing. Let's say that the area code property for the JBKing user object has changed because his friendly neighborhood global telecommunications company has added yet another area code. When he changes his area code information, the USN for that property is advanced. If for some reason the change doesn't take or the server chooses that instant to crash, then when it comes back up the USN will back out, just as in a transaction. The process is atomic; it either worked and the USN incremented by one, or it didn't and the USN remains the same.

For this reason, every domain controller has a unique USN. This USN increments every time a change is made to any property in its copy of the Active Directory, and an internal transaction log tracks what changes were made for which USN. Each domain controller also has a table of USNs for other domain controllers with which it's a replication partner. The table is updated with the last update (i.e., the highest USN) from each partner.

When a partner domain controller decides that it needs to replicate its changes, the local domain controller simply looks up the USN in its internal table (the last changes from that domain controller it knows about) and asks for all the changes made since that sequence number.

With all this work going on in replication, it seems as though it would take over available server and network resources just trying to keep the Active Directory internally consistent. It isn't as bad as it sounds, though; replications are made at the atomic level, which means that only changed objects are replicated around the domain. If someone changes his email address, for instance, only those few bytes will be replicated. Nonetheless, minimizing replication is a major goal of a good Windows 2000 design.

For more details on replication and how replication collisions are handled, see "Microsoft Windows 2000 Active Directory Technical Summary," available from `http://www.microsoft.com/windows/server/Technical/default.asp`.

FSMOs
In a few instances in the Active Directory, a single master model must be used:

- Schema master—To control updates to the Active Directory schema.

- RID pool master—To control generation and allocation of a chunk of Relative Ids (RIDs), to use for SID generation. When a domain controller is upgraded to Windows 2000 or is promoted from member status, it asks for ownership of the RID master from the domain controller that currently has it. When it owns the resource pool of RIDs, it allocates a number of RIDs from the pool with which it will generate SIDs on an as-needed basis.

- Primary domain controller advertiser—To interact with Windows NT 4 domains.

- Domain naming master—To ensure that domains don't get name conflicts.

- Infrastructure daemon—To keep references to objects in other domains, such as keeping group members up to date.

These special cases are handled with *operations masters*, originally called FSMOs—floating (or flexible, depending on who you ask) single master objects. For example, the schema master is the only place in the enterprise schema where updates can be made. It can move from one domain controller to another over time, which is why it's called the "floating" single master. Each of the cases previously listed has its own FSMO.

You can see what domain controller is the FSMO for any of these operations by accessing the Active Directory Users and Computers snap-in, also known as Directory Management from the Administrative Tools menu. Click on the target domain to expand its contents in the results pane (the rightmost pane), and then right-click on the same domain and choose Operations Masters. Microsoft is changing its terminology from FSMO to Operations Masters to make the concept a bit easier to understand.

You can also query and change the FSMOs with the command-line utility NTDSUTIL.

ADSI

In most large environments, one or more directory services have been around long before the Active Directory came along. Groupware systems (such as Notes), email, and, of course, network operating systems (such as Novell Directory Services) all have their own directory services. As you might expect, they all have different interfaces and requirements as well. Add NTDS (the original Windows NT directory service) and its APIs to the mix, and life really gets confusing. That's why Active Directory Service Interface (ADSI) was developed to provide a single, consistent, open set of interfaces for managing and using multiple directories. ADSI is Microsoft's preferred API set to access the Active Directory. In Windows 2000, you can use ADSI to write to any LDAP V2-based directory service, NetWare 3, NetWare 4, NTLM (NT 4 for downlevel compatibility), and NTDS (the Windows 2000 directory service).

ADSI communicates with each service in its own protocol—Net APIs for Windows NT 4, and LDAP for the Active Directory and NetWare 5. The Active Directory has an LDAP "listener" on port 389, the well-known port for LDAP packets.

If you want to write any kind of tool to access the Active Directory (and just about every tool will need to), you'll want to use ADSI. ADSI is easier to write to than LDAP because it's a higher-level interface than LDAP's raw C API set. Unlike the LDAP API set, developers or system administrators can write to ADSI using Visual Basic, Perl, REXX, or C/C++. This opens up lots of custom tool possibilities. For example, a custom version of User Manager could be written in Visual Basic to allow the Human Resources administrators to change an employee's work shift and pay grade in the Active Directory, and nothing else. The account administrators could have a tool for adding user accounts following specific guidelines and using simple customized interfaces.

Active Directory Comparison

Table 3.1 lists the major differences between Windows NT 3.x/4 domain architecture and the Windows 2000 Active Directory:

Table 3.1   Differences Between Windows NT 4 Domain Architecture and the Active Directory

Feature	Windows NT 4	Windows 2000
Trusts	NTLM one-way trusts	Kerberos transitive trusts, NTLM
Naming	NetBIOS	RFC 822, HTTP, LDAP, UNC
Scope	Security boundary	Security, replication boundaries
Domain types	Master/resource	Domain tree, OUs, forest
Server types	PDC, BDC, member	Domain controller, member
Replication model	Single master, multiple backups	Loosely consistent multimaster
Groups	Global, local	Universal, global, domain local

In describing the Active Directory, I've thrown around a lot of concepts (and certainly acronyms) that are probably new. Basically, Active Directory is a highly flexible database and directory service that is designed to hold all the information about the network. You can populate it with so many objects that the cost of keeping the whole thing on an individual server— and keeping replicas of it on other servers—would be too high. To avoid this, the sum total of the Active Directory is distributed across an entire Windows 2000 forest and is broken up so that in any given domain in an enterprise you have direct access to only part of it. You get to the rest by querying the Global Catalog and then contacting the remote domain.

Security

We've already discussed a lot of security topics in the section "The Active Directory" earlier in this chapter, which indicates how tightly security is integrated with the Active Directory. In Windows NT 4, the architecture of the SAM as a secured part of the Windows NT registry, and the limitations of the NTLM trust, meant that security was limited to three levels inside a domain (global groups, local groups, and users) and two outside a domain (master domains and resource domains).

When you store security information in a flexible, distributed database such as the Active Directory instead of the Windows NT registry, this enables a lot of new features such as OUs, directory trees, forests, and delegated administration that weren't possible before.

Now that your company has stored all this useful information in the Active Directory, you must be able to easily control access to it. Because the Windows 2000 security components are integrated into the Active Directory, the Active Directory objects and attributes (properties) are protected by ACLs. As a result, you can define access control of these objects down to the attribute level. In other words, you can grant access to almost all of Jim Bob's 300 user object properties but restrict access to his email address. When you add the concept of inheritance, you can set up an administration model where any user object has a set of administrators that can control only phone numbers, and another set that can control only passwords.

Protocols

Windows 2000 uses three security protocols: Kerberos, X.509 V3 public key certificates for public key infrastructure, and NTLM. Kerberos is the default protocol, public key security is used to grant Windows 2000 resource access to users outside the network who can't use Kerberos, and NTLM is used for compatibility with downlevel Windows NT 3.5x/4 domains and clients.

Both Kerberos and public key infrastructure are multileg authentication protocols. Client and server engage in a dance of exchanging certificates or keys, or tickets, to mutually authenticate one another. NTLM doesn't perform mutual authentication, and that recently has been its weak spot for crackers looking to break into a network, or at least to cause trouble for Windows NT clients. Although the Windows NT server authenticates the Windows NT client, the client assumes that the server is valid. This can allow a malicious program masquerading as a server to gain access to a Windows NT client.

Public key infrastructure, although popular on the Internet as the basis for Phil Zimmerman's Pretty Good Privacy security program, is only now starting to make its appearance in large enterprise systems.

Public Key Infrastructure

Unless you've been doing some work with secure Internet email, the concepts behind public key security are probably completely foreign to you. In the Windows NT world, security is a matter of challenge-response authentication and ACLs. The only encryption we think about, if we think about it at all, is what's done to the user's password. But public key security, or what's more commonly known as public key infrastructure (PKI), will soon be an essential security protocol for businesses working with other businesses over the Internet.

In our intranets, we use Windows NT security to authenticate who can and can't have access to resources on the network. If a user isn't on the network and doesn't have a Windows NT account, then that user can't get to the goodies—period. This presents a problem to the growing number of businesses that must work with other companies in electronic commerce: how to securely exchange information over the Internet between individuals and companies so that the sender can be verified and the data encrypted against prying eyes. These individuals don't have accounts in each other's networks, so they can't use the standard Kerberos or NTLM authentication protocols. PKI will be that solution. It uses digital certificates to confirm the identity of the data's sender and uses encryption to protect the data itself.

Two types of encryption are most widely used today: *private key* and *public key*. Private key encryption uses a shared secret, such as a password, between two parties to encrypt and decrypt data. There's a problem with shared secret encryption, though: Somehow you must transmit the password to the other party so that your data can be encrypted. How do you do that securely? Whispering in one's ear doesn't scale very well. For more on shared secret security, take a look at the "Kerberos" section that follows.

Public key encryption uses a pair of keys—one private, one public— to create *ciphertext*. These two keys are called a *key pair*. The private key is protected, but the public key is freely available. Only the public key is needed to encrypt a message, and only the private key is required to decrypt it. Both are *one-way* functions; that is, after the public key has encrypted the data, it can't be used to also decrypt it. And even though the private key can decrypt data that has been encrypted by the public key, it can't itself be used to encrypt data. In Windows 2000, both public and private keys are stored in a *certificate authority* (CA); public and private keys are determined by the access control.

Confused? Just be patient. A simple example of how public keys work is a good start (see Figure 3.12).

In this example, Alice wants to send a secure, encrypted message to Bob. (Alice and Bob are the names traditionally used for the first two users of cryptography on a system.) Windows 2000 Certificate Services has previously created a key pair for Bob; his public key is freely available from the CA (step 1). In step 2, Alice writes the message and encrypts it with Bob's public key. (Remember that the public key can only encrypt.) In step 3, Alice sends the encrypted message to Bob. Bob then uses his private key to decrypt the message (again, a one-way function—decryption only) and then reads it.

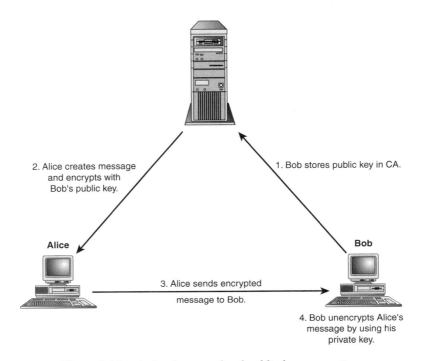

Figure 3.12 *A simple example of public key encryption.*

If you expand this example to have everyone in the enterprise create a key pair and store it in a CA or a hierarchy of CAs, you have a public key infrastructure that encrypts messages without having to share any secret passwords. Can you see how this would also be expandable beyond the boundaries of an enterprise? As long as two certificate authorities (say, one inside a company and the other on the Internet, such as Verisign) support cross-certification (i.e., they trust each other and therefore each trusts each other's users), this security infrastructure knows no bounds.

But how do you know—really *know*—that Bob's public key really is *his* key and not from someone else who just says that he's Bob? If this happened, you'd encrypt a message intended for Bob that could actually be decrypted only by the adversary spoofing Bob's account. This proves that, once again, with computers it isn't as simple as in real life. (Or, it proves just how sophisticated real life is when we try to break it down into individual processes.) In real life, we know when we're looking at Bob that it's really Bob. (Unless we've been watching reruns of *Invasion of the Body Snatchers.*) We know that if we hear Bob on the phone, it very likely is Bob.

We know if we meet someone and he shows us his driver's license (with picture), we have a high degree of confidence it's really him. This isn't the same for digital data, though, so we must come up with a way to verify that Jim is really Jim and that Bob is really Bob.

The verification is done with *digital certificates,* stored in the certificate authority. Windows 2000 PKI uses X.509 v3 digital certificates; these hold the name of the user or server, the user's public key, and the certificate's validity period and function, such as encryption or verifying digital signatures. The certificate authority attests to the validity of the digital certificate, so you know that you truly are getting Bob's public key. The certificate authority in Windows 2000 is Certificate Services, and it's managed—through the Microsoft Management Console, of course—by Certificate Manager.

These certificates can be mapped onto Windows 2000 security groups so that users who are trusted but who are outside the corporation can gain access to network resources without requiring Kerberos Two credentials.

To learn more about public key security, check out `http://` `www.entrust .com/resources/whitepapers.htm`; for everything you ever wanted to know about cryptography, go to RSA Lab's FAQ at `http://www.rsa.com/ rsalabs/faq/`.

Kerberos

Kerberos is a network authentication protocol, developed by Massachusetts Institute of Technology for transmitting data across an insecure network. It's the default protocol for Windows 2000, although public key cryptography and NTLM authentication are used when appropriate. Kerberos is a complex and powerful animal. The combination of Kerberos and Active Directory are the two biggest enabling technologies that make Windows 2000 so different from Windows NT 4.

Kerberos uses *private key* or *secret key* cryptography to do its authentication. No password ever goes across the wire, and (unlike NTLM authentication) neither the client nor the server trusts each other until the secret keys have been exchanged *(mutual authentication).* Kerberos acts as a trusted third party to handle Windows NT authentication and keep the secret keys between a client and server. Standard extensions to it allow Windows NT privileges to tag along and to be used after Kerberos has answered the critical question, "Is this guy valid?" for each party.

Where Does the Name Kerberos Come From?

Kerberos was developed out of MIT's Project Athena in 1988. The three-headed dog in Greek mythology that protected the gates of Hades was named Cerberus. However, because Athena was a Greek goddess (and, after all, it is Greek mythology), the Greek spelling of Kerberos was used instead. That's a skill they never teach you in project management class: how to choose a good metaphor for your project name so that you can have good names such as "Kerberos" for the deliverables. Imagine what Kerberos would be called today if the project manager had chosen a Marx Brothers metaphor!

Where Kerberos Is Used in Windows 2000

Kerberos is Windows 2000's default authentication protocol. A short list of the subsystems that depend on it includes the following:

- Logon authentication
- Session setup between a client and server
- Active Directory trusts
- LDAP authentication
- DNS secure dynamic update
- Distributed file system
- Host-based IP security

The Kerberos server service runs on every Windows 2000 domain controller. A Kerberos client service runs on every Windows 2000 client. All passwords and identities are stored in the Active Directory.

Why Kerberos Instead of NTLM?

NTLM is the original authentication protocol for Windows NT. Though powerful, a number of problems have become apparent as Windows NT has matured. Kerberos both solves these problems and presents a number of other advantages:

- NTLM performs only one-way authentication, from the client to the server. This means that a server that provides the right kind of bogus information can spoof the client into providing secure data. Kerberos performs mutual authentication before any sessions are set up.
- The trusts NTLM creates are non-transitive, which means that all domains that trust one another must be set up in a direct one-to-one relationship. This is hard to manage, and it doesn't scale well. Kerberos trusts are transitive—if A trusts B, and if B trusts C, then A trusts C. Put in more relatable terms: If you trust your parents, and if your parents trust the Joneses next door, then you trust the Joneses. This property is what allows Windows 2000 to create domain trees.

- As part of the workings of the transitive trust, Kerberos allows delegation of authentication. NTLM allows a network service to impersonate the user who calls it on the local system or a trusted domain, but no farther. Kerberos allows a service to make another call on behalf of the user to another domain, perhaps several hops away. This is a big help in creating truly secure, distributed systems.

- Kerberos is faster than NTLM. Despite all the tickets that appear to fly back and forth, it actually takes less time than NTLM pass-through authentication. In addition, after a Kerberos session ticket has been granted (providing user access to some network service), no re-authorization is necessary for the life of the ticket (a default of 10 hours).

- Kerberos is a well-established IETF (Internet Engineering Task Force, the main standards body for the Internet) standard, so Microsoft's implementation should be interoperable with other flavors of Kerberos provided by different vendors. This means that a UNIX network using Kerberos V5 should (theoretically) be capable of authenticating with aWindows 2000 network.

Kerberos in a Mixed-Mode Environment

Kerberos itself works only among Windows 2000 servers and clients. However, the Windows NT security subsystem is designed to work with all types of clients. Windows 2000 systems will use NTLM whenever they must pass security information to a downlevel system (i.e., anything that isn't Windows 2000) that understands it. In general, Windows 2000 acts like Windows NT 4 to downlevel systems. Of course, one of the consequences is that to get full Windows 2000 functionality, both client and server must be upgraded.

Do I Need to Learn How Kerberos Works?

It depends. Most Windows NT administrators don't need to understand the intricacies of Kerberos authentication, just like most don't understand the inner workings of NTLM authentication and session setup. But if you're a Windows NT architect or security administrator, or if you're responsible for troubleshooting a large Windows NT network, you need to understand the authentication process. The follow sections are a relatively high-level description of the logon authentication and session setup process that takes place with Kerberos Version 5 in a Windows 2000 network. What makes it harder is that Kerberos authentication introduces about seven new terms and acronyms for just logging on and accessing a server! For simplicity's sake, assume that the domain is in native mode—everything in sight is running Windows 2000.

In addition to the terms I introduced earlier, here are a couple more that make following Kerberos processes easier:

- Key—A key is simply a password. It may be encrypted by many methods, or it may be clear text. In Kerberos, the key is always encrypted. The most common keys you'll hear about in Kerberos are the session key and the server key.

- Ticket—A Kerberos ticket is like a driver's license. It's a way to positively identify the holder to the reader. It's issued by some authority, and it contains information about what the bearer can and can't do (e.g., I can drive, but not without glasses). The ticket is good for some period of time, after which it must be renewed. Of course, Kerberos tickets must use a different kind of positive identification of the bearer than a photo. Unlike a driver's license, the Kerberos method of authentication also verifies to the ticket-holder that the ticket examiner is also who it says it is. (It's like being able to tell the cop who pulls you over for speeding to show you his driver's license, too. If he fails his credential check, you can leave!) There are session tickets, server tickets, referral tickets, and even ticket-getting tickets.

- Key Distribution Center (KDC)—The KDC is a storage area and an authentication service, sort of a central clearinghouse for Kerberos tickets. Clients get authenticated at the KDC. The KDC gives authenticated clients a ticket-granting ticket so that they can access other network services. Network services store their service tickets in the KDC, and everything is stored securely in the Active Directory so that it can be distributed wherever it's needed. The KDC service runs on every domain controller.

Logging on with Kerberos

Jim Bob attempts to logon to his Windows 2000 workstation to see if his buddy Billy Ray has sent him email about the new chili seasoning he has been experimenting with. The Local Security Authority SubSystem (LSASS) finds a domain controller at Jim Bob's site by querying DNS. It also takes Jim Bob's password, hashes it, includes Windows NT-specific security information, and bundles it (now called the session key) into what's called an *AS* (authentication service) *request* to be sent to the KDC. (A *hash* is a number generated from a string of text. The hash is generated by an encryption so that it's extremely unlikely that anything else will produce the same hash value.)

The KDC verifies that it's indeed Jim Bob trying to log on by comparing the password hash to what it develops from its own copy of Jim Bob's user key. (Remember, Kerberos is a shared secret protocol.)

If Jim Bob remembered his password, the KDC authenticates his logon by issuing a ticket-granting ticket (TGT) back to his workstation (Figure 3.13). The TGT is used by the workstation to get other service tickets in the user's domain. Jim Bob's Windows NT account rights and groups are also bundled into this package.

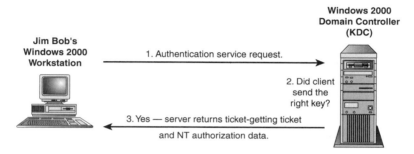

Figure 3.13   *An AS request, and the KDC returning the ticket-granting ticket.*

Jim Bob is logged on, but he must go through more authentication before he can actually access any services.

Session Setup Using Kerberos
Because he has successfully logged on, Jim Bob's workstation has a ticket-granting ticket (TGT) in its LSA cache (see Figure 3.14). The TGT originally came from the KDC.

Suppose Jim Bob wants to check his mail. To do that, he must have access to an Exchange server. To be specific, he must access the Exchange service running on the particular Exchange server, BRAHMA, that has his message store. In Figure 3.15, Jim Bob's workstation sends his TGT, along with a ticket-granting service (TGS) request for that Exchange service, to the KDC. The TGS request is simply a request to access the BRAHMA Exchange service.

The KDC opens the TGT and confirms that it's indeed the same TGT it sent to Jim Bob in the first place. If he has permission to access that service, the KDC uses this information to construct a session ticket and sends it back to Jim Bob. (This is why the TGT is called that; its purpose in life is to help Jim Bob get other tickets, such as session tickets, granted to it.)

**Domain
Controler
(KDC)**

**Jim Bob's
NT 5.0
Workstation
(JBWKS)**

TGT

**\\BRAHMA
(Exchange)**

Figure 3.14   *Logged on, with TGT, before accessing any resources*

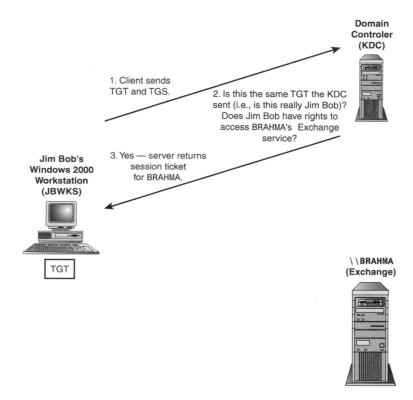

Figure 3.15 *Acquiring the session ticket.*

Jim Bob now has a pass (the session ticket) to get him access to his message store. His workstation sends the session ticket to the Exchange service on BRAHMA.

In Figure 3.16, The BRAHMA Exchange service opens the session ticket. The KDC is the only other entity that knows the server key, the hashed password that identifies the server to the KDC. Because the KDC could decrypt (read) the ticket using its server key, this proves that the ticket was encrypted with the same key, so it really did come from the KDC after all.

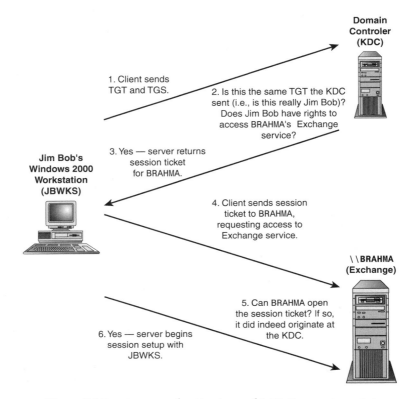

Figure 3.16   BRAHMA *authenticating and initiating session setup*

Now that everyone is satisfied, BRAHMA does a session setup between itself and Jim Bob's workstation. There's some more traffic back and forth, but the most important part is finished and Jim Bob can look for that chili seasoning suggestion that Keith sent him.

An Example: Kerberos at the Company Party
As an analogy, imagine that you go to a company party where all ages are allowed and where alcohol is served (see Figure 3.17).

To get into the party, you must show your driver's license (the AS request containing your password) to the big, ugly bouncer at the door in a too-small tuxedo (the KDC).

The bouncer looks at you, looks at your license, and looks at the party's invitation list. You're either confirmed and can go in (logon), or you're out of luck. Furthermore, the bouncer stamps your hand with one of two stamps (step 1) to show that you're over 21 (the TGT). For this analogy's sake, assume that it's an open bar, but you must ask the bouncer for a drink ticket you can give to the bartender. You can see what an important service the KDC is!

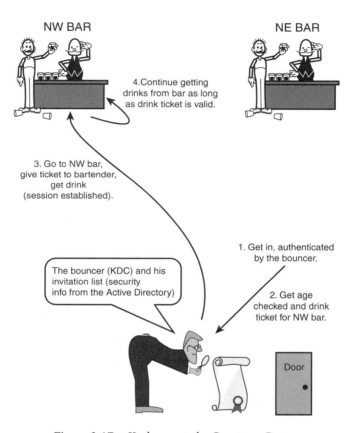

Figure 3.17   *Kerberos at the Company Party.*

Now that you're in the party, you'd like a drink. You go to the bouncer and ask him for a drink ticket. The bouncer looks at your hand stamp (he's so busy with this crazy setup that he has forgotten your face already) to check that you're authorized to access the bar and gives you a ticket (step 2) that's good for drinks only at the bar in the northwest corner of the room, at the bartender's discretion, and only for the next few hours. The bouncer writes the time he gave you the ticket on the back. (The client presents the TGT to the KDC. Based on the TGT, the KDC gives the client a session ticket for the BAR service. The session ticket is of short duration, only for a specific service, and doesn't contain any hash of the user's password. That way, if somehow it's hacked or otherwise compromised, the client's password is never in danger.)

You go to the bar and give the bartender the ticket. He examines it, sees that it's real and from the bouncer, makes a note of when the bouncer gave it to you, and keeps it at the bar (step 3). You (finally) get a drink. Now that you've gone through all this checking and double-checking, you can continue to go to that particular bar for the next few hours for more drinks. You don't need to go back to the bouncer; the bartender simply checks the ticket he has stored at the bar (his cache), sees your time isn't up, and gives you another drink (step 4). It's very fast and direct. (The network service examines the session ticket, authenticates it, and grants access to the service. For the lifetime of the ticket, the client can access the service, and all the service has to do for authentication is check that the ticket hasn't expired.)

You can see how the KDC will handle a lot of requests and also how tightly it controls access to network services. There's a lot of requests and responses back and forth between the KDC and the client, but they're small; after session tickets are granted, there's virtually no overhead for the life of the ticket.

Dumbing Down Kerberos

Microsoft has had to deal with another effect of using Kerberos: export restrictions. Data encryption techniques using keys larger than 40 bits are considered munitions by the U.S. government, and Kerberos uses 56-bit keys for bulk data encryption and message integrity checks. As a result, Microsoft had to come up with a routine to derive a 40-bit key from the original 56-bit key before the company could sell Windows 2000 overseas. Note that these restrictions apply to data only; authentication is exempt from these restrictions and so uses the original 56-bit keys.

Kerberos Across Domains

Earlier, I said that a TGT is good only for the domain in which it's issued. For cross-domain authentication, Kerberos does another dance on top of the existing one, and it explains how a transitive trust actually works.

Jim Bob has learned from Billy Ray's email that their friend Donnie Joe in the Memphis office has some recipe tips on a server in the Tennessee domain, `tenn.bigcorp.com`. (They're in the Texas domain, `texas.bigcorp.com`.) Jim Bob attempts to connect to the `tenn` server.

The request for `tenn.bigcorp.com` goes to a KDC in `texas.bigcorp.com`, usually the one Jim Bob authenticated with. This KDC doesn't know anything about `tenn.bigcorp.com`, so it asks the friendly neighborhood Global Catalog service for the name of an adjacent domain that may know more about `tenn.bigcorp.com`.

The global catalog passes the domain name and an associated KDC to the local KDC, which passes it back to the client in a *referral ticket*.

The client sends an AS request to that KDC to get a TGT for that domain. Now it can ask that domain, "Where is `tenn.bigcorp.com`?" and the process begins again until the `tenn.bigcorp.com` is finally reached.

How does the Global Catalog know the domain to which it should refer the client to find its eventual target domain? The Active Directory uses a *spanning tree* algorithm to optimize the request routing. Spanning tree is an algorithm, usually used in network equipment, to determine the most desirable path between domains. It disables all other paths to eliminate unnecessary redundant loops. The spanning tree algorithm first determines a root domain, and then each domain determines the one best path to the root domain. Combining the one best route from each domain to the root domain forms the spanning tree.

Windows NT 4 (NTLM)

Despite all the hoopla about Kerberos, good old NTLM authentication hasn't gone away in Windows 2000. In fact, it's critical to Windows 2000's domains coexisting with Windows NT 4 domains. Windows 2000 uses NTLM authentication to establish trusts with downlevel domains and clients. Partly because of this, Windows 2000 systems appear to be Windows NT 4 to non-Windows 2000 systems. NTLM is fully supported and is one of the protocols that ADSI understands, so application programmers can write for that interface as easily as they can write for the primary LDAP communication protocol.

Management Services

A number of new management services are built into Windows 2000, but I'm going to talk about only the two most important: Group Policy and the Microsoft Management Console. One controls the user and computer environment in a domain, and the other is the basis for managing all Windows 2000 services.

Group Policy

Group Policy is a very powerful tool for administrators that allows them to set a policy for how the user environment in a domain should be configured. After it's set, the system enforces the policy for all users or whatever subset the administrator has established. Group policy will be a major tool in Windows 2000 for configuring systems and users.

With Group Policy, the administrator can control the following:

- All kinds of scripts—logon, logoff, startup, shutdown.
- Software installation and policies.
- Security settings.
- User documents, the default Documents folder. There's now a common User Documents and Settings folder, one for each user on a machine. You can add files, folders, or shortcuts to the user desktop by controlling these settings.

The administrator can do all these things on a per-user or per-computer basis. The per-user policies follow the users around the enterprise, wherever they log on. The per-computer policies apply to the computer, regardless of who logs on to it. These policies, stored in the Active Directory, are referred to as *Group Policy objects* (GPOs).

Group Policy is an evolution of Windows NT 4's System Policy Editor. That tool's scope was basically limited to removing functionality from the desktop, locking it down so that, for example, the Run command couldn't be accessed. Group policy can certainly still do that, but it has become much more powerful.

Some general observations about Group Policy are listed here:

- A GPO affects all computers and users in an Active Directory container, but you can filter it with security groups.

- Group policy isn't inherited across domains, but you can access and use a group policy from another domain. You will probably face network issues if you do that, though, because just about every client operation in the other domain will require a reference back to the domain with the GPO ("Can I do this?").

- Group policy is very powerful and consequently can be very dangerous. If you mess around with it and don't know what you're doing, you could easily deny logon access to everyone in a domain. Group policy must also set some kind of record for how deep you can drill down into the user interface.

- When thinking about how group policy is applied, think SDOU—sites, domains, and OUs. This is the order in which GPOs are processed. Additionally, at the bottom of the order is the default domain group policy.

- Be very careful in setting the default domain policy. It's at the bottom of the hierarchy, but it will apply to *every* object in the domain. This includes domain controllers, workstations, everything.

- Use "log on locally" from servers, DC OUs, and default domain policy as an example of the different scopes

For detailed information on Group Policy in Windows 2000, read the 51-page "Windows 2000 Server Group Policy" white paper (`WNT5GroupPolicy.exe`) at `http://www.microsoft.com/windows/server/ Technical/management/grouppolicy.asp`. Thanks to the product renaming, the URL might change, so you may have to search for "Windows 2000 Server Group Policy."

MMC

MMC was created in an effort to centralize and standardize the administration interface for Windows NT-related functions. In Windows NT 4, administration of the network is done through a whole collection of different utilities: User Manager for Domains, Server Manager for Domains, Policy Editor, Performance Monitor, Event Viewer, DHCP Administrator, WINS Administrator... the list goes on and on.

One of the reasons for this profusion of tools is the kind of interfaces they must use. Windows NT systems have two interfaces for management and instrumentation: the Win32 Registry and PerfLib. Windows 95 clients also have a Registry, but it's different from the Windows NT version. Each of these interfaces has its limitations, so various administration tools have sprung up to work around them.

MMC uses the new Windows Management Infrastructure (WMI) to provide a single model for all management and instrumentation. In Windows 2000, just about everything uses MMC. Even if you don't like it—and I might be one of those—you'd better learn to use it.

MMC is an empty framework, a multiple document interface in Microsoft parlance. If you launch MMC all by itself (Start, Run, MMC), Figure 3.18 is all you get.

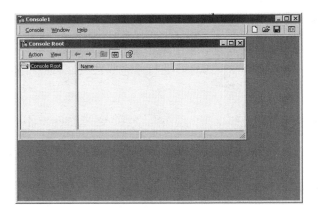

Figure 3.18   *An empty MMC.*

MMC's usefulness comes when you add *snap-ins*. A snap-in is a management tool that runs in its own child window. Everything that needs to be managed on a Windows 2000 system has its own snap-in. One instance of MMC that has one or more snap-ins running is defined as a *tool*.

Microsoft is clearly creating a do-it-yourself, home improvement analogy with the concept of a snap-in. Imagine a string trimmer that contains many attachments. The power head isn't much use by itself, but if you snap in the string trimmer attachment, it becomes a tool to be used for weed-whacking. Snap in another attachment such as a blower, and it's a very different kind of tool. The MMC becomes whatever snap-in is loaded into it.

Figure 3.19 shows the basic components of the MMC and their naming, using the Computer Management snap-in as an example. The *scope pane* is really a tree control that shows the scope of what the snap-in can manage. There's only one scope pane per snap-in.

The *results pane* shows the results of your selection in the scope pane. More than one results pane can exist in a snap-in. There are toolbars for both the snap-in and the MMC itself.

To add a snap-in to an MMC instance, click on the Console menu item. This presents the Add/Remove Snap-in dialog box, which shows the snap-ins currently running in the MMC. Click the Add button, from the Add Standalone Snap-in pick list choose the snap-in, and press Add. (Annoyingly, you can choose only one at a time.) If the snap-in has particular requirements, they will appear. Repeat until you've added all the snap-ins you desire for this MMC. Close all the Add/Remove dialog boxes. Figure 3.20 shows the Services snap-in being added to an MMC.

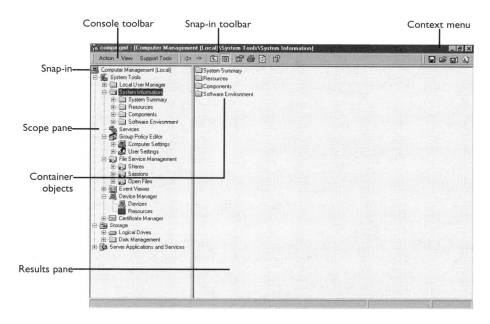

Figure 3.19   *MMC components.*

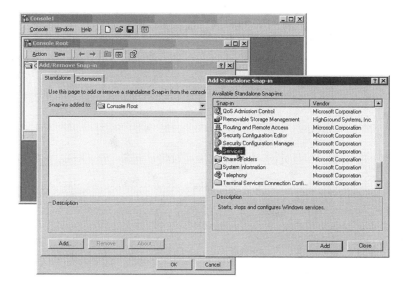

Figure 3.20   *Adding a snap-in.*

Because MMC is a multiple document interface, you can add another snap-in to the existing instance by following the same steps.

If you want to keep the configuration, you can save it as an .msc file. The OS will also add it to your Start Menu under My Administrative Tools.

A few basic tips will make using the MMC a little less confusing:

- Right-click all the time. This brings up the context menu for the object. Whatever can be done to the object (e.g., add a user to the Users container in the Directory Manager snap-in) can be done from this menu. If you double-click an object, you get only whatever action is highlighted on the context menu.

- When you explore the objects in the scope pane, it helps to play around a bit. Sometimes the little plus sign next to a container indicates that there's stuff in it to be expanded, and sometimes nothing happens at all.

- Always explore the properties of an object. Often the context menu for an object is pretty simple, but when you look at the properties menu item, you find a very complex "book of property sheets" view, such as that shown in Figure 3.21.

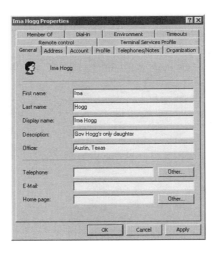

Figure 3.21   *User object properties.*

Network Services

The network services of DNS, Dynamic Host Configuration Protocol (DHCP), and WINS are assistants that get us started and then tell us where everything is on the network. They're critical components to the Windows 2000 network because the client needs to use them before ever doing useful work. At the same time, when these systems are working well, the client shouldn't even know of their existence. Let's take a look at how they work in Windows 2000.

DNS

It should be pretty apparent by now that DNS is a critical component in a Windows 2000 network. It's the new version's location service. A client (which could be a PC or a server, depending on the situation) supplies a name to a DNS server, and the server returns the name's IP address. DNS is also used by the client to find a domain controller and Global Catalog server, which together contain all the objects in the Active Directory.

> ### Note
>
> *It's beyond the scope of this book to talk about DNS concepts; a whole book could be written just about DNS on Windows NT. As a matter of fact, there are two:* Windows NT DNS *(written by Masterson, published by New Riders Publishing), and* DNS on Windows NT *(written by Albitz, published by O'Reilly). I recommend both books; the Masterson book has very good explanations about the interaction between DNS and WINS.*

Windows 2000 DNS is the third generation of DNS on Windows NT. The first version, released in the Windows NT Resource Kit, was not well received. The next version, which is available with Windows NT 4, is much better and widely used in the Windows NT community. Windows 2000 DNS builds on this foundation and adds several features that are key to the whole Windows 2000 network.

Dynamic Updates

Based on RFC 2136 ("Dynamic Updates in the Domain Name System"), dynamic update adds the UPDATE opcode (API, in the Microsoft world) to the DNS instruction set. UPDATE allows an application to add or remove resource records (RRs) on the fly instead of manually editing the zone master file (the database that maps DNS names to IP addresses). This transforms DNS from a static naming system to a dynamic system that keeps up with the constantly changing IP addresses of a DHCP-enabled network. The UPDATE opcode ensures integrity of the zone master because it works atomically, (i.e., transactionally). The update either worked and the zone master is updated, or it didn't and the zone master is left in its original state; it can't be left halfway completed.

The two applications we're immediately concerned with that will be updating DNS are the DHCP service and the Windows 2000 client.

DHCP assigns IP addresses to computers on the network, and each DHCP server maintains a database of the IP address-to-name mapping. Windows 2000 DHCP uses the UPDATE opcode to keep DNS's distributed databases of IP addresses in synchronization with what DHCP is dynamically managing. Windows 2000 DHCP will do this on behalf of non-Windows 2000 clients (which aren't aware of DNS dynamic update) and can also do this for Windows 2000 clients if it's configured that way. The two services are now an integrated method for assigning and resolving names to IP addresses.

The Windows 2000 client can perform updates to DNS directly without using DHCP as an intermediary (see Figure 3.22). After the client has completed its DHCP D–O–R–A sequence, it updates its DNS server directly with its forward lookup ("A" record—the name-to-IP-address mapping). The DHCP server updates the client's reverse lookup (PTR record—the IP-address-to-name mapping) in DNS, just as it does for downlevel clients.

Note

DORA stands for client Discovery of a DHCP server, Offer of a lease from the DHCP server to the client, client Requesting the proffered lease, and DHCP server Acknowledging the lease.

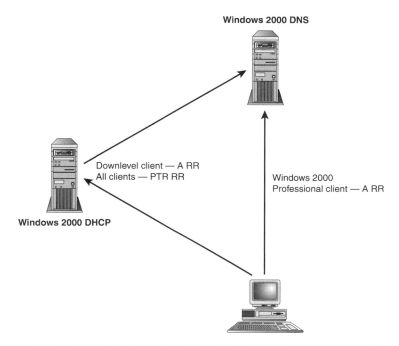

Figure 3.22   *A dynamic update of A and PTR resource records.*

Support of the SRV Resource Record

RFC 2052, "A DNS RR for specifying the location of services," describes a new DNS resource record that specifies the location of the server(s) for a specific protocol and domain. This new record is the SRV (Service) location resource record.

SRV RRs tell the Windows 2000 client where to find the following and the domains in which they're located:

- Domain controllers
- Global Catalog servers
- Kerberos KDC servers

This allows the Windows 2000 client to query DNS and locate the three key services it needs for authentication and locating resources. SRV records can be specialized for other uses, such as locating other services, looking up sites, and selecting a subset of domain controllers with special characteristics.

These SRV records can be seen under the tcp folder in the DNS Manager snap-in, as shown in Figure 3.23.

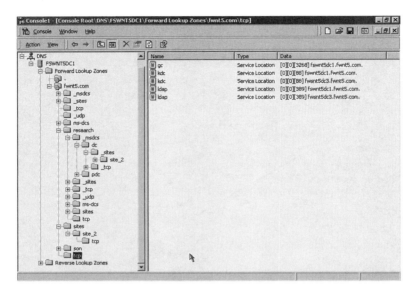

Figure 3.23   *The SRV resource record.*

gc refers to the Global Catalog service, kdc records are servers that run Kerberos Key Distribution Centers, and ldap records point to domain controllers (remember that LDAP is the Active Directory's primary protocol).

Incremental Zone Transfer

When DNS has needed to update zone files on its secondary name servers, the primary has always had to transfer the entire zone file, regardless of how many records had actually changed. To increase speed and efficiency, RFC 1995 ("Incremental Zone Transfer in DNS") was proposed. Simply put, when an update is requested by a secondary server, only the changed records are sent instead of the entire zone file. Windows 2000 DNS supports this RFC.

Active Directory Integration

We've already discussed the single biggest impact of DNS integration into the Active Directory: DNS is used to locate domain controllers, which are registered with the SRV resource record. The other integration piece has to do with database duplication.

DNS has its own distributed databases of zones that are spread among the enterprise. It uses a single master model, such as the Windows NT 4 domain model, where in any given zone there's only one primary domain server with the master zone file. All the other DNS servers in the zone are secondaries that have read-only copies of the zone file, and all updates to the zone must be made to the primary server. If this server goes down, no changes to DNS configuration for the zone can be made.

The replication of zones from primary to secondary servers is called *zone transfer*, and it transfers the entire zone file. It's triggered from a secondary server when it initializes or when its database gets out of synchronization with the primary.

So, what we have in DNS is a replication topology that parallels replication already going on in the Active Directory. Admittedly, the DNS replication process is pretty well-proven, especially compared to Active Directory's; the largest DNS implementation covers the planet supporting something called the Internet. As an administrator, though, it sure would be nice to have one less replication topology to worry about.

To pull DNS replication into Windows 2000, DNS has the option of directory integrating primary DNS zones. In other words, DNS stores its zone information in the Active Directory instead of in text files on each DNS server. This has quite a few benefits:

- DNS records become Active Directory objects that use its replication engine. The replication frequency is much higher than with your average DNS server, and the replication between sites can be adjusted to take WAN bandwidth into account.

- If you configure your DNS servers to be domain controllers, updated records are available locally as the Active Directory is kept synchronized.

- Active Directory replication uses a multiple master topology instead of single master—multiple slaves, so updates to DNS don't depend on a single server.

- Zone information stored in the Active Directory gets a boost from its enhanced security. You can use ACLs to control access to a zone object container or even down to a resource record level. You could use this feature to distribute administration of DNS zones to a much deeper level in the company than has ever been possible. This could be very handy when you have an enterprise with many non-DHCP clients such as UNIX engineering workstations; you could empower many administrators in one DNS zone (which may encompass many buildings on a campus) the rights to add static host names for only their building.

• As part of the Active Directory, DNS data will be replicated on a per property level instead of an entire zone file—a faster method and a more efficient use of bandwidth.

If you're a pessimist, this Active Directory integration can be thought of as a drawback because it puts all your eggs in one basket. If you're a pragmatist, however, you realize that if Active Directory replication isn't working correctly, DNS is only one of your worries!

Most of us already have DNS implementations in place. Windows 2000 DNS Active Directory integration supports BIND 8.1.2 and later; basic zone transfers can be done with much older versions. You can use other versions of DNS in your Windows 2000 implementation, but it *must* support the SRV RR—and it's *recommended* that it support dynamic update. I'd try to use Microsoft's version of DNS if at all possible. It's a critical component to the Windows 2000 network, and you just don't know what kind of compatibility issues will pop up in the middle of your implementation.

MMC Integration

Hardly a big surprise, DNS management is now an MMC snap-in. As you can see from Figure 3.23, it has the quickly-becoming-familiar interface. It also has a few wizards, including the reverse lookup zone wizard, to make the configuration job easier. This graphic interface has really become necessary because Windows 2000 DNS has many options related to its Active Directory integration that don't exist in other implementations. Every DNS server, every forward and reverse lookup zone, and every domain all have their own properties and configuration settings.

DHCP

DHCP is the solution to a basic problem all TCP/IP networks face: how to assign all those clients their own unique IP address and give them some other network configuration at the same time. It's a priceless tool for administering all TCP/IP networks larger than a small office. DHCP has been around in Windows NT for a while, and it gets significant enhancements in its Windows 2000 incarnation.

DHCP and DNS Integration

DHCP maintains a database of all its clients that contains their names and IP addresses. Sounds a bit like DNS, doesn't it? DHCP has the goodies, but it didn't have a way to update DNS with them. Over time, all sorts of custom applications have been written to link the two together. Unfortunately, they all fall short in one area or another, the most common being that they aren't very dynamic. There must always be some kind of static load of the new or changed addresses from DHCP into the zone files, and this isn't practical to do every second or so.

DHCP in Windows 2000 offers two kinds of dynamic updates to DNS. The default method updates only the A (forward lookup—name to IP address) and PTR (reverse lookup—IP address to name) records in DNS when requested by the client. Figure 3.24 shows this setting, reached from the properties of the DHCP server. The other method is to always register the A and PTR record with DNS. This is enabled by selecting the radio button Always update forward and reverse lookups.

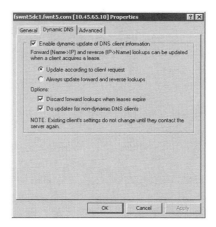

Figure 3.24   *Configuring Dynamic DNS hooks in DHCP.*

DHCP IP Auto-Configuration
One difficulty with DHCP is the problems it creates when it isn't available. If a DHCP-enabled client that doesn't yet have any lease boots and no DHCP server is available, it has no network connectivity until it can reach one. The same result happens if a client's lease has expired and no DHCP server is to be found.

Windows 2000 clients can get around this problem with IP auto-configuration. Microsoft has kindly donated one of its internal Class B subnets—169.254.0.0, with the subnet mask, 255.255.0.0—for use by these afflicted clients. When a client can't reach a DHCP server, an IP address from this network will be assigned (and checked for conflicts on the network) until a server becomes available. Although this feature isn't of much use on routed networks, it's a plus in small business and home office environments.

DHCP User Classes

A nice DHCP feature is the scope option—the capability to provide other information—such as default gateways, DNS & WINS servers, WINS/NBT node type, and so on—along with the IP address in the lease. You can cut this information only one way, though, by scope. Because a scope is a range of IP addresses, you can't change the options for a certain type of hardware or physical location that doesn't map exactly to a scope or scopes.

Windows 2000 DHCP offers *user classes*, a way to separate DHCP options by classes you define. An immediately useful example would be to create a desktop class and a mobile class. A typical DHCP scope configuration would have short lease times for conference room and traveler's area subnets because that's where mobile users and their laptops land. If you configure your clients with desktop and mobile user classes and then set short lease times for the mobile class, it won't matter *where* the mobile users land—they'll get a short lease time. It's a nice feature, but it works only with Windows 2000 clients (who recognize the existence of the user class).

DHCP and MMC Integration

As with every other management tool in Windows 2000, DHCP Manager has become an MMC snap-in. With this, the administrator gets (besides lots more right-clicks) some common task wizards and enhanced icons that show the state of the servers and scopes. The icons are helpful once you understand them, that is; Windows 2000 DHCP Help actually has an Icon Reference.

DHCP Multicast Scope Support

Windows 2000 DHCP supports Multicast DHCP (MDCHP) multicast scopes. Multicast scopes are used to assign a range of IP addresses used only for multicasting. Multicasting works like a broadcast, but only to the addresses in the multicast scope. Anyone in the multicast scope can send directed communications to everyone else in the scope. Clients can be dynamically assigned to and dropped from the multicast scope.

DHCP and Active Directory Integration

As I've said before, every Windows 2000 network service that has a data store seems to have some kind of Active Directory integration built into it. DHCP is no exception, but because DHCP leases are too dynamic to be published in the Active Directory, only static addresses are published. The Active Directory then acts like a backup of the static data. It also compares its stored entries with what's on the server when the DHCP service starts, as protection against corruption.

Rogue DHCP Server Detection

Because DHCP is implemented by client broadcast, part of a good DHCP design must ensure that a client can contact only the right DHCP servers. A non-standard server brought up in some office, configured with DHCP (for example, by someone who wants to learn how it works) can wreak havoc on DHCP clients. When a client broadcasts for a DHCP server, it may get this rogue DHCP server that gives it who-knows-what kind of address and lease time.

Another aspect of DHCP's Active Directory integration is how the Active Directory plays Santa Claus; that is, it determines who's naughty and who's nice. Before a Windows 2000 DHCP server can accept client broadcasts, it must be authorized in the Active Directory by someone with administrative rights. Even then it ain't an obvious process.

Figure 3.25 shows DHCP Event Log entry 20057 that resulted when DHCP server HARPO1 attempted to service clients without authorization.

Figure 3.25   *Event ID 20057—Rogue DHCP server not authorized.*

To authorize a DHCP server, from the DHCP Manager you must choose Action, Browse Authorized Servers. Then you must add the name or IP address of the DHCP server and close the dialog box (see Figure 3.26). The setup is a little goofy; you don't press an Authorize button; you see who's on the authorized list and then add the server to it.

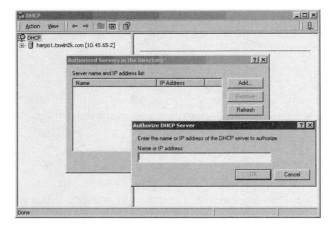

Figure 3.26   *Authorizing a DHCP server.*

Figure 3.27 shows a DHCP event log entry from HARPO1 after it was authorized.

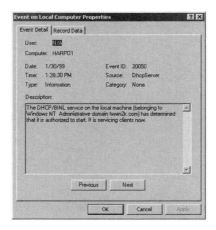

Figure 3.27   *Event ID 20050—DHCP server authorized to start.*

WINS

WINS manages NetBIOS-to-IP-address name translation in a routed network. Even though DNS becomes the primary name resolver in Windows 2000, WINS isn't going away anytime soon. As long as you have clients that depend on NetBIOS names (i.e., everything before Windows 2000), and as long as NetBIOS applications are on the network, you need WINS. So, WINS support continues in Windows 2000 with some enhancements to the basic product and a lot to the management interface.

WINS Product Enhancements
The following are the biggest WINS product enhancements, in relative order of importance:

- Persistent network connections between replication partners. Instead of creating connections to its replication partners and dropping them each time, the WINS network of replication partners will stay connected. This should improve replication performance a bit.

- The Windows 2000 client will be capable of specifying up to 12 WINS servers in the network configuration, either explicitly or via DHCP. It'll also be capable of dynamically (i.e., without rebooting) re-registering itself in WINS when an incorrect static entry exists, or when a database problem corrupts the entry.

- Autodiscovery of replication partners. A useful feature in small networks, this shouldn't be used in large networks because of the extra traffic it will generate. Each WINS server will announce itself on the network and listen for other WINS servers that do the same on a multicast address reserved for WINS. This option is turned off by default.

WINS Management Enhancements
The following are the biggest WINS management enhancements, in relative order of importance:

- The WINS Manager is now part of the MMC, enabling a lot of the other features that weren't available in the previous versions. Thanks to the MMC interface, management is now multithreaded so that you don't have to go get a cup of coffee while waiting for the database to display. The interface has improved monitoring capabilities, so you can check for communication problems and verify replication setup. You can resize the columns, sort the view by clicking on column headers, and open more than one instance of WINS manager if you want.

- Filtering and record searching from the MMC console lets the WINS administrator find specific records without searching the entire database.

- Administrators can now delete dynamic addresses from the database in addition to static ones. They can also select a range of addresses with standard Shift/Ctrl+click techniques.

- Administrators can now manually tombstone records.

- Here's a really nice feature that's long overdue: You can export data from the database into a comma-delimited file. Because it is exported from what's displayed in the detail pane (the right one), you can apply filters and searches to the data before you export it. After it's in a comma-delimited file, you can easily import it into Excel and analyze the heck out of it.

Summary

The distributed services in Windows 2000 are arguably the most complex components to understand. They're also the most important to understand when you're designing, deploying, or supporting Windows 2000. You must develop over time a deep, intuitive knowledge of how the Active Directory, Kerberos, DNS, and group policy work. You can get away with less-than-perfect knowledge of these components when you're designing your Windows 2000 network, but woe be unto you when you try to troubleshoot what you've designed.

There's a difference between *knowing* something and *understanding* it. Lots of people will very quickly say that they know Windows 2000. Far fewer will truly understand it on an intuitive level in which you jump to the correct answer but have to stop and think of the steps you raced through to arrive at the conclusion. You should strive to be one of these people; it will be such a valuable skill that it will pay you back many times.

Part II

Choosing Hardware for Windows 2000

4

Choosing the Box

Along with the actual network design, selecting your server hardware is one of the most important decisions you'll make in creating your Windows NT network. Hardware platforms are the building blocks of your network because every choice you make in the server's configuration is repeated each time one is built. In a large network where hundreds or thousands of servers are created, it's likely that once a server has been built, it won't be closely examined again until it's time to upgrade or until something breaks. As in a software development project, it's much cheaper to get it right early in the development/deployment cycle than to later fix a problem on hundreds of servers around the country or the world.

Choosing a brand of server is one of the big religious issues in a network design; it ranks right up there with operating system decisions. This chapter covers all the important aspects of choosing the right vendors—and you'll learn that their technical qualifications are only part of the process.

You'll always have to consider four main subsystems when choosing the box: processor type, memory, the I/O subsystem (including mass storage), and the network interface. You configure these subsystems to provide availability and scalability. It's important to remember that no single one of these subsystems can completely outweigh the others. A fast processor in a server with slow disks can act just as sluggishly as one with a slower processor. When shopping for hardware, you must consider all the subsystems that comprise a server.

The Processor

The microprocessor is always the first thing people look at when choosing a server, so let's consider the basic questions of what kind and how many.

When Windows NT was being designed, one of principal architect Dave Cutler's goals was that it should be independent of server hardware architecture. To do this, a layer in Windows NT's architecture was inserted between the operating system microkernel and the hardware itself. This layer, the Hardware Abstraction Layer (HAL), maps physical server resources to the Windows NT microkernel and eliminates the need for major code modifications when any PC architecture changes. (I wonder how long the Windows NT development team cast around in their dictionaries until they hit on the words that distilled to *HAL*?)

When Windows NT was introduced, it was available in three flavors: x86 for Intel architecture, MIPS, and Alpha. A fourth version for PowerPC was added when that chip—from the consortium of Motorola, Apple, and IBM—was introduced. Since the high-water mark of four architectures, Windows NT builds have decreased to two: x86 and Alpha. MIPS and PowerPC were victims of the market; few companies bought these architectures, so there wasn't enough demand for the chips by OEMs. In the case of the PowerPC, IBM stopped selling PowerPC-based Windows NT systems before Microsoft stopped making its Windows NT version. People who wanted high-performance Windows NT boxes were already buying Alphas.

When deciding what kind of server architecture to focus on, consider two issues, one technical and the other commercial. The technical choice is well known: Do I stick with the majority and buy an Intel architecture machine, or do I choose a Digital Alpha machine that's faster but that occupies only a small market share? It's reminiscent of my mainframe days when a truism in purchasing was, "No one ever lost their job choosing IBM."

Alpha Processors

The 64-bit Alpha chip, developed by Digital Equipment Corporation (now Compaq) has long been the fastest and most powerful PC-based microprocessor on the market. A drawback to these and all RISC chips has historically been that IBM PC-based applications executed directly on the server (such as backup software) ran in an emulation mode that did not support enhanced-mode (Intel 386 and later) 16-bit applications. The Windows NT 4 operating system itself is a 32-bit system running on a 64-bit processor. Windows NT 4's Alpha release now supports 16-bit applications, and Digital has released FX!32 emulation, which supports end user x86 32-bit applications that run on Windows NT 4 and use the standard Windows NT application programming interfaces (APIs). Applications such as device drivers, services, screen savers, and debuggers are not end user applications because they include system-level code that FX!32 does not support. FX!32 performance increases or decreases depending on the Alpha's clock rate.

Early Alpha 150MHz systems running x86 32-bit applications were approximately comparable to 60MHz Pentium processors. But performance on the newest generation of 21264 Alpha processors exceeds that of Intel's newest processors. It's a very difficult area to pin down because everybody uses different benchmarks, system configurations, operating system versions, and so on to make their systems look the fastest.

The commercial point to consider when choosing a server architecture is Alpha's uncertain future. Since the merger of Compaq and Digital, strategic support of the Alpha hasn't been a sure thing by any means. Compaq has begun marketing Alpha machines under the Compaq brand, but a small market share translates into a smaller number of software vendors with applications that are Alpha-compatible and, more importantly, peripherals that have Alpha drivers beyond what's in the base OS media distributed by Microsoft.

Intel Processors

The Intel Pentium III Xeon processor is currently the standard bearer for 32-bit Intel Architecture (IA-32) servers. It has a 100MHz system bus and a Slot 2 interface (an enhanced Slot 1 with a modified cartridge that supports up to four processors). This processor can scale to eight-way and larger configurations with specialized chipsets. The Pentium III Xeon processor has up to 2MB of Level 2 cache (secondary high-speed storage on or near the processor) and uses a custom Intel-built chip to transfer data to the CPU at its full clock speed. (Previous Pentium II processors before the Xeon line had Level 2 cache that ran at one-half clock speed.) Several cycles of latency exist, so the large Level 2 cache isn't as fast as the 32KB Level 1 cache; when a transfer starts, however, successive data items are transferred at the processor's full speed. The Pentium III Xeon processor runs floating-point operations at up to 2 GFLOPS (billion Floating-Point Operations Per Second; I know it's confusing; why didn't "billion" just become "biga" instead of "giga"?), which is twice as fast as the fastest Pentium II.

The first entry in Intel's IA-64 product line is code-named Merced (pronounced "mer-said"—there's nothing more embarrassing than knowing a code name and pronouncing it wrong). Merced will be fully compatible with x86 code and will not require emulation or translation software. This chip will be the first of a 64-bit processor family called IA-64 (*IA* for *Intel Architecture*). Microsoft and leading hardware vendors such as Compaq are working with Intel to optimize a 64-bit Windows NT and to ensure good hardware integration testing and compatibility.

The next IA-64 processor after Merced, code-named McKinley, is supposed to be the first IA-64 processor to fully realize the performance potential of IA-64 architecture. McKinley will have the largest on-chip Level 2 cache of any Intel chip. More importantly, perhaps, the McKinley architecture will support a memory large enough to fit almost all databases within it, resulting in high-speed queries and other executions. IA-32 will continue for awhile, as most desktop hardware and applications won't need the 64-bit data path of IA-64.

Chapter 5, "Building, Maintaining, and Tuning the Box," discusses system component choices in more detail, including general recommendations for server types.

VLM Support in Windows 2000
One of Windows 2000's features will be Very Large Memory (VLM) support, something the Alpha is perfectly positioned to take advantage of. Windows NT is currently a 32-bit operating system and can address memory up to 4GB, 2GB of which is reserved for the operating system. VLM support requires a 64-bit operating system and can theoretically address memory up to 16 million terabytes; Windows NT's support will address 4GB to 32GB of virtual memory. One of the biggest benefits of a VLM model is that it can load very large, multigigabyte databases such as SAP, Oracle, and SQL Server into memory to minimize paging out to disk. Because memory I/O is approximately 100 times faster than disk I/O, this makes a huge performance difference.

Alpha's 64-bit architecture is already being used with VLM UNIX operating systems, and it will support the Windows 2000 VLM model. IA-32 Xeon processors handle very large memory (more than 4GB) with a Windows NT device driver called PSE36 (Page Size Extension 36-bit). The IA-64 processors will handle very large memory natively.

Warning

Windows 2000's VLM support will be in non-paged pool memory. This means that it will never be paged out to disk, so you must have real memory to support what you're addressing. This puts the burden on hardware manufacturers to build systems that will match this new memory model; as of this writing, the Compaq

ProLiant 7000-Xeon server will support 8GB of system memory. In addition, memory modules for systems of this size are many times more expensive than the commodity memory 16MB and 32MB DIMMs found in PCs. ✦

The other issue, one that designers don't usually like to deal with, is commercial. Microsoft no longer develops Windows NT for two of the four PC architectures originally supported by Windows NT 3.1. Even though Cutler's vision was a good one, the market chose to follow where the greatest number of applications were. It has come down to a two-horse race between Intel architecture and Alpha. The good news is that there's room in the industry for both of these architectures.

There's no question that a purely homogeneous environment of Intel architecture servers will be less expensive to maintain than a mixed environment of Alphas and Intels. A two-architecture server environment requires duplication of support directories, OS code, many types of documentation, and operator training; it also complicates hardware support contracts and server software. However, servers using the Alpha chip do fill a need in the business environment until the Merced and McKinley chips are available and have applications that can use them. In addition, if you have applications that can benefit from VLM support, the DEC servers will probably be the first to offer such support.

Symmetric Multiprocessing

If one fast processor in a server makes it fast, isn't more better? Well, yes—mostly. Symmetric multiprocessing (SMP) systems have two or more identically configured processors sharing the same main memory, system bus, and I/O subsystems. Windows NT is one of about six server operating systems that support SMP; Windows NT Workstation supports up to two processors, and Windows NT Server 4 supports four processors out of the box. A typical Windows NT-based SMP system can have up to four processors; beyond that, the server manufacturer must supply a special HAL to interface with the Windows NT operating system.

Tip

Windows NT 4 performance improvements begin tapering off after the second processor, so the bang per buck beyond four processors can be small indeed. Windows 2000 has SMP improvements that are supposed to remedy this problem. Other problems in designing SMP systems with more than four processors are related to shared memory and cache coherency, but that's beyond the scope of this book. If you want to learn more about SMP and how it compares to clustering, pick up Dr. Greg Pfister's excellent and readable book, In Search of Clusters, *published by Prentice Hall PTR.* ✦

As an SMP consumer, you don't have to be concerned with the esoteric problems of maintaining cache coherency in common main memory with four processors. You won't care, as long as it works well and doesn't trash your CIO's spreadsheets. From that point of view, you have just a few things to consider when deciding whether to use SMP.

When should you choose an SMP machine? An SMP machine has more processor resources than the garden-variety uniprocessor server, so it offers the biggest impact on processor-intensive applications. Excellent examples of this are database servers such as Microsoft's SQL Server, Lotus Notes, or SAP R/3. Client/server databases typically use lots of processor memory for query manipulation in memory, and lots of disk I/O to and from the database. Relatively little network I/O is generated in a good database design because only the database query and the result set goes over the wire. Most databases automatically take advantage of the extra processors and have tuning parameters that on dedicated database servers can boost performance even more. Remember, though, that you'll get the best SMP performance out of one application per SMP server. Running multiple applications on an SMP server can show a very disappointing performance boost if you aren't careful in choosing your coexisting applications.

Adding processors will benefit a file server—it never hurts—but probably not as much as adding memory will. Because a file server pushes data stored locally back and forth over the wire, its performance is characterized by lots of memory used for opening all these files, lots of network I/O for moving the data over the wire, and processor utilization to get all this done.

Tip

My recommendation when buying new servers or researching a new standard is to choose an IA server with a Slot 2 interface. Then order two processors. The two processors may initially be overkill, but the extra cost is outweighed by the inevitably higher cost of adding a processor in the field. In Windows NT 4, if you're budget conscious, the performance boost above four processors is not worth the expense. If you have a very large, compute-intensive application, consider a server based on one or more 21264-series Alpha processors. Be careful with the add-on hardware you choose, though; without updated or adequate Windows NT drivers the processors are useless. ◆

One of the design goals of Windows 2000 is increased scalability. In the SMP arena, this means achieving nearly linear performance increases as additional processors are added. The design team hopes to achieve this level of performance with up to eight processors.

Memory

Physical memory is the second of the four major subsystems you need to consider when planning a server. Its purpose is to provide a fast working space between the processor and disk storage for the server's operating system, programs, and data. I won't go into detail about memory optimization and tuning here; refer to the section "Monitoring Performance and Tuning the Box" in Chapter 5. Just remember that speed is the name of the game. Every subsystem of a server is trying to get faster, to avoid being the bottleneck that slows down the server. The positions are well established. The microprocessor has long won the battle for first place, and memory is a solid second. Network I/O is third if you use high-speed optical technology. And disk I/O pulls up the rear because, after all, it's the only subsystem that's moving real hardware around instead of just pushing electrons.

What Kind of Memory?

As new technologies are adopted to speed up memory access, researching what kind of memory to choose reads like a history of the memory business. In reality, you don't have a lot of choice about what kind of memory comes in the server you buy, but you should understand the differences among the basic types of RAM.

Dynamic Random Access Memory (DRAM)

Have you every wondered how RAM really works, right down in the bits? (Probably not.) The concept is amazingly simple. What's confusing is the rapid progression of technology wrapped around this simple concept to make memory faster and more reliable.

A basic electronic component is the capacitor. The capacitor's purpose is to hold an electric charge—and that's it. How much of a charge it can hold, and how long it can hold it are part of the capacitor's design. Capacitors for even standard consumer electronics can hold quite a charge, which is why you don't want to fumble around on the back of a television set—even if the set's unplugged.

On the other end of the scale is the capacitor designed into a silicon wafer, about .25 microns (one quarter of a millionth of a meter) in size. Just like a larger capacitor, it holds a charge for a certain length of time. But because it's so small, this type of capacitor holds only a small charge (3.3 volts) for only a very brief period (128 milliseconds, about one-tenth of a second), and the charge must be refreshed before it's lost. That's why it's called *dynamic* RAM. The charge in a given location is either there (3.3V, a 1), or it isn't (0V, a 0).

The circuit layout of the memory chip looks like a grid, with rows and columns. Just as with choosing a cell in a spreadsheet by its row and column (such as, cell C5 in Figure 4.1 is the fifth row and the third column), choosing a particular row and column in a memory device yields either a 1 or a 0. With this technique, you can access any memory location on the device in any order. That's why it's called *random access memory*. Now go ye forth and amaze your friends with your arcane knowledge.

	A	B	C	D	E
0	1	0	1	1	1
1	0	0	0	1	0
2	0	0	0	1	0
3	0	0	0	0	0
4	1	1	1	1	1
5	1	1	1	0	1
6	1	0	0	0	1
7	0	1	1	0	0
8	1	1	0	1	1
9	0	0	1	0	1

Figure 4.1   *Accessing a memory location in random access memory.*

The *access time* of a memory device is the time between when you ask the device for data from a memory location and when you get it back. Remember that this is only access time for the device; it doesn't take into account the entire path from memory to processor.

A standard DRAM, called fast page mode DRAM, has access times at 40–60 nanoseconds (*ns*, 10^{-9} seconds). This type of RAM can supply memory requests at a maximum rate of 28.5MHz, which is a lot less than the 66–100 MHz that the processor needs to stay busy. (You can find more information about synchronous DRAM at http://www.chips.ibm.com/products/memory/sdramart/sdramart.html.) An improvement called EDO (extended data out) DRAM takes advantage of the fact that most data accessed is contiguous. In other words, it's very likely that the next piece of data the processor needs to access will reside next to—contiguous to—the piece it just previously accessed. EDO DRAM "bursts" extra data from contiguous addresses, achieving a 10% performance improvement. Fast page mode DRAM is almost never used in PC designs anymore.

Synchronous DRAM (SDRAM)
Synchronous dynamic RAM improves on EDO DRAM in two major ways. SDRAM architecture allows two pages of the DRAM device to be opened simultaneously rather than just one, with the delays that normally occur in between memory requests. This means that data can be recalled faster from the device. SDRAM has an access time of just 10ns, equivalent to a frequency of 100MHz. The data path has also been widened to 64 bits and 128 bits to increase the throughput of the devices. SDRAM is the standard for PCs, but servers have been slow to adopt the technology. It's very possible that server manufacturers will move from EDO DIMMs directly to direct RDRAM.

Direct Rambus DRAM (RDRAM)
SDRAM offers a great speed improvement over DRAM, but the target (in this case, processor speed) doesn't stand still. Memory frequency has moved up to 100MHz, but processor frequencies are now hovering around the 500MHz mark—a huge gap.

Rambus is a memory design company (http://www.rambus.com/) that has developed a high-speed memory interface that boosts DRAM performance to a peak bandwidth of 1.6GBps from a single device. That's more than twice the speed of conventional SDRAM. Getting more speed from conventional memory has been sabotaged by physics; you can't push electrons through silicon any faster than current designs do. To solve a problem where previous designs ran out of gas, Rambus didn't try to remain compatible with them. In direct RDRAM, the memory bus frequency is increased one-third, to 800MHz, and the data bus width has been doubled, from 8 bits to 16 bits. The Rambus architecture also defines separate row, column, and data buses to increase the speed of the control signals. Finally, the memory architecture is pipelined so that a single Rambus device can support four interleaved memory operations simultaneously.

> **Warning**
>
> *RDRAM is not compatible with other types of DRAM. It's an integrated system of memory modules, motherboard chipsets, clock chips, and connectors. Your system is either RDRAM–compatible or it isn't. If it isn't, you won't be able to upgrade it to RDRAM.* ◆

Even though Rambus memory offers a welcome speed increase over conventional SDRAM, it still doesn't keep up with processor speeds. Processor designers must design larger cache to hold and fetch data from slow memory.

How Much Memory?

Windows NT 4 memory requirements aside, you need to set your goal toward buying what's right for Windows 2000. This is by far the more memory-hungry of the two operating system versions.

Windows 2000 Server requires a minimum of 64MB to even install, and Windows 2000 Professional requires 32MB. If you're in the market for new server purchases or are revising your server hardware standards, 256–512 MB should be the amount you consider. There are two good reasons for requiring this much memory, even though you could initially make do with a smaller amount.

First, if you buy a server with a good safety margin of memory, you don't have to install memory later at a higher cost. (This involves not just the cost of the memory itself, but also the cost of installation, tracking the changes, and so on—that total cost of ownership thing again.) This also follows the guidelines of keeping your server network homogeneous—in other words, minimizing the number of different configurations you must support.

Second, in its production lifetime, it's likely that the server will change roles. It may start out as a simple member server providing file services, but in Windows 2000 it's very easy to promote servers to domain controllers and then demote them again. Domain controllers of large organizations will need more memory to support the Active Directory and Global Catalog services. You want the greatest amount of flexibility possible in your server network; you don't want to be unable to add domain controller services at a site just because you saved a few bucks on memory two years ago.

The best advice I can give is to not be stingy when you're considering server memory. After all, have you ever seen Windows NT Server memory requirements go down? All of us in the profession continue to be amazed by the advances in processors, disk space, and memory. We know it's going to happen, yet when the next big jump in what is "standard," occurs we all stand around and gawk. Buy more, and stave off server obsolescence for a few months.

At the 1996 Microsoft Professional Developer's Conference, Dave Cutler, the original architect of Windows NT and still its greatest influence, said, "Processors are getting faster and memory is getting cheaper—and we are going to use every cycle and byte we can get." Everything we've seen since then has proven him right: The minimum "real" (as compared to Microsoft recommended minimum) memory requirement for Windows 2000 Professional is 128 MB.

The I/O Subsystem

If you're like many system administrators, you may be somewhat hazy about the I/O architecture of an Intel Architecture server. It isn't as glamorous as processors, but knowing how the I/O subsystem is put together is something all server folks should know about.

The majority of servers sold today by well-known manufacturers use the peripheral component interconnect (PCI) specification on their expansion bus. The simplest technical reason is that it's faster than Industry Standard Architecture (ISA) and Extended ISA (EISA) buses. What follows is a thumbnail reference of the different expansion bus architectures you may run across in a server.

The System Bus

The system bus—or internal bus or local bus—is the data and control pathway that connects the microprocessor, the main memory, and the cache subsystem. The *front side bus* is the bus that connects the CPU with main memory. In contrast, a *back side bus* connects the microprocessor to a Level 2 cache.

Because the back side bus connects the microprocessor with the Level 2 cache—the highest speed and the most expensive memory after the Level 1 cache on the microprocessor itself—it has traditionally run at the processor clock speed. In contrast, the front side bus has run at 66MHz, long outpaced by generations of microprocessors.

The Intel 440BX AGP chipset was the first PC chipset that offered a front side bus that ran at 100MHz and therefore enabled a higher memory bandwidth, as the common 66MHz front side bus used to.

> *Tip*
>
> *What's the point behind this system bus primer? When you're shopping for a server, keep in mind that a design with chipsets that incorporate the 100MHz front side bus will give you improved performance over the older 66MHz versions. ◆*

ISA

The ISA bus first showed up on the IBM PC AT. It evolved from the expansion bus found on the IBM PC and XT. With the exception of the server (which is really a PC turned on its side), the ISA architecture is just about unheard of anymore in the server world. There are several aspects to remember about the ISA bus as it sails off into hardware Valhalla:

- The ISA bus is designed to support a single processor that, in addition to executing all software, also controls all I/O.
- The ISA bus has an 8-bit architecture, which allows it to address up to 16MB (although higher addresses can be reached via a very slow technique called *double buffering*).
- The bus has a clock speed of 8MHz.
- It can handle 8-bit and 16-bit components.
- Bus mastering is primitive. This works like a disk controller, taking control of the expansion bus away from the CPU during the I/O request and thus freeing it to perform other operations.

EISA

The EISA bus was designed by committee to extend the capabilities of ISA while keeping backward-compatibility with the large installed base of ISA expansion boards. The big features of EISA are listed here:

- Multiple processor support
- Bus mastering support
- 32-bit architecture, so all devices can access 4GB of memory and support 8-bit, 16-bit, and 32-bit expansion boards
- Clock speed at 8MHz (but up to 33MBps data transfer rates [in burst mode] may be gained for bus masters and Direct Memory Access)
- Automatic configuration of the system board and EISA expansion devices via the EISA configuration utility

EISA was the standard for server bus architecture for many years. EISA servers are still used everywhere, especially among companies that can't afford to throw out their installed server base every few years.

PCI

PCI is a local-bus design developed by Intel, Compaq, Digital, IBM, and NCR in late 1991. Local bus technology is designed to eliminate bottlenecks caused by slow expansion buses by allowing the bus to operate at the speed of the CPU instead of the original AT bus speed of 8.33MHz. Its key features, which go above and beyond those of EISA, are listed here:

- Initially designed to provide a high-performance bus for Pentium processors, the PCI bus is separated from the system bus by a PCI bridge chip, which makes it processor-independent. This allows PCI to become a standard for all manufacturers, not just IA systems.

- The bus provides switchless and jumperless support (hooray!).
- The bus offers 64-bit support, which makes it very well suited to IA implementations.
- Plug and Play capability is enabled. PnP is a hardware and software specification that, when all aspects of the system (hardware, BIOS, and operating system) are compatible, will automatically configure all components. (Also known as *plug and pray*.)
- PCI supports bus mastering and burst-mode transfers of 132MBps. In addition to bus master support, the PCI bus may buffer read or write activity to allow the processor to continue with other tasks rather than wait for the I/O operation to complete.

Because of its performance characteristics and processor independence, PCI will be the standard for the system bus in the foreseeable future. Of course, it's easy to say that because the "foreseeable future" in this industry is about two years!

The PCI specification has recently been advanced by a 2x performance improvement because of the introduction of a 64-bit-wide 66MHz bus and multisegmented PCI support in the 450NX chipset. An extension to the PCI bus, PCI-X, is being promoted by IBM, Hewlett-Packard, and Compaq as a way to increase overall server performance by up to six times. It supports bus speeds of up to 133MHz and transfers data at up to 1GB per second.

Mass Storage

There's lots of activity going on in mass storage technology today, but to understand the technology you must also understand the terminology. This section discusses mass storage interface standards, most importantly SCSI and Fibre Channel.

It's easy to confuse mass storage interface standards with bus architecture standards; how many three- and four-letter acronyms can a body remember? We can simplify things with this summary:

- IDE, and its brawny offspring EIDE, will continue to be the standard mass storage (disk drives and CD-ROM drives) interface for desktop systems for some time.
- SCSI is currently the dominant mass storage interface for servers.
- The SCSI hardware interface in servers will be replaced by Fibre Channel, though still using the SCSI software protocol.

IDE

Integrated Drive Electronics (IDE) represents a significant advance over the old Enhanced Small Device Interface (ESDI) and Modified Frequency Modulation (MFM) standards (we're talking PC Stone Age here). IDE and Extended IDE (EIDE) are far and away the most popular hard disk drive interface for the personal computer today. IDE has the following features:

- The drive controller is integrated onto the drive, eliminating the use of a system board expansion slot.
- It's faster, smaller, more reliable, and less expensive than its predecessors.
- It has buffers or cache onboard the drive to increase performance.
- It has a maximum throughput of 2.5MBps, unsuitable for high-performance environments such as servers.

EIDE

EIDE has several very useful extensions to the IDE standard. It requires BIOS support, however, so old systems may not be able to take full advantage of it:

- It removes the 528MB barrier—disks can be up to 8.4GB.
- It supports CD-ROM drives and tape drives.
- Four devices can be supported on a system, compared to IDE's two hard drives only.
- Throughput is raised to 11–13MBps.

EIDE-compatible interfaces are standard on all new motherboards for both desktop systems and servers. These interfaces may go unused on servers, however, because a SCSI controller (also known as a *SCSI host adapter*) is used to connect its mass storage devices.

SCSI

SCSI (small computer system interface) has been around for a long time and has grown considerably from its beginnings. As a result, you'll find a bewildering variety of SCSI implementations:

- SCSI-1 is an 8-bit protocol that supports a data transfer rate of 5MBps. You can identify it on old systems by its 50-pin Centronics connector (which looks like an old printer connector).
- SCSI-2, also 8-bit, supports a data transfer rate of up to 10 MBps. Sometimes called Fast SCSI-2, it uses a 50-pin high-density min-DIN connector. You won't find vendors marketing new SCSI-2 systems.

- Fast Wide SCSI-2 is a 16-bit protocol with data transfer rates of up to 20 MBps. This is achieved by simply doubling the data path of SCSI-2. It uses a very similar connector to Fast SCSI-2, but it has 68 pins. This is a very common SCSI implementation, but again, most vendors have moved on to Ultra SCSI and its variants.

- Ultra SCSI comes in two flavors: Narrow, at 20MBps, and Wide, at 40 MBps. Wide Ultra SCSI is also, annoyingly, called Wide Ultra2 SCSI. These implementations are popular in workstations and many mid- to high-end servers.

- Wide Ultra SCSI-3 is the latest in this endless dance of adjectives. (Personally, I think it's part of the club mentality: If you can't spit out the terms as though it's second nature, you can't join the club.) Wide Ultra SCSI-3 gets a data throughput of 80 MBps by doubling the SCSI-2 clock speed. This protocol is used in high-end enterprise-class servers, usually along with 10,000 RPM drives.

Fibre Channel

Fibre Channel is the industry's answer to the need for increasingly higher-speed channels to devices and a standardized interface between them. As I/O speeds kept increasing, expansion bus protocols became increasingly hard to remember ("Was that Fast Wide SCSI or Wide Ultra SCSI?"), and a growing list of physical interfaces started cropping up. It was apparent that a new standard for high-speed serial I/O needed to be defined.

Fibre Channel was developed to solve three problem areas: A new serial drive interface, a high-speed system interconnect for server-to-server communications, and a networking medium that's an alternative to 1GBps Ethernet (a.k.a. Gigabit Ethernet). Unlike Fiber Distributed Data Interface (FDDI, another fiber-optic–based protocol), Fibre Channel is designed to be a standard interface that supports a number of protocols, including SCSI, IEEE 802.2 (the standard for the Data Link Layer in the seven-layer OSI reference model), Internet Protocol (IP), and Asynchronous Transfer Mode (ATM) over a much faster physical medium. By providing a standard interface, Fibre Channel relieves manufacturers from supporting multiple interfaces. Using optical fiber as its medium, Fibre Channel will predominantly use the Fibre Channel Arbitrated Loop (FC-AL) device interface. IBM is using its own Serial Storage Architecture (SSA) interface instead of FC-AL, but it has limited support in the industry.

A few advantages of Fibre Channel are:

- It's fast, with a transmission rate of 100MBps per link in both directions. It's also targeted to increase to 200MBps and 400MBps in the future.
- It offers a great advantage in transmission distance over older technologies such as parallel SCSI. That protocol has a maximum distance of about 3.5 meters, whereas with 9-micron single mode optical fiber, Fibre Channel can span distances of up to 10 kilometers! This enables all sorts of interesting possibilities with data centers and storage area networks (SANs). By eliminating the distance barrier in storage configurations, a truly distributed computing network can be designed.
- It's the only interface designed to support simultaneous hot pluggability. You can add or remove multiple drives from an active loop without interfering with the operation of the loop.

As with any fiber optic carrier, Fibre Channel is somewhat fragile and requires extra care in layout and maintenance. It's not suitable for all environments, nor is it yet the most cost-effective solution for all storage situations. Still, it's rapidly growing in acceptance. It can be found in enterprise-class storage solutions today and will continue to trickle down to more mainstream server solutions as cost drops.

Hard Disk Drives

Disk drives are and always will be the slowest component of the server because this is the only component that's physically flinging something around at high speeds. The rate at which you can get data into and out of a drive is determined by two simple factors: how fast you can get data down the wires to other system components, and how fast you can get data off the platter.

The first has been improved by the ever-escalating SCSI alphabet soup: Wide Ultra SCSI-3 has data rates of 80MBps. The second is achieved by spinning the disk at higher speeds. The quicker you can get the next sector of platter under the drive's read/write heads, the faster a data rate you'll get. Take a look in your Sunday paper at the computer store advertisements, and you'll see that a standard-issue consumer hard drive spins at 5400 revolutions per minute (RPM). A newer generation of high-performance drive rotates at 7200RPM. The newest drives have rotational speeds of 10,000RPM and benchmark at up to 35% higher throughput than 7200RPM drives.

The raging demand for more disk space has made drive capacity the most important factor, with the device interface (SCSI-2, Fast Wide SCSI-2, Wide Ultra SCSI) determined by the server's specifications. Should you be carefully peering at access times and disk latency figures for all the disk drives before you purchase them? Though it certainly can't hurt to know the specs, it's a good idea to use drives specified by the server manufacturer. Unless they've specified something horrendous, the small performance boost you may get is outweighed by the benefit of simplified maintenance by having the drives covered under the same warranty and hardware contracts as everything else—not to mention the advantage of removing one more variable from the support equation.

For *really* big storage requirements, mainframe-class storage devices from the likes of EMC and Hitachi are available and usually are attached by Fibre Channel. These devices, which are arrays of up to 256 disk drives, offer gargantuan amounts of storage (up to 9TB!) as external storage to either servers or mainframes.

Tip

Through all the confusion of drive types and interfaces, just remember this: To get the maximum throughput from your disk drives, go for the newest, fastest interface protocol (such as Wide Ultra SCSI-3) and the highest rotational speeds. If you're more interested in capacity than ultimate speed, you can often find it in slightly slower drives with higher area densities. The 36GB drives are the latest contenders for big storage. ◆

Hot Pluggable Drives

A hot pluggable drive is a drive that can be pulled out and replaced while the system is running. You don't need to have a system down when a drive goes bad. This sleight-of-hand feat requires a disk controller that supports the feature and hard drive carriers designed for it. The drive must also be functioning in a RAID scheme that will allow the operating system to continue. If you remove a hot pluggable drive from a two-drive unmirrored system, the drive will spin down gracefully, but something ugly will happen to the running system. Hot-plug drives are essential for any server that claims to be fault-tolerant.

The Network Interface

The network interface cards (NICs) are one of the less fascinating server components, but they're every bit as critical as the microprocessors. After all, what good is the fastest server if it can't get to the network or if it has only a tiny little pipe to push data through?

As with the other major components in a server, you usually choose a NIC as part of the server purchase package. This is a good thing, and you should go with it if the card fits your network; life is hectic enough without the added trouble of supporting a non-standard NIC that either saved you a few pennies or that was a little bit faster than the standard offerings.

The basic factors to look for in a NIC are listed here:

- Network type—It should support 10MBps or 100MBps and should offer an autosensing feature so it can set itself up. Remember that a server will always be a focal point of network activity, so its network interface should always be faster than a client network interface. The vast majority of client networks still run at 10Mbps, so your servers should run at 100Mbps. If they don't, you're setting yourself up for a bottleneck. For higher throughput situations you can consider FDDI or Gigabit Ethernet, but your choices are limited by the type of physical network infrastructure you already have in place.

- The card should be PCI, and preferably hot-pluggable so that it can be swapped out with no downtime if it goes bad.

- If the NIC follows the "Wired For Management" initiative, it will be remotely manageable.

- Do everything you can to minimize the number of NICs you install in a server. A multihomed server may sound like a good idea, but in reality it can be a pain to support. Windows NT has a history of routing packets unpredictably through multiple network interfaces. The exception I would make to this rule is an interface to a backup network.

- Multiple ports in a NIC can be a good thing, but they don't necessarily provide higher performance.

- If you do use multiple NICs, look for a feature called *asymmetric port aggregation*. This technology distributes outbound server traffic between two or more cards, providing a wider data pipe. The NICs appear to be a single device with one network address. This also provides a measure of fault tolerance.

Availability and Scalability

High availability is one of the most sought-after goals for Windows NT servers. Fault tolerance, the ability to take a licking and keep on ticking, is the traditional means of achieving high availability in IA servers. A fault-tolerant server can take a single failure in many of its subsystems and continue to function, at least in a degraded mode, until the fault can be repaired.

Clustering, which is very new to the Windows NT world but well understood by the UNIX and VMS communities, is a way to achieve extremely high availability and scalability on a larger scale than simple fault tolerance. With two or more servers and disk subsystems in a cluster appearing over the network as a whole computer, the failure of any one system won't bring down the cluster.

Fault tolerance and scalability are complementary approaches and should be used together.

Fault Tolerance

Fault tolerance in servers can be implemented in every major component in a server. You must determine how much you're willing to spend on fault-tolerant equipment by determining how much downtime costs your business. There's fault-tolerant equipment for every business size, from relatively inexpensive commodity servers to extremely expensive Tandem Himalaya servers. This section talks about ways you can create fault tolerance in commodity servers offered by companies such as Compaq, IBM, Hewlett-Packard, and Dell.

The processor for these servers still isn't fault-tolerant in the sense that the server stays up if a processor dies. It doesn't. Some manufacturers, however, offer an offline backup processor. If a server with this option fails, it's powered down, reconfigured, and restarted from the backup processor. It's not transparent, but at least the processor doesn't stay down. Redundant processor power supply modules are also available to prevent processor failure from a dying power supply.

Memory protection for servers comes in the form of parity memory, error checking and correcting (ECC) memory, and advanced ECC memory. In parity memory, 1 extra parity bit is appended to every 8 bits of data. Parity memory really isn't fault-tolerant because even if it does detect a memory error, this type of memory can't correct. Thus, the server halts operation—abruptly. (See the entry for "BSOD" in the Glossary.)

ECC memory adds some redundancy to the data bits that allows it to detect single- and double-bit errors and then to correct single bit errors. Advanced ECC memory uses single-bit and adjacent-bit addressing code; system memory populated with advanced ECC memory DRAM can tolerate a single DRAM device failure without server failure.

In short, for maximum memory fault tolerance, choose advanced ECC memory whenever possible.

The network interface card (NIC) can be made fault-tolerant by installing a redundant card. Available in some servers, a redundant NIC stays inactive but shares the device driver with the active NIC. When the device driver detects an unrecoverable error on the NIC, the driver switches the roles of the active and standby interfaces without interrupting service. Of course, this means you must have two network drops for each server, even though only one will be active at a time. If the NIC supports PCI Hot Plug (discussed in the next section), you can also replace the card without shutting down the server.

The hardware backplane can be available in a divided configuration. This enables two disk controllers to be installed—and with that, you can have disk duplexing or even storage array mirroring.

Dual and N+1 power supplies can be installed to avoid system failure due to failure of any one supply. Even fans are available in redundant, hot-pluggable pairs so that a failed fan won't let the box overheat and go into thermal shutdown.

PCI Hot Plug

PCI Hot Plug is an emerging industry standard endorsed by Compaq, Hewlett-Packard, Intel, Microsoft, Adaptec, Novell, Texas Instruments, and others. PCI Hot Plug is simply the capability to remove and replace any PCI adapter card without powering down the server. The first beneficiaries of this technology are disk controllers and NICs. PCI Hot Plug allows a server to undergo a hot replacement of a failed card, an upgrade of an existing adapter, or a hot expansion of a server by plugging in an additional adapter into an empty PCI slot.

Disk Controllers

Because hard disks are one of the most numerous components of a server, one of the more likely to fail, and the component that contains user data, a lot of effort has been spent on increasing their fault tolerance. The important things to know about a disk subsystem are the disk controller, its fault-tolerant configuration, and the disks themselves.

An often overlooked part of the disk subsystem is the disk array controller, the hardware responsible for managing disk I/O. Unsung heroes, the best of this breed perform a number of functions that are critical to both the speed and the fault tolerance of the I/O subsystem. As bus-mastering controllers, they take control of I/O requests and free the processor(s) for other duties. As RAID controllers, they manage I/O to a disk array. They can rebuild data from a failed drive in the array without the operating system's knowledge, and recently they have been made capable of extending a RAID set without breaking and rebuilding the array. Array controllers can be a single point of failure and can take down an entire fault tolerance array.

Redundant Array of Inexpensive Disks (RAID)
RAID, which is an acronym for redundant array of inexpensive (or independent) disks, is essentially a method of writing data across multiple disks instead of to a single disk at a time. RAID was first proposed in a 1988 paper titled, "A Case for Redundant Arrays of Inexpensive Disks," written by three researchers from UC Berkeley: David Patterson, Garth Gibson, and Randy Katz. The 1988 RAID paper cited three main objectives for RAID: increased performance, increased reliability, and reduced cost. Of the three, increased reliability is certainly RAID's best-known feature. Putting together a RAID set requires an intelligent RAID disk controller.

RAID is generally accepted to have the levels shown in Table 4.1. The Cost column is a relative measure of how expensive it would be to implement disk storage in that configuration. For example, the cost of storage in a server with two drives formatted and partitioned into two volumes is N, where N is the price of the drives. If you take those two drives and configure them into a RAID 1 mirror, you have great fault tolerance—but you've used up the entire second drive for fault tolerance. You only get half the storage you paid for, or 1/2 N.

Table 4.1   RAID levels

RAID Level	Description	Fault Tolerance	Performance	Cost
0—Striping	Data is striped across the RAID set of disks; no parity is maintained.	None. If one disk fails, the data is lost.	Excellent. The fastest RAID level.	N Equivalent to the cost of disks in a non-RAID system.

continues ▶

Table 4.1   continued

RAID Level	Description	Fault Tolerance	Performance	Cost
1—Mirroring (Duplexing, if two RAID controllers are used)	Identical data is written simultaneously to two disks.	Excellent. Depending on the implementation, failover can occur immediately.	Very good. Reads a bit faster than it writes.	*1/2 N* The most expensive level.
2	All data is striped across both data and parity disks. All disks must be accessed in parallel.	Good.	Superseded by RAID 3.	Approaching *1/2 N*
3—Striping + parity drive	Similar to RAID 2, but parity data is stored on a dedicated drive.	Very good, but all fault tolerance is lost if the parity drive fails.	Moderate.	$N/(N-1)$
4	Similar to RAID 3, but with multiple independent disk reads instead of synchronized read and writes to the array.	Very good.	Moderate.	$N/(N-1)$
5— Distributed data guarding	Instead of a dedicated parity drive, data and parity information is interleaved over all drives in the array.	Excellent. Two drives in a RAID 5 array must fail to cause the array to fail.	Read: excellent. Write: moderate, as two I/Os (one data, one parity) must be performed for each write operation.	$N/(N-1)$
6	RAID 5 + extra parity information.	Most excellent. Three drives in a RAID 5 array must fail to cause the array to fail.	Similar to RAID 5, but writes are a bit slower.	$(N/(N-1))+N$

RAID Level	Description	Fault Tolerance	Performance	Cost
10	RAID 1, but with mirrored pairs instead of single drives.	Excellent. Two drives must fail for the array to die.	As fast as they come on reads; almost as fast on writes.	*1/2 N* (Heinously expensive.)

The most common RAID choices available today are RAID 0, RAID 1, and RAID 5. When combining a number of physical drives into one logical volume (as in RAID 0 and RAID 5), RAID controllers "stripe" the data across the entire logical volume. This means the original file is broken down into many smaller blocks, which are then evenly distributed across the physical drives that make up the logical volume. Disk striping offers several benefits, but the biggest advantage is a boost in performance. This boost comes from a reduction in *latency*, or the amount of time a disk head must wait for the target sector of the physical disk to come under the head. Latency is a big performance factor because this is the transition point from electrical signals (measured in nanoseconds) to mechanical movement (measured in milliseconds). Latency is reduced in striping because if the system must wait for the disk in Drive 0 to find a free sector, why not find another drive in the array that is positioned over a free sector right now?

RAID 0, or disk striping without parity, isn't fault-tolerant at all, so you should think twice before ever considering it for use in a production server. As you can see from the previous discussion, it's the fastest configuration, but if any disk in the array fails, all the logical volumes built from the array also fail. The data can be recovered only from backups after the disk has been replaced. Look carefully at performance claims in product bench-marks. If they're using RAID 0 in their configuration, they're cheating to get better numbers because this isn't a realistic configuration for a high-availability server. A possible use for a RAID 0 set would be in a server that contains read-only data that's refreshed on a daily or weekly basis, and one that has high speed but not high availability requirements.

RAID 1, also known as *mirroring*, is a popular choice for fault-tolerant systems because it makes a duplicate image of all your data. If you enable mirroring in hardware (the recommended method), then if one of the mirror set drives fails, the controller will failover to the functioning drive without any interruption. Assuming that you have hot-pluggable drives, you can simply replace the offending drive with a new one and the controller will dynamically rebuild the mirror. The advantage: no downtime.

Mirroring is also fast. Because data is written to and from each disk simultaneously along two I/O paths, the I/O throughput is the same as that of a single standalone drive. Unlike the higher RAID schemes, no parity data is written to the drive. You don't need no stinkin' parity—you have an entire backup drive.

If mirroring is so great, why not use it for everything? It's expensive compared to other RAID options because you're buying two drives for the storage space of one. By its nature, disk mirroring is also limited to pairs of drives—you can't create a mirror set larger than the capacity of a single drive. This is less of a problem than in the past; 36GB hot-pluggable drives are now available, and the trend will certainly continue.

Good environments for mirroring are applications with high availability requirements that don't require lots of disk space (meaning now less than 36GB total). You also must be willing to pay the premium of losing the capacity of one drive to the mirror. Some examples are listed here:

- Windows NT 4 primary domain controller or Windows 2000 domain controller
- WINS/DHCP
- DNS
- Dfs (Windows 2000)
- Web server

Windows NT Server can also do both RAID 1 and 5 in software. This is a cheap way of getting fault tolerance out of hardware that doesn't support it, and it works. This method two major drawbacks compared to hardware-based RAID, however:

- It's much slower than hardware. A truism of computing is that performing a function in software is always slower than hardware. Seymour Cray, the famous supercomputer architect, once said, "You can't fake what you haven't got." Well, you *can* fake it here, but it isn't as fast as the real thing.
- If you have a drive failure, a down is required to replace the failed drive. You can schedule the down, however, for an off-peak period because the system will limp along after the failure.

Software fault tolerance has one major advantage: It's free. If your server doesn't have fault-tolerant hardware, and if you can live with the slower performance, it may be just what you need.

Duplexing is for people who think mirroring isn't safe enough. The single point of failure in a RAID 1 mirror set is the disk controller. If that card goes to meet its maker, the system crashes. Worse than that, the controller, in its death throes, could have theoretically fed both mirrored drives bad data as its last evil act, so both drives would be trashed. Duplexing simply adds a second controller to the mirror system so that each drive has its own controller, eliminating that pesky single point of failure.

RAID 5 is a descendant of RAID 0 in the evolution of disk array fault tolerance. It takes the idea of disk striping and adds parity data to it, striping the parity data right along with the data itself. RAID 5's biggest benefits are listed here:

- If one disk in a RAID 5 array fails, the system will continue with no interruption. If you have hot-pluggable drives, you can simply pull out the bad drive and plug in a fresh one. Once in, the disk array controller will rebuild the data on the new drive based on parity information striped across the remaining drives.

- The penalty in lost disk space for fault tolerance is low compared to RAID 1. RAID 1 costs 50%—half your drive space—for its mirroring, whereas RAID 5 costs one physical drive—(N–1)—to protect its array. As drive capacities get larger, this impact also can grow. A 14GB RAID 5 array of seven 2GB drives loses 2GB to parity. A 12GB RAID 5 array of three 4GB drives loses 4GB—twice as much.

RAID 5's drawbacks are also listed here:

- Only one drive in an array can fail at a time. Until it has been replaced and rebuilt by the array controller, the array isn't fault-tolerant.

- While a drive is down, and until the disk array controller has rebuilt the new drive, the array is in degraded mode and system response time will suffer slightly. This is because for every read or write request to the failed drive, an I/O operation against all the other drives in the volume is required. Information that would have been on the missing drive must be derived from the parity information striped across the remaining drives. A RAID 1 set doesn't have this problem; it just has a drive that's offline.

- It's very fast for reads but relatively slow for writes. Therefore, it's best in read-mostly, write-occasionally environments.

In my experience, most companies use at least a partial implementation of RAID 5 in their server's disk arrays. It's very difficult to support a variety of RAID schemes; if you must pick one or two configurations, RAID 5 is a good bet. And the more drives you can put in a RAID 5 array, the better performance it will have.

A new variant on the scene, RAID 10, has begun to appear on some systems. RAID 10 is essentially a striped array whose segments are RAID 1 arrays. Think of it as RAID 1 in a RAID 0 configuration.

RAID 10's advantages are as follows:

- It offers the same fault tolerance as RAID 1.
- It has the same overhead for fault-tolerance as RAID 1 alone.
- High I/O rates are achieved by striping RAID 1 segments.
- It acts like RAID 1, with an additional performance boost.

RAID 10's drawbacks are listed here:

- It's very expensive—at least double the cost of a RAID 0 stripe set.
- All drives must move in parallel to properly track lowering sustained performance.
- It offers very limited scalability at a very high inherent cost.

Industry testing of various RAID 1 and RAID 5 arrays has shown that more and smaller disks are best for systems with large numbers of users, high I/O rates, and high concurrency. Fewer, larger disks work best for environments with a few users, high I/O rates, and low concurrency requirements. However, this doesn't really take into account the practical aspects of increasing drive capacities and dropping prices. If you can shoehorn more space into a new server because the drives have more capacity than the previous generation, will you say, "I'd like lots of 1GB drives, as expensive as the 4GB drives with one quarter the capacity, because I can squeeze more performance out of a RAID 5 array?"

Note

With the sad state of disk capacity management in the Windows NT environment today, I'd always opt for more disk space at the cost of a slight performance loss in the array. ◆

Extending a RAID set in Windows NT 4 isn't a trivial exercise, but it's getting better. The traditional method for enlarging an established RAID set (who ever heard of *decreasing* storage capacity?) has always been to accomplish these aims:

1. Back up all data
2. Break the RAID set
3. Install the new drive(s)
4. Re-establish the RAID set with the new drives
5. Restore the data

New system BIOS chips and RAID controllers now can extend a RAID set dynamically. Unfortunately, Windows NT 4 doesn't recognize the increased size in a dynamic manner. You must reboot the server before the OS becomes aware of the extension. This is changing in Windows 2000; you will be able to add and remove disks from a RAID set, and both the hardware and Windows NT will recognize the change.

Tip

Remember that RAID doesn't replace backups. All the fault tolerance in the world won't help you if one of your users accidentally erases a critical file and you don't have a backup copy of it. ◆

If you want to become a RAID expert, an excellent resource is *The RAID Book, A Source Book for Disk Array Technology*, published by The RAID Advisory Board.

A major enhancement to RAID performance is beginning to show up in servers. Intelligent RAID uses I/O processors such as the Intel i960 to offload much of the I/O processing requirements from the microprocessor. This is a building block of a fully I_20 (intelligent input/output)-compliant subsystem. (Chapter 1, "Base Services in Windows 2000," discusses I_20 in more detail.)

Disk Subsystem Recommendations

The structure of a disk array has three different levels, with each layer hiding the true characteristics of the layer below. (In this aspect, it's similar to the well-known seven-layer OSI reference model.) These layers are shown in Figure 4.2.

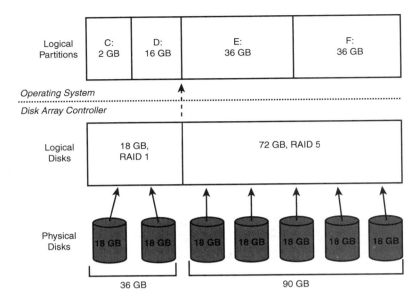

Figure 4.2   *Logical to physical disk mapping.*

In this example, seven 18 GB physical disk drives are configured as two logical disks. One logical disk is a RAID 1 mirror set; another is a RAID 5 set comprising the remaining five drives. The operating system sees these as an 18GB disk and a 72GB disk, with four partitions built on these two virtual disks. It's important to note that under normal circumstances (when you haven't done any fancy footwork with Windows NT's Disk Administrator to create volume sets or software RAID), you can't define a partition to bridge these virtual drives.

A fact of life in this business is that no matter how you size the partitions, sooner or later you're going to run out of room on one or all partitions. A really nice product called ServerMagic by PowerQuest has appeared to save us all many weekends of rebuilding partitions. This tool allows you to resize partitions by simply stepping through a resizing wizard. It does all the other work, recalculating partition sizes, determining cluster sizes, moving data, and so on. It works so well that the suffix "Magic" is appropriate. Even though it works like magic, it will take quite some time to resize a multi-GB partition. However, it's at least an order of magnitude faster and easier than the old backup/FDISK/restore method.

When an array of disks is built into a RAID structure, the number of physical disks in the array and their capacity comprise the lowest layer. The next layer, the logical disk layer, is where the RAID structures for these physical drives are configured. In the previous example, two physical drives have been built into a RAID 1 mirror set, and the remaining five are assembled into a RAID 5 configuration. This work is done in a system configuration utility, and the actual construction of the sets is performed by the array controller. Windows NT will believe there are two physical drives on the system: a 4GB drive and a 16GB drive.

The top layer, the logical partition layer, is built by the operating system based on the "physical" drives it believes are available. (They're virtual drives, actually.) They can be partitioned any way you want, but you can't create a 5GB C: partition because the "physical" drive isn't big enough.

Tip

What all this means is that after you define your logical disks, it's very time-consuming to change them. If a RAID set (other than RAID 1) is broken up, all data on the set will be lost. Therefore, part of the process of reconfiguring a RAID set is time-consuming backups and restores. There is a new exception to this rule, however. Some new array controllers have the capability of dynamically adding a volume into an existing RAID 5 set. Unfortunately, Windows NT 4 doesn't have the capability of dynamically extending existing partitions to take advantage of the new features. Windows 2000, however, will allow you to dynamically extend a logical drive or partition. This complements the capability of RAID controllers to dynamically extend RAID arrays by adding hard disk drives to them; before Windows 2000 you could extend the RAID array, but you had to use the old backup/FDISK/restore method before the operating system could use it. (See Chapter 1 for more information.) ◆

Fault Tolerance Recommendations

Before you choose a final configuration for your servers, you should split them up into the types of service they'll be providing (see the section "Homogeneous and Heterogeneous Hardware Environments"). Then decide what level of fault tolerance you want for each service type and how much you're willing to pay for it. What follows are some examples, with increasing cost, of fault-tolerant configurations and the servers that could use them.

Figure 4.3 shows a basic disk configuration suitable for a file server. This configuration provides full fault tolerance for the entire server at the lowest possible cost. It doesn't do any separation of disk I/O by partition, however; no matter where the data resides on the server, it gets striped across all the disks.

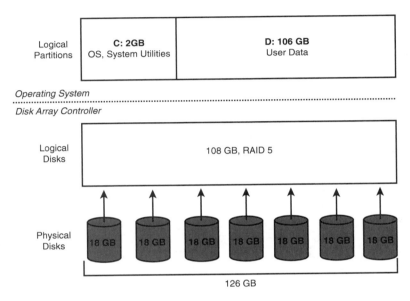

Figure 4.3   *A basic file server configuration.*

Figure 4.4 shows another file server configuration, one that separates the operating system partition from the user data. This example combines the best fault tolerance for the best price. The mirror set makes the server's operating system both very rugged against any hardware failures and also independent of any user data disk failures. It's more expensive than the previous example, but it greatly increases the fault tolerance of the server. The extra space on a big mirror pair could be used for data that needs to be highly available (the D: partition, in this example).

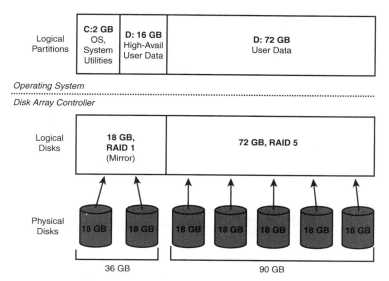

Figure 4.4   *Another file server configuration.*

Figure 4.5 is a good configuration for an infrastructure server such as WINS, DHCP, DNS, or a dedicated domain controller. These types of servers have important availability and performance requirements, but they don't require scads of disk space. Smaller drives would be perfectly adequate, but the market usually dictates that they be nearly as expensive as larger ones. The added expense of a mirror set here is minimal because of the low space requirements, and the extra space of the D: drive could be used for some special storage.

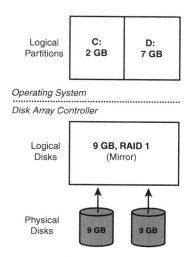

Figure 4.5   *A small infrastructure server.*

Figure 4.6 is the most complicated configuration, but it's a good one for a relational database server such as SQL Server. The operating system is a separate mirror set, as in the previous example, and a second mirror set has been added that contains the database transaction log and database dump files. The final volume partition contains the database. The log/dump partition is separate because logging and dump processes are characterized by heavy sequential I/O that's different than database I/O's random reads and writes. Transaction logs are written to in a steady stream, and database dumps or load are heavy bursts of sequential writes or reads. A RAID 1 mirror set provides a high–performance, fault-tolerant foundation for these operations. The nature of relational databases tends to spread their data throughout the physical devices of the database. The striping of RAID 5 complements this randomized I/O by spreading the data across many disk drives.

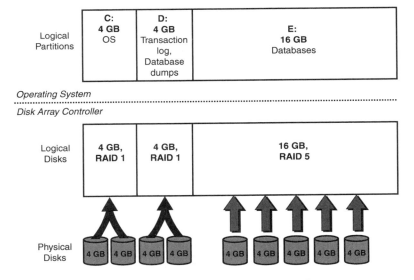

Figure 4.6 *A relational database server configuration.*

Clustering

I won't attempt to go into clustering in great detail; several excellent books have been written on the subject, and the market is changing so rapidly that it would be pointless to dwell on specifics. Instead, I'll cover enough of the basics to acquaint you with the terminology. Then I'll talk about the advantages the general categories of clustering solutions, and recommendations on what you should do about clustering now.

To understand the basics of clustering, let's get a few definitions out of the way:

- A *whole computer* is pretty much what it sounds like: a conventional server, with processor, disk, memory, and at least one local hard drive. In Windows NT 4 clustering, this hard drive holds the Windows NT Server 4 Enterprise Edition operating system and the clustering software.

- A *node* is the same as a whole computer, but it's a more commonly used term. When a cluster is said to have two nodes, it means that two whole computers are connected in a clustered configuration.

- A *cluster* is a collection of two or more whole computers, loosely coupled together, that appear to function as one. ("Loosely coupled" in this case means that each node runs its own copy of the operating system.) When you access a cluster's shares over the network, you don't type in a specific server's name; you enter the cluster's name, and the clustering software directs the query to the correct place, depending on the state of the cluster. A network user shouldn't even know that the cluster exists; he's just accessing a computer with a different naming convention. This appears to be a *single system image* to the client.

- *Failover* is the act of the cluster software automatically moving resources from a failing node to an available node to keep them available. An application literally "fails over" to another node. The time it takes for a failed node to execute failover varies from a few milliseconds to several minutes, depending on the clustering software. The failover speed is usually directly related to the cost of the clustering solution.

- A *failover object* is a resource or group of resources that must move together when failover occurs. This ensures that if, for example, one disk in a database fails, the entire application will pause for failover with no damage other than a slight (or extended) pause. Failover objects are defined by the clustering software and the application or administrator. They're also called, somewhat confusingly, a *group* by Microsoft.

- *Failback* is the operation of returning the failover object(s) back to their original node.

- A *heartbeat* is a signal generated by each node in the cluster along a *hardware interconnect* between the nodes that tells the cluster software "I'm alive... I'm alive... I'm alive...." When the node stops generating this signal, the clustering software assumes that the system has failed and executes the failover process.

- The three software models used in clustering are *mirroring, shared disk,* and *shared nothing.* Mirroring software (as with offerings from Network Specialists (NSI), Octopus, Veritas, and Vinca) works like RAID 1: The software mirrors every write to one server to a copy of the data on at least one other server. This offers a lot of advantages, especially in disaster recovery, because the mirror could be in another state. However, it's an availability rather than a scalability solution; you can't increase the processing power of the cluster by adding nodes.

  In shared disk clusters, every system can access every disk at any time. Obviously, there must be a traffic cop to lock cluster resources so that only one node accesses a resource at any instant and to keep the data in synchronization, if needed. This software is generally called the *distributed lock manager* (DLM). The DLM generates a fair amount of overhead that increases rapidly as nodes are added to the cluster. As a result, this model isn't as scalable as the shared nothing model.

  In the shared nothing model, each system within the cluster owns a subset of the resources of the cluster. Only one system may own and access a particular resource at a time. (On a failure, however, another dynamically determined system may take ownership of the resource.) In addition, requests from clients are automatically routed to the system that owns the resource. This model is the most scalable and is used by Microsoft and Tandem.

Benefits of Clustering

If one or more nodes crash, that doesn't necessarily mean the cluster will crash. If you need to bring a server down for maintenance, fail it over manually and work on it while the cluster stays up (called the "rolling upgrade"). This solution also helps you get more bang for your buck; a cluster of commodity servers is much cheaper than a Tandem or Stratus high-availability system, and it scales better than any SMP system can. While you're doing all these things, the client continues to do useful work on the cluster.

Despite all the hype and overactive public relations on clustering, it isn't for everyone. Exactly what kind of high availability do you require, and how much are you willing to pay for it?

Clustering is expensive. In Windows NT, it costs only about 20% of a UNIX clustering solution, but that doesn't go very far with your manager. ("But, honey, look at all the money I *saved.*") As in any business decision, you must compare the cost of clustering to the cost of not having it when you need it. You can use the same process that you (hopefully) used when putting together a budget for a disaster recovery plan: What does the solution cost versus the cost of a disaster to your business, weighted against the likelihood of its occurrence? Clustering isn't limited to a glass house data center. You can use relatively inexpensive software such as Octopus to mirror disk data to another server—and that server can be 10 miles away. How's that for disaster recovery of critical data?

Clustering isn't just for a grand and glorious 99.99% available transaction processing system. It can provide a good return on investment in many situations if you think creatively. Say, for example, that your company has a site that is isolated from your hardware support vendor. The contract you have for a one-hour response time is very expensive. The four-hour or eight-hour response time contract is thousands of dollars cheaper per year. If you install a two-node-high availability cluster in this remote site, you can change your contract from one-hour to eight-hour response and pay back your cluster investment in a year or two.

Clustering Solutions
Cluster advantages, and the solutions themselves, fall into two categories: high availability and scalability. Many clustering solutions are available today, so in most cases it's better to talk about representative types of clustering software than an exhaustive list of products.

High-Availability Products
High-availability clusters are designed to seamlessly cover the failure of one node in the cluster so that the client experiences no (or very little) downtime. The products themselves fall into two categories: hardware/software, and software only. Qualix's OctopusHA+ is a standout example of the software-only solution, while MSCS is the key hardware/software product.

OctopusHA+ mirrors data between two or more servers (up to 16 nodes) so that you have multiple complete copies of your data. If a hardware failure or a break in the network connection occurs, the target server you choose will automatically assume the identity of the failed device and will maintain network operations. Though all it requires is the software, license keys, and Windows NT 3.51 or 4, it will also work with Microsoft Cluster Server.

For better or worse, any talk of clustering on Windows NT systems begins and ends with Microsoft's clustering solution: Microsoft Cluster Server (MSCS).

> **Note**
>
> *There's an interesting bit of lore about MSCS. During its initial development, its code name was Wolfpack (a much more interesting name than MSCS). This code name was created in honor of an analogy in Dr. Greg Pfister's book* In Search of Clusters. *Dr. Pfister compared the advantages and disadvantages of a savage multiheaded pooch (an SMP server) against a pack of dogs (a server cluster). ♦*

MSCS is a feature of Windows NT Server 4 Enterprise Edition, which in practical terms means that to get clustering you have to buy at least two copies of the product.

In addition to the clustering management software, MSCS is a set of clustering APIs that allows the cluster and the applications that run on it to communicate with each other. The software is only part of the solution, however; there's still this messy business of putting together a number of computer systems and storage devices.

By far the simplest way to start working with clusters is to buy an MSCS prepackaged solution from IBM, Compaq, Hewlett-Packard, or a number of other vendors. All the hardware and software you need is installed or available out of the box. This is a big advantage because clusters can be complex hardware environments, and you can't just slap together whatever you have in the lab, install MSCS, and off you go. It might work, but it's only a coincidence. There's an MSCS Hardware Compatibility List (go to http://www.microsoft.com/hwtest/hcl/ and choose "cluster" for the category) that contains specific configurations of hardware that are validated and supported to work with MSCS. It's a good attempt to prevent clustering's early adopters from being sunk by the weight of hardware problems encountered when trying to piece together a cluster. This isn't to say it can't be done; I just don't recommend it at this phase of MSCS clustering development.

MSCS is currently available in the first of two phases. MSCS Phase I is a high-availability configuration, more accurately described as a two-node failover cluster. Two servers, each with an internal hard disk, are connected to a disk storage subsystem and directly to each other. Each node does useful work. If a node fails, the clustering software transfers ownership of system resources, such as disk drives and IP addresses, from the failed system to the surviving system, and then restarts the transferred resources on the surviving server. Though not instantaneous, it usually takes less than a minute to perform the failover.

Scalable Clustering Products
The scalable cluster doesn't just have high-availability features. Additional nodes can be dynamically added to the cluster to increase the overall power of the cluster without any downtime.

Tandem, a pioneering clustering company that's now a division of Compaq, specializes in fault tolerance, high availability, and scalable computing, and it's the most sophisticated Windows NT clustering solution on the market. Its non-Windows NT servers have by far the largest market share in the high-availability markets of banking, financial services, and telecommunications. One U.S. stock exchange that relies on its NonStop Himalaya solutions has had no downtime at all for 18 years.

The company has two Windows NT-based offerings. One is an original equipment manufacturer (OEM) version of MSCS; the other uses the company's own ServerNet technology to interconnect cluster nodes. ServerNet uses ASIC-based switches to move data from any system component in a cluster to anywhere else—for example, from CPU to CPU, from CPU to disk, or from disk to disk. Because all processes are handled by the switching fabric, the server CPUs contribute about one-tenth of the overhead compared with a Fast Ethernet interconnect. Leading server vendors such as Compaq, Dell, NEC, and Unisys have announced support for ServerNet, and Vinca has said that its Co-StandbyServer for Windows NT is optimized to work with ServerNet. ServerNet drivers are included in MSCS, making it as close to a de facto standard as you can get.

Microsoft spent a considerable sum of money learning how NonStop clustering and ServerNet system area network technology work, and a key technical officer in their clustering area comes from Tandem. In November 1998, a 72-node NonStop cluster of dual-processor Compaq ProLiant 1850R servers at Sandia Labs (christened "Kudzu") set a world record for sorting a terabyte (1000GB) of data. Running Windows NT 4 Service Pack 3 on its nodes, the cluster finished in 50 minutes, almost three times faster than the previous record on a shared-memory supercomputer.

Challenges for Clustering
MSCS has been slow delivering on Microsoft's promises. Phase I provides high availability, but it's not scalable beyond two nodes. Phase II will be a highly scaleable cluster that will support up to 16 nodes. Unfortunately, it also has fallen victim to Microsoft's wildly optimistic ship dates. It was

originally supposed to ship in 1998, but now it won't be available until after Windows 2000 ships. Some other important features also won't debut until post-Windows 2000:

- Fibre Channel support
- A single programming model that provides true clustering support for application services, based on Microsoft Transaction Server and COM/COM+
- A true single-system image that will support unified management
- Software RAID support (in conjunction with Veritas Software)

Clustering requires applications software to handle failover as well as the hardware. This means that Microsoft must write good cluster-aware applications to show that it can be done and must create good software development kits (SDKs) that let independent software vendors (ISVs) make their applications cluster-aware.

Clustering Recommendations
My clustering recommendations are as follows:

- Dive in. Clustering is complex enough that your Windows NT engineering staff needs to be working with the technology now so that you can determine when it's ready for your company. It takes a seasoned Windows NT administrator to work with clusters at this stage in their development cycle. Develop a cluster in the test lab (you do have a test lab, don't you?), or put a simple two-node file and print cluster in production.

- Carefully examine your needs; for your first clustering experience, choose only the top one or two situations that will have the best chance of success. This pilot will accomplish several goals: You'll achieve an early win with your customers, management will see that clustering can work, and you'll gain real-world experience with the technology.

- Keep it simple. Buy a prepackaged cluster from a single vendor, and migrate your data to it rather than attempting to upgrade your current systems to a cluster.

- Pay close attention to the development of the shared nothing disk model. This is what MSCS and Tandem use.

- Pay close attention to Tandem NonStop architecture. This clustering technology is years ahead of Microsoft, and it's where MSCS is headed.

- Remember that as much as it's hardware, clustering is also software. The cluster manager software handles the failover and failback process. The MSCS APIs allow applications to be cluster-aware. Most critically, the applications themselves must be cluster-aware before that expensive hodge-podge of hardware is good for anything. Without applications that use all the features clusters have to offer, this technology will never gain wide popularity. It's a chicken-and-egg problem: Software vendors are reluctant to spend lots of money developing cluster-competent applications because the installed base of Windows NT clusters is small—and there aren't a lot of clusters installed because there are few applications for them. Of course Microsoft can't and won't allow this to happen because clustering is the way to scale Windows NT to enterprise-class applications currently reserved for mainframe and UNIX platforms.

Clustering for Windows NT is still just out of its infancy. Good solutions are available now if you fit the right profile, but it still will be a couple of years before enough applications are available to make a Windows NT cluster as ubiquitous in the enterprise as UNIX and VMS clusters are today.

Other Factors in Choosing the Box

In a good Windows NT Server network design, you have a few more hardware-related decisions to make. These might not be as much fun as picking processors, but they have a dramatic impact on your support costs.

Homogeneous and Heterogeneous Hardware Environments

As you begin browsing through the glossy brochures of the many Windows NT server manufacturers on the market, you need to consider a general issue first. How many server brands will you need? Does one manufacturer (or OEM) supply a wide enough range of servers to fit your needs, or will you need several? To make this decision, you must think about what applications are planned for your network. These services generally fall into the following categories:

- File servers—The most basic type of server, a file server is simply a data repository on the network where users store and share data. Users have personal or common shares to the server, and the applications that use this data are usually run from the client and may not even be network-aware. A variant of this is the *data server*, which is essentially a file server dedicated to storing large amounts of data for fewer users. File services are handled directly by the Windows NT operating system via the Server service.

- Print servers—A print server manages network printers and their queues. The printers can be shared between other network operating systems such as UNIX by using the Microsoft TCP/IP printing services. Print services are a low-overhead operation, and unless a great number of print queues are run on a server, they're often incorporated into a file server.

- Application servers—These make up the middle tier of a three-tier application design such as SAP. This server does the actual processing of the data that it receives from the client and the database servers.

- Database servers—These servers are dedicated to running database engines. Some of the best-known examples are SQL Server, Lotus Notes, Oracle, and SAP R/3.

  The database server may work directly with the client, as in Lotus Notes, or indirectly through an application server, as in SAP. It's important to realize that in the case of a dedicated database server, the Windows NT OS is running one or several services. Those services handle all the clients, not the operating system.

- Infrastructure servers—These servers provide support for the network and its basic functionality. Some examples of infrastructure servers are listed here:

  Windows NT 4 domain controller—A server that manages authentication for a Windows NT 4 network

  WINS (Windows Internet Naming Service)—A service that registers and maps NetBIOS names to IP addresses

  DHCP (Dynamic Host Configuration Protocol)—A service that dynamically provides the TCP/IP configuration for computers on the network

  DNS (Domain Name System)—A service that resolves DNS names (such as *mycomputer.mydivision.mycompany.com*) to IP addresses

  RAS (Remote Access Service)—A service that enables remote clients using dialup networking or other PPP or Serial Line Internet Protocol (SLIP) dialup software to access the network

  Microsoft SMS (System Management Server)—A network client manager that provides hardware and software inventory, remote control, and software distribution

  Microsoft IIS (Internet Information Server)—A system that enables file and application sharing using the HTTP and FTP protocols

  Dfs (Distributed File System)—A system new to Windows NT 4 and Windows 2000 that provides a logical namespace for network shares

  Windows 2000 Domain Controller—A server that performs authentication and any kind of activity that queries the Active Directory

Windows 2000 Global Catalog Server—A Windows 2000 domain controller that also contains a copy of all the objects (though not all their attributes) in the Active Directory

Windows 2000 Certificate Server—A server that manages the issuing, revoking, and renewing of public key certificates (see "Public Key Infrastructure" in Chapter 3, "Distributed Services in Windows 2000," for more information)

That's a lot of servers if each service had one or more servers dedicated to its use; in reality, more than one service often coexists on one server in a complementary manner (for example, DNS and DHCP).

- Firewall servers—This server runs firewall services to block most kinds of incoming Internet traffic, but it allows outbound traffic from a corporate intranet.

The natural tendency of a network architect—especially one being bombarded by hardware vendors seeking referrals on hardware purchases—is to choose the best technical fit between a server and the business need it's supposed to serve. Let's call this the "heterogeneous hardware environment" and look at its advantages and disadvantages.

A heterogeneous hardware environment offers certain advantages:

- The hardware is cheaper, assuming that you shopped around for the best price (or even constructed the servers yourself). You may also be able to get volume pricing from a single vendor.

- Each application has the most appropriate hardware supporting it. You can spend the money you saved from buying cheap CD-ROM server hardware on a fast fault-tolerant system for your CEO's online news service.

However, there are more disadvantages to a heterogeneous hardware environment:

- Hardware support costs. Each server is different, which affects everything from the initial build ("Oh—the system bug checks on Windows NT installation, and the motherboard isn't on the Hardware Compatibility List.") to its decommissioning ("Server 'Harpo' is being removed from service because its hardware doesn't support the newest Windows NT release and the manufacturer's support can't even spell 'NT.'").

- Hardware maintenance contract costs. If you're thinking of maintaining your server hardware by using maintenance contracts, no reputable company of a size to handle support across a WAN will touch a wildly diversified server environment. If anyone does support it, the cost will bankrupt you.

- Software support costs. You or your system administrators will have a different environment to deal with on every server you encounter. The last thing you need on a large network are servers with personalities! (Server "Groucho" has a tendency to hang under heavy load because the box will support only 64MB of RAM, while the accounting department's servers are slow with network traffic because you got a great deal on a case of 16-bit network cards.)

- Every manager in the company that's just read the latest "server shootout" in the trade magazines will come by and suggest the top-rated server for your company's next location.

In a homogeneous hardware environment, you limit yourself to one or two OEMs, and one or two types of servers within their product lines. The goal is to simply reduce the total cost of ownership by eliminating variables whenever you possibly can.
Advantages of a homogeneous hardware environment include these:

- You'll have more clout with a vendor because you're buying more hardware from them.

- You'll negotiate less-expensive hardware support contracts because the support vendor has a limited number of spare parts to keep onsite (which *you* often have to pay for).

- You'll have greater knowledge of the hardware internals of one or two server types instead of a working knowledge of more.

- You'll need only one or two versions of server build programs with their associated UNATTEND.TXT and .UDF files.

- Although the user interface will appear the same, the hardware configurations will be different, which means less operating training. For example, the boot sequence of a RISC processor is different from that of an IA machine.

- It's easier to track the software configurations of hundreds of servers when the different types are kept to a minimum.

Tip

To keep your software support costs as low as possible, be a follower, not a leader. Choose a popular vendor whose product line offers you the options discussed in this chapter. This increases the chance that bugs in the newest OS release or service pack that apply to you will have already been encountered by someone else. It's also more likely that the vendors are working with the Windows NT development staff on new features, thus sparing you from unpleasant surprises during OS upgrades. ◆

Disadvantages of a homogeneous hardware environment include these:

- Your hardware costs will be greater. Sometimes you may have a less than perfect fit between the server and the application. If the difference isn't unworkable, the advantages in continuity among many servers may outweigh the disadvantage of the occasional poor fit.
- Every manager in the company who has just read the latest "server shootout" in the trade magazines will demand to know why the top-rated server isn't all over the network.

This issue really comes down to a tradeoff between hardware/software costs and support costs. Hardware costs are mainly one-time expenditures, while you'll be supporting the network long after the hardware has depreciated. A Windows NT network consisting of mostly well-known, mainstream servers with a few specialized servers scattered around for special applications seems like a pretty safe and boring recommendation to make. Standardizing your hardware is a very big step to controlling the total cost of ownership (TCO) of your network.

> **Tip**
>
> *No matter how large or small your Windows NT network, the following is always true: As a Windows NT network architect, you must look at what's important to your customers and support staff, not what's interesting to you. In this business, you don't win prizes for having the most technologically interesting servers; your users judge you by how reliable, convenient, fast, and expandable your Windows NT network is.* ◆

Homogeneous and Heterogeneous Networking Operating System Environments

A brief comment on mixed network operating system environments: Most of us don't have a choice about whether we build a Windows NT network in a mixed environment or a homogeneous Microsoft network. It's like dating someone in their 30s or older; everyone has a history, and you simply have to deal with it. Unless you're building a new network from the ground up, you already have existing servers, different network operating systems, and applications that you must either peaceably coexist with or convert to Windows NT.

Fortunately, Windows NT was designed to be a good neighbor with other network operating systems, especially NetWare. Gateway Services for NetWare, File and Print Services for NetWare, and the Client Service for NetWare allow Windows NT servers and their clients to interact with NetWare servers and their clients.

Dedicated Servers Versus Multiple Applications

There's nothing in the Windows NT Server documentation that says you cannot install as many applications as you desire on a server. As with many Windows NT Server areas, however, just because you *can* do it doesn't mean that you *should* do it. By far the most common practice in the industry is for each server to be dedicated to a certain function (for example, an SQL server isn't also running Lotus Notes). Having your Windows NT network built of dedicated servers offers a number of advantages:

- They're easier to build because the build is a simpler process.

- They're easier for configuration management to maintain.

- They're easier to troubleshoot because a dedicated server has at most only two major software components to investigate: the operating system and the server's main application. In the case of file servers, the operating system is the only component. For example, imagine that a Notes server is suffering from slow response time. Further investigation shows that processor utilization is high, that the system is paging heavily, and that the Available Bytes counter is hovering around 1.5MB–2MB. On a dedicated server, it's pretty straightforward to discover whether one of the services running the Notes application is the culprit. If this server were also running file services and RAS, it would be more difficult to determine which component was the troublemaker. A longer troubleshooting period would be required to isolate each application.

- If you have problems, or if emergency maintenance is required on an application, bringing the server down affects only the users of that application, not everyone using all applications on the server.

- Dedicated servers are much easier models for capacity planning. The long-term performance statistics of a dedicated server guarantee that the figures reflect the trends of a certain application, which gives you valuable information about the popularity of the application itself (in addition to forewarning you when the server needs to be upgraded).

- The Windows NT operating system is constructed to tune most easily with one application. For example, SQL Server has tuning options for dedicated servers that can significantly increase its performance. These options, if enabled on a multi-app server, would significantly beat down performance on the other applications.

- A dedicated server initially also may give you extra user capacity in the beginning because its resources aren't being shared by other applications.

The biggest disadvantage of dedicated servers is that they are more expensive than a network of Windows NT servers, where most every processor cycle is used by one application or another. Some servers will inevitably be lightly loaded, while other, more popular applications will be begging for hardware upgrades.

Tip

Remember that support costs are more expensive than hardware costs. Perhaps this will put things into perspective: Who would you rather have running after you with pointed sticks—a few accountants because of the money you're spending on servers, or the IT support staff because it's so difficult to maintain these servers? If you need a hint, the support staff is usually located much closer to you than the accountants. ◆

Multi-app servers can be the right design choice in several circumstances:

- Infrastructure servers—Logical choices for complementary applications are WINS and DHCP, and file/print services.
- Small or remote offices—Small offices that aren't capable of using the resources of the corporate network due to a slow link are excellent candidates for multiple applications. For example, a field sales office with 30 people can't justify the expense of dedicated RAS, Notes, and file/print servers, but these particular applications can be configured to coexist in a reasonable manner. RAS servers tend to have prime time schedules opposite of other applications; employees tend to dial into the network after hours rather than during the day. Lotus Notes on Windows NT is very demanding of memory and processor resources, while file and print services focus on memory and network I/O. You must test out these combinations as best you can before putting them out in a remote office—unless you like walking into an office full of people upset with you, or unless the office is in Hawaii!

Miscellaneous

When choosing a server, don't fixate on just the processor. Processors sell boxes because it's an easy way to categorize and simplify the perception of a computer's power for Joe Consumer. You aren't Joe Consumer, though! Remember, it's a system, not an isolated bunch of components. The amount of memory, the I/O bandwidth, and the network interface are all critical to the design of a successful server. All the processor horsepower in the world won't help your server if the I/O subsystem can't get data to and from the processor fast enough. Instead, look for the following:

- Expandability and upgradeability—Will the server be obsolete before the cover has gotten dusty? Can you plug in more processors if it becomes memory-bound? Can you upgrade the existing processor? How much total system memory can it support? Does it require proprietary memory (that is, expensive memory) available only from the manufacturer? How much disk space will it support? How many slots in the chassis?

- OEM support—Does the manufacturer support its product directly? Do they have a dedicated technical area for server support? When your distributed payroll system is down, your urgent call to the vendor's support line shouldn't be dumped in the phone queue behind the home user that can't get CD audio over his multimedia speakers. When you do get a support rep, he had better know a lot about how Windows NT Server works with the hardware. A number of computer manufacturers, mostly those whose product lines focus on single-user PCs, have servers that are regarded highly, but their Windows NT server support is abysmal. So caveat emptor; check out the support!

- Reliability—Does this brand have a good track record? Does it offer any kind of a pre-failure warranty on its parts? What is the part availability in the areas your servers will be deployed? Are you willing to pay the price for high reliability, or can you live with the occasional down as long as the data is protected?

Summary

When you're planning on buying a large number of servers for your network from a vendor, the honest truth is that beyond ensuring that the hardware is decent, well-made, and reliable, you should be focusing your criteria on less-tangible aspects. Does the vendor have a good reputation for service? Will the company support you worldwide directly, or through a third party?

Are the servers highly manageable through remote control, Wired For Management, or other elements? If you're in a position to recommend servers, you must also focus on the total cost of owning and supporting them after the purchase. Your operations staff may complain about some aspects of a particular server, but if you're able to keep TCO for servers down because they're highly manageable, your managers will compliment you.

5

Building, Maintaining, and Tuning the Box

After you've selected the server hardware, you must deal with the other half of the equation: the server software. You must build the operating system, maintain it properly to maximize the server's availability, and be able to diagnose and head off performance problems.

Understanding Partition Types and Requirements

Partition sizing and configuration for a server is one of those planning tasks that, although mundane, will affect your entire Windows NT network. The ability to run utilities, perform automated upgrades, service applications, and store system dumps depends on how much free space you have on your operating system partition. It's very important to get it right ahead of time because it's very difficult and intrusive to reconfigure a partition. Before you can make intelligent decisions on how many partitions to have and how large they should be, you must understand the different partition types and their requirements.

The *system partition* contains the hardware-specific files, such as `Ntldr`, `Boot.ini`, and `Ntdetect.com`, needed to load Windows NT. This term *system partition* is also used by some hardware manufacturers for a partition to put system hardware configuration utilities and diagnostics in a fast and available location instead of always having to load a CD-ROM or set of disks. It's small (less than 50MB), and it doesn't have a drive letter. It requires a special BIOS, which makes it accessible before the Windows NT loader takes control.

The *OS partition*, sometimes called the *boot partition,* should contain the Windows NT operating system, critical system utilities such as the backup program and logs, and little else. The system utilities are on this partition so that full system functionality can be recovered by restoring the C: partition. This partition needs to be big, much bigger than you'd expect. The partition size you choose now must keep pace with Windows 2000, which is vastly larger than its predecessor. The partition can also incorporate many different services, each taking varying amounts of space.

Some of the unexpected disk hogs are listed here:

- Page files—You can move the page file off the OS partition, but if you want a system crash to dump the contents of memory to a disk file, the page file must be equal to the real memory size.

- Dump files—The partition must be large enough to hold the dump file in addition to the page file. Its default location is `%Systemroot%\memory .dmp`, where `%Systemroot%` is the environment variable assigned to the operating system directory (usually `c:\Winnt`). On a system with 512 MB of RAM, these components have already chewed through 1GB— and that's not even considering the operating system. If you want to store more than one copy of the dump file, add another chunk of space equal to the system's memory size.

- Large SAM support—A domain controller in a large Windows NT 4 domain requires a significant boost in the Registry Size Limit setting to accommodate the resulting large Security Account Manager (SAM) database. This, in turn, boosts the paged pool requirements, which require an increase in page file size.

- Active Directory—Large Windows 2000 domains require a large directory service database, `%Systemroot%\Ntds\Ntds.Dit`. A large company with 60,000 user accounts, 54,000 workstations, and the full complement of attributes associated with these can have an `Ntds.Dit` of almost 800MB. You can choose on which partition to locate this, but you should definitely allocate plenty of room.

- Spool files—The directory where temporary printing files are stored is in `%Systemroot%\System32\Spool\Printers`, on the OS partition. If you print large files or have a large number of active printers attached to the server, you need to account for this occupied space.

- The operating system—The Windows NT 4 Server operating system directory takes a minimum of 130MB, excluding the page file. Windows 2000 disk requirements vary, from merely voracious for a member server to monstrous for a domain controller in a large enterprise. Big surprise, eh? The Windows 2000 %Systemroot% directory alone takes 600MB installed. This doesn't include the files it creates in \Program Files, and the installation process requires significantly more.

Table 5.1 is a quick reference of conservative disk space recommendations for a server's OS partition.

Table 5.1   Recommended Server OS Partition Sizes

Server Type	OS Partition Space Requirement
Windows NT 4 servers that will be retired for Windows 2000	2GB
Windows 2000 server, moderate domain size	4GB
Windows 2000 large enterprise domain controller, including Global Catalog	9GB

Note that these partition requirements don't say whether a server is a domain controller or a member server. That's because in Windows 2000 it's a simple task to promote a member server to a domain controller. If you're parsimoniously allocating your disk space to a member server, the time will certainly come when you need to promote one in an emergency and can't because you don't have the free space.

Tip

Remember that hardware—especially disk space—is cheap compared to support costs. Disk space is an area where it's much better to err on the conservative side. And these estimates don't include room for expansion. ◆

FAT or NTFS?

When Windows NT Advanced Server 3.1 appeared, administrators argued with fervor over the benefits of formatting the operating system partition with the venerable FAT file system versus NTFS. There are valid points for both sides, but without getting into too much gory detail, the battle has been won. If you spend any time at all looking at the future of Windows NT and examine the space requirements previously discussed, it's pretty obvious that only NTFS is capable of managing the impending space, speed, and security required of a Windows NT server partition of any size. A FAT partition of a decent size would have a cluster size of 32KB, which means that every file would occupy at least 32KB of disk space, regardless of its size.

The FAT file system is best for drives or partitions under approximately 200MB and is faster for sequential I/O. FAT32 can address much larger disks, but it still has none of the security features of NTFS. NTFS works best for file systems above 400MB. NTFS has its own log file for internal consistency; FAT has none. Additionally, an NTFS Version 5 volume is required for the Windows 2000 SYSVOL. Finally, NTFS has detailed security built into it. This is important now for user data, and its granular security is becoming more important as many different Windows NT components that are managed by different groups are being incorporated into the %SYSTEMROOT% directory (usually c:\WINNT).

The FAT32 file system fixes a lot of FAT's problems, especially for larger disk sizes, but it's no more appropriate for a large Windows NT server than FAT is.

Tip

The single most important first step you can take in securing your servers against security attacks is to use NTFS on all partitions. ♦

Windows 2000 will have FAT32 support to ensure compatibility with Windows 98 and the OSR2 release of Windows 95. You'll finally be able to dual boot Windows 98 and Windows 2000, or to actually install Windows 2000 Professional on a system that has an OEM install of Windows 98 on a FAT32 partition. Windows NT 4, however, is incompatible with FAT32. You could get around this incompatibility, if you're a little daring, with a utility called FAT32 from www.syssolutions.com. FAT32 is a driver for Windows NT 4 that allows the operating system to access a FAT32 volume. The freeware version allows read-only access, and the $39 full version grants full access. This would allow you to dual boot between Windows 98 and Windows NT 4—but why would you want that on a server anyway?

Windows 2000 Startup Options and Automated System Recovery

Windows 2000 now comes with a Win9x-like boot menu, called Advanced Setup, that allows you to choose from a number of startup options:

Note

The following options are documented in Windows NT 5.0 Server Beta 2 ADVSETUP.TXT. ♦

- Safe mode—Starts Windows 2000 using only basic files and drivers, without networking. Use this mode if a problem is preventing your computer from starting normally.

- Safe mode with networking—Starts Windows 2000 using only basic files and drivers—as with safe mode—but also includes network support.

- Safe mode with command prompt—Starts Windows 2000 using only basic files and drivers, and displays only the command prompt.

- Last-known good configuration—Starts Windows 2000 using the last-known good configuration. (Important: System configuration changes made after the last successful startup are lost.)

To start your computer using an Advanced Startup option, follow these steps:

1. Restart your computer.
2. When the OS Loader V5.0 screen appears, press F8.
3. Select the Advanced Startup option you want to use, and then press Enter.

Partition Recommendations

Here's a list of recommendations that apply to most partitions:

- To ensure that you have enough room to grow (and my, how it does grow!), your OS partition should be no less than 2GB, under any circumstances.

- Keep all partition sizes down to what you can fit on one backup job (and, therefore, one restore job). If a partition takes 16 hours to back up, either it's too big or you need to upgrade your backup hardware.

- If your fault tolerance setup allows it, keep the page file on the fastest disk possible.

- Don't use Windows NT volume sets. A Windows NT volume set is a collection of partitions over a number of disks that allows you to create a large, contiguous volume out of several smaller ones. Once it spans more than one disk, however, you'll have jeopardized all your carefully planned fault tolerance. If one component partition of this volume set is on a non–fault-tolerant volume and it dies, the volume set will fail and your only recourse will be to recover from backups.

- Seriously consider a disk defragmenter, and run it from the beginning of the server's life. It has much lower user impact to continuously correct small amounts of defragmentation than to schedule massive defrag sessions. If your fragmentation is bad enough that the defragger can't do a good job, your only choice is to back up, reformat, and restore to start clean before you enable the defrag service. Windows 2000 has built-in disk defragmentation courtesy of Executive Software. It's only manual, however, and is the equivalent of their DisKeeper Lite freeware product. To get fully automated defragmentation—which is obviously a useful feature—you must buy DisKeeper just as with your Windows NT 4 systems.

Building the Box

Now that you have unboxed the hardware, put it together, and performed initial partitioning and formatting, you're ready to install the operating system. This isn't a thorough treatise on how to install Windows 2000; as with everything related to this new version, it's a very big subject so I'll leave that to the doorstop books (so named because they make good doorstops on a windy day). Instead, I want to point out some issues on naming the box and cover some highlights of the SYSPREP utility for automated builds in Windows 2000.

In both Windows NT 4 and Windows 2000, all servers and workstations must have a unique name of up to 15 characters to identify them on the network. This is called the NetBIOS name, computer name, or machine name. In Windows NT 4, this name is the primary way clients locate a Windows NT system; Windows 2000 doesn't care much about it, but you choose one for compatibility with downlevel systems. Unlike DNS, which has a hierarchy separated by periods (*myserver*.*mydepartment*.*mycompany*.com), NetBIOS is a flat namespace. This means that the name *myserver* must be unique across the entire Windows NT network. This isn't a big deal for a small company whose naming convention can follow the Marx Brothers, but ensuring uniqueness can be a big headache for a large corporation.

Some pointers in choosing workstation and server naming conventions include these:

- Choose a unique identifier by which each node on the network can be mapped to a person responsible for it. The simplest way to do this is by naming workstations with an employee number, which can then be looked up in the company's HR database. The key is to be able to look up the name; a workstation named JIMBOB might be acceptable as long as you can make a directory services query to discover that the owner is James Robert Worthington III. Perhaps the simplest method is to name the workstation after the owner's Windows NT account name.

- Name your servers alphabetically ahead of your workstations. In Windows NT 4, the domain master browser has a buffer size of 64KB. This limits the number of workstations and servers displayed in the browse list to 2,000–3,000 computers, easily reached in a large Windows NT domain. When this happens, names beyond the limit simply won't appear on the list. Because servers are more heavily browsed than workstations, define a naming convention so that servers are alphabetically ahead of workstations. That way, in a large domain, workstations will drop off the browse list instead of servers.

Warning

Beware of the forward-compatibility problem between NetBIOS names and DNS names. In Windows 2000, the NetBIOS restriction will be lifted and network nodes such as servers and workstations will use DNS names to identify themselves. Remember that in Windows NT 4, NetBIOS names may contain special characters. In general, DNS domain and host names have restrictions in their naming that allow only the use of characters a–z, A–Z, 0–9, and "-" (hyphen or minus sign). The use of characters such as the "/," "." and "_" (slash, period, and underscore) are not allowed.

Servers or workstations with NetBIOS names that don't fit into the DNS naming convention will have problems under Windows 2000. Windows NT 4 will warn you before attempting to create or change a NetBIOS name with a slash (/) or period (.), but it will allow an underscore. The underscore is allowed in Microsoft's implementation of DNS, but it doesn't comply with RFC (Request for Comments) 1035, "Domain names—implementation and specification." This means that if you use an underscore in your naming convention, it will work with Microsoft but probably won't work with other industry-standard DNS servers—and Microsoft could clamp down on this loophole in the future. Even this rudimentary character checking isn't done if you've upgraded from a previous version of Windows NT. The most common name violation is use of the underscore in NetBIOS names. Start stamping out incompatible names now! ◆

Automating a Windows NT build has historically been very time-consuming and error-prone. Automating the final 20% was very tedious—and sometimes almost impossible. Microsoft has had much feedback from its customers to make automating a Windows NT rollout much easier to do. A very popular method has been to build a "template" Windows NT system, and clone it to hundreds of other systems by copying the template system's hard disk to the new systems. Cloning, as it's known, is no longer a no-no, but you should be aware of two issues.

Because you've exactly duplicated the template system, you've also duplicated its security identifier (SID). I won't get into SIDs here, but strictly speaking they are supposed to be unique on a Windows NT network. If you've cloned hundreds of workstations, you'll have hundreds of duplicate SIDs on your network.

Duplicate SIDs cause security problems in a Windows NT network in two situations: Workgroups (no Windows NT domains) and removable media, formatted with NTFS. Problems with the former happen because user SIDs on one workstation, with no domain component, can be identical to user SIDs on another. For instance, this allows the first-created user account on one workstation to access files of the first-created user account on another's workstation. The removable drive problems occur because NTFS ACLs depend on the SID for security. If the system is cloned and the security references a local account instead of a domain account, a removable drive could be inserted into a cloned machine. The hacker logs onto an account with the same name, such as Administrator (the password needn't be the same), and the data can be read.

So, duplicate SIDs aren't as big a problem in a domain-based environment as everyone thought. There is a basic requirement for cloned systems, though. Windows NT Setup goes through all sorts of hardware detection, so a cloned machine must have the same hardware of the template machine, or funny things start happening.

Note

This hardware exactness applies especially to hard disk controllers and the HAL. In one situation, cloned machines began breaking for no discernable reason. After many weeks of troubleshooting, the team discovered that all the broken machines had a slightly newer version of a hard disk BIOS. ◆

Third-party tools such as Ghost from Symantec to clone systems have been very popular, and now that GhostWalker (a SID-scrambling tool) is also available, systems can be cloned and still have unique SIDs.

For Windows 2000, Microsoft has given in and provided the SYSPREP utility. SYSPREP is used after the template system has been configured, just the way you like it. The utility is run as the last act before shutting down the system. The template system's hard drive will then be cloned by a third-party tool. When the target machines are first booted, SYSPREP generates a unique security ID for the machine and then pops up with a short menu used to generate a few last items such as computer name and domain membership. SYSPREP has switches to do useful things such as run in unattended mode, re-run the Plug and Play detection on first startup, avoid generating a new SID on the computer, and automatically reboot the system when the final configuration is complete.

For system rollouts that will use different kinds of hardware, the old method of unattended setup with a customized answer file is still around. It has been expanded to take care of the differences in Windows 2000, but it's essentially the same as Windows NT 4.

The final, most sophisticated, and most restricted method of rollout is available via the Remote Installation Service of Windows 2000 Server. The "empty" workstation boots, contacts a Remote Installation Server, and downloads and installs the OS. Pretty slick, eh? Before you start jumping up and down, you need to know that you must have your Windows 2000 server infrastructure (including Active Directory) in place and Remote Installation Service up and running. Only then can you install Windows 2000 Professional on it. This option could be useful down the road, most likely after you've upgraded your clients to Windows 2000 Professional and when you're ready to begin replacing existing systems or installing new ones.

The situations where you can automate a rollout fall into three categories: cloning systems with exact hardware, building systems with unattended setup and answer files, and using the new Remote Installation Service to remotely install the Windows 2000 operating system.

Maintaining the Box

Four of the most important areas of maintaining a Windows NT server are backing it up, scanning for viruses, performing hard disk defragmentation, and maintaining software. All of these are discussed in the following sections.

Backing Up Windows NT Servers

Backing up server data, and coming up with a system recovery strategy have always been low on a network administrator's list of fun things to do. If you do the job right, people complain about the money spent on tape drives, tapes, and operators. If you don't do the job right—or if you do it right but don't constantly monitor the backup and tune the strategy—you can jeopardize the company, lose your job, or at least get yelled at.

Your Windows NT network's system recovery strategy should be designed at the same time you determine the type of backup hardware and backup media. This is because the implementation of a system recovery strategy depends on the media, while the amount the media is used (therefore influencing the choice of media type) depends on the strategy. This section does not include a thorough analysis of disaster recovery because much fine material has already been written about it (for example, John McMains and Bob Chronister's *Windows NT Backup & Recovery*). This section *does* cover the basics of putting a good strategy in place.

Using Storage Management Software

One of the first and most important choices you must make when putting together a backup strategy is that of the storage management software. (We all refer to these things as backup software, but the biggest packages do much more than just backups; *storage management software* is really more accurate.) After storage management software is in place, it becomes deeply entrenched in the environment because of the software expense, the operator training, the customer training (if customers can perform their own restores), and certainly the backups themselves if the software uses a proprietary format.

The storage management software must be capable of growing with your company's needs. You may not initially need enterprise management utilities for multiple servers, but with good fortune you'll need it in the future. You don't want to be forced to switch storage management software because yours couldn't stretch to fit your growing company's needs.

Another advantage to fully featured storage management software from a major vendor is consistency. Whenever possible, you should have one vendor for all your storage management needs, simplifying management, taking advantage of the integration within the vendor's product line, and reducing your total cost of ownership.

Following these guidelines, you should choose your storage management software from one of these four vendors:

- ADSTAR Distributed Storage Manager (ADSM), by IBM
- ARCserve, by Computer Associates
- Backup Exec, by Seagate Software
- Networker, by Legato

I haven't listed these products in any particular order. All are very good and offer a wide range of utilities; they've been the market leaders ever since Windows NT's inception. Ntbackup, the backup utility included with the operating system, is a lobotomized version of Backup Exec, and most of these company's products have existed for many years for other operating systems.

The following are recommendations to keep in mind when choosing your storage management software:

- Clearly define your requirements. Do you want to back up your clients as well as your servers? Do you want your clients to be able to do their own restores? Do you need Web-based administration?

- Think big. Choose a solution once that will do all you'll ever need so that you never have to do it again. And do your research carefully: If you haven't looked at storage management solutions recently, you'll be astounded at the depth and breadth of what they can do. Of course, this makes you continually re-examine your requirements. When you realize what these suites can do, you'll be able think of new ways to handle data you didn't know were possible.

- Choose a vendor that supports the widest variety of client operating systems possible—not just Windows NT. You want to be able to back up all your business's clients, not just your Microsoft-based ones.

- Make sure the software you're considering also supports all the databases you're using—and those you may ever possibly use in the future. Look carefully into the support so that you're sure you understand what it can and can't do. SQL Server, Oracle, SAP, and Exchange all may require additional software that not every solution may support. For example, if you use the OpenIngre database, of the four mentioned only ARCserve for Windows NT has an agent to back it up.

- The storage management software must support the broadest range of backup devices, from 4mm DAT up to tape libraries with terabyte capacities. Again, think about your company's growth and a single-vendor solution.

Choosing a Backup Hardware Format

It's worth noting that when you're perusing the brochures for different backup types, most have split numbers such as 4/8, 7/14, 15/30, 35/70, and so on. This is a capacity description of each tape, uncompressed and with maximum 2:1 hardware compression with the right data (such as bitmaps). Obviously, your mileage will vary depending on the type of data you're backing up. If you have a good mix of data in your backup stream, splitting the difference between the two extremes will probably yield a valid estimate. I've seen a solid 27GB per tape on a 15/30 DLT when backing up standard file server data: Word documents, Excel spreadsheets, Dilbert® cartoon archives, and so on.

> **Note**
>
> *There's a very important trend to be aware of in data storage: The ability to put more data on disk drives has in no way kept up with the ability to back them up. With the exception of network backup servers using autoloaders and tape libraries, file servers of enterprise scale cannot be adequately backed up without using tape autoloaders. You must take this into consideration when you're putting together a purchase order for servers. Don't cut corners on your backup solution; if anything happens—and, of course, it will—you'll be reviled more for not having adequate backups than for the redundant power supply you just had to have.* ◆

A number of tape formats are available. You can quickly narrow your choices, however, to one or two formats based on how much you must backup and automation you need, what speed you need, and how much you're willing to pay. The next few sections talk about the most popular formats and their strengths and drawbacks.

QIC

The QIC (quarter-inch cartridge) format and capacity has evolved over the years. Originally limited to 100MB or 200MB per tape, it's now capable of up to 8GB using Travan cartridges. QIC been a mainstay of PC backups for many years. Its throughput can rival that of 4mm, but because it won't scale to larger systems through use of magazines, it's limited to workstations and workgroups.

8mm

8mm tapes are about the size of a deck of cards and use the same helical scan technology found in the family VCR. Backing up between 7GB and 14GB, 8mm tapes can be found with autofeeders to increase its capacity. As with your family VCR, however, the drive demands regular cleaning when subjected to heavy use.

4mm DAT

DAT (digital audio tape) is only about two-thirds the size of an audio cassette. Relatively inexpensive and fast, DAT also uses helical scan echnology in which data is recorded in diagonal stripes with a rotating drum head while a relatively slow tape motor draws the media past the recording head. DAT tapes hold 2GB–24GB depending on the compression achieved by the backup hardware, and they have some popularity in the IA server world. To increase their capacity, DAT tapes are available with loader magazines that can exchange up to 12 tapes without operator intervention. DATs can back up data at about 1GB–3GB per hour. (These are conservative numbers based on actual experience rather than product brochures.)

DLT

DLT (digital linear tape) is a fast and reliable backup medium that uses advanced linear recording technology. DLT technology segments the tape medium into parallel horizontal tracks and records data by streaming the tape across a single stationary head at 100–150 inches per second during read/write operations. Its path design maintains a low constant tension between the tape and read/write head, which minimizes head wear and head clogging. This extends the operational efficiency of the drive as well as its useful life by as much as five times over helical scan devices such as the 4mm and 8mm formats. DLT is the most expensive, per unit, of s tandard tape backup solutions, but for your money you get the fastest throughput (3GB–9GB/hour real-world), greatest capacity (35GB–70GB in the newest drives), and best reliability (minimum life expectancy of 15,000 hours under worst-case temperature and humidity conditions; the tapes have a life expectancy of 500,000 passes) of all drive types. The current standard is 35GB uncompressed or 70GB with 2:1 compression, and it's been around for a while. On the horizon is 50/100, but it still isn't keeping up with the increase in disk capacity.

DLT cartridges look disconcertingly like old 8-track cartridges. Loaders to handle multiple tapes and increase capacity without operator intervention are also available from many vendors, and these are a necessity if you have a number of servers to back up and limited operators to swap tapes.

Network Backup

One problem with traditional local tape backups is that when you have a lot of servers, you have a *lot* of tapes and tape drives to manage. An unattended network backup solution moves the backup media to one server specifically designed to back up massive amounts of data as quickly as possible. Truly awesome amounts of storage can be built into supported devices: an ADIC Scalar 1000 DLT library integrated into ADSM can hold up to 5.5TB. Whatever its advantages and disadvantages for server backups, network backups are a huge win for lowering the total cost of ownership in a network. All backup operations are automated, which means that the single most expensive overhead item for operations—the operators themselves—aren't needed for changing tapes at all hours and performing tedious data restores.

Tape Format Recommendations

Table 5.2 shows a comparison of backup methods. I've listed the advantages and disadvantages in relative order of importance, based on a goal of high availability. Your business priorities for your Windows NT network may be different, perhaps compromising on longer restoration times to save hardware money. Keep in mind, however, that mainstream backup hardware and tapes almost always cost far less than the price of tens or hundreds of workers sitting on their hands because the server's down.

My recommendation hands-down is DLT for a shop of any size. Besides speed and reliability, it comes up the winner in an area most people haven't thought about: longevity of the format. If you're backing up design data to be archived for 5 years, or company financials for 10 years, you have to think of the environment at the time of restore. Will a tape drive of the right format still be around? I know of a large company that kept a Digital Equipment Corporation RV20 write once-read many (WORM) optical drive around (and had to pay for maintenance) for years after the technology was obsolete because it was the one piece of hardware that could read their archives.

Table 5.2   A Comparison of Backup Methods

Advantages	Disadvantages
Network Backups	
Lower support costs; very little operator intervention is needed for regular backups.	Very expensive for large tape storage devices.
No "end of tape" to deal with; extremely large storage capacity.	High-speed network required.
	Problematic for remote sites with slow links.
Full remote control of backups (you don't need an operator to change tapes).	Must have guaranteed network connectivity during (potentially long) backup or restore process, or else backup/restore job fails.
Built-in disaster recovery if tape silo is offsite.	Restoration time may be unacceptable for large volumes, or the network may be too unstable for restoration even to be possible.
Also has optional DRM (Disaster Recovery Manager) to assist in removing media from silo for offsite storage.	
	Some products (Networker) use parallelism for increased speed.
Backup policy changes are easy to enact.	Disaster recovery is compromised if the silo is onsite.
	Total costs are not as well understood as with standard tape.
Tape Backups	
Dramatically lower local hardware cost: $1,000–$5,000 per server	Higher operations costs.
Faster backup and restore.	Remote management available within the tape, or tape magazine only (need an operator to change tapes).
Tapes can be carried offsite in all cases for disaster recovery.	
Not dependent on network bandwidth or reliability, if backing up local server only.	
Good remote management.	

continues ▶

Table 5.2   continued

Advantages	Disadvantages
4mm DAT	
Inexpensive. Good capacity, approaching 72GB with 12-tape magazine. Good throughput, 1GB–3GB/hr.	Higher maintenance—heads must be cleaned frequently, magazines jam, and so on. This can be a problem with high duty-cycle backups (8–12hrs/night). Tapes wear out relatively fast.
DLT	
High capacity: 35GB–70GB per tape. Densities as high as 100GB achievable when backing up design data. Highest throughput, 3GB–9GB/hr. Low maintenance, rarely need cleaning. Better for high duty-cycle backups than 4mm.	More expensive than DAT. Autoloaders are much more expensive than comparable DAT autoloaders.

Building a System Recovery Strategy

Before you begin designing a system recovery strategy, you must ask your customers, your managers, your operations staff, and yourself a number of questions.

Gathering Customer Requirements

Here are some questions to ask your customers and their managers:

• How long should a file exist before it gets backed up? In a typical backup scenario, any file that has existed more than 24 hours gets backed up. This doesn't mean, however, that it will stay backed up for months or even weeks. If a document is created on a Tuesday and erased on a Thursday, its chances of being recovered after several weeks are less than if it was created on a Thursday and erased on a Tuesday. This seems arbitrary, but due to standard business hours, full backups are best done over the weekend. This period where files greater than 24 hours old on any day of the week are backed up can be described as the *high-detail backup period*. So be aware: Depending on when they are created and erased, a file's life on backup media will vary. Fortunately, most people's habits keep them from quickly erasing any data they deem valuable. When's the last time you saw disk space utilization on a server volume go down?

- How many copies of a file should be kept? Is it important that users can retrieve a specific version of a file? In most file server environments, the number of versions created by several weeks of full backups is often enough, but special applications may require more.

- How far back in time should a file be recoverable? Certainly, everyone would like to be able to recover that year-old weekly report of accomplishments for the following year's annual review. In reality, however, most people ask for restores within the last two or three weeks—and most of these ask for recovery from yesterday's backup! Increasing backup media storage time, known as the *retention period,* beyond three to six months dramatically increases the cost of media.

- Should the customer be able to restore the file himself? This would be a nice feature, but server backups don't currently allow users to restore their own files. It's a server backup, so it must be restored by server operations. This could be done in an indirect manner, however, if you have a network backup system such as ADSM. ADSM can back up client workstations with a simple user interface that allows workstation users to restore their own files. If the client includes a personal share on the server as part of the workstation's backup, he will also be able to recover the server share. Of course, this raises a number of other problems, one of which is multiple backups of the same data. The server may back up the same client share as the workstation backups because it has no knowledge of the workstation backups, and vice versa. Another problem is network shares on the user's workstation. After backing up his personal share, the simple marking of a checkbox may allow the user to back up a 1GB department share (which is already being backed up by the server backups).

- How long may restoration of the user data to the server take? If the integrity of the data is more important than its restoration speed—and especially if you have lots of data—a network backup product may be acceptable. As availability requirements increase, the backup data storage possibilities move from local tape to online copies, to network mirrored data, to clustering.

Gathering Data Center Requirements

Here are some questions to ask your management and other IS managers:

- How long may the server itself be down? If the Windows NT operating system is dead but the user data is fine, you need to be able to recover the operating system quickly and with as little pain as possible. This is a balance between your business needs of server availability and what you're willing to pay for it. If you require instant availability, you should have a clustering or network mirroring solution. Data on the OS partition changes slowly, so if you have partitioned it correctly, a weekly full backup to tape will ensure that the operating system can be rebuilt within 30 minutes or so. If recovery time isn't important and the server receives its data from replication, backups of the operating system partition may not even be necessary.

- Do you have SLAs (service-level agreements) signed with your customers stating the maximum recovery time? If you do, you must base your calculations on this. If it turns out that you were hopelessly optimistic in your recovery time estimates, you'll have to crawl back to the negotiating table for more money or renegotiate the recovery times based on realistic expectations with the business.

- What level of disaster recovery does the company believe should be implemented? Despite your belief in the importance and irreplaceability of your Windows NT systems and data, the company may not share your convictions. Assuming that your company has an existing disaster recovery plan for its existing systems, the decision needs to be made whether to include the Windows NT systems in it. Certainly the simplest solution is to incorporate Windows NT into an existing DR plan. Disaster recovery can imply several levels, too; when you say "disaster recovery" to a server operator, she may think of two hard drives failing simultaneously. When you say it to a DR planner, he may think of a 747 crash-landing on the roof. These require different levels of planning, and the disaster scenarios must be thought out ahead of time. If your company doesn't have a disaster recovery plan for its computers, run—don't walk—to the bookstore where you bought this, and buy a book on disaster recovery planning! Do something, even if it means carrying one set of tapes home weekly.

- Is there an operations staff at each server site? You need operators to change tapes. This is where network backups shine. No operators are needed for network backups to a tape library, only for assistance in catastrophic system recovery. If operators are unavailable or must make limited trips to the site, consider an autoloader tape magazine that can hold a number of tapes. You can schedule various jobs to run on different tapes in the magazine, and you can even include a cleaning tape that runs at scheduled intervals. Of course, in this scenario there's limited disaster recovery potential because the backup tapes are sitting next to the computer!

- What are their hours and how busy are they? Even if the computer room or server area is staffed 24x7, you need to consider operator availability when scheduling tape changes, tape drive cleaning, offsite disaster recovery shipments, and so on. Balance this with the need to run backups at off-peak hours, and you have defined certain time windows in which tapes must be handled.

- What is the network bandwidth at each server computer room and between these locations? This factor determines whether network backups are practical. In large installations, at least a 100Mbps network backbone is necessary to provide enough bandwidth to back up multiple servers in a practical amount of time and without saturating the network.

- Has the recovery plan been tested, and have all operators been trained on it? Too often, the recovery plan isn't really tested until a failure happens.

- Have you factored performance degradation into your recovery times? Be very conservative in estimating the amount of time required to recover a system, especially if it's to be restored from a network backup system. If you don't have a dedicated backup network, the length of time required to restore the server depends on the network traffic. Indeed, you may have a service agreement in place that requires data restores to wait until the evening if network traffic is above a certain level. If you run this kind of risk, you shouldn't be using network backups.

- If chargeback (billing customers for your services) is not used, how much is the information systems department willing to spend on backups? In most shops I've encountered, the IS department simply eats the cost because the amount billed isn't worth the overhead for journal entries. In other words, what's your budget? Be prepared to go back for more after you've done your research. You could also consider offering a tiered pricing structure based on the level of service being offered.

- Do you have any way to automate the review of backup results? You must have a way to notify your operators if a backup has failed. Enterprise-scale storage management software now has automated alerting functions, but unless you're prepared to write your own log-viewing facility, you also have to buy the coordinating systems management software.

- How important are all these to you and your customers (i.e., what are they willing to pay for these things)? Every one of these costs money— some much more than others. A 4mm DAT drive can be acquired for $1,000 and will hold between 4GB and 8 GB, while an automated tape silo costs well into five figures and holds terabytes of storage. You and your managers need to establish where the balance lies between high server availability and the cost to keep it high. Unfortunately, braggin' rights tend to focus on the 99.9% availability your servers averaged last month; it's harder to crow about how much less your servers cost to maintain!

Types of Backups

Regardless of your choice of backup hardware or media, the type of backup being performed usually falls into three categories:

- Full—Everything on the selection list is backed up, period. The archive bit, a property of all PC-based files that indicates whether the contents of the file have changed since it was last set, is unconditionally reset to 0. Full backups are often broken into two categories: weekly and monthly. They perform the same function; the difference is that weekly backups are once a month, while monthly backups are cycled for the length of the tape retention period. For an example, take a standard configuration where a month equals five weekly cycles and tapes will be retained for one year. In this case, a weekly job will be reused every five weeks, and a monthly job will be reused once a year. Any file that exists during a weekly job and that is less than five weeks old may be recovered. Any file that exists during a monthly job and that is less than a year old may also be recovered.

  The advantage is that because all data that was selected was backed up, this is a snapshot in time of an entire disk volume or server (if you built the selection list correctly). With this set of tapes, you should be able to restore a server to some level of service. Full backups are the foundation of the remaining backup types.

The disadvantage is that because everything gets backed up, this chews up a lot of tape. Full backups are the most time-consuming backups. If backups are run across a network, they consume a lot of network bandwidth during this long backup time.

- Incremental—Everything on the selection list with the archive bit turned on is backed up. After the backup completes successfully, the archive bit is reset to 0. From a practical point of view, this means that every file that has changed since the last backup (full or incremental) gets backed up. In backup documents, this is usually (but not always) the type of job defined as a "daily."

The main advantage of this type of backup is that it is much speedier than a full backup because, if incrementals are run daily, relatively few files have changed compared to all files on a volume (typically 5% or less on a file server). Incrementals allow versioning: If they run daily and the contents of a file are also changed daily, the file's archive bit gets set to 1 and the incremental job backs up a new version every day.

The main disadvantage of an incremental backup is that it usually cannot be used by itself to restore a volume or server; it must depend on the data from a full backup being restored first. On a system such as a database server, where data files are interrelated and depend on each other's versions, all incrementals must be applied to a restore job. This can be a time-consuming process, and the time required for restoration will eventually outweigh the convenience of a speedy backup. For example: An SQL server's database files are backed up with a full backup on Sunday and incrementals early every morning during the week. If the database becomes corrupted Friday afternoon, the restoration process requires 1) restoring Sunday's full backup, and 2) restoring the five incremental backups taken Monday through Friday morning.

- Differential—Everything on the selection list with the archive bit turned on is backed up. Unlike an incremental, the archive bit is not reset to 0. As with an incremental, every file that has changed since the last backup gets backed up. This type of backup job is occasionally used as a "daily" is much speedier than a full backup.

Differential backups also offer versioning. Unlike an incremental backup, a volume or server can be restored more quickly to a "snap-shot in time" with a full backup plus a differential. This is because the backup contains all the changes made since the last full backup; an incremental may contain only changes since the last incremental. (Though it's possible to run differentials after incrementals, it gets very complex and isn't recommended.)

Because the archive bit isn't reset to 0 after a differential is run, the number of files to be backed up grows every day. A system recovery strategy that uses daily differentials consumes more tape than one that uses daily incrementals, but unlike incrementals, you don't have to restore multiple differentials to rebuild a snapshot of the system.

As with an incremental backup, a differential backup usually cannot be used by itself to restore a volume or server; it must depend on the data from a full backup being restored first.

- Copy—A copy job is identical to a full backup job, with the exception that the archive bit isn't reset. It is usually used for special jobs such as disaster recovery, where a complete copy of the system is desired but won't normally be available for file restoration.

In a world with unlimited backup storage and tremendous backup speeds, a full backup every day would be the simplest system recovery strategy. Because this would require a tremendous amount of time and tapes, a good system recovery strategy balances retention period, high-detail backup period, disaster recovery, operator availability, and minimizes tape use. It's no wonder that a good system recovery strategy is hard to find.

A Backup Example

As a real-life example, let's answer many of the questions ourselves:

- *How long should a file exist before it gets backed up?* 24 hours.
- *How many copies of a file should be kept?* This isn't as important to the customer as recovery time—let's say three copies.
- *How far back in time should a file be recoverable?* Six months.
- *How long may restoration of the user data take?* Within four hours.
- *How long may the server be down?* Two hours.
- *What kind of disaster recovery should be implemented?* Data will be stored offsite. Because of operational considerations, it will be between three weeks and six months old.
- *What is the site operations staff's hours?* Staff are available 7AM–4PM, Monday through Friday.
- *What is the network bandwidth at each site and between these sites?* The servers are on FDDI rings at each site, and the major sites are linked by an ATM network. Remote sites are connected to the main campus by T1 WAN circuits with apparent bandwidth of 10Mbps.
- *What kind of backup hardware will be used?* 35-70GB DLT, single tape (not changers).

Armed with this information and data on the available backup options, we can put together a system recovery strategy. For the sake of an interesting example, let's assume that ADSM is already being used for workstation backups across most of the company, including remote sites.

Figure 5.1 is an example of a backup schedule for systems with a dedicated DLT tape drive. It covers an entire month and handles full and incremental backups, cleaning, and disaster recovery jobs. The letters A–E in Figure 5.1 stand for the following tape operator duties:

A	Dismount Daily tape. If needed, mount cleaning tape and allow drive to clean heads and eject tape. Mount corresponding coded Weekly tape into drive.
B	Ship third-oldest Weekly tape offsite for storage as Disaster Recovery tape.
C	Dismount Weekly tape. Relabel Weekly tape as Monthly tape, and store. Mount corresponding coded Daily tape into drive.
D	Dismount Weekly tape. Mount corresponding coded Daily tape into drive.
E	Manually clean drive, if necessary.

	Sunday	Monday	Tuesday	Wednesday	Thursday	Friday	Saturday
Week 1							
Job(s) Scheduled	20:00 Daily Append	20:00 Daily Append	20:00 Daily Append	20:30 Weekly	20:00 Daily Replace	20:00 Daily Append	20:00 Daily Append
Operator Duties				A, B, E	D		
Week 2							
Job(s) Scheduled	20:00 Daily Append	20:00 Daily Append	20:00 Daily Append	20:30 Weekly	20:00 Daily Replace	20:00 Daily Append	20:00 Daily Append
Operator Duties				A, E	D		
Week 3							
Job(s) Scheduled	20:00 Daily Append	20:00 Daily Append	20:00 Daily Append	20:30 Weekly	20:00 Daily Replace	20:00 Daily Append	20:00 Daily Append
Operator Duties				A, E	D		
Week 4							
Job(s) Scheduled	20:00 Daily Append	20:00 Daily Append	20:00 Daily Append	20:30 Weekly	20:00 Daily Replace	20:00 Daily Append	20:00 Daily Append
Operator Duties				A, E	D		
Week 5							
Job(s) Scheduled	20:00 Daily Append	20:00 Daily Append	20:00 Daily Append	20:30 Weekly	20:00 Daily Replace	20:00 Daily Append	20:00 Daily Append
Operator Duties				A, E	D		

Figure 5.1   *A sample backup schedule: a calendar for file server with DLT drives.*

The following are more complete descriptions of the individual jobs:

- Weekly and monthly jobs—Full backups will be taken weekly and be kept for five weeks. Ideally, these long-running backups would be taken over the weekend when there is little user activity. In this case, however, the operator's schedule dictates that they must run on a weekday. (Let's choose Wednesday.) The full backup jobs are called weeklies; monthly jobs will simply be weekly jobs that are removed from the five-week backup cycle and kept onsite.

- Daily jobs—Incrementals will run on the remaining nights of the week. They will be kept for two weeks, and they'll be called daily jobs. These jobs will be of two types: Daily Append and Daily Replace. Daily Replace will run once a week after the weekly/monthly and will overwrite (replace) the contents of the tape. Daily Append will run on the remaining days of the week and append its data to the tape. The combination of these two jobs creates a single tape with a week's worth of incremental backups.

- Disaster recovery jobs—Disaster recovery jobs can be created in two ways. If you have 24x7 or 24x5 operator support, a DR job can be run one night a week after the nightly job has completed. This requires one more intervention by the operator than described on the calendar, but this will assure that disaster recovery tapes are no more than one week old. If you don't have the luxury of 24-hour operator support or an autoloader, unless you are able to run backup jobs during the day (not recommended due to open files and server load), you must use the simpler method indicated in the backup schedule. In this case, disaster recovery jobs will be the third-oldest weekly job, rotated offsite until the next weekly job is run. The obvious drawback to this method is the age of the data; it's always at least three weeks old. The reason for this method is because a single tape drive doesn't allow you a way to change tapes without operator intervention, and your operator's schedule ensures that no one will be around to perform the change required for the DR job after the regular nightly job. Other possibilities are to substitute a DR job for a daily (losing 24-hour recoverability for one day of the week) or pay an operator overtime one night a week to drive in and swap tapes. Only one set of DR tapes is kept offsite; you may want to increase that to two sets for redundancy.

- Cleaning—DLT drives don't need to be cleaned nearly as often as 4mm tapes, and an indicator light tells the operator when it's needed. The CLEAN job on Wednesday that uses a special cleaning tape is optional and needn't be performed unless the cleaning light is on.

- Open files—Any file on a Windows NT system that has an exclusive lock on it—whether it's an open Word document or the SQL Server master database—may not be backed up. I say *may* because most storage management software offers optional open file backup modules, but if you don't get it and a file is open, the backup program will skip it. This has very large and unfortunate consequences (especially related to database systems) if you aren't aware of this. That SQL server you've been backing up for six months with the native Windows NT backup tool actually has no worthwhile data on tape because SQL wasn't shut down before backups and has locked all its data structures open. As a result, the master database and all the database devices have been skipped by the backup program. This is an excellent reason to examine your backup logs on a daily basis, because these errors show up there.

If you must have high availability on your databases and you either won't buy an open file backup module or your software doesn't offer it, a simple process can provide data integrity:

1. On a nightly basis, just before the scheduled backup time, dump the databases to dump devices. The scheduled job will then be capable of backing up these files.

2. If possible, perform a full backup of the server with the database shut down. This should ideally be done whenever a physical database device has changed on the system because those are the files that the operating system sees. To minimize the number of database downs, you'll want to change this device as little as possible. The advantage of a full physical backup of the database devices is that in the event of a failure, the rebuilding of the database system will be greatly speeded. SQL Server won't have to be reinstalled and the database devices won't have to be re-created manually.

3. If you can't bring the database system down for the occasional backup, keep printed copies of database device information. After a failure, you'll have to rebuild them manually before you can load the database dumps from tape.

Restoration of service will be slower with this method because you must reinstall SQL Server and rebuild the database structure before loading your database dumps. If you shut down the database before backups and backed up everything at once, a simple restore job would bring back the entire database and its executables and data structures at once. It's a compromise you must make between availability and restoration speed.

To determine the right number of tapes to purchase for this backup scenario, we need to add up the number of tapes needed for each kind of job, the number of times they run, and factor in the various retention periods. Let's figure it out by job type:

Daily:

(# of tapes needed for dailies)	=	(Total # of daily jobs) × (# of tapes per daily job)
	=	(6 dailies/week × 2 weeks) × (1/6 tape per daily job)
	=	2 tapes

> **Note**
>
> *"1/6 tape per daily job" really means that the same tape is used for dailies all week. ◆*

Weekly:

(# of tapes needed for weeklies)	=	(Total # of weekly jobs) × (# of tapes per weekly job)
	=	(5 weekly jobs) × (4 tapes per weekly job)
	=	20 tapes

Monthly:

(# of tapes needed for monthlies)	=	(# of tapes per weekly job) × (# of tape sets pulled from rotation)
	=	(# of months that weeklies are in rotation)
	=	(4 tapes per weekly) × [(6 months)—(1 month of weeklies)]
	=	20 tapes

> **Note**
>
> *In this case, "# of tape sets pulled from rotation" is equal to the retention period of six months because a set of weekly tapes is set aside every month for six months. Likewise, "# of months that weeklies are in rotation" means that you don't need to account for special monthly tapes when you can pull a valid weekly tape (one that's in current backup rotation) off the rack. In most cases, this will be equal to 1. ◆*

Disaster Recovery:

(# of tapes needed for DR)	=	(# of tapes per weekly job) × (# of tape sets pulled from rotation)
	=	(4 tapes per weekly) × (6 months)
	=	5 tapes

These formulas may seem like overkill when you can probably work it out with a little head scratching, but they will work in a situation where it gets too large or complicated for seat-of-the-pants reckoning. Having said that, don't forget to add Finagle's Constant of about 10% to cover bad tapes, underestimation of how many tapes you think you'll need, and so on.

Virus Scanning

It's well known by now that Windows NT is susceptible to viruses. The boot partition and users' files are especially at risk, with much resulting pain and anguish. A server can be infected with a boot sector virus through infected service disks such as system configuration utilities, Windows NT boot disks, BIOS updates, and others. It's vital that you practice safe hex by scanning these disks regularly with an up-to-date virus scanner.

Building a comprehensive virus policy for Windows NT servers is more complicated than it might first appear. The most obvious requirements of a virus scanner are listed here:

- Detection and correction—The scanner must be capable of finding and fixing as many viruses as possible.

- Unobtrusive operation—The scanner must interfere with normal server operations as little as possible.

- Comprehensive notification and reporting—It's very important to have flexibility in how virus alerts are sent. A scanner with a highly configurable alert utility will allow you to distribute file disinfection to local administrators by partition or share.

Selecting and configuring a Windows NT Server virus scanner is the easy part of building a virus scanning policy; figuring out what to do with a virus when you find it is the hard part. Before you sneer, "Automatically clean it off—Duh!", think ahead to the consequences.

Whose responsibility should it be to disinfect viruses? It's pretty clear that the administrations/operations group should keep the boot sector and OS partition clean. What about the user partitions?

What is the process for cleaning a virus off the server? The only way some viruses can be cleaned requires erasing the infected file. How will that be handled? *"Dear sir: We erased your critical spreadsheet from the server because it was infected with a virus (even though you could read the data). Have a nice day, MIS."* If the virus is on a personal share, the owner can spread it by emailing the file to others. If it's on a group share, it may be infecting many other people. The moral: Automatic correction on user partitions is okay if the file is not deleted, but get the alert about the virus out to the user right away so the user can notify others who may have been infected. If the virus requires that the file be deleted, move it to a special directory and notify the user immediately.

Who gets notified if a virus is detected on a user partition? The server administration staff? If the infected file is on a group share, where does the alert go?

Don't forget that here economies of scale work against you. If you have 1,000 users on a server and have 5 servers, and if 35% of them have at least one virus on their files, that's 1,750 cases that need to be dealt with. If you roll out a virus scanner across multiple servers in a short period, the help desk will be swamped with calls.

Suppose that one day you get all the viruses off the server. You now have a clean server with hundreds or thousands of dirty workstations reinfecting it every day. To work effectively, a comprehensive server virus policy must dovetail with a workstation virus policy. Fortunately, workstation virus scanners have become quite sophisticated and can catch many viruses the instant they're loaded into memory. You also need a process of regularly updating the virus signature database on all servers.

Fragmentation

Yes, Virginia, there *is* disk fragmentation on NTFS volumes, and it can affect your system's performance. Although they don't fragment as quickly as FAT, NTFS partitions can be badly fragmented by normal operations. Take print spooling, for example. The process of printing a file to a network printer requires a spool file be created and almost immediately deleted. This process alone, repeated hundreds or thousands of times in the course of a normal working day, can defragment any type of partition.

Disk fragmentation is measured by how many fragments a file is broken into. A completely defragmented file has a fragments per file ratio of 1.0: The file consists of one fragment. Executive Software, the company that literally wrote the book on the subject, believes that any partition with a fragments per file ratio greater than 1.5 is badly fragmented and severely impacts performance. An analysis I did of a Windows NT file server whose disk array had been around for three years yielded a fragments per file ratio of 3.64! Historically, the only thing that could be done about fragmentation was to back up the volume, format it, and load the data. With the advent of Windows NT 4, however, hooks have been added to the operating system's microkernel to allow real-time defragmentation, and several products are on the market.

Software Maintenance

The task of keeping Microsoft operating system software up-to-date is pretty straightforward once you understand the concepts of hotfixes and Service Packs. Equally important, you should understand how much Microsoft itself trusts each of these updates.

Using Hotfixes

As problems are reported with Windows NT, Microsoft develops fixes for them. (We'll leave the subject of how quickly and how well for another time.) Called *hotfixes*, not much regression and integration testing is done on them before they're posted here:

`ftp://ftp.microsoft.com/bussys/winnt/winnt-public/fixes/`

Hotfixes can be installed in one of two ways. The simplest way is to save the hotfix executable in a temp directory and run it. A more organized way, especially if you have a number of hotfixes, is to run the executable with the /x switch. This will extract the hotfix and its symbol files. You can then install the hotfix with the HOTFIX command. Table 5.3 lists the switches (that is, options) for the HOTFIX command.

Table 5.3   Switches for the HOTFIX *Command*

/y	Perform an uninstall (but only with /m or /q switches)
/f	Force applications closed at shutdown
/n	Don't create an uninstall directory (not recommended)
/z	Don't reboot when the update completes
/q	Use Quiet mode—don't ask the user for anything
/m	Use unattended mode, very similar to quiet mode
/l	List the hotfixes already installed on this system

There are two other ways to quickly check whether hotfixes have been applied to a system. The first is to check in the `%systemroot%` directory for hidden directories:

`$NTUninstallQxxxxxx$`

Here, *xxxxxx* is the hotfix number.

The second method is to look directly in the registry:

`HKEY_LOCAL_MACHINE\Software\Microsoft\Windows NT\CurrentVersion\Hotfix`

If the `\hotfix` key isn't there, or if it's empty, no hotfixes have been installed.

Tip

If you come to Microsoft operating systems from a different background, be careful about your assumptions on software maintenance. Unlike IBM mainframe maintenance (which recommends that you keep up with monthly fixes and believes these program update tapes [PUTs] are safe), Microsoft takes a different position. Don't apply hotfixes unless they fix a specific, critical problem you're encountering—and then be prepared for something else that had a dependency on the hotfixed files to possibly break. Microsoft doesn't hide the fact that most hotfixes are only minimally tested and certainly aren't for all the dependencies in the OS. So don't apply a hotfix unless you really need it, and then test it thoroughly in your environment before releasing it to your production servers. As always, make sure you have a good backup of your server before you apply any maintenance of this type. ◆

Using Service Packs

As a large number of hotfixes are accumulated, they'll be rolled up into an overall maintenance package called a *Service Pack*. Service Packs are infrequent events; there were only five for Windows NT 3.51, and there are four so far for Windows NT 4. Service Packs also developed in size and sophistication over their history. Besides becoming easier to install, since Windows NT 4 SP3 they've featured an uninstall option. The original files are stored in a hidden directory named `%systemroot%\`
`$NTServicePackUninstall$`. Unlike individual hotfixes, the updates in a Service Pack are regression and integration tested to ensure that they're more stable than an ad-hoc collection of individual hotfixes. Service Packs are cumulative, which means that updates from previous Service Packs and hotfixes are rolled up into later ones. Service Pack 4 is 100MB in size and has more than 1,200 files.

Service Packs are more thoroughly tested and theoretically are more stable than hotfixes, but again Microsoft's policy has long been, "If you aren't having problems, don't apply it." There are several reasons to cautiously change that mindset. The first is that as the world has begun to pay attention to Windows NT, the security attacks against it have dramatically increased, and therefore so have Microsoft's security hotfixes. Test carefully before you install an individual security hotfix, but applying a Service Pack with a tested suite of these updates is a good idea.

The second reason is that Service Packs have evolved into providing new features as well as fixing existing ones. Password filtering in Windows NT 4 Service Pack 3 is a good example; it provides a higher level of password security if you choose to implement it.

You should read the release notes *before* installing a Service Pack, and carefully consider all the implications of what you read. For example, Service Pack 4 updates the NTFS file system driver, so a Windows NT 4 system will coexist with NTFS Version 5. Does this affect your disk utilities, such as your defragmenter or your virus scanner? You need to have answers to questions like these before you apply the newest Service Pack.

The Windows NT Service Pack site (for all releases of Windows NT) can be found at this address:

```
ftp://ftp.microsoft.com/bussys/winnt/winnt-public/fixes/
```

Using System Dump Examinations

When a system bugchecks and generates the infamous blue screen of death (BSOD) and a dump file, symbol files are needed during dump analysis to determine where in the operating system code the problem occurred. The symbol files can be found on the Windows NT Server CD at `\support\debug\`*processor type*`\symbols`; the dump analysis tools are at `\support\debug\`*processor type*. However, you don't have to keep all this straight because the batch stream `\support\debug\expndsym.cmd` will install the symbol files in the correct place. The syntax is as follows:

```
Expndsym <CD-ROM_drive_letter> %systemroot%
```

Here's an example:

```
expndsym d: c:\winnt
```

You could easily substitute `%systemroot%` or even hard code it into any copies you make of the batch stream. This would work as long as you were actually running under the operating system on which you wanted to use the symbol files.

Symbol files take up a lot of space (approximately 100MB) and must be kept up-to-date. To accurately debug a dump with symbol files, every Service Pack or hotfix applied to the OS must have its corresponding symbol file updated in `%systemroot%\system32\symbols`. When repeated over hundreds of servers, this can obviously be a configuration management nightmare. Fortunately, you don't need to install symbol files on every server. Instead, install them on a single troubleshooting server that runs the OS release and fix level of your production baseline. If you have more than one OS baseline, install that baseline with symbols in another directory. When a bugcheck occurs on a production server, send the dump to the troubleshooting server—you may want to zip it if you have slow links—and perform the dump analysis from there. The DUMPEXAM command is the starting point for reducing the dump:

```
dumpexam  -v  -f output_filename -y
        symbol_search_path, usually "c:\winnt\system32\symbols"
            crashdumpfile
```

Obviously, it's easier to write a batch program to take care of the dump file processing. Listing 5.1 is a simple batch stream called DUMPSHOOT that runs DUMPEXAM, writes it to a text file, then displays it for you.

Listing 5.1. *A Batch Stream to Simplify the Dump Processing*

```
@Echo off
if "%1"*=="* goto a
if "%1"*=="/?"* goto help
if "%1"*=="?"* goto help
set dumpfile=%1
goto exam

:a
set dumpfile=memory.dmp

:exam
Echo Attempting to extract information from c:\dumpster\%dumpfile%...
dumpexam -v -f c:\dumpster\dumpshoot.txt
        (continued) -y %systemroot%\symbols c:\dumpster\%dumpfile%

Echo Would you like to view the crash dump analysis?(CTL-C if not!)
pause
notepad c:\dumpster\dumpshoot.txt

goto exit

:help
Echo "DUMPSHOOT <dump file>"
Echo DUMPSHOOT condenses NT crash dumps into a useable format.
Echo DUMPSHOOT invokes DUMPEXAM with the right parameters.
Echo If no dump file is specified, the file is assumed to be
```

```
Echo found in C:\DUMPSTER\MEMORY.DMP.
Echo If you specify a dump file, I still assume it's in C:\DUMPSTER.
Echo The output is C:\DUMPSTER\DUMPSHOOT.TXT

:exit
```

The output from DUMPSHOOT is dumpshoot.txt. Most of the time it contains all the information that Microsoft product support needs to move forward in problem resolution, without having to ship a 128MB dump file to their ftp server.

Software Maintenance Recommendations
Here's a summary of my software maintenance recommendations:

- Only apply hotfixes if you really need them, and test them in your environment before putting them in production.

- As with anything else brand new, don't be in a rush to install a new Service Pack. Microsoft has had a mixed record on the reliability of its Service Packs; unless you're dying for the updates, wait until they've aged just a little.

- Be sure you pull down the hotfix for the right server architecture. The IA architecture hotfixes end in *i*, and the Alpha ones end in *a*.

- For Windows NT 4, apply maintenance such as hotfixes and Service Packs only after you've installed and configured all the system's software. If you install a Service Pack and then install a software component, the installation process will overwrite the updated components with the original media components. This recommendation therefore leads into the following one.

- If you *have* installed software after applying maintenance on a Windows NT 4 system, reapply the maintenance. This unfortunately means that more OS partition disk space is chewed up because a new uninstall directory is created every time a Service Pack is applied.

- Service Packs in Windows 2000 are supposed to be intelligent enough that if you install software after the Service Pack has been applied, you won't have to re-apply the Service Pack.

- Print and read the documentation very carefully. This is *not* some program you want to just install without looking! Even though it has an uninstall option, a service pack often changes the basic structure of the SAM database or the registry so that it's not possible to completely back out without restoring from backups.

- Take a full backup of your boot partition, and update your Repair Disk, before you install a hotfix.

- Don't keep hotfixes older than the most recent Service Pack. At this point, they've been rolled into that pack; if they haven't, it's because the hotfix has been withdrawn. If that's the case, you don't want it on your system anyway!

Monitoring Performance and Tuning the Box

Windows NT is the most self-tuning operating system ever devised for the commodity server market. As a result, there are very few knobs the Windows NT administrator can turn to alter the performance of a Windows NT server—and turning them without restraint will probably degrade the system more than if you had left it alone. However, it's important to understand the performance characteristics of Windows NT and learn where it's most likely to get clogged up. I'll just hit the high points of detecting bottlenecks and tuning a Windows NT server by subsystems, sprinkled with some general rules. For a complete treatment on Windows NT performance, look in the *Optimizing Windows NT* volume from the *Windows NT 3.51 Resource Kit* (a similar volume doesn't exist in the 4 Server Resource Kit).

Note

A note on Windows 2000: Even though performance documentation may say 3.51 instead of 5.0 or Windows 2000, 98% of it is perfectly relevant. At all but the deepest level of detail, performance characteristics and bottlenecks of Windows NT are the same from versions 3.5 to 5.0. Indeed, the basics apply almost exactly across any virtual memory operating system, whether IBM, Sun, Compaq, or Microsoft is on the box. ♦

What follows are four of the basic tenets of system performance diagnosis and tuning for all computer systems. The fifth (Task Manager) is specifically for Windows NT systems:

- Thou shalt not change more than one system parameter at a time. It's important to look at performance problems logically because you will always have these four dynamic variables interacting with one another in a system—and it's easy to lose track of where you are in a four-variable equation. If, in your hurry to get your boss off your neck, you tune several system parameters at one time to correct a problem, you'll never know exactly what fixed the problem and what didn't. Ask your boss if he really wants to see the problem appear again because a good problem analysis wasn't done the first time, or would he spend some extra time and fix it just once?

- There is always a bottleneck; tuning just minimizes it and moves it around. One subsystem will always have more load than another, even if just a little. A bottleneck occurs when a task on the system must wait for a system resource (processor, memory, disk, or network) because it's tied up with another task. Bottleneck equals wait.

- One bottleneck may mask another. A heavily loaded system may have several bottlenecks, but until the first bottleneck is corrected, often only one shows. A common example is a database system without enough CPU resources. The processor is pegged (old analog gauge slang, for you new technocrats) at 100%, but disk I/O is at manageable levels. Upgrade the processor or add a second processor, and that bottleneck is removed, allowing the database engine to make I/O requests to its database unhindered by a slow processor. Suddenly the disk I/O goes through the roof! This is something you need to warn your boss about *before* it happens so that you don't look like an idiot.

- The Heisenberg Uncertainty Principle also applies to performance monitoring. To paraphrase an important tenet of quantum mechanics: "You can interfere with the performance of a system simply by monitoring it too closely." (Mr. Heisenberg was specifically referring to the momentum and location of subatomic particles.) Performance Monitor, when recording lots of data over short intervals, can impact the performance of a Windows NT system. The Perfmon utility uses CPU, memory, and disk I/O. If you monitor the server remotely, you reduce these three, but you increase network I/O as the performance data is sent over the network to the computer running Perfmon. This isn't normally enough to worry about but, it's good to be aware of. If, for example, you're remotely collecting log information and have selected the process, memory, logical disk, and network interface objects, a moderate but continuous load has been put on your network interface.

- Use the Task Manager. In Windows NT 4 and Windows 2000, the Task Manager (shown in Figure 5.2) has been greatly expanded from its original role as a simple way to shut down unruly applications. Launched from the three-finger salute (Ctrl+Alt+Delete) or by simply clicking on an empty spot of the taskbar with the secondary mouse button, it now has Processes and Performance property sheets that can provide a great deal of detail on the current system status. The Processes property sheet allows you to quickly view processes that were previously more time-consuming to reach; by clicking on the column headers, you can sort for the highest values in each field. The menu item View, Select Columns allows you to add up to 13 object to monitor and sort. A limitation of this expanded tool is that it can be run only locally. To view system processes remotely, you must use Performance Monitor.

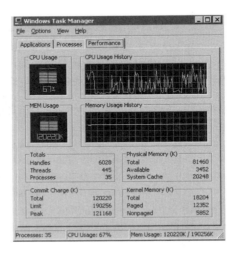

Figure 5.2   *The Task Manager.*

Because Windows NT is such a self-tuning operating system, performance and tuning often distill into two steps. Step 1 is finding the Windows NT subsystem(s) with the bottleneck, and step 2 is throwing hardware at it! To use an old Detroit saying, "There ain't no substitute for cubic inches." Most of us don't have unlimited hardware budgets, however, so a detailed performance analysis will tell you exactly where the problem lies, will offer the best course of action to fix it, and will provide documentation to support your conclusion when the bean counters get upset.

What about performance and tuning for Windows 2000? There's no need to get worked up over the new release in this area because performance basics are the same for any server. The user interface to find the right knobs has definitely been pushed around, however. Where there's a difference, I'll show how to get there. For example, Performance Monitor from Windows NT 4 has been moved to the MMC as a snap-in (Perfmon.Msc). It functions pretty much the same as its predecessor (see Figure 5.3).

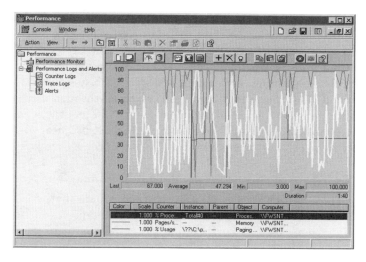

Figure 5.3 *Performance Monitor in Windows 2000.*

A Windows NT system can be analyzed in four sections: processor, memory, disk I/O, and network I/O. Use this organization to logically investigate any performance problem you encounter on a Windows NT server.

Tuning the Processor

People who don't know much about Windows NT performance always seem to focus on the CPU as the source—and the solution—to server performance problems. Although that isn't true, it's pretty easy to spot CPU bottlenecks.

The following are recommendations of the Performance Monitor processor-related counters to watch:

- System % Total Processor Time—Performance Monitor object consistently near 100%. A snapshot can also be seen from the Windows NT 4 Task Manager Performance property sheet, CPU Usage History section.

- Here's an easy way to see what processes are hogging the CPU: In Perfmon, select the Process object. Select the % Processor Time instance associated with the Process object. To the right of these, click the second instance (below "_Total"), and drag the mouse down to include every instance. Now either scroll up and Ctrl+click to remove the Idle instance, or delete it later. Click the Add button. You're now tracking every process on the system by percentage of processor utilization. To make the chart easier to read, click Options, Chart, or the rightmost button on the display. Change the Gallery section from Graph to Histogram, and click OK. Hit the backspace key to enable process highlighting. Perfmon now displays a histogram of all the active processes on the system. You can scroll through them with the up and down arrows, and the instance that's in focus will be highlighted in white. If you haven't deleted the Idle instance, you can do it now by selecting it from the list and pressing the Delete key.

The following are recommendations about how to tune your processor:

- Take the doctor's advice: "If it hurts when you do that, don't do that." At least not during prime time. Schedule CPU-hungry jobs for off-hours, when possible. For example, programs that read the SAM of a large Windows NT 4 domain to process user accounts for expired passwords can peg the primary domain controller for quite a while.

- Upgrade the processor. If you're considering whether to switch from an Intel architecture to an Alpha, look at the System Context Switches/Sec. object. Don't switch if this counter is the primary source of processor activity; relatively speaking, an Alpha takes as long as an Intel to do context switches. (A context switch occurs when the operating system switches from user mode to kernel mode, or vice versa.) And, of course, you shouldn't make big decisions like this based solely on the System Context Switches counter!

- Add processors if the application in question is multithreaded and can take advantage of multiple processors.

- Use fast network cards. A 16-bit network interface card (NIC) uses more CPU than a 32-bit card.

- Use bus-mastering SCSI controllers. A bus-mastering controller takes over the process of an I/O request, thus freeing the CPU.

- Use the START command. This command has /low, /normal, /high, and /realtime switches to start programs with varying levels of priority. This is the only way to externally influence the priority of individual programs.

- You can also tune the foreground application response time with the Performance property sheet, found in the System applet of the Control Panel. In Windows NT 4, it's a three-position slider. Figure 5.4 shows how it looks in Windows 2000.

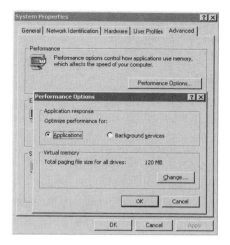

Figure 5.4   *Foreground application response in Windows 2000.*

This alters the following:

```
SYSTEM\CurrentControlSet\Control\PriorityControl\Win32PrioritySeparation
```

This code has a value from 2 (highest foreground priority) to 0 (all programs have equal processor priority).

> **Tip**
>
> *It's interesting to note that in Windows NT Server 4, this counter is tuned to give foreground applications priority over the background applications that are, after all, the main business of a server. The reasoning may be that if you do run a program from the console, it's not done casually, so you want good response time. You should consider setting this counter to None. In Windows NT Server 5.0, it's correctly set to Background Services. ◆*

Understanding Memory Performance

Memory, not processor utilization, is the first thing administrators should look at when a Windows NT system is experiencing performance problems.

Paging is a necessary evil—bad, but unavoidable. Okay, to be fair, it's an integral part of memory management, so "bad" may be an overstatement, but avoid it as much as possible. If you're reading this book, you've probably heard the term "paging" for a while, have seen it occurring with Perfmon, and can even convince your boss that you know what it means—but you probably would hate to be cornered into defining it or explaining the concept to a new hire. Here's a (hopefully) simple explanation.

Windows NT uses a demand-paged virtual memory model. That's four adjectives attached to one noun, so it deserves explanation. Windows NT is a 32-bit operating system, so programs that run on it can see 2^{32} GB, or 4GB, in a flat address space. ("Flat" means that there are no segments or other compromises to worry about, as in previous versions of Windows.) The upper 2GB is reserved for system code, so the lower 2GB is available for user programs. The basic problem is obvious: You can run a program that may try to load data up near a 4GB memory address (location), but you probably don't have 4GB of physical RAM shoehorned inside your servers. This is where the term "virtual" comes in. Windows NT juggles its limited amount of memory resources by pulling data into main memory when it's asked for, writing it out to disk when it has been written to in memory, and reclaiming memory by writing the least recently used data to a page file. This process is called *paging*. For efficiency's sake, this data is moved around in chunks called *page frames* that are 4KB in size for Intel systems and 8KB for Alpha systems. Virtual memory is how the operating system lies to everyone and everything that asks for memory by saying, "Sure, no problem, I have room in memory for you!" and then scurrying around under the covers to page data in and out of main memory to provide it. (A good definition I heard for *virtual* memory is that the word that follows it is a lie.) Good virtual memory managers are masterful at maximizing the use of system memory and automatically adjusting their actions to outside conditions.

So, the page file (PAGEFILE.SYS) is the space on your hard disk that Windows NT uses as if it were actually memory. Why is it a problem if the system pages out to the page file? (Paging to get data from disk is unavoidable, so it doesn't matter in this discussion.) Isn't that how it's designed? Well, yes, it is, but it's *slow*. How slow is it, you may ask? Average computer memory today has an access time of 50 nanoseconds, or 5×10^{-8} seconds. Very fast disk access time today is about 6 milliseconds, or 6×10^{-3} seconds. This means that memory is 120,000 times as fast as disk!

A good analogy is to increase the time scale to something we're more comfortable with. A Windows NT program executing in the CPU asks for data. If that data is already in main memory, let's say it takes 1 second to return it. If the data it needs is out on disk, it will have to wait almost a day and a half to get the data it needs to continue. Now, the virtual memory manager mitigates this wait by passing control to other programs that don't have to wait, but it's obviously a tremendous performance impact. When paging rates go too high, the system gets caught in a vicious cycle of declining resources and begins "thrashing."

The two best ways to avoid paging are to add physical memory and to tune your applications (especially database applications) carefully to balance their needs with the operating systems needs. Unfortunately, the most obvious Performance Monitor counter of Memory Pages/Sec can be misleading, as explained here.

The following are recommendations of what Performance Monitor memory-related counters to watch:

- Memory Available bytes consistently less than 4MB (Intel) or less than 8MB (Alpha). A snapshot of this can also be seen from the Windows NT 4 Task Manager Performance property sheet, Physical Memory section, Available counter. As an indicator of the amount of free memory pages in the system, when this value drops below 1,000 pages (4MB in an Intel system using 4K pages), the system paging rate increases in an attempt to free up memory. This was also seen in Windows NT 3.51 from the WINMSD utility, Memory section, as memory load. In that utility, a memory load of

  0 = 1100+ available pages

  and a load of

  100 = 100- available pages

  Any values in between have an appropriate load. For example, a memory load of 25 indicates that 3MB are available, and a memory load of 75 means that only 1MB is available. Several shareware or freeware memory load monitors can be found to monitor this important indicator.

- Memory Available bytes decreasing over time. This indicates a memory leak condition, where a process requests memory but never releases it—there's a bug in an application. To determine the culprit, monitor the Private Bytes counter of the Process object, and watch for an increasing value that never goes down. (Actually, the term "memory leak" is a misnomer; memory isn't leaking out of the system—it's being kept by a process.)

- Paging File: % Usage, % Usage Peak is near 100%. Don't let the page file grow, as it will have a significant impact on system performance. All disk I/O ceases during page file growth. Not only that, but page file growth very likely causes fragmentation of the page file. This means that during normal paging operations, the operating system will have to jump the physical read/write heads all over the disk instead of one contiguous area. The simplest way to avoid this is to make the page file larger than its default size of physical memory plus 12MB, especially on memory-constrained systems. The next simplest way, after the page file has already become fragmented, is to move it to another partition, reboot, defrag the original partition, and move the page file back. This will create a contiguous page file.

- Memory Committed Bytes is less than RAM. Memory Committed Bytes is the amount of virtual memory actually being used. If the system is using more virtual memory than exists in physical memory, it may be paging heavily. Watch paging objects such as Memory Pages/Sec and Memory Page Faults/Sec for heavy usage. The Task Manager equivalent of Memory Committed Bytes can be found in its Performance property sheet, Commit Charge section, Total counter.

- If Memory Committed Bytes approaches Memory Commit Limit, and if the page file size has already reached the maximum size as defined in Control Panel, System, there are simply no more pages available in memory or in the page file. If the system reaches this point, it's already paging like a banshee in an attempt to service its memory demands. The Task Manager equivalent of Memory Committed Bytes can be found in its Performance property sheet, Commit Charge section, Limit counter. This is the same as %Committed Bytes In Use. A number less than 80% is good.

- Memory Pages/sec can be a misleading counter. For performance reasons, in NT 4 Memory Pages/Sec was moved from the memory subsystem to the file subsystem. Instead of detecting actual page faults in memory, it simply increments every time a non-cached read (i.e., from disk) occurs. This makes the counter somewhat unreliable in a file server where many open file activities take place and very unreliable where a database server (that manages its own memory) may be doing much database I/O.

The following are recommendations on how to optimize your memory performance:

- Add physical memory. Generally, the best thing you can do to boost Windows NT performance is to add memory. Lack of memory is by far the most common cause of performance problems on Windows NT systems. If your boss corners you in your office and asks why server XYZ is so slow—and you didn't even know XYZ existed—answer, "It's low on memory," and you'll probably be right. You can approximate (or, guess) how much memory you need by looking at the page file(s) and using the following line of reasoning: If you had a system with no memory constraints, it would almost never page and the page file utilization would approach zero. You don't, so the operating system needs some number of megabytes in the page file to back its memory requests. The worst-case amount can be found in the Paging File % Usage Max counter of the Paging File object. So, if the system in question has a page file of 100MB and the Paging File % Usage Max counter is 75%, at its most heavily loaded point the system required 75MB more than it had available in physical memory. Therefore, adding 75MB of physical memory would be a good guess. Of course, the Paging File % Usage Max counter measures an instantaneous maximum, so if an operator quickly launched and then canceled three big utilities from the server console during your monitoring period, the value will be too high. On the other hand, if you already have a processor or I/O bottleneck, the value may be too low. As I said, it's just a guess.

- If one application is the troublemaker, run it during off-peak hours. Remember that it will have to share time with long-running system utilities such as backups, anti-virus scanners, and defragmenters.

- If the page file utilization hits 100% and its size is less than the maximum set in Control Panel, System, Performance, Virtual Memory, Paging File, the page file will extend itself. You don't want this to happen, for several reasons. First, all system I/O will halt while the page file extension occurs. Secondly, the odds are good that no contiguous space will be available after the page file, so it will become fragmented. This means that whenever the system becomes heavily loaded enough to use the extra space, the disk heads must jump around the disk to simply page, adding extra baggage to a system already in trouble. Set the initial page file size sufficiently large when the system is built or recently defragmented so that it won't need to extend. Disk space is cheaper than a fragmented page file.

- If the system in question is a BDC of a large Windows NT 4 domain, consider converting it to a member server. All Windows NT 4 domain controllers have a SAM database that is stored in paged pool memory. This means that when a domain controller authenticates a user's logon, it must page the entire contents of its SAM into main memory to get the account's credentials. If it doesn't perform any more authentications for a while. the dirty pages will get reused for other programs; however, authentications on a domain controller usually happen frequently enough that this doesn't happen. So, a domain controller has a chunk of main memory semi-permanently allocated for user authentications. How much memory is used depends on the size of the SAM.

Tuning Disk I/O

Because of the mechanical nature of hard disk drives, the mass storage subsystem is always the slowest of the four subsystems in a computer. As we've seen so far in this section, it's 120,000 times slower than memory. As a result, all sorts of elaborate data caching and buffering schemes have been devised to minimize the disk's performance penalty. This subsystem can be the most important area you tune. If you have a 500MHz processor but your hard drives came from a salvage sale, you've effectively put a ball and chain around its leg whenever the system has to page!

When working with hard disk drives, a good analogy to use is that of an LP-playing jukebox. Inside the drive's case are one or more constantly spinning aluminum-alloy platters, arranged one on top of another in a stack. When you are at work on your computer, you enter commands through your keyboard or mouse. The hard drive's actuator arm—much like a jukebox's tone arm—responds to these commands and moves to the proper place on the platter. When it arrives, the drive's read/write head—like the needle on the tone arm—locates the information you've requested and reads or writes data.

The following are recommendations of which Performance Monitor disk I/O-related counters to watch:

- Physical Disk % Disk Time counter consistently at or near 67%. This is the percentage of time that this particular disk drive is busy servicing read or write requests.

- Physical Disk Queue Length > 2. Any time the queue length on an I/O device is greater than 1 or 2, it indicates significant congestion for the device.

The following are recommendations of how to tune your disk I/O:

- *Minimize head movement.* The slowest actions of a hard drive are the time expended waiting for the disk's actuator arm to move its read/write heads to the correct track (the *seek time*)—and once it's there, you must wait for the correct sector to come under the heads (*rotational latency*) so that data can be read or written. There isn't much you can do about rotational latency, but you can minimize head movement. The most effective way to minimize head movement is to defragment your disk and to make sure that your page file(s) are contiguous. You can tell if the page file is fragmented by looking at the text mode results of a disk analysis from DisKeeper. The operating system won't allow disk defragmenters to defragment the page file, so you must do it yourself. The technique is simple: Create a page file on another partition and remove the original, reboot, and recreate the original configuration.

- The second way to minimize head movement is to think about what kind of data is on the disk. Place large, heavily accessed files on different physical disks to prevent the heads from jumping back and forth between two tracks. For example, let's say that you create an SQL server with the operating system on disk 0, the database device on disk 1, and the transaction log on disk 2. A little later, you discover that the database device is both heavily accessed and isn't large enough, so you extend it with a second database device on disk 2. You now have a case of head contention on disk 2. The read/write heads focus on the heavily accessed database device (at the inside of the physical disk platters, because it was created last), with constant interruptions from the transaction log (at the outside of the physical disk platter because it was created first). The transaction log is written to in small bursts whenever a transaction is made to the database device.

  The heads continuously bounce back and forth across the full extent of the disk. For the same reasons, you shouldn't install Office components on the same physical disk if you're not using RAID.

  This won't apply in systems where the disk subsystem has been striped in a RAID 0 or RAID 5 configuration. Data is evenly striped across the physical RAID set regardless of where it appears to be on a logical partition.

- Use NTFS compression sparingly. Disk compression is a great way to squeeze more data onto a disk. It's also a great way to increase the average percentage of processor utilization and to fragment the disk. I recommend that compression be used for low-access document shares and to temporarily buy back disk space when a server's data drive is almost full. In Windows NT 4, compressed files on disk must be decompressed by the server before the data is sent to the client. Windows 2000 Professional will support compression over the wire, which keeps the data compressed until it reaches the client where it is then decompressed. This offers two big benefits: It offloads the CPU cycles required for decompression from the server to the client, and it decreases network bandwidth. Compression load on a processor will be less of an issue if you're buying a new server with the latest high-speed processors.

- Use fast disks, controllers, and technology. Almost all modern disks and controllers supplied with servers are SCSI. Fibre Channel technology (133MB/sec) is faster than Wide Ultra-2 SCSI (80MB/sec), which is faster than Wide UltraSCSI (40MB/sec), which is faster than Fast Wide SCSI (20MB/sec), which is faster than Fast SCSI (10MB/sec), which is faster than SCSI-2 (5MB/sec), which, finally, is faster than IDE (2.5MB/sec).

- Use mirroring to speed up read requests. The I/O subsystem can issue concurrent reads to a pair of mirrored disks, assuming your disk controller can handle asynchronous I/O.

- If you are using a RAID 5 array, increasing the number of drives in the array will increase its performance.

Tuning Network I/O

Network I/O is the subsystem through which the server moves data to its users. This is the server's window to the world. You may have spent money on the fastest server in the world, but if you use a cheap NIC, it will look just as slow as your oldest servers. Here are some recommendations to help your network I/O:

- The more bits, the better. The number of bits in a NIC's description refers to the size of the data path, so more is better. 32-bit NICs are faster than 16-bit NICs, which are faster than 8-bit NICs. A caution to this is that you should match the NIC to the bus. If you have a PCI (32-bit) bus, you should use a 32-bit card. An EISA bus will support 8-, 16-, and 32-bit NICs, but if you follow the previously stated rule, a 32-bit NIC will be the best performer.

- Install the Network Monitor Agent service—but leave it in Manual mode. If you have Network Monitor Agent installed, a very useful Network Interface object will be added to Performance Monitor. This provides 17 different counters on the virtual interface to the network. I say "virtual" because, in addition to any physical NICs you have installed, it also includes an instance for every virtual RAS adapter you have defined on your system. For the NIC that you're probably interested in, however, it monitors the physical network interface. Leave the service turned off until you need it to reduce system overhead.

- The server should always have a faster network interface than its clients. A server is a focal point of network traffic and should therefore have the bandwidth to service many clients at one time. This means that if your clients all have 10BaseT, the server should have 100BaseT. If the clients are running at 100, the server should have an FDDI interface.

The following are recommendations for what Performance Monitor network I/O-related performance counters to watch:

- Network Interface Bytes Total/sec is useful to figure out how much throughput the card is getting compared to a theoretical maximum. For instance, a bytes total/sec of 655,360 for a 10baseT NIC on standard Ethernet is shown here:

  (655360 bytes/sec)×(8 bits/byte)/(1024 bits/Kb)×(1024Kb/Mb)=5Mbps

  Because the theoretical bandwidth for standard Ethernet is 10Mbits/sec, this card is running at 50% of its theoretical maximum. In reality, it's much closer to its maximum because the Ethernet collision rate begins to rise dramatically when network utilization rises above 66%.

- Broadcasts/sec or Multicasts/sec is greater than 100/sec. A certain number of network broadcasts or multicasts are normal; for example, DHCP requests from clients are broadcasts. However, excessive broadcasts or multicasts are bad because every card on the network segment must examine the broadcast/multicast packet to see whether it's destined for its client. This means that the NIC must generate an interrupt on its clients' CPU and allow the packet to be passed up to the transport for examination. This can cause serious processor utilization problems.

- Network Segment % Network Utilization should be considered when things start slowing down to the point at which they are no longer acceptable. Some say that this point is around 40%–50%. Then the network is the bottleneck.

The following are recommendations for how to tune your network I/O:

- Analyze network I/O based on the OSI model. (For more information on the 7-layer OSI model, search for "OSI model" at http://technet.microsoft.com/cdonline/default.asp.) This allows you to look at network I/O performance problems from the bottom up.

- Consider the following at Layer 1 (the Physical Layer): Is the network overloaded? Is the NIC handling too much data? Are there excessive network broadcasts that the NIC must receive and analyze?

- Consider the following at Layer 4 (the Transport Layer): Is your primary protocol first in the network binding order? If it isn't, you've unnecessarily increased the average connection time to other network nodes. Figure 5.5 shows the most common situation on a Windows NT 4 system. When you request a connection to shared resources on a remote station, the local workstation redirector submits a TDI connect request to all transports simultaneously; when any one of the transport drivers completes the request successfully, the redirector waits until all higher-priority transports return. For example: The primary protocol for your network is TCP/IP, and that's the only protocol most of your workstations are running. You have TCP/IP and also NetBEUI installed on your server because you must still service the occasional NetBEUI workstation. NetBEUI is first in the network binding order. When the server attempts a session setup with another network resource, the server must wait for NetBEUI to time out before completing the TCP/IP session setup.

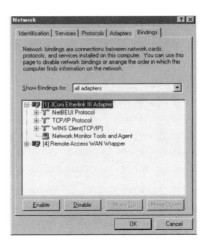

Figure 5.5   *Poor binding order for a TCP/IP network*

- Consider the following at Layer 5 (the Session Layer): The Server service's responsibility is to establish sessions with remote stations and receive server message block (SMB) request messages from those stations. SMB requests are typically used to request the Server service to perform I/O—such as open, read, or write on a device or file located on the Windows NT Server station.

You can configure the Server service's resource allocation and associated nonpaged memory pool usage. In Windows 2000, it's buried in the Network Control Panel applet, Local Area Connection properties, then File And Print Sharing For Microsoft Networks Properties (see Figure 5.6).

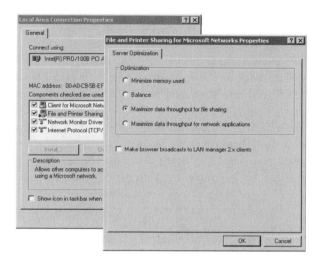

Figure 5.6   *Server memory optimization.*

You may want to consider a specific setting, depending on factors such as how many users will be accessing the system and the amount of memory in the system. The amount of memory allocated to the Server service differs dramatically based on your choice:

- The Minimize Memory Used level is meant to accommodate up to 10 remote users simultaneously using Windows NT Server.

- The Balance option supports up to 64 remote users.

- Maximize Throughput for File Sharing allocates the maximum memory for file-sharing applications. You should use this setting for Windows NT servers on a large network. With this option set, file cache access takes priority over user application access to memory. This is the default setting.

- Maximize Throughput for Network Applications optimizes server memory for distributed applications that do their own memory caching, such as Microsoft SQL Server. With this option set, user application access to memory takes priority over file cache access.

Tuning Database Servers

Database servers deserve special mention here because they are so often accused of poor performance. Using the following rules will help you understand the performance characteristics of a database server.

Most of the time, poor performance isn't the server's fault—it's the application's design at fault. It's much easier to write inefficient relational database queries than to mess up the tuning of a Windows NT system. Unfortunately, you will almost always have to prove beyond the shadow of a doubt that the system is performing adequately before the application developers will go back and begin optimizing their code. It's all too common to be forced into throwing hardware at a poorly designed application.

Allocate enough memory for Windows NT, and then give the rest to the database. It may seem obvious, but after the operating system, the most important entity in a database server is the database engine. Most databases designed for Windows NT have a parameter to reserve physical memory for their own use—and most databases voraciously gobble up every byte you can give them. Exactly how many bytes to give them is an inexact process, but the general process for Windows NT 4 is listed here:

- Give 24MB to Windows NT and the rest to the database.

- Watch Windows NT's paging rate. If under normal conditions Windows NT pages excessively (consistently more than 30–40 pages/sec), give it more memory by reserving less for the database. Keep doing this until the average paging rate is manageable. Because the Performance Monitor Memory Pages/Sec object can't separate database paging from operating system paging, to get Windows NT paging rate you must subtract from that number the sum of SQL Server Page Reads/Sec and SQL Server Single Page Writes/Sec.

- Watch the databases paging rate. Again, you want to minimize database paging because it incurs a high performance penalty. If the database paging rate is too high (consistently more than 10–20 pages/sec), you must add physical memory to the system.

- Database servers are the biggest beneficiaries of multiple processors. By adding a second processor to a uniprocessor database server that's a bit processor-bound, you may almost double your throughput. Adding additional processors will continue to boost performance, but the single biggest gain will come from adding a second processor. Don't forget: In addition to running the system setup utility, in Windows NT 4 you must update the Windows NT OS to a multiprocessor kernel and HAL before it will be recognized. The UPTOMP.EXE utility in the Windows NT Resource Kit automates this process.

- Watch the database server subsystem loads. The load on database server subsystems is listed here, in order:

Processor

Memory

I/O subsystem

Network I/O

Processor, memory, and disk I/O are heavily used by a database, while network I/O is relatively low. This is because a well-designed client/server database passes only the database query and the query results over the wire. The operations to form the query are done on the client, and the execution of the query is done on the server.

Even though you use a logical approach to performance analysis, there are so many variables out of your control that, in the end, there's still some black art to it. You must look at your systems regularly, understand the applications they are running, and be able to read the tea leaves to come up with a feel for a system's performance problems.

Tuning Control Panel Settings

The Control Panel is the place to go for 90% of a Windows NT 4 server's general tuning. The other 10% are sketchily documented or undocumented keys and values in the Registry. In Windows 2000, you can forget almost everything you learned about where controls are located in the user interface; most have changed out of recognition. Fortunately, beta feedback has pointed this out to Microsoft, so the help system has a specific section on how to find the new ways to do old tasks. What follows are tips on Control Panel settings to make managing a server a bit easier:

- The Console—In the Layout tab, change the screen buffer size height to 999. This will give you a scrollable command prompt window that will display the last 999 lines of data or commands. In Windows 2000, the easiest way to reach this is to launch a command prompt from the start menu, click the icon in the upper-left corner, choose Properties, and then select the Layout tab.

Tip

In a command prompt window, you can view the buffer of your previously entered commands by pressing F7. ◆

- Network—Review your bindings to be sure that you have removed or disabled all unnecessary protocols.

- Server—Update the description field with pertinent information about the server. This might include the server model, the owning organization, the purpose, and the location. In Windows 2000, the Description field is buried in Control Panel, Computer Management. Right-click the uppermost icon labeled Computer Management, choose Properties, and then choose Networking ID.

- Services—Review the services. Do they all need to be started? For example, the Messenger service can be disabled on most servers because they rarely need to receive a message sent via NET SEND to the console. In Windows 2000, there are a ton of new services; services administration has also moved to the Computer Management tool.

- System—The System applet controls basic functionality (such as startup and shutdown options), the paging file, and general performance options. In the System applet, you'll find the following tabs:

  - Startup/Shutdown tab—Set the Show List timer to 5 seconds. On a dedicated Windows NT server, there's no choice to be made other than the base video mode. Ensure that all check boxes in the Recovery section are checked.

  - Performance tab—In Windows NT 4, consider sliding the Foreground Application Boost slider to None (see Figure 5.7). The setting for this control can be argued two ways. The first theory is simpler: A server's primary purpose is to serve its network customers, so foreground applications should always take the back seat to the customer's needs. The second one proposes that if an operator *does* need to do something on a server console, it's for a very good reason and is worth taking cycles away from paying customers to get good response time. Foreground boost set to None on a heavily loaded, bottlenecked server could result in very slow response time for a console operator. In Windows 2000, this boost control changes to a radio button, shown previously in Figure 5.3.

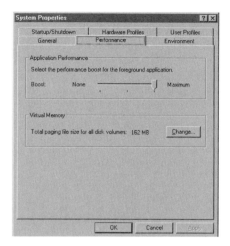

Figure 5.7   *Foreground application boost*

- Display—Don't use a screen saver. If you do, set it to a simple one such as Marquee or a blank screen. I know it doesn't look nearly as cool as a row of monitors running 3D textured flags, but elaborate screen savers chews up CPU for no good reason. If you must have some kind of a high-tech screen saver to impress your boss when he visits the computer room, choose Beziers and back the speed down a bit.

Summary

This chapter covers many of the basic practical matters in assembling a server and then keeping it in good working order. It's a really big subject, so I've skimmed over some intimate details. Instead, I've included lots of important points in these areas to help keep you on a straight course as you wade through all those intimate details. Server performance, backup media and jobs, software maintenance—there are hundreds of pitfalls you can encounter. This chapter has laid out principles you can use to avoid them.

Part III

Planning for and Migrating to Windows 2000

6

Designing Your Windows 2000 Core Services

As mentioned in the book's introduction, there are no universal right or wrong answers in Windows 2000 design. The goal of Part II, "Choosing Hardware for Windows 2000," is to provide many design principles that you can apply to your own unique situation, not to provide a cookbook for a finished design. The chapters in this part point out issues and ask questions that should make you think about how these apply to your situation.

This chapter discusses the core services of Windows 2000: Active Directory (domains, OUs, sites, domain controller, and Global Catalog server placement), DNS, DHCP, and WINS. Many more services can be added, but these are the most important—the services that everything else depends on.

Four major phases exist in a Windows NT design process:

- *Learn*—First learn how the new technology works and begin collecting information for your design. This is a huge step in Windows 2000.

- *Design*—Create the preliminary design based on the information you have and your knowledge of the customer's environment.

- *Teach*—Visit the major Windows NT sites in the enterprise, show them the preliminary design, and solicit input. For a major upgrade such as Windows 2000, this will require you to teach a number of new concepts to them. Some may have learned on their own, but you must ensure an even level of knowledge. Remember that your design will have the most productivity impact at the local level. A side benefit of teaching is that it will help *you* learn the product better.

Tip

Put together a nice-looking, thorough presentation of basic Windows 2000 concepts and the overall design. Include the Active Directory, domains, domain trees, forests, OUs, sites, trusts—and all with pictures. I know you're too busy executing to take the time, but doing so will repay you many times over the course of the project. Many people will want to find out what's going on and will give you their largely uneducated opinions. By creating a good presentation with detailed backup slides (try making a hyperlink in the presentation to hidden slides at the end), you can describe the problems, make your case, and get a lot of the tedious education out of the way. Just steer interested parties to the presentation before you talk to them.

• *Collaborate*—Work with your key customers in a cooperative relationship to finalize the design. Remember, however, that you have different priorities; theirs is to their local site or area of authority, while yours is to the entire enterprise. Beware! This can get very political. "The good of the company" or "the needs of the many outweigh the needs of the few" doesn't cut much slack when it comes to the local administrator's performance review time.

As you work through your Windows 2000 design, there's a critical point you must always keep in mind. Your design must not only work in the end state when all clients and servers are running Windows 2000 Server and Professional, but it must also work in the mixed environment when you've deployed Server but all clients are running downlevel Windows NT 4 or Windows 9x operating systems. The differences between how these two environments function—that is, the loads different server types experience, network traffic patterns, and client response time—are often dramatic. Every time you come up with part of a design, ask yourself, "How will this work in a mixed environment?"

Tip

If you use Microsoft Exchange for your email system, leverage the knowledge and experience of your Exchange designers for Windows 2000. Exchange uses several concepts similar to Active Directory constructs. Don't take their knowledge as absolutes, however; in most cases, Windows 2000 has refined these constructs. For example, Exchange performs replication at an object level among its servers, but Windows 2000 replicates objects at a per-attribute level.

Project Management

Because we always seem to be under tight deadlines—and because it's much more fun to execute than to plan—software projects such as Windows 2000 are often weak in the project management aspect. Experience has convinced me, however reluctantly, that project management and planning must be done for a project of this size. It's very hard to be sitting around thinking and filling out various risk assessments instead of *doing* something, but it pays dividends in less surprises and more peace of mind.

I won't go into project management principles here, but I will touch on a number of suggestions for your Windows 2000 project that will save you time and money. These will also save you from some unpleasant surprises from your customers—some of whom are the company's managers.

Have a good *project description*. Remember that you're selling your project's deliverables to a lot of people in the company, both to management and to individual contributors. And by selling, I don't mean just the project go-ahead; you have to sell the concept of what you're doing and why you're doing it to everyone it will affect—the whole enterprise. With Windows 2000, this means that your team will be teaching as well as selling.

A good project description should contain these steps:

- Define clear objectives, in simple language. State what you're going to do.

- Establish a clear scope. Describe what you're going to do and, equally importantly, what you're not going to do.

- Run the project descriptions past your sponsor (probably your management) so that everyone understands and agrees with what's going to be done.

- Define your success criteria (e.g., a 20% decrease in the number of domain controllers to support the network). It's best to keep the success criteria high-level (but measurable) at this point in the project because you don't know yet how the details will work out.

Define and interview your major stakeholders (where a "stakeholder" is defined as anyone who affects or is affected by the project). You should worry only about major stakeholders, because a Windows 2000 project will affect a significant percentage of the company. The following are things to keep in mind when defining the major stakeholders:

- What does the stakeholder expect of the project? This serves as a chance to get—and set—expectations. Does this major manager think that Windows 2000 will reduce the number of administrators he needs, or has he heard that it will make his coffee in the morning? (Don't discount this; it seems as though they've thrown everything *else* into the product.)

- How much do you foresee their lives changing when the product is rolled out?
- Are they all for it, neutral, or against it?
- What is their influence? What's their ability to impact the project if they aren't happy, and in what area? Can they take away budget or stop the rollout? Can they force you to do extra work that was outside the original scope of the project?
- How will you communicate the project's progress regularly to this person? If not to them directly, who's a good contact person?
- Don't forget to also interview your own team. What are their priorities? Do they have other, higher-priority projects that prevent them from spending all their time on this project?

You should record all this information in a *stakeholder analysis*, which is also a good beginning document for the political implications of the project.

You may not be doing this yourself, but someone needs to work up a good *communication plan*. This should include communication methods (e.g., email, brown-bag lunches, intranet, flyers), when to send out communiqués, and ways to provide feedback from the stakeholders. This plan will be followed for communicating first to other project members, then to managers, then eventually to all the company's affected employees.

Do a *work breakdown structure* with the team. This is a list of all the tasks that must be done, but not in any particular order. Start brainstorming at a high level, and then drill down into as much detail at a task level as occurs to the team. This kind of activity makes you think of tasks, and relationships between them, that wouldn't have occurred to you until much later in the project.

Define your *deliverables*. What are "must haves," and what are "nice to haves"? You should create something concrete, such as a document, set a delivery date, and identify a person or team responsible for it. These can also be *milestones*, deliverables that mark a significant achievement in the project's life span.

The minimum deliverables for a Windows 2000 design project are listed here:

- The network services design document, which should include the Windows 2000 DNS namespace design, DHCP plans, WINS plans, and NetBIOS end-of-life statement of direction.
- The domain namespace design document, detailing the domain and forest structure.

- The OU and group design documents. These can be integrated into the domain design document.

- The site design document, including Global Catalog server and domain controller placement.

Each document should detail the requirements and constraints figured into the design and reasons why a decision was made. In short, these papers aren't just a publication of design, but they are fully reasoned technical papers that interested parties can read to understand why the team made its choices without contacting the team members.

With your work breakdown structure, put the tasks in the order they must be done to create a *network diagram*. Be sure to account for any periods where you must wait for something outside of your control (e.g., ordering hardware). This is the earliest point that you should be using a project management tool such as Microsoft Project.

You also need to do a thorough *risk assessment* of the project. Sit down with your sponsor and team, and brainstorm all the things that could impede or stop the project. For each constraint or obstacle you come up with, think through these points:

- What's the honest chance that this constraint will occur?

- If it *does* happen, what is the impact? The combination of these first two items becomes the real risk level. A good chance that you'll find a bug in the code isn't an important risk; it'll happen, but it's not a big deal. A small to moderate chance that the management review committee will disapprove the project *is* an important risk, and you should have Plan B (the mitigation plan) already figured out and ready to roll if it does happen.

- How far into the project will the risk occur?

- Will it affect the budget, the scope, the schedule, or the quality of the project?

You must always remember the *business reasons* for this project. Contrary to what you might think, business managers don't want to upgrade to Windows 2000 just because it's cool; they need reasons why it will either save the company money or enable it to make more money. Therefore, you need to have a good long list of how Windows 2000 will help your company. Analyze how the company uses and administers Windows NT today, and determine how Windows 2000's new features could reduce administration costs, provide better service to the customers, and enable customers to do things they haven't done before. One example is how distributed administration brings account administration closer to the user through the use of Organizational Units, thereby reducing the cost of centralized administration and allowing problems to be resolved within the user's workgroup.

Several big benefits of project management outweigh the pain of doing all this up-front work. Going through all these exercises in the beginning points out areas where you haven't thought things through and reveals significant risk so that you can have a "plan B" ready and waiting. It shows where the schedule might be impacted and how optimistic you really were around that in the first place. Finally, it gives you some peace of mind because you know you've really taken the effort to look deeply ahead into the project.

What Flavor of Windows 2000 to Choose?

When all this design work is finished, don't forget that eventually you must order the actual product from Microsoft Select or your favorite VAR. (I know—details, details.) Let's take a minute to go over the way this new product is being marketed.

Microsoft has broken up Windows 2000 into four versions: Windows 2000 Server, Windows 2000 Advanced Server, Windows 2000 Datacenter Server, and Windows 2000 Professional. The first three are aimed at the server, and the fourth is the only client being offered at this time. The base product—the Windows NT kernel—is the same in all the products; where they differ is by the number of bells and whistles hung off this base:

- **Windows 2000 Server** is geared for the small to medium business segment. It supports up to two processors and 4GB of addressable memory. It contains all the main features of the other variants, including Active Directory, Kerberos security, and public key infrastructure.

- **Windows 2000 Advanced Server** will be the mainstay of the enterprise. It supports up to four-way SMP and addressable memory to 64GB. This product also is the first Microsoft offering to have clustering built in. Current Windows NT 4 Enterprise Edition customers are being steered toward this product.

- **Windows 2000 Datacenter Server** pushes the envelope of Big NT beyond where it has previously been. It supports the same amount of memory as Advanced Server, but its SMP support takes the roof off at 32 processors. According to product literature, Microsoft believes that (appropriately sized) servers running Datacenter Server "will support

more than 10,000 simultaneous users in some workloads." As you
might expect, it supports clustering and component load balancing as
Advanced Server does. However, this variety won't be released until at
least four months after Server and Advanced Server.

- **Windows 2000 Professional** is the successor to Windows NT
  Workstation. Like its predecessor, it supports up to two processors. It's
  geared toward the corporate client; at this time, there's no home version planned.

Note

*I can't help commenting on how these product names crack me up. I like to com-
pare a product against its antonym, because surely that's why they're pointing it
out. For example, Microsoft has returned to the "Advanced Server" moniker originally used in Windows NT 3.1. Does this mean that the "Server" flavor isn't
advanced? Or is it compared to "Ordinary Server"? What about "Windows 2000
Amateur" for the home client?" And don't get me started about the whole
"Windows 2000" business!*

Microsoft has backed off on its original intentions of creating a Windows
2000 for the home market and will continue the Windows 9x family a while
longer.

The limiting factor for most businesses will be how many processors they
need to support. If you don't have any four-processor systems and have no
intention of clustering, Server will be perfectly adequate and certainly the
least expensive option. If you have a few four-way systems, buy Advanced
Server just for those or for systems you intend to cluster. Datacenter Server
should be purchased for only the very largest SMP systems.

Namespace Design

When Microsoft uses the phrase *modeling the enterprise* in relation to
Windows 2000, it implies that you will be using the operating system to be
deeply integrated throughout every branch of your company. Namespace
design for your Windows 2000 network means creating a DNS design and,
within it, designing your forest, domain trees, OUs, Global Catalog and
domain controller placement, and your site design.

DNS Design

Because Windows 2000 is so tightly integrated with DNS, any design of a Windows 2000 network must start with a DNS design. In addition to meeting Windows 2000 requirements and standard requirements such as supportability and fault tolerance, this design has one big hurdle: It must fit into the existing DNS topology without disrupting current operations. This makes designing the DNS topology perhaps the toughest part of Windows 2000 namespace planning.

The vast majority of companies planning for Windows 2000 have a DNS namespace in production. Because DNS is a core infrastructure component for UNIX servers, workstations, and the company's intranet, any changes to it must be examined very carefully. In its Windows 2000 documentation, Microsoft has taken the approach that companies will willingly redesign their DNS infrastructure to fit Windows 2000's needs, or at the most will create a separate namespace for Windows 2000 servers and clients. If Windows 2000 is ever to be thoroughly integrated into the enterprise, the issue of integrating the Windows 2000 DNS namespace into the existing DNS infrastructure must be resolved very early in the planning process. Without knowing the DNS design, domain design and migration scenarios can't be finalized.

An example of the kind of problem you may encounter is the split DNS namespace. For example, say you upgrade a resource domain in MyCompany named RESOURCE01, located in Dallas, to Windows 2000. A Windows 2000 client, DHCP-enabled and therefore dynamically registered in a Windows 2000 dynamic DNS server, will use this DNS to find resource01.namerica.mycompany.com. Locating a non-Microsoft server, such as an Auspex file server in the same location but in the long-established DNS domain dallas.mycompany.com, requires contacting the pre-existing static DNS server that's authoritative for the il.mycompany.com zone. Microsoft clients can list several DNS servers in their network configuration, but requiring different DNS servers for Windows 2000 and UNIX systems is not an acceptable solution.

What are the possible scenarios for integrating the Windows 2000 DNS namespace into the current DNS infrastructure? Another way to ask the question is, "How do I share my company's top-level DNS domain with Windows 2000?" Five possible ways exist, each of which has advantages and disadvantages:

- Replace the existing DNS servers with Windows 2000 DNS servers. This is the simplest, cleanest, and most obvious solution, but it's also the most politically charged. Not only does it dive headfirst in the Windows NT versus UNIX religious war, but it makes the enterprise dependent on the stability of new Windows 2000 servers. This solution may well be the best if your existing DNS infrastructure uses Windows NT 4 DNS servers.

- Add Windows 2000 DNS servers into every DNS zone. Make them the primary servers, and make the existing DNS servers secondary. The new features of the Windows 2000 DNS servers can then be used, and they will perform zone transfers to the legacy DNS servers (now secondaries). This keeps the existing namespace intact, but it means that the enterprise must depend on Windows 2000 servers for its namespace. It also means that DNS update tools and processes must be updated because they'll be hitting Windows NT servers instead of UNIX servers.

- Create a separate DNS root domain, such as `myco.com`, alongside `mycompany.com` in MyCompany's intranet. This completely separates Windows 2000 servers and clients from the existing DNS infrastructure. It's pretty non-intuitive, and because it isn't integrated with the rest of the company's DNS it leads to confusion when locating resources on the intranet. A UNIX Web server's DNS name—`home.mycompany.com`—would be different from a similar one—`library.myco.com`—just because it's Windows 2000-based. `myco.com` would reside only in the company's intranet, but its `myco` domain name should be registered with the Internet DNS registration authority if it will ever be accessed from the Internet.

- Create a separate DNS subroot domain, such as `windows.mycompany.com`. This is an approach that Microsoft recommends, and offers has some advantages. Unfortunately, clarity isn't one of them. A client trying to reach a resource on the company's intranet runs into the same problem as the previous scenario, only it isn't quite so bad. In this scenario, the URL of a UNIX server for the online library would be `library.mycompany.com`, while a Windows 2000 Web server servicing the same site would appear as `library.windows.mycompany.com`. Both this method and the previous one suffer from the same shortcoming: They expose the operating systems to the user and force him to remember them. The user doesn't care what kind of operating system the Web site is using; he just wants to access the data. Of course, the administrators like this method for the same reason. They can immediately tell that a server is Windows 2000 from its host name.

- Add Windows 2000 DNS servers into every zone, and make them primaries in addition to the existing primaries. The Windows 2000 servers service the DHCP clients, and the legacy servers handle the rest. The big requirement here is that you must have a tool that reliably synchronizes the two servers. The Windows 2000 DNS server will be much more active, with dynamic updates from its DHCP service.

In addition to the logical design problems, the physical infrastructure must be upgraded to support Windows 2000. Should you replace your UNIX DNS servers with Windows 2000 DNS servers? Most of these companies—especially the large ones—use DNS on UNIX servers instead of Windows NT. Even though Windows 2000 will work using any DNS that supports RFCs 2052 (SRV record) and 2136 (dynamic update), most companies aren't in a hurry to upgrade their UNIX DNS to these standards and prefer to use Windows 2000 DNS in their Windows 2000 design.

DNS Design Recommendations
DNS design is one of the toughest areas to complete, and every company has to find its own answers based on the existing DNS infrastructure, UNIX versus Windows NT politics, and operational requirements. In a perfect world, the solution I'd recommend is to migrate your DNS infrastructure to Windows 2000 servers, either by themselves (as in the first method) or by using (presumably) UNIX DNS servers as secondaries. The latter method provides a bit more fault tolerance, but if you run DHCP from your DNS servers as well (recommended), there isn't any easy way to redirect the clients to the UNIX servers because DHCP will be down also.

Whenever possible, keep the names from the various protocols and contexts (i.e., NetBIOS names and Windows 2000 domains) the same as the DNS names. This tremendously reduces the administrative overhead and keeps the user's search for a resource as simple as possible.

If you want to support Windows 2000, your non-Microsoft DNS servers must support the SRV record, and you really do want dynamic update as well to integrate DNS and DHCP. On a Windows 2000 DNS server, you must specifically enable dynamic update; it's disabled by default.

Should DNS servers be member servers or domain controllers? If you put DNS on a domain controller, the Active Directory updates to the DNS database take place on-server and never use the network, so it's more efficient. However, if you put DNS (and DHCP, as recommended later in this chapter) on a domain controller, the Active Directory updates also must share the system's resources with authentication processes. Because these processes are part of the operating system, they run at a higher priority than DNS or DHCP will. This means that if some major event (such as a power outage) causes hundreds or thousands of clients to start up at the same time, the DNS and DHCP services will lose out to the Kerberos services, causing many clients to fail logon. Their natural reaction is to reboot and try again, which only makes the situation worse. Thus, I recommend pairing DNS with DHCP on a member server.

Timing is also important. The DNS design is an early and critical path deliverable for any Windows 2000 design, so it should be an early and high priority in your Windows 2000 project. Work closely with the DNS administrators to ensure a model that works for everybody.

Domain Design

Domain design encompasses a number of areas: the domains themselves, OUs, forests, domain controller placement, Global Catalog server placement, and sites. They all affect each other, so at each stage in the design you must review what you've already done in light of your latest decisions.

Unless you're building a new network from scratch, you already have an existing Windows NT 4 network from which you must migrate to get to the Windows 2000 Promised Land (and promised, and promised...). Do you create a design that's perfect for Windows 2000 but tear apart your existing Windows NT 4 network piece by piece to get there? Or is your end state model a compromise between the Windows 2000 domain model while remaining Windows NT 4-ish so that the upgrade is less complicated? What do you want to do with your resource domains? Do you upgrade them to Windows 2000 and leave them in place? We'll discuss this in more detail in Chapter 8, "Migrating a Windows NT 4 Network to Windows 2000," but the examples in this chapter follow the philosophy of designing a clean Windows 2000 end state model and then migrating the users to it.

The Root Domain

A tree starts at its roots, so a domain tree must start at the root domain. All other domains in the tree are named extensions of the root domain, so you'd better choose a name that represents the company and that is as short and simple as possible. In the best of worlds, MyCompany would use the name mycompany.com for its root domain (refer to Figure 3.8 in Chapter 3, "Distributed Services in Windows 2000"). Each directory tree has a root domain, so if your design requires a forest, you may have more than one root domain. For example, Figure 3.10 in Chapter 3 has five root domains in its forest.

The root domain has different requirements than other domains in the tree. No user accounts or resources exist in it, so the directory objects don't change and there's little replication traffic. (There's nothing to prevent you from adding accounts or resources, but the very existence of a root domain implies that you've already decided to distribute resources among child domains.) However, all Kerberos session ticket requests from one branch of the domain tree to another branch that isn't a parent or child domain must be referred through the root domain (refer to Figure 3.9 in Chapter 3). Kerberos referrals from anywhere in the root domain's tree to any other domain tree in a forest must also go through the root domain. The domain controllers for the root domain don't necessarily need to be Global Catalog servers.

Based on these requirements, servers for the root domain don't need much disk space, but they should have two fast processors and good I/O bandwidth. You also need high availability for this domain, because without it the domain tree falls apart.

Note

Of course, for small companies the root domain will really just be a single domain; is it still called a root domain if no child domains are underneath it? In this case, the domain will obviously have all the servers and replication traffic for the company.

A disclaimer here for DNS purists busily red-inking the preceding paragraphs: Yes, in the purest DNS terms, mycompany.com isn't the root domain. .com isn't even the root domain; . is the true DNS root, but it is hidden from most everyday activities. The domains underneath the root—.com, .edu, .org, and so on—are called top-level domains, or TLDs. Therefore, mycompany.com is really a second-level (or layer) domain in the grand scheme of things. Because we're working within a company's intranet, however, it's less confusing to call the highest Windows 2000 domain in the enterprise the root domain. There's one more reason that can't be ignored: Microsoft uses this terminology. You can revel in the knowledge that you're correct when referring to mycompany.com as a second-layer domain, but you'll confuse everyone else in the room.

The First-Layer Domains

In a domain tree, the first-layer domains are the ones whose parent domain is the root domain (or domains, in a forest). These are the domains that do the heavy lifting; in your end state model, they should contain most of the users and resources for the company.

These domains should be permanent—or as close to permanent as one gets in the modern company. The reason is simple: naming. The higher a domain sits in the domain tree structure, the greater the impact its name will have on every directory object beneath it in the tree.

Renaming a domain isn't allowed in the initial release of Windows 2000, and the following example demonstrates what a task it would be. Let's say `mycompany.com` has child domains of `atlanta.mycompany.com` and `sales.atlanta.mycompany.com`. If MyCompany went under new management and some rocket scientist Marketing VP decided that the company should be renamed for "a newer, fresher feeling," every object in `mycompany.com`, `atlanta.mycompany.com`, and `sales.atlanta.mycompany.com` would have to be renamed. You couldn't phase the change in anything smaller than domain size because the users couldn't keep track of the naming convention. Plus, DNS would have to swallow the changes (made easier if it were running in Directory Integrated mode, but what about the legacy DNS servers?). And as if that wasn't enough pain, all the object renames replicating to Global Catalog servers would bring them to their knees, disabling users for who knows how long. Enough said?

Note

I suppose you could rename a domain by demoting all domain controllers to member servers, and then running DCPROMO again and giving it the right name. But what would be the point? In demoting all the domain controllers, you've collapsed the domain and lost all the domain's objects, including little things such as accounts, groups, printers, and so on. In addition, this action would orphan a child domain beneath the collapsed domain.

In that light, my domain naming recommendations are as follows:

- Your root domain should be something that identifies the company. If you have an existing DNS infrastructure, the best name is probably already in use. If you decide to create a new one, make it related to the existing one and register it with an Internet naming authority.

- Don't name domains by organization. Name them something that won't soon change—perhaps after a continent. Countries can be a little chancier (especially if you're in Eastern Europe), but these are generally a safe bet as well.

- Give domain names at least three letters because approximately 250 two-letter names are reserved for the ISO 3166 two-character country codes used on the Internet.

- Try to strike a balance between short names (the higher-level domain names will appear as part of every object name below them in the tree and in all Global Catalog servers) and names that are too long. After NetBIOS is removed from your Windows 2000 network, users won't choose their domain from the domain pick list any more; they'll simply type in their UPN name (e.g., `james.robert@mycompany.com`). Take the number of letters in the domain names you choose, and multiply that by hundreds of thousands of keystrokes across the company to get a feel for the impact of your choice.

- You can assign *friendly names* to the domain, such as `myco.com`, `itsmine.com`, or whatever you like. These aliases are assigned in the domain's properties and can be used wherever a user would type `mycompany.com`. This somewhat frees up the need to make the real domain name completely user-friendly.

If your company isn't spread out geographically and separated by WAN circuits, or if it is spread out but has pretty good network connectivity between its locations (i.e., WAN circuits of 128Kbps or greater), these domains should be few and large. Fewer domains give you the following:

- Simpler replication topologies.

- Fewer domain controllers.

- More practicality. It's more practical (i.e., less costly) to place domain controllers for the other regional domains and root at a central location, usually a point of high connectivity. This technique will speed up authentication in the other domain.

- Simplicity of moving machines (computer accounts move less between domains).

- Simpler location of resources.

- Less mobile user confusion (greater chance that DHCP at a visiting site will point to same domain as the traveler's home site).

- Less chance of needing shortcut trusts. (See the section "When Would I Want a Shortcut Trust?", which follows.)

- An easier link among forests with shortcut trusts. (See the section "When Would I Want a Shortcut Trust?", which follows.)

If your company is separated by slow WAN links, you may need to create more domains (see the section "What About More Domains?" later in this chapter.) Because these domains are so large, your domain controllers (especially the Global Catalog servers) must be built big for the role. See Chapter 5, "Building, Maintaining, and Tuning the Box," for details on sizing the server.

Figure 6.1 shows a very simple domain tree with a root domain and two first-level domains, each of which have three domain controllers.

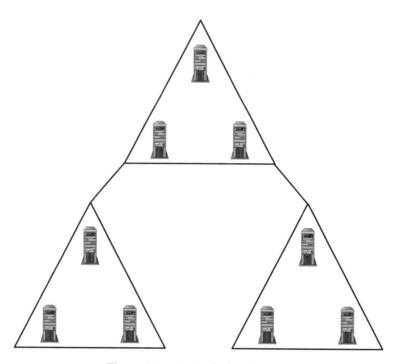

Figure 6.1   *A simple domain tree.*

What About More Domains?

Microsoft recommends creating child domains for countries, such as under a regional first-layer domain. (Technically, a first-layer domain is also a child domain—of the root—but for this discussion, a child domain is second-layer and beyond.) However, I see only a few compelling reasons to have child domains in an end-state domain model instead of OUs. OUs can handle all the security and administrative partitioning requirements, and sites can be used to manage replication if the physical location where the OU's members work is separated from the rest of the domain by a slow link.

There are a few reasons why you might want to have child domains, at least temporarily, in your domain model:

- Child domains can be used as an intermediate step when migrating between Windows NT 4 resource domains and Windows 2000 OUs.

- If you have an organization with account policy requirements that are different from those of the rest of the enterprise, a child domain would be appropriate because account policies are applied domainwide. For example, a university might want to put all its student accounts in a child domain with tighter account restrictions than for the computer center administrators.

- If an organization operates almost completely autonomously from the parent organization, both administratively and in its network topology, a child domain might be appropriate because the only replication that will take place between the child domain and its parent is that of the Global Catalog servers. For example, if you worked for a retail company that had large branch locations connected by satellite links, it could be a good candidate for a child domain. The only replication taking place over the link would be for the Global Catalog objects.

- Remember that a domain is a unit of replication; in other words, domain controllers replicate only to other domain controllers inside their own domain, not outside of it. Therefore, if it's important to limit replication traffic in a corner of the enterprise, you can achieve this by creating a child domain. For example, if your business has a branch in a controlled country (for example, China) and you don't want regular corporate data from the large regional (first-level) domains to replicate into that country, you can create a child domain just for that country. Domain objects between the controlled country and regional domains won't be replicated across the network firewall between your corporate intranet and the controlled country (although the Global Catalog will).

For all circumstances besides those listed here, I'd recommend an OU.

When Would I Need a Forest?

My short definition of a forest is that it's like a domain tree, but without a contiguous namespace. The best example that always comes to mind is General Motors. This company has five divisions with completely separate naming (refer to Figure 3.10), but if it implements a forest the company can still have enterprisewide connectivity because each division can reach the others through transitive trusts. (I haven't asked them if they're going to implement Windows 2000 this way, and they haven't consulted with me either.)

In a few special cases, you may require even more than one forest. The main requirement for what I'll call a *voluntary* separate forest is when a schema must be different than the enterprise schema. The best example of this situation is your corporate presence servers. They should be completely isolated from the rest of your intranet, and a separate forest is the only way to do it Windows 2000. Another good reason is for development or piloting purposes. If something you're testing messes with the schema, it won't affect the production forest.

You'd end up with an *involuntary* separate forest as the result of acquiring a company that's already migrated to Windows 2000. (At least it's involuntary on the part of IT.) The company has its own forest, its own schema, and there is no way to combine them. This is a situation where shortcut trusts could be used to create some connectivity between individual domains in each forest. The initial release of Windows 2000 has no tools to merge new forests into existing forests.

When Would I Want a Shortcut Trust?
A shortcut trust (also called a *cross-link trust*) is a specific use of an explicit trust. Explicit trusts are one-way trust relationships you set up manually through the Active Directory Sites & Services Manager. As with NTLM trusts, you must set up a one-way trust in both directions to get two-way functionality. Unlike NTLM trusts, however, an explicit trust is transitive as long as the two domains it joins are in the same tree or forest. This means that it's not transitive when it joins downlevel domains or a domain in another forest.

Shortcut trusts are used to minimize the number of Kerberos referrals required to get a user from one branch of a domain tree authenticated in another (see Figure 6.2). Users in `sf.us.research.mycompany.com` would use the shortcut trust to access `fr.sales.mycompany.com` without traversing the domain tree.

Sounds great, eh? Why not have shortcut trusts all over the place? Because they're trusts to keep track of, as in the Windows NT 4 days. Standard Kerberos referrals should work just fine in most cases. Here are some rules about shortcut trusts:

- Don't apply any at first. Use them only to fix a documented problem. If you start out using them, how will you know if there really was a problem to be corrected in the first place?

- Use a shortcut trust when you have two or more peer domain trees in your forest, much traffic between a domain in one tree and another domain in another tree, and slow authentication times.

- Not enough or slow domain controllers in the root domain might contribute to this problem also.
- Use a shortcut trust if you have a slow link anywhere in the standard (through the root) referral path.

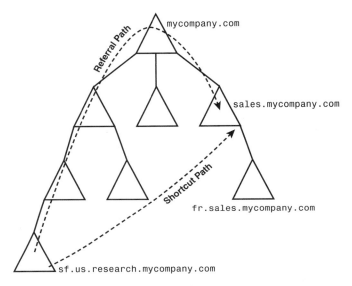

Figure 6.2   *A shortcut trust.*

Here's yet another reason why having fewer domains, or at least fewer child domains (i.e. making the tree "deeper"), is a good idea. A "wide" domain design means that fewer Kerberos referrals are necessary to get a user in one domain authenticated in any other domain. Therefore, you have less chance of needing a shortcut trust.

Shortcut trusts can mitigate the difficulties of multiple forests that result from acquiring companies with their own Windows 2000 network. You can use shortcut trusts to enable non-transitive trust relationships between two domains in different forests; fewer domains means fewer shortcut trusts are required for full interoperability between the forests.

Domain Recommendations

The following are my domain recommendations:

- Minimize the number of Windows 2000 domains in your forest. Just because you *can* have a lot of domains (after all this time fighting over account domains with your customers) doesn't mean you *should*. Domains should be used to control replication; use OUs to give customers the distributed administration they've been clamoring for. You must also factor in your network bandwidth; intradomain replication requires more of it than interdomain replication, so if your WAN circuits are small or busy, you may need more domains (see the section "Replication Classes" later in this chapter.)

- If you want to minimize the number of domains in your enterprise, why not just have one big domain? It comes down to replication again. In a North American-based company, the North American domain will probably hold the bulk of the company's user accounts and resources. This also means that most of the changes to the Active Directory that must be replicated between domain controllers will take place in this domain. If you had one domain for the entire enterprise, all the international sites would get replication traffic from the North American directory object changes—which they don't need. Splitting off the North American users into their own domain eliminates this problem. What's the rule that comes from this? You can use domains to segregate replication, but do it sparingly!

- Name your domains for objects that don't change very often, such as geographic regions. This does *not* mean naming a domain after your department. I don't know about yours, but mine seems to reorganize every six months. Because you can't currently rename a domain, you would be stuck with an obsolete domain name until the rename capability is added. Another advantage to geographic naming is that replication tends to stay in the local geography (as long as the WAN circuits are configured that way also).

- Replication is bad. Okay, that's an overstatement, but the design principle is to be always thinking, "Will this complicate the replication topology in my network?" It's a cost, and so there had better be a visible benefit to any increase in replication that you incur. Repeat after me: Minimize replication, minimize replication....

- Remember that replication traffic will *never* decrease. The Active Directory is just getting started, and Active Directory-enabled applications will increase dramatically in the next few years.

- Name your domains carefully because you can't rename them.

- After spending all this time talking about replication, it seems as though it's the biggest component of network traffic going over the link. In the grand scheme of things, though, it isn't. The most traffic generated in a typical corporate office network is—big surprise—email. You need to factor the requirements of your biggest customer, Microsoft Exchange (or whatever you use) into your planning.

- Put together a well-reasoned and as technical as possible document that explains the criteria for when a domain should be created. This document is separate from a "road show" presentation, and it helps if the document is big and heavy. One of the biggest reasons for this document is so you can throw it at every manager that demands his own domain! To add more power to the document, it should be written to steer these people toward an OU.

- Consider distributing the several domain controllers of the root domain(s) to centers of high connectivity around the enterprise. This has several advantages, with no real disadvantages. First, it speeds up Kerberos referrals because a root domain controller will be "closer" to other domain controllers. Second, it increases fault tolerance of the root domain because they aren't all vulnerable to a building power failure or other site disaster. Third, the domain controllers make good Global Catalog servers in this position (see the section "Global Catalog Server Placement and Recommendations" later in this chapter).

- Keep the domain namespace and the DNS namespace as closely related as possible.

- Ask yourself, "How will this design work in a mixed environment?".

- Finally, don't forget the advice of a very knowledgeable colleague of mine: "It's very important to use equilateral triangles when drawing your domains so that all the transitive trusts line up correctly."

Consider an example of MyCompany, as shown in Figure 6.3. It's a multinational company, based in the United States. It has North America locations in Dallas, Seattle, Toronto, and New York. Its international locations are in Tokyo, Singapore, Sydney, London, Oporto (Portugal), and Oslo.

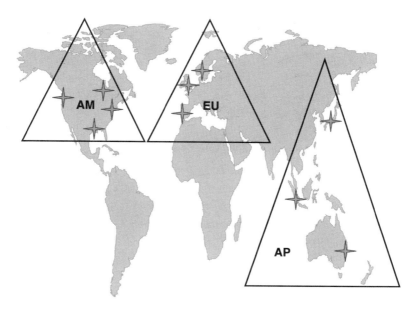

Figure 6.3 *MyCompany's locations worldwide.*

MyCompany's existing Windows NT 4 domain architecture (shown in Figure 6.4) consists of three master domains (NAMERICA, EUROPE, ASIAPAC) and 10 resource domains (DARD01, STRD01, TRRD01, NYRD01, NORD01, UKRD01, PORD01, JPRD01, SIRD01, and AURD01). The domains are trusted in a classic multimaster domain configuration where the master domains have two-way trusts between themselves, and where each resource domain trusts each master domain. (The trusts are omitted for clarity.)

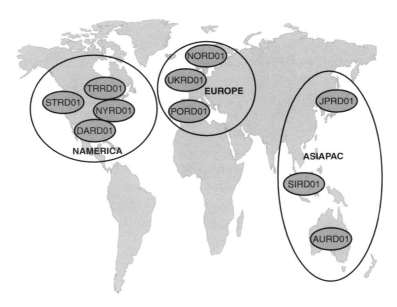

Figure 6.4 *MyCompany's Windows NT 4 domain architecture.*

Following is a recommendation of large regional domains. MyCompany's Windows 2000 domains might look as shown in Figure 6.5.

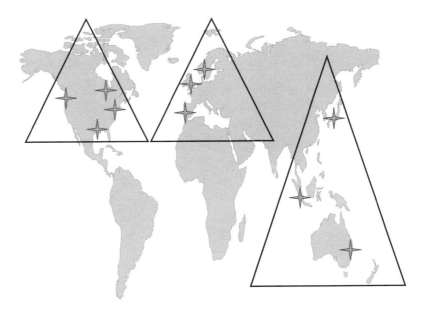

Figure 6.5 *MyCompany's Windows 2000 domain namespace.*

Three regional first-layer domains—AM, EU, and AP—globally encompass the entire company. (For clarity, the root domain linking these domains isn't shown.)

OU Recommendations

Organizational units are a really great idea in Windows 2000. They provide most of the functionality of a domain, and they don't require their own domain controllers or otherwise complicate the replication scheme. They're the key to resolving the problem that has dogged Windows NT since its inception: how to give customer groups their own administrative control without adding domains to the trusted Windows NT network.

Start with your existing account and resource domains, and decide on which Windows 2000 domains they should reside as OUs. Try to standardize the rights as much as possible to make administration simpler when you have a lot of OUs.

My OU recommendations are listed here:

- Involve your stakeholders in the creation of the OU structure for the domains they reside in. If they did have their own domain, they probably won't in Windows 2000, and it's up to you to prove how they can still administer themselves with OUs. If they didn't have their own domain, you have the happy task of showing them how they now *can* administer themselves.

- Remember to always think in terms of the requirement, not the solution. Windows 2000 is so different from Windows NT 4 that old solutions aren't necessarily needed. In other words, keep refocusing yourself and the customer on the problem you're trying to solve.

The customer says, "We must have our own domain!"(fist on the table).

You reply evenly, "What's the *requirement*? You're proposing a solution when we haven't clarified what it is you need."

The customer, being the extremely reasonable type I can create (but that doesn't often exist), says, "Well... we need to be able to administer our own accounts and fix our customer's passwords without waiting for a centralized help desk."

You say, "We can do that. We can create an organizational unit that gives you complete control over your user's accounts, *and* give you the ability to grant each site's administrator access to just the accounts at that site. In addition, the corporate help desk will still be able to fix passwords for your users if no one at your local help desk is available. Does that meet your requirements?"

- You need to decide to what level you're willing to delegate administration. By all means, move it out to the businesses, but don't go too deep; the deeper into a business you push an administrative structure, the more likely it will be caught up in a reorganization.

- OUs are cheap, so when you create domains, also create a standard set of OUs for administration categories that are common across the enterprise. The Active Directory already has containers for servers and domain controllers; consider creating OUs for PCs, for application servers of a certain type (such as SQL Server), or for any collection of Active Directory objects that should be administered together.

- Always try to use an OU to get a requirement satisfied before you resort to using a domain.

- Try to name OUs along administrative lines, not by organizations. Organizations reorganize, and even though OUs are much easier to set up and take down than domains, they're deeper in the organizational structure and therefore are more likely to be made obsolete by a reorganization. The object here is to simplify administration by delegating it—not to exchange one type of administrative overhead (accounts) for another (OUs).

As MyCompany plans for Windows 2000, IT and the customer agree that the resource domains will become OUs in the regional domains. Note that the two-letter location names embedded in the resource domain names have been changed so that they don't conflict with official ISO 3166 country codes, as shown in Figure 6.6.

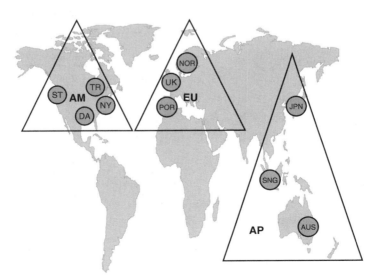

Figure 6.6 *MyCompany's Windows 2000 organizational units.*

Site Design

Sites are a collection of well-connected subnets. Their purpose is to bring some knowledge of the physical network topology and relative connection costs into Windows 2000. Think of them as islands of high connectivity in a sea of lower connectivity. Now in reality, it isn't so much a sea as a number of discrete WAN links that have the lower connectivity. But the analogy still works insofar as each site must reach another site by going across a region of lower connectivity.

> **Note**
>
> *Allow me a short digression here on terminology. In the rest of the chapter, I use the term network-proximate a fair amount. My definition of network-proximate is that two network nodes (specifically, two computers) are network-proximate when they're near each other in the realm of network bandwidth; that is, there's high connectivity between the two. This is a relative term, not an absolute one. It comes into play, for example, in discussions of how clients contact a domain controller. You want a client to choose the "closest" domain controller for performance—but it's not necessarily the closest physically.*

Sites serve two purposes:

- They provide greater control over replication between sites (intersite) than is possible with replication inside a site (intrasite).
- They provide a means for Windows 2000 clients to favor Active Directory and Global Catalog servers (i.e., domain controllers) in their own sites. This means that clients in a well-designed site topology will always choose a nearby domain controller for their authentication and Active Directory and Global Catalog queries.

Site topology is almost always a compromise. It must be the buffer between the domain design and the WAN topology. The domain design is based on geographical or organizational constructs, while the WAN topology is derived from physical realities such as available circuit capacity, circuit cost, and (hopefully) network traffic patterns.

The Importance of Network Circuit Maps

Before you get any further in your site design, stop here and go dig up your company's network circuit maps. If you work in a large company, these maps (and the WAN engineers) are probably far from your daily circle of coffee buddies. Well, you need to introduce yourself and learn how the map was put together. The WAN engineers will be happy to hear from you—and very willing to help when they learn how the Windows 2000 site design can drastically affect their beloved WAN traffic flow patterns.

After you've learned to decipher the maps (hint: 1536Kbps = T1 circuit) they're pretty interesting. In my experience, large United States-based multinational companies rarely connect all their locations around the world in a mesh; usually all the major circuits go to and from the United States. This is especially true in the Asia-Pacific region, where land-based circuits are few and far between. After all, many of the major economic players in this region—Japan, Taiwan, Hong Kong, Singapore, and Malaysia—are islands. If the company is United States-based, the network traffic patterns tend to go into and out of the states rather than between international locations.

Inside a site, and within a domain at that site, replication between domain controllers is automatically configured in a bi-directional ring by the Knowledge Consistency Checker, or KCC. This ring topology means that if any one domain controller bites the dust, replication can still be done by going the other way around the ring. The ring algorithm is designed so that any one domain controller is no more than three hops to another domain controller. This means that if you have seven or more domain controllers in a site, other connection objects—christened *optimized edges*—will be created between domain controllers. This also increases the fault tolerance of the replication topology. The connection objects that link domain controllers are unidirectional like NTLM trusts; two connection objects are necessary for each link. The object is shown as belonging to the server that receives the data.

The KCC is an intelligent agent that configures, and reconfigures, the replication topology between servers in a site and also between sites. It automatically designates "bridgehead" servers that are the gateways for intersite replication. If a bridgehead server goes down, after several failed replication attempts the KCC reconfigures its site connector to go through a new server.

You can override the KCC at any time. The best idea, however, is to let the KCC do its work and influence it by varying the relative cost of each site connection in the Active Directory Sites and Services Manager.

Remember, if you mess around with the settings too much, you'll have to mess with them again when your configuration changes. Why add extra-administrative headaches unless it's absolutely necessary?

> **Note**
>
> *Intersite compression of replication data is very efficient. The data is compressed down to 10–15% of its uncompressed form within a site.*

Site Design Recommendations

The following are my site design recommendations:

- Keep the number of sites to a minimum, based on your network topology. Start with one site for the entire enterprise; then on a case-by-case basis, establish why a different site should be established. Repeat after me: Minimize sites, minimize sites, minimize sites....

- Microsoft's WAN circuit threshold recommendation for a location to be its own site is 128Kbps.

- Sites are relatively easy to create from larger sites, so start with fewer sites and allow yourself to be goaded into more sites if necessary—not the other way around. After a location has been established as its own site, it will be politically more difficult to consolidate it into another site.

- Every site should have at least one domain controller. This isn't required, but the whole point of creating a site is that connectivity is lousy between the site and the rest of the enterprise. If you don't want to land a domain controller there, a site serves no purpose.

- The domain criteria document mentioned in the previous section "Domain Recommendations" should also include site criteria, known internally to the architects as "Why Everyone Can't Have Their Own Site." This document should also be very technical. This won't be as much of an issue as the "Why Everyone Can't Have Their Own Domain" section, because most managers won't understand it anyway.

- If for some reason you can't use TCP/IP site connectors to a location, you can use SMTP replication (i.e., replication as mail) if you make the location its own site and configure it appropriately. This is a good approach if you have an office in a controlled country.

- Keep Global Catalog replication in mind when configuring a site.

- Ask yourself, "What influence do sites have in a mixed environment?"
- Try to keep one domain to a site if at all possible. Keeping track of replication among multiple domains in a site can get very complex, very quickly.

Let's look at MyCompany's locations again, this time overlaid with the wide area network circuit topology (see Figure 6.7).

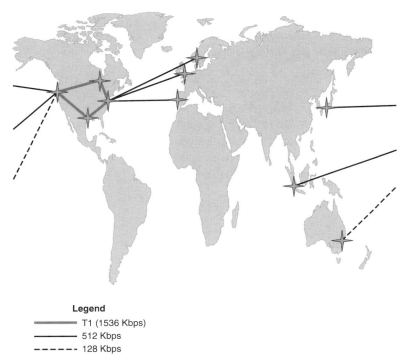

Legend
━━━━━ T1 (1536 Kbps)
───── 512 Kbps
- - - - - 128 Kbps

Figure 6.7   *MyCompany's WAN circuit topology.*

The North America locations are connected by T1 circuits and are laid out in a ring so that no one site outage will prevent them from communicating with each other. However (international circuit costs being what they are), the loss of the Seattle or New York hubs will disable Asia-Pacific or European connectivity, respectively. Also note that most of the international circuits are lower-bandwidth (512Kbps) than the domestic circuits. The Australian circuit is only 128Kbps.

Overlaying a possible site design gives us four sites, as shown in Figure 6.8.

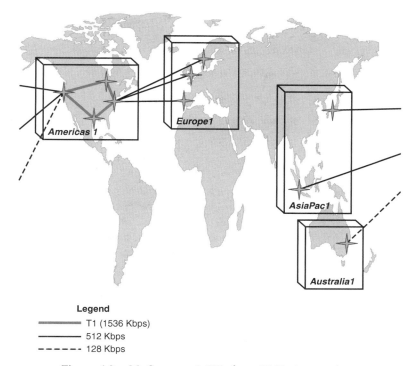

Legend
▬▬▬▬ T1 (1536 Kbps)
———— 512 Kbps
– – – – – 128 Kbps

Figure 6.8 *MyCompany's Windows 2000 site topology.*

You should think about a couple aspects of this design. First, following the principle of minimizing sites, I've placed all the European locations into one site. Because they're also in one domain, this means that intrasite replication traffic must go over the international circuits. This choice entirely depends on the amount of available bandwidth you have on the international circuits. My suggestion is to start with one site, and if the traffic is unreasonable, break it into three sites and schedule replication traffic for off-hours. This will ease the network burden, but everything has a price: Users in Oslo won't see updates made in London for several hours rather than in just a few minutes. A similar situation exists in the AsiaPac1 site.

Second, I put the Australian office into its own site. The main reason is because it has only a 128Kbps link to the rest of the company. This is definitely a case where user convenience must take a back seat to WAN circuit costs. Intersite replication for this link is scheduled during non-business hours.

Domain Controller Placement and Recommendations

As in so many other areas of Windows 2000 design, domain controller placement is a compromise between two opposing requirements. The first—the client point of view—is that you want clients to have a "'local" (i.e., close to the network) domain controller for authentication purposes. The second—the enterprise point of view—is the fact that fewer domain controllers means less replication, therefore less complication, and less network traffic. How to reach a balance?

Three factors control where you place domain controllers:

- Availability. You must have enough domain controllers that are network-proximate to any given client population so that if one croaks, another can pick up the load without severely impacting the clients. Remember that this doesn't necessarily mean physically close; if you're lucky enough to have a good network, a network-proximate domain controller could be several states away.

- Load balancing. You can scale up Windows 2000 domain controllers compared to Windows NT 4 domain controllers, but there's always a reasonable size limit. If you have more than one domain controller that's network-proximate, the load will be balanced between them.

- Locality. If you have a domain that spans two sites because the locations are separated by a slow link (less than 128Kbps, or high latency as in a satellite link), you'll need a domain controller on each side of the link to ensure that clients get adequate response. Indeed, there's little point to a site without at least one domain controller.

My domain controller placement recommendations are listed here:

- If you have good connectivity in your network and consequently few sites, your domain controller philosophy should follow the same guidelines as your domains: few, but large. These servers must authenticate many users but will have relatively few replication update requests from other domain controllers. A limiting factor to this is the number of sites in your enterprise.

- If your network is already somewhat bandwidth-constrained, and if you have many sites, you must have more domain controllers; still, they needn't be as large as the ones just mentioned. These domain controllers won't authenticate nearly as many users, but they will have to deal with replication update requests from many other domain controllers.

- The placement of domain controllers for the root domain is very important. Because each Kerberos referral between domain trees must touch a root domain controller, placing one in each high-connectivity area for your first-layer domains will speed up intra- and intertree authentication.

- Every site should have its own domain controller. If you balk at this, reconsider why you want a site there in the first place. The whole point to having a separate site is to control replication to domain controllers in that site. If there aren't any domain controllers, why bother?

- Don't go off placing domain controllers at every remote site as you did for Windows NT 4. Windows 2000 is not the same paradigm! Windows 2000 uses Kerberos for its logon authentication, not NTLM. The actual Kerberos traffic has a different pattern than NTLM (see Chapter 3), and the logon process requires that a Windows 2000 domain controller touch other servers that probably won't be on the user side of a slow link (such as a Global Catalog server). In addition to hardware costs, then, an extra domain controller might not speed up the user's logon.

  Remember, however, that for some time in the future you'll still have Windows NT 4 and Windows 9x clients to service. If you have existing Windows NT 4 remote backup domain controllers, don't tear them out right away.

- Fewer domain controllers means less replication traffic.

- Fewer domains means fewer domain controllers, which means less cost. Enough said.

- Ask yourself, "What are the implications in a mixed environment?" This is very important for domain controller placement, because unlike Windows 2000 clients, downlevel clients have much more traffic with domain controllers.

- Consider landing an extra-beefy (i.e., domain controller hardware size) member server in important network centers. It can run whatever standard set of applications you desire. If a network-proximate domain controller will be taken out of service for maintenance, this member server can be promoted to domain controller status (using DCPROMO) to temporarily handle the workload.

  Note: In large domains with many objects, the DCPROMO operation will replicate the Active Directory database from another nearby domain controller—and this could be several gigabytes of network traffic. If a domain controller in a large domain crashes, the act of promoting another server in its place will put a lot of strain on the network and create other problems. If you must build a large domain controller quickly, promote it on the same segment as an existing domain controller, and then drive the darn thing to the dead controller's location in someone's truck.

Note

I haven't shown any domain controller placement recommendations for MyCompany because it's entirely dependent on the size and configuration of each location. Therefore, it's too messy to show in a simple figure.

One constraint in Windows NT 4 that forced the system designer to create more domains is the recommended 40MB limitation on how large the SAM should be on Windows NT 4 domain controllers. This constraint has been lifted in Windows 2000, and test numbers by Microsoft and Compaq seem to agree. The equivalent of SAM in Windows 2000, the actual directory store database on a domain controller, is Ntds.dit. When planning for the eventual size of Ntds.dit, here are experimental results and recommendations:

- A scaling test created an enterprise of 100,000 users with 30 attributes loaded for each user, 2,000 OUs, 30,000 groups(!) loaded with 8 attributes and 100 members per group, 90,000 workstations loaded with 6 attributes, printers loaded with 8 attributes, and all string attributes set to a random size from 1 to 100 characters.

  The resulting Ntds.dit size was 1.6GB. The objects were loaded into the Active Directory in a stepped manner, 10% at a time, and then Ntds.dit size measured. The database size growth was completely linear and predictable with the number of objects, and this sizing experiment has been carried to larger numbers of Active Directory objects as well; Compaq has documented linear growth up to 16 million objects with a resulting Ntds.dit of 68.6GB, and tests of up to 40 million are being done. (Of course, how you'd actually manage such a behemoth is another matter.) The point is, *you can accurately estimate the size of your Active Directory database* Ntds.dit *for your company, regardless of its size.*

- As with SAM, when objects are deleted from the Active Directory Ntds.dit doesn't shrink in size. However, unlike SAM, the server can be taken offline and compressed with the NTDSUTL utility (available on every server). When compressed, Ntds.dit shrinks down to exactly the size it's supposed to be with the smaller number of directory objects. There's no problem with unreclaimed space.

- As you migrate to Windows 2000, `Ntds.dit` will grow as objects are loaded and changes are made. When you come up with `Ntds.dit` size estimates for your own company, be sure to provide lots of extra space (100%) on your SYSVOL partition just in case. A few extra MB or GB on your domain controllers is less expensive by far than discovering that your SYSVOL is running out of room midway during your migration!

Here are recommendations for estimating the size of `Ntds.dit` for your company:

- A basic user object (containing information only in the account name, name, and email attributes) occupies 3600 bytes in the Active Directory.
- A basic OU container (with nothing in it) occupies 1100 bytes in the Active Directory.
- Treat security principals like users—add 3600 bytes per object.
- Treat non-security principals like OUs—add 1100 bytes per objects.
- To be safe, at least double your estimated size.
- As you add attributes to your objects (for example, loading a telephone number for every user object), add about 100 bytes for every string attribute. Add more if the string size is greater than 10 characters.
- If you've loaded binary data into attributes, use the size of the data plus 25% for a buffer.

Note

Have you ever looked for an Active Directory service such as the Kerberos Key Distribution Center, the directory service engine, or the Global Catalog on a domain controller? You won't find them broken out in any listing of services (such as the Control Panel Services applet). That's because they're all part of the `Lsass.exe` *service.*

Global Catalog Server Placement and Recommendations

You can think of a Global Catalog server as a domain controller on steroids: In addition to doing everything a domain controller does, it has an index that contains every object (but not every attribute) in the forest.

You can designate a domain controller as a Global Catalog server in the Active Directory Sites and Services Manager (see Figure 6.9):

Figure 6.9 *Designating a domain controller as a Global Catalog server.*

1. In the console tree, right-click NTDS Settings.

2. Launch Active Directory Sites and Services Manager from the Administrative Tools menu.

3. Click Sites to expand, and select the site that has the domain controller you're interested in. This will expand it to show the Servers container.

4. Click the domain controller you want to designate as a Global Catalog server. This will reveal the NTDS Settings object.

5. Right-click the NTDS Settings object, and choose Properties. The Global Catalog Server checkbox determines whether it will be a Global Catalog server or not.

Tip

A key fact to remember about Global Catalog servers is that they are much higher replication targets than ordinary domain controllers. Anything that needs information from the Global Catalog hits the server (read only), and anything that updates the Global Catalog causes replication to this server (read/write). You may want a lot of Global Catalog servers for better client response time, but you'll pay the price in replication traffic.

So when does a client need information from the Global Catalog?

- With the PC as client, the Global Catalog is queried whenever a directory object that can't be found in the local domain is requested.
- With a domain controller as client, the Global Catalog is queried on behalf of the user to find what universal groups he's a part of. Without this information, the user's logon can't complete successfully.
- With an Exchange Server as client and the Active Directory Connector enabled, the Global Catalog is queried for user email addresses.

So what updates the Global Catalog? Anything that changes Active Directory objects or some of their attributes. For example, adding a new user or computer account is an example of object changes; changing a user's email address or phone number is an example of attribute changes. Any of these changes must be replicated to Global Catalog servers across the enterprise.

The contents of the Global Catalog originate in domain controllers; they're loaded into a Global Catalog's indexes by domain controllers in the Global Catalog server's site. After it's in a Global Catalog server, the data is then replicated to other Global Catalog server across the forest (enterprise).

The first domain controller created in the forest will be automatically designated as a Global Catalog server; after that, you must manually designate the domain controllers that will also host the Global Catalog.

My recommendations for Global Catalog servers are listed here:

- The Global Catalog has only five or six attributes per object by default; this translates to 15–25% of a domain database that is replicated to the Global Catalog. The size of the Global Catalog is directly affected by how many universal groups you create.
- A starting point for Global Catalog server placement is one per site. If you have many sites, you should cut down on this ratio; if you have only a few sites for a large company because you have a good network, consider having more than one per site.
- Remember that Global Catalog access (by a domain controller) is required for Windows 2000 network logon. This means that if a Global Catalog server isn't located at every site, it should be reachable from the site.
- You must strike a balance between having enough Global Catalog servers for good response time to Active Directory queries, and the replication overhead that comes from having too many Global Catalog servers.

- Consider making the root domain controllers Global Catalog servers if the root domain's controllers are distributed through your major sites. The root domain controllers should be lightly loaded, which matches well with the heavy database activity of the Global Catalog.

- Domain controllers also serving as Global Catalog servers should be designed for high processor and file I/O loading. Because the Global Catalog contains all the objects in the Active Directory (though not all the attributes), these domain controllers should have a mirrored pair of 10K RPM drives. Current drive sizes of 9GB or 18GB are plenty for most enterprises Global Catalogs; 36GB drives will take care of the largest corporations as well. The mirror set provides the high availability for the Global Catalog's critical role in most aspects of Active Directory operations.

- Exchange servers are especially heavy users of the Global Catalog. Exchange 5.5 servers that use the Active Directory Connector to access Active Directory information will hit a Global Catalog twice: once on behalf of the user who's resolving a name to email address, and again in the transmission of the mail. You want to be especially sensitive to the location and number of Global Catalog servers near your Exchange data center.

- Remember to account for the extra disk space requirements (usually much greater than the domain data) when configuring Global Catalog server hardware.

- Ask yourself, "What are the implications, if any, in a mixed environment?"

Returning to MyCompany, Figure 6.10 shows a possible Global Catalog server layout, overlaid with the domain and site topologies.

This is a conservative approach; I'd prefer not to have so many Global Catalog servers. Because of the WAN circuit topology, however, if an international circuit went down, all international locations could log on only if they had cached credentials on their workstations. The two Global Catalog servers in North America would be part of the root domain; located at network hubs for Asia-Pacific/North America and Europe/North America, they would both provide Global Catalog lookup and speed Kerberos referrals. A suggestion to experiment with few Global Catalog servers would be to install Global Catalog servers only in Seattle and New York during the pilot, and to take response time, traffic, and server load metrics. You could deploy no Global Catalog servers internationally, but you could have hardware ready to install if the need became apparent. Just remember to not check that Global Catalog checkbox until off-hours because it will kick off a lot of replication from a remote Global Catalog server.

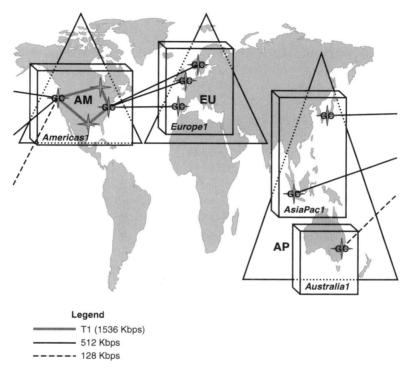

Figure 6.10   *MyCompany's Global Catalog server placement.*

Group Design

Groups in Windows 2000 have become more useful and also more confusing. First there's the addition of universal groups. Then there's the redefinition of local groups into "domain local" (for local groups that can be accessed only within a domain) and "local" (for local groups that can be accessed only on a member server). Global groups can be called domain global groups, and you can now nest them. Finally, these all fit into the new paradigm of the Active Directory.

Group Design Recommendations

These are some general recommendations of what groups to use and when:

- Use domain local groups to control access to resources in a single domain. In Windows NT 4, this wasn't necessarily a good idea because anyone with Account Operator rights in the domain could add a user to this group, granting him access to the resource. In Windows 2000; however, you can be more granular in your permissions and specify exactly who has the rights to a directory object or network resources. You can grant permissions to modify a local group to only a very specific list of individuals, not all Account Operators.

- After you've set up domain local groups to control resource access, most of your work should be done with global groups. Even though a global group's membership can be accessed from outside a domain, it contains only users and computers in that domain. Therefore, only domain controllers in the global group's domain get replication from changes to the group. In other words, you can change a global group's membership on a regular basis without causing enterprisewide Global Catalog replication.

- Remember that you can nest global groups. For example, if you have OUs A and B in a nested structure and you want A to be capable of administering B, you can nest a global group containing B's users in a global group containing A's administrators.

- Unlike Windows NT 4, Windows 2000 member servers can access Windows 2000 domain local groups.

- When you migrate your Windows NT 4 domains to Windows 2000, you will potentially have far more groups in the Global Catalog than you want. Remember that every object in every domain will go in the Global Catalog, so if you upgrade a bunch of resource domains to Windows 2000, every little group that's in them will go in the Global Catalog. Reduce and clean up your groups before you migrate.

- Apply domain global groups uniformly across domains to consolidate users who will be granted similar rights and permissions. For example, in a network with two domains—Europe and NorthAmerica—if there is a global group called GLAccounting in the NorthAmerica domain, there should also be a group called GLAccounting in the Europe domain (unless the accounting function does not exist in the Europe domain).

- To keep Windows NT security groups straight, I used to tell people to consider the following:

  Users in global,

  Global in local,

  Local in resource.

In Windows 2000 it has become:

Global in universal,

Users in global,

Domain local in resource.

- Set up universal groups and leave them alone. Whenever you change them, there's a big price to be paid in replication. Because universal groups reside only in the Global Catalog, any changes to them are replicated to Global Catalog servers across the enterprise. Use universal groups to consolidate functional groups that span domains, and put only global groups in them. For example, in a network with two domains—Europe and NorthAmerica—with a global group called GLAccounting in each domain, create a universal group called UAccounting that contains the two GLAccounting groups, NorthAmerica\GLAccounting and Europe\GLAccounting. The UAccounting universal group can then be used anywhere in the enterprise. Any changes in the membership of the individual GLAccounting groups will not cause replication of the UAccounting group because nothing has changed in that universal group; it still has just two global groups.

Group Policy

Group policy is a tool that's a little bit ahead of its time. It's designed to provide unparalleled power and flexibility in controlling the complex Windows 2000 environment, but a side effect of that power and granularity makes it potentially very dangerous to use and difficult to support.

One inadvertent setting in group policy can lock out every user in a domain; a goof in another direction can set security wide open. This is especially troublesome from a support viewpoint. If a customer calls into a help desk because he's having trouble accessing a share or logging onto the network, or if an application in another domain is failing, the help desk representative has a potentially complex environment to troubleshoot. In addition to the Windows 2000 environment itself, if group policy objects (GPOs) of any complexity have been implemented on clients in the domain, it can be nearly impossible to figure out what the user can and can't do. At this time, there aren't any tools to help troubleshoot a user with GPOs in an environment. (Ironic, isn't it? You need tools to help support the support tools.) For what it's worth, Microsoft is going easy on its own internal implementation of group policy for these very reasons.

One area in which you might consider carefully implementing group policy is on the server side of things. A few choice GPOs that control access and rights to all servers in a domain—regardless of whether they're domain controllers or member servers—would be a welcome addition to the domain management scheme. These GPOs don't have to be very complex, but you should follow a conservative policy nonetheless. Testing the GPO in a test environment, slowly applying one policy at a time while testing the results, is the way to go. Remember that you can as easily lock all users out of the servers as all the workstations.

WINS Planning

A long time ago, in the days of non-routed networks and Microsoft LAN Manager, NetBIOS was used as a method of establishing and maintaining a name space on the network. Because NetBIOS is broadcast-based, larger routed networks were not suited for such an implementation.

The introduction of the LMHOSTS file enabled computers in both routed and non-routed networks to resolve NetBIOS names to addresses without broadcasts. However, because LMHOSTS files are static text files, they required constant manual updating as new clients are added and as IP addresses change.

The Windows Internet Name Service was developed to be a "dynamic LMHOSTS" system. Its primary functions are to maintain a cross-reference of client NetBIOS names and IP addresses, and to resolve NetBIOS names to IP addresses when queried. However, WINS is more than just name resolution to facilitate net use commands; it has dependencies that include trust relationships, domain logins, and pass through authentication, to name a few. A poor design can cause severe problems with client operation and general network stability.

> **Note**
>
> *So that you can bone up on WINS services, Microsoft has put forth an excellent whitepaper on the subject. I highly recommend printing out a copy for your bathroom literature collection. The paper, "Windows Internet Naming Service (WINS): Architecture and Capacity Planning," can be found at* http://www.microsoft.com/ntserver/nts/techdetails/techspecs/winswp98.asp.

It bears repeating that WINS will be around for quite a while. Even if you magically were able to banish all your NetBIOS applications from your network, every Microsoft client except Windows 2000 Professional relies on

WINS for NetBIOS name resolution. Until you've completed your Windows 2000 client upgrade, WINS will be vital. So, a good WINS architecture is every bit as important as the other network services.

The most important topics in WINS planning are how many WINS servers the network should have, the replication topology, and the server configuration. These topics are covered in the following sections.

How Many WINS Servers?

A common trap that large networks fall into is to deploy too many WINS servers. This is due to several reasons, among them an overemphasis on redundancy. Exacerbating this tendency are ego and turf wars that we are all too familiar with—every shack that houses more than two employees is considered a "site," and "my site must have two WINS servers" to keep up with xyz site. This is an unfortunate side effect of distributed organizations.

So the central question is: What is the ideal number of WINS servers for my network? The answer to this question, of course, will vary primarily upon concentration of your user base and speed/reliability of network connections. What are proper levels of redundancy? Microsoft provides good recommendations in this area, advising to err on the side of fewer WINS services. Their stated capacity for a single WINS service is 10,000 clients, hardware permitting.

The first step in designing the architecture is to land the appropriate number of WINS servers. Ignore site-secondary WINS considerations for now; you'll want no more than one service at each large geographic location. For those locations with more than 10,000 clients, you should consider a second WINS service.

Smaller locations may not need a WINS service at all; they may be able to use another site's WINS. You'll want to evaluate reliability of the link(s) to the adjacent site in making the decision. One good rule of thumb is to compare the WINS replication traffic to the site against the number of registrations and queries that would come from the site. If there will be more replication traffic than registration and query traffic, you probably don't need a WINS service there. For example, if you have a small site of 50 users and your enterprise has 100,000 clients, do you really want to continually push 100,000 entries to that service? You're better off having the 50 clients use a remote WINS.

After you have identified the location of your WINS servers, you'll need to identify site secondaries. Outside of political considerations, there is no need to add services to each site for redundancy. Select an adjacent site's

WINS as a secondary service. Do not designate site secondaries in a recipro-cal fashion (i.e., site A's secondary is site B, and site B's secondary is site A). In the event of a WINS failure, the two sites are now dependent on one server, with no secondary available for either.

Instead, chain them so that site A uses site B's as secondary, site B uses site C's as secondary, and so on.

WINS Replication Topology

For large enterprise networks, you can use several "exotic" designs. These exotic designs are intended to reduce replication traffic. Avoid any replica-tion scheme that does not locate a full copy of the database at each WINS service. This ensures high performance to WINS queries, as well as redun-dancy.

Your replication architecture should follow a basic hub-and-spoke topol-ogy. Each spoke will be a push/pull partner with the hub. The hub should be a dedicated server whose sole responsibility is to replicate with each of the site spokes. This design guarantees a maximum convergence time of two times the replication interval. The number of spokes should be kept to 30 or fewer (see Figure 6.11).

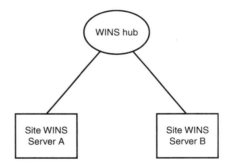

Figure 6.11   *WINS hub-and-spoke architecture.*

For very large enterprise networks, additional hubs may be deployed regionally and may be set up to replicate with one another. Ensure that they replicate in a serial relationship, as shown in Figure 6.12.

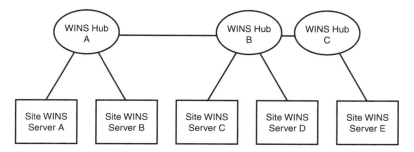

Figure 6.12   *WINS large network hub-and-spoke architecture.*

WINS Server Configuration

Most network administrators follow Microsoft's advice and locate their WINS services on domain controllers. If your WINS server supports a large number of users, it should be on a dedicated member server. Locating WINS on a domain controller can cause problems in high-volume environments because WINS and domain resource demands peak at the same time.

To illustrate what can happen, consider a power failure that knocks down a whole office location (say, about 5,000 users). Power is typically restored all at once, so every client in the location goes through its startup sequence at the same time. This sequence includes broadcasting to find a DHCP server, which among other things returns an address for a WINS server, which in turn gives the client a list of domain controllers (the 1C list of available domain controllers), which it then queries to get authenticated. The local security authority subsystem (LSASS) service is responsible for the domain authentication process, and it runs at a higher priority than the WINS service. This means that as thousands of users are starting up, the WINS service will have to wait until LSASS gives it processor time. The result in the client environment is that the first several hundred clients contact WINS and get authenticated before LSASS is overwhelmed with authentication requests, causing it to dominate the processor. WINS is therefore essentially locked out, so the vast majority of users get "Unable to locate a domain controller" message and are—how shall I delicately put it—hosed. To make things worse, the first thing most users will do upon experiencing this kind of failure will be to reboot and try it all again. You can see how the situation can spiral downhill quickly; it's dangerous to locate a WINS service on a server that can potentially become overused.

For this reason, you should implement WINS on a dedicated server. The server can be light on disk space but heavy on processor and memory (dual-processor, Intel Pentium II, 256MB). The goal here is to throw power at the WINS infrastructure to ensure that it can easily handle peak loads.

Your WINS servers should be located on a central network location such as the site backbone. You'll want to use a high-speed NIC such as 100MB Ethernet. One NIC only is recommended; there have been so many hot fixes for multihomed WINS—do you really want to take the chance that it works flawlessly now?

Further WINS Recommendations

A number of optional settings should be used to prevent problems and keep WINS operating smoothly. Many of these recommendations are the result of bugs that were or will be addressed with service packs. In any case, you lose nothing from putting these into practice. Detailed write-ups of many of these configuration parameters and their benefit can be found in TechNet.

The following are good practices for keeping your WINS servers healthy:

- Compaction for large enterprise networks should be performed monthly, at a minimum. Use the command scheduler (AT, or WINAT.EXE from the Resource Kit) to execute a batch file in interactive mode. The batch file should follow the following general algorithm:

```
Net stop WINS
Jetpack wins.mdb wins.tmp >> compact.log
Net start WINS
```

- Defragmentation should be strongly considered, as WINS is physically disk-intensive. Defragmentation is discussed in Chapter 2, "Storage Services in Windows 2000," and Chapter 5.
- Fill in the Backup Path section so that WINS will perform periodic backups. A backup directory will be created, so it is only necessary to state the path to the WINS files (C:\WinNT\System32\WINS).
- Use the WINS server's own IP address for both primary and secondary. A few problems have been associated with the TCP/IP properties, in particular the primary and secondary WINS settings. Using different WINS servers for primary and secondary can cause WINS registrations to be split between the configured servers. Under certain circumstances, leaving the secondary blank can block the server from acting as a WINS client, although incoming registrations and queries will be serviced.

- Use the following registry key to set the WINS service to a high priority class:

```
HkeyLocalMachine
  System
    CurrentControlSet
      Services
        WINS
          Parameters
            PriorityClassHigh
```

Although less critical on a dedicated platform, this will reduce the drag of other less-important processes on WINS.

- To ensure low convergence time, replication intervals on all servers should be set to 30 minutes.

- Service timers (Renewal, Extinction, Extinction time-out, and Verify Intervals) should be left to defaults, as Microsoft recommends.

WINS Client Recommendations

The following are recommendations for WINS-related settings in the client's TCP/IP Protocol Properties:

- DNS lookup will allow the resolution of non-WINS clients, assuming that a static entry has not been made in WINS (in which case, it would have been resolved by WINS). If your network does have non-WINS clients, it's a good idea to check the "Use DNS lookup" checkbox, as well as other DNS options such as DNS Name Servers and DNS Searchlist.

- For DHCP-enabled WINS clients, LMHOSTS lookup should not be enabled. If individual users wish to maintain their own LMHOSTS files, they can modify their individual configuration for this.

- The same recommendations apply to WINS clients that aren't DHCP-enabled, primarily servers. On servers, you might consider using LMHOSTS as a backup to WINS. In the event of WINS failure or corruption, the LMHOSTS file could provide resolution for Domain group entries that are critical to interdomain authentication and login. For example, your resource domain controllers must be capable of identifying MAD controllers to process client logins. If WINS is not available to pass IP addresses of MAD controllers, your users (and their managers) will not be happy. Having an LMHOSTS file with #DOM entries may save the day.

The problem with this argument is that your clients will also need WINS to identify their resource domains controller address(es); therefore, to maintain functionality in the event of the failure of both WINS servers, an elaborate network of LMHOSTS files will need to be implemented and maintained. You're better off putting the effort into ensuring that your WINS servers are on solid, fault-tolerant platforms.

- Every WINS client must have both primary and secondary WINS configured, even if they are to the same WINS server. The reason for this is that Windows NT will swap the primary and secondary entries if resolution or registration with the primary fails. If the secondary entry is left blank, this swapping will move the blank entry to the primary setting, in effect preventing the machine from acting as a WINS client.

Note

In some unique cases you may not want a client to register with WINS. For example, imagine an isolated network subnet that's used for backing up servers to a network backup server. A subnet like this is inaccessible to normal user subnets. Servers that use this backup network must obviously have a NIC attached on this backup subnet and an IP address associated with the NIC. Registering this interface with WINS will cause resolution failures because users might obtain this address from WINS, but they can't access the subnet. The solution is to leave the primary and secondary WINS fields blank for the NIC addresses you don't wish to advertise to clients.

- Once you've deployed Windows NT 4 Service Pack 4 to your static (non-DHCP) clients, a useful option, NBTSTAT -RR, will be available. This allows changes to the client's TCP/IP properties dynamically (without reboot), enabling the refreshing of WINS entries and changing of WINS configurations without downtime.
- The manual delete function in WINSADMIN works fine if your network contains a handful of WINS services. For managing several dozen, you'll want to have the capability of deleting entries from all WINS services on your network. This may be used to clear invalid addresses or corrupted entries. A batch file using the WINSCL tool in the Windows NT Resource Kit can be hacked together, taking a list of WINS servers and NetBIOS names as arguments. The time spent hacking up such a tool will be well worth it.

DHCP Planning

DHCP is critical to the success of a Windows 2000 implementation because it's the very first service in a series of services that the client uses to configure itself and then to locate services in the network.

The particular area in which DHCP is important to Windows 2000 is that it tells the client what DNS services to use. DNS is used to locate everything else in a pure Windows 2000 network. DHCP also configures WINS settings, the NetBIOS node time, the default gateway, time servers, and just about any other network client service you can think of.

Fortunately, DHCP is one of the few areas that hasn't changed radically for Windows 2000, so my recommendations are pretty straightforward:

- Locate your DHCP services on DNS servers. This has a couple of advantages. The first is that if you have set DNS to be Active Directory-integrated, every DNS server is a primary and therefore updateable. Installing DHCP on this server ensures that dynamic updates to DNS from DHCP happen within the server instead of over the network. The second advantage is that if you land two DNS servers per zone for fault tolerance, you've set the servers up for split DHCP scopes.

- Split your DHCP scopes for fault tolerance. In other words, take the range of IP addresses you wish to be dynamically allocated, split it in half, and assign each to the DHCP service on your two DNS servers (a *DHCP service pair*). This ensures that if one service is unavailable, the remaining one can continue to provide leases until its scope fills up.

  Figure 6.13 is an MMC console showing how this is done. One DHCP server is displayed in each window, and together the two cover an address range from 10.45.65.1 to 10.45.65.254. The top DHCP server, FWSNT5DC1, covers the first half of the range from 10.45.65.1 to 10.45.65.127. The first 20 addresses are excluded from the pool for non-DHCP network equipment. The bottom DHCP server, FWSNT5DC2, covers the second half of the range from 10.45.65.128 to 10.45.65.254. (It also has a 20-address exclusion range.)

- Put one of the services on a DNS server (assuming you have local DNS services). Much communication takes place between DNS and DHCP in Windows 2000; co-locating the services can only help.

- Keep the services off domain controllers. They'll have enough to do in Windows 2000 as it is, and the Active Directory services on the server will have a higher priority than DHCP.

- Traditionally, servers have had static IP addresses to ensure that they remain stable in DNS's static zone files. Now that DHCP and DNS are tightly integrated, you can enable DHCP on servers. You should be careful to distinguish the network information you supply a server via DHCP, however. Use DHCP user classes to configure DHCP options by server type. For example, DHCP options for a user class of "WINS" on one DHCP server will have the WINS server's own address (as recommended), while a file/print server will have the same WINS addresses as a client might.

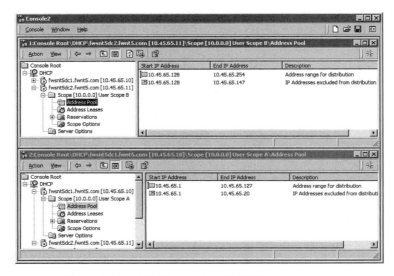

Figure 6.13   *MMC console of DHCP service pair.*

Replication Miscellany

Replication is a complex topic, so it can't hurt to look at it from a different perspective in hopes of explaining it better.

The Layered Look

All the areas in domain design affect replication, and they also all affect each other. This can get *very* confusing, so let's look at the various naming contexts again in a layered manner, in a simplified example. Figure 6.14 is a simple three-domain tree showing domain boundaries, trust relationships, and domain controllers.

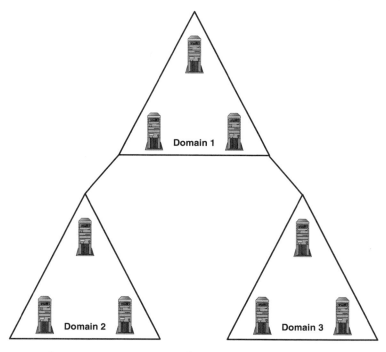

Figure 6.14 *Domain topology with domain controllers.*

Figure 6.15 adds a layer that shows replication within a domain.

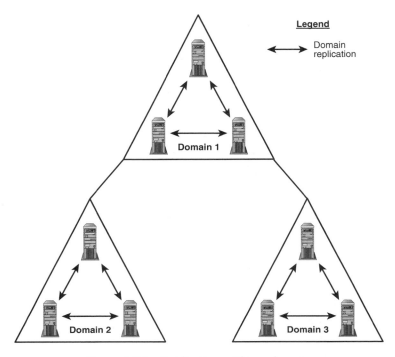

Figure 6.15   *Replication within a domain.*

Figure 6.16 adds sites to the picture. Note that that intersite replication is different than intrasite replication.

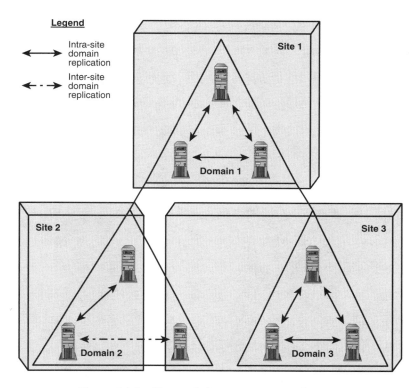

Figure 6.16 *Sites and their impact on replication.*

Figure 6.17 adds site connector objects. Notice the servers in Site 2. The lower-right server is in another site, and this server is a bridgehead server along with its partner to the left.

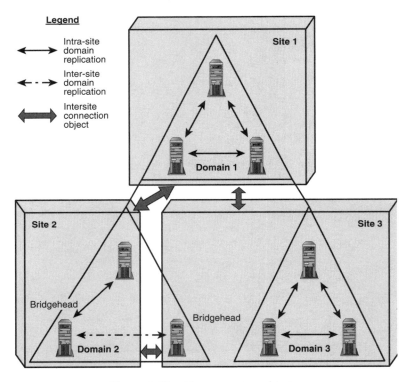

Figure 6.17   *Site connector objects.*

Figure 6.18 adds a layer that shows replication between Global Catalog servers. This is a logical representation; Global Catalog replication traffic doesn't go directly between Global Catalog servers in different sites.

We've built up a somewhat accurate representation of the replication that takes place in this very simple example. However, Figure 6.18 still doesn't show the true bridgehead server replication paths. It also doesn't show replication between the Windows 2000 domain controllers and downlevel Windows NT 4 domain controllers that your entire client population will be using until they migrate to Windows 2000 Professional.

This example helps demonstrate why you need to KISS (keep it simple, stupid) your domain and site architecture as much as possible. With a moderate number of domains and sites, your support staff will *never* be able to keep track of replication. (And you thought Windows NT 4 trust management was bad!)

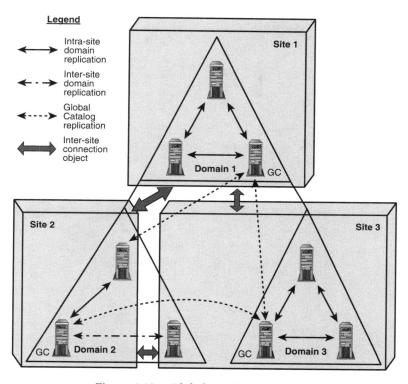

Figure 6.18 *Global Catalog replication.*

Replication Classes

You can classify the amount of Windows 2000 replication traffic that will go across any given network segment (LAN or WAN) into four categories, from the highest amount of traffic to the lowest (Figure 6.19):

- Class A (intradomain, intrasite): Figure 6.19, location A. Full, uncompressed domain. Global Catalog replication traffic takes place at regular (default is 5 minutes) intervals. *Typical use:* LAN connectivity inside a campus or over a very high-quality WAN topology.

- Class B (intradomain, intersite): Figure 6.19, location B. Both domain and Global Catalog replication traffic occurs over the segment. This traffic is schedulable and compressed via site connection objects. *Typical use:* Business locations whose users belong to a regional (i.e., large) domain, but whose WAN circuits require extra control over replication.

- Class C (interdomain, intrasite): Figure 6.19, location C. The segment is between domains, so only Global Catalog replication traffic takes place. However, because the segment is inside a site, the traffic is not schedulable (by default, it occurs every 5 minutes) and is uncompressed. (This is a bit confusing, because site connectors between bridgehead servers are shown in the figure only in a logical sense, with block arrows. In reality, a site connector would be established between the two servers bracketing point C.). *Typical use:* Business unit that requires a different account policy for its users (or some other factor that forces a domain instead of an OU), but whose connectivity is good enough that it doesn't need special control over its replication schedule.

- Class D (interdomain, intersite): Figure 6.19, location D. No domain replication traffic takes place over the segment because it's between two (or more) domains. Global Catalog replication occurs, but because the segment is intersite (between sites) it's schedulable and compressed via site connection objects. *Typical use:* Slow link/autonomous location, or controlled country.

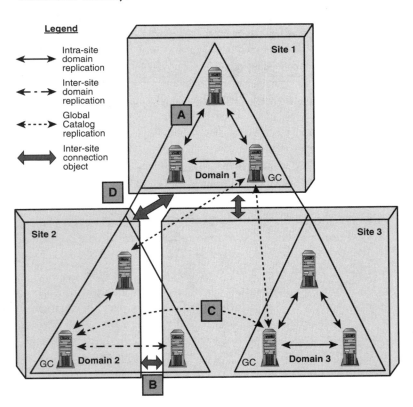

Figure 6.19 *Replication classes.*

Summary

A good Windows 2000 core services design is a well-balanced work of compromise. Every major component you're trying to minimize—domains, sites, replication, domain controllers, Global Catalog servers—conflicts at some level with every other component and with the client's goals. Much of it reduces down to an interplay of replication versus bandwidth; how much of one are you willing to give up for the other? After a while, you find yourself going around and around in an endless loop of changing variables. To move forward, you must take one aspect of the design, such as the number of sites (because it's based on something physical) and put a stake in the ground. Only then can you proceed with the rest of the design.

Keep your design as simple as possible. Hopefully this chapter has demonstrated the many interrelating layers that must fit together in a Windows 2000 network. You can see how administration in a multidomain, multisite, multi-OU Windows NT network could quickly grow far beyond the ability of a group to manage it. Troubleshooting this environment—especially when it's mixed between Windows 2000 servers and Windows NT 4 servers, Windows 2000 clients, and Windows NT 4 clients—will be challenging enough (to put it nicely); don't make it harder on yourself than you need to. Don't design yourself out of a job! Remember that unlike its predecessors, Windows 2000 allows you to dynamically create and remove domains, sites, and OUs, so you aren't stuck forever with your initial design. Start conservatively, and wait until the dust settles before you begin experimenting with new features. There are enough of them in Windows 2000's initial release to keep you busy for a long time.

7

Preparing a Windows NT 4 Network for Windows 2000

If you've just read Chapter 6, "Designing Your Windows 2000 Core Services," you might be thinking, "What does he mean, preparing a Windows NT 4 network? Isn't that what the last chapter was about? Don't I have enough to do on this project already?" The point behind this chapter is to help you work smart early in the project's life cycle so that you don't find yourself out of time or resources in some major areas.

Let's assume that you're a diligent Windows NT administrator or designer and that you're attending all the briefings, reading all the documentation, and generally trying to figure out how to use the product. That's a fairly safe assumption; after all, you *are* reading this book. What else should you or your company be doing to get ready? Because you're a few white papers ahead of the pack, you're treated as the default Windows 2000 guru. Use this position as a bully pulpit—tell other groups in the company what they should be doing *now* to prepare them for the Windows 2000 project.

Getting ready for Windows 2000 does include quite a few areas that need advance preparation—besides just learning the product and getting the technical design right. Some of this is design-related, but a lot of it is boring grunt work that we've all been putting off for months or years. I'll break my recommendations down into similar areas as Chapter 6: servers, domains, network services (such as DNS, DHCP, and WINS), plus various support items such as project issues, a pilot program, third-party tools, and politics.

Servers

Servers are the building blocks of a Windows NT network, the bricks or timbers that hold the structure together. You can take some actions on your servers now to make your Windows 2000 upgrades or rebuilds easier:

- Prepare for hardware upgrades, especially memory. Chapter 4, "Choosing the Box," goes into more detail in this area, but in short, both domain controllers and member servers will probably need memory and/or processor upgrades.

- Consider moving resources (e.g., file and print services) off your domain controllers. Unlike member servers, NT Server 4 domain controllers can't be moved from domain to domain. It's true that you can demote Windows 2000 servers from domain controllers to member servers, but to bring a Windows NT 4 domain controller to this point, you must upgrade its domain. If you aren't ready to deal with those issues just to move some file services, you have more flexibility if your domain controllers are dedicated to only authenticating users.

- Ensure that all your Windows NT 4 servers are running at least Service Pack 4. This is probably a no-brainer because it's required for Y2K compatibility; I'm more interested for its compatibility with NTFS Version 5. If you must perform a Windows NT 4 system recovery as a result of a failed Windows 2000 upgrade, and if the backed-up system doesn't have SP4 installed, it won't recognize any pre-existing NTFS partitions.

- Here's another variation on the dedicated domain controller theme: Be sure that DNS, WINS, and DHCP are removed from the domain controllers that you intend to keep for Windows 2000. This way, you can perform a clean Windows 2000 install rather than an upgrade, and not worry about keeping the various service databases intact during the upgrade.

- Standardize all your servers on Windows NT 4 and the latest Service Pack to minimize the number of variables you must deal with in the upgrade/migration process.

- When you're selecting hardware, be sure to choose server configurations that support I_2O, hot plug PCI, and (eventually) Microsoft Clustering Service.

Domains

Clean up your directory. Now is the time get your resources straightened out so that you don't have to move them. You need to investigate and clean up these areas:

- User accounts—unused accounts, special accounts, disabled accounts
- Groups—redundant or extinct global and local groups
- Naming conventions—accounts, servers, workstations, printers
- Network shares—extinct personal and group (especially group) shares

Cleaning up your directory is a long, tedious task. You can use third-party reporting tools that extract information you can't normally get to, such as how many days (or years) since an account logged on.

As part of this trimming, you need to identify and determine ownership of all your Windows NT resources. This includes the following:

- Personal shares—Check out resources named and shared with the user's Windows NT account.
- Group shares—This will require more detective work. Identify the owner and description of the share.
- Servers—Make sure that the description field has updated information on its hardware, ownership (if not IT), and location.
- Workstations/PCs—When these systems have a single owner, make sure their names reflect that ownership.
- Customer global and local groups—As with a group share, you need owner and backup owner information and a description of the group's purpose.
- Printers and printer queues—Include printer type, black-and-white or color, any other special characteristics (such as paper type), and location.

Get at least two names for each resource: the owner and the manager. This will ensure that you still have a contact name if one person changes position.

Windows NT 4 isn't capable of storing all the information that can be loaded into the Active Directory; you must come up with your own database. For small networks, Microsoft Access will probably do the job. For medium to large networks, you should use Microsoft SQL Server—not so much for its power as for its capability to allow many users to read from and write to a table simultaneously. A larger network is much more likely than a small network to have several account clerks writing resource information at the same time. When you build the tables, you should use the exact object and attribute names in the Active Directory so that there's no confusion about where it should go. Again, this is where a reporting tool can be invaluable; you can use it to tell you what has been named so that you can zoom in on what hasn't.

Examine the Active Directory schema and decide what objects and attributes you're going to populate. The Active Directory's usefulness is directly proportional to how much interesting data you populate it with. For example, if you put a user's manager in his user object (and make it part of the user organizational move process to ensure that it stays updated), you can track the organization's structure right up to the CEO.

Examine the Active Directory schema and decide whether you must extend it with new objects or attributes. Extending the schema isn't something you should do before thinking very carefully about the consequences, however. Add objects or attributes to the schema only if you've examined all the existing objects and attributes and have decided that there's nothing already there than can do the job.

Get the word out to independent domains—if you expect to join the enterprise forest, don't upgrade before your time. An independent domain is a domain that isn't part of the trusted network. After you have upgraded a domain to Windows 2000 and have chosen its DNS name, the domain can't be changed to a new name (i.e., to join an existing tree) without demoting all domain controllers and starting over. Of course, this means that if a Windows NT 4 domain is upgraded, all the objects from the original Windows NT 4 domain will be destroyed.

Fallout from this restriction is the realization that your customer groups (and other groups that weren't your customers) will be pushing for Windows 2000 migration sooner that you expect. The other alternative is for the really stiff-necked independent domains to perform their own upgrades independently—and wait or hope for an integration tool to eventually be released from Microsoft.

Make corporate HR aware of the value of feeds from the HR database into the Active Directory. All large corporations have some kind of human resources database with employee information. This is the reference for active employees and is immediately updated when employees take different positions or are terminated. This is priceless information for the Active Directory, especially to populate the User object and keep it current. These are some of the User object fields you might populate from the HR database:

- User's first and last name.
- User's display name—This is the name the user prefers to go by
- Office location—This may be available from the HR database, but at least the building code is quite useful.
- Telephone, pager, fax, cell phone numbers—There's an attribute for every possible number you could think up.

- Email addresses—Include information for work and home email addresses.

- Personal (intranet) Web site—Here you can find information on the employee's projects, weeklies, and so on.

- Organizational information—This includes the user's title, department, and division.

- Manager's name—If kept up with feeds from an HR database, this data outlines the organizational structure when rolled up.

Figure 7.1 shows some of the many attributes of the User object. Many of the individual pages have push buttons that lead you deeper and deeper into less-commonly used attributes, creating a very complex user interface.

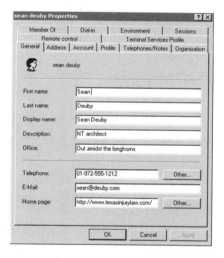

Figure 7.1   *The User object properties dialog box.*

When the Active Directory is populated with this data, every Windows 98 and Windows 2000 client can perform directory searches for people's email and phone numbers right from their Start menu. This is similar to a trick you can perform with Exchange and Outlook: Instead of looking up the user in the corporate HR database, simply create an email and put their name in the subject line. When Outlook resolves the name, simply double-click on it to get all the information Exchange has on the user—in particular, his phone number. It's usually much faster than an HR lookup.

Figure 7.2 shows the dialog box that results from choosing Start, Search, For People.

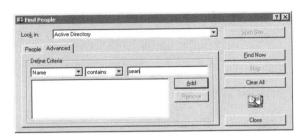

Figure 7.2   *The advanced Find People dialog box.*

If you chose to search MyCompany's Active Directory for all users whose name contained "Sean," you might come up with an interesting search result (see Figure 7.3).

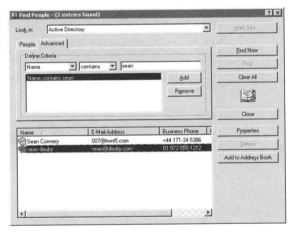

Figure 7.3   *Search results for names that contain "Sean".*

By double-clicking on a name, you can review five property sheets full of information. (Of course, all of Mr. Connery's information is classified.)

You can use this same method to find specific printers. For example, let's assume that you travel from one office location to another for a meeting. In the conference room (which is wired to the office LAN) you discover that you need to print a report. Using the same search engine, you can request a color printer located on your floor of the office building. You don't have to know the name; the Find tool will locate the best printer for you based on your selection criteria (assuming that the resources were input correctly into the Active Directory).

Network Services

WINS and DHCP network services don't change that much in Windows 2000, but the impact of DNS on this new release more than makes up for them. The following sections list recommendations (or warnings) for these services.

DNS

The following are my recommendations for using DNS:

- Become familiar with DNS. By this, I mean get really comfortable with it—now. Understand your company's DNS namespace inside and out. You will have to work with the DNS and Internet team to figure out how to integrate the Windows 2000 namespace into the existing DNS namespace.

- Change your NetBIOS names to fit standard DNS naming conventions. To support the legacy NetBIOS naming rules, Microsoft DNS will support underscores in resource names, but RFC-standard DNS servers such as BIND won't. Change your resources by using underscores to hyphenate—and don't use spaces.

- Establish a good rapport with the naming services team. Traditionally, the DNS environment has been the realm of UNIX administrators who move in different circles than Windows NT folks. It's time for this to change. Windows NT has long since come out of the broom closet and into the data center; we aren't (necessarily) minions of The Evil Empire. A good DNS namespace design is critical to the success of Windows 2000. This requires that you actually *talk* to the naming services people. Have lunch with them on a regular basis. Stay on top of what they're doing, and keep them updated with the naming issues you're encountering. Team members should become familiar with Windows NT domain basics so that they begin taking Windows 2000 considerations into account. The final DNS namespace design for Windows 2000 must be integrated into your corporate namespace as much as possible.

- Begin your DNS namespace design, teamed with DNS support, as early as possible. (I've harped on this already in Chapter 6. but I'll repeat it at every opportunity.)

DHCP

The Dynamic Host Configuration Protocol is a vital network service for a Windows NT network of any size, not only because of its assignment of IP address but because it configures all the other critical network services as well.

The following are my recommendations for preparing your DHCP services for Windows 2000:

- Here's a really basic recommendation: If you don't use it yet, get it deployed now! Search with the keywords "DHCP" and "deploy" at www.microsoft.com for more information.

- Move the DHCP service pair off domain controllers to member servers. As I've mentioned before, you should rebuild domain controllers rather than upgrade them to Windows 2000, and you can't do this if you have service databases on the server to keep intact.

- At least one—and preferably both—of the DHCP service pair at each location should be relocated to a DNS server. This prepares the pair for DHCP/DNS integration in Windows 2000.

- In DHCP options for each scope, specify primary and secondary WINS, as well as WINS/NBT node type.

- Take advantage of DHCP to configure WINS settings for your clients. This also allows you to easily reconfigure client's WINS settings as you work toward "end-of-lifing" that service.

- Your "WINS/NBT node type" setting dictates the order of operations in which your WINS clients will attempt name resolution. The recommended setting for most circumstances, H-node (hybrid), will first attempt WINS resolution, then attempt broadcast, and then try DNS and LMHOSTS resolution if those options are configured.

  If at least the primary WINS server is specified in the client configuration, the node type defaults to H-node. Because of this, it's not required to specify the node type, but it should be done anyway to avoid confusion.

WINS

Most of you are not in the enviable position of deploying a brand new WINS infrastructure; rather, you have probably inherited an existing WINS environment that is less than ideal. The typical dysfunctional environment will probably have the following characteristics: too many WINS servers, underpowered domain controllers, and an inefficient replication topology.

Some of the problems you are probably experiencing center on replication and general performance:

- Domain login problems ("No domain controller could be found" messages)
- Credential authentication failures
- WINS services that spontaneously shut down
- New WINS entries that fail to propagate
- Old, invalid WINS entries that persist with bad IP addresses
- Client resolution failures due to lack of timely response, outdated entries, or lack of entries
- Inconsistent drive mappings
- Secure channel trust failures

You can take some corrective actions immediately with a small amount of effort:

- Apply the latest Service Pack to your WINS servers immediately.
- Audit the configuration of your WINS servers and apply the recommended options as described in this chapter—in particular monthly compaction of the WINS database and priority class upgrading.

You can get additional infrastructure improvements from the following tips, but they will require some planning and potentially additional hardware:

- Evaluate your replication scheme. Changing the replication scheme of your environment will not affect operations if you plan it intelligently. If your architecture does not already follow a hub and spoke model, implement a new topology following the recommendations in Chapter 6. This may require the addition of dedicated WINS servers to support the hub topology. Set your replication intervals at 30 minutes.
- Replace shared WINS servers with dedicated WINS servers. You can do this by using the same IP address for the new server as the old WINS server and by quickly bringing one offline and the other online. This avoids the time-consuming and risky repointing of client and servers to new IP addresses.
- If your WINS service resides on a domain controller, and if an excessive amount of BDCs exist in your environment, the BDC can be rebuilt as a member server and the WINS database can be restored. This method requires no incremental hardware usage. However, if the BDC cannot be spared, a new one can be brought up with a new IP address.

- If the server is shared by multiple services such as DHCP, Web, or applications, you must take another course of action. Some of these services are dependent on either IP address or NetBIOS name consistency.

- Retire excess WINS services. This step is the most time-consuming and potentially dangerous in terms of user impact because clients and servers may find themselves without WINS. The Windows NT Resource Kit tool WINSDUMP will enable you to track all WINS entries and their owning services. When a WINS service no longer owns registrations, make use of the Persona Non Grata feature when retiring services (see Microsoft TechNet for details).

WINS Group entries are limited to 25 IP addresses; therefore, domains with more than 25 controllers will see IP address drop (the first into the group are the first kicked out) as new controllers are added. The simple solution here is to have fewer than 25 domain controllers per domain.

Support

Start re-examining your support model, and begin a series of meetings toward distributed administration. This should involve fairly high-level managers; your job is to make a presentation to them that forcefully conveys the need/opportunity surrounding this new product. Is it centralized or decentralized now? Where should it be in the future? This is a chance to fix old fissures.

You must also evaluate your support tools. The odds are good that none of them will work with Windows 2000 in their current version. You must look to the vendor for a new version, or—if you've written your own—write a new one. (This is one of the many drawbacks of building your own tools.) It's also a good opportunity to examine the tools that have been written especially for Windows 2000. Tools new to Windows 2000 don't have to provide continuity with a Windows NT 4 model, so they may better take advantage of the new version's features.

The Windows 2000 Project

As with any major project, up-front preparation is very important. Because Windows 2000 can change the entire support model, all the stakeholders in this current model must be involved. Here are some recommendations related to the Windows 2000 project itself:

- Begin with the end in mind. What exactly is the business case to be made for what Windows 2000 can provide?

- Form a coherent, enterprise-wide design team. One very important piece of preparatory work must be done for Windows 2000, and it's so obvious that it can be overlooked: To create a coherent directory architecture across the enterprise, you must have a coherent, enterprise-wide design team. In the easiest implementation, this may mean a centralized IS department responsible for the entire corporation. This also could be as complex as a team with voting and non-voting members from divisions around with world, with the resultant turf wars and cultural differences thrown in for spice.

- You need warm bodies. If you plan to move from your existing Windows NT 4 model to a completely new Windows 2000 model, you need resources—lots of human resources that understand how the Windows 2000 Active Directory works. You need resources to help in the design, testing, pilot, requirements, communications, organization, resource identification and cataloging—the list goes on. Send up a flag to your high-level managers (including the CIO) right away; this will be a big project.

- Consult members of your Exchange team on the design—they've worked with similar concepts for quite a while already. Windows 2000 is more sophisticated in how it handles the concepts, but it's similar. Exchange will also immediately be your biggest Global Catalog load and will be your biggest Active Directory customer with Release 6.0.

The Windows 2000 Pilot

As in any project of significant size, you must run a production pilot. The pilot accomplishes several things:

- It puts your Windows 2000 design in a proving ground, a middle environment somewhere between your test lab and full production. This is where you begin getting user feedback on how well the thing works.

- It gives you and your team a first pass at what supporting such an environment will be like. You get to first encounter and document user difficulties unique to Windows 2000. These findings will be passed on to the help desk.

- Metrics taken during the pilot help set expectations for your production release.

If it's successful, a Windows 2000 pilot can turn into the production environment. An alternative is to create a new production environment from the lessons of the pilot and then keep the pilot environment for a new release or feature testing outside the test lab.

Your Windows 2000 pilot should have the same domain configuration, go over similar WAN topology, use similar sites, and have similar percentages of domain user populations as the production effort. In essence, it *is* the production design, only in miniature form. Unless you have a terrific lab, this means involving people from all over the company in the major locations at which you intend to deploy Windows 2000.

Your pilot must have a clear definition of success or failure, and it must be measurable. If your client's requirement is that client logons should take no longer than they do in Windows NT 4, then you need numbers of how long an average Windows NT 4 client logon takes. You also need to find out where these numbers were taken and determine whether you can take yours at the same location.

You must decide what metrics are important and then take them throughout the pilot. For example, do you want to monitor replication traffic? That particular one is tough because although you can measure the traffic with a network monitor, the amount of traffic generated depends on about 10 or 15 different variables. A simpler metric, such as memory utilization on a domain controller, can be better represented because it has fewer variables that must be accounted for. This is not to say that you shouldn't track whatever metrics you need to; just account for all the factors that influence them.

Take measurements in a reproducible manner. First take baseline measurements. For example, how much memory utilization does an idle domain controller have? Next introduce your users into the environment in batches, and take a measurement. Continue the process until your pilot is fully populated. If you've done it right and understand what you're measuring, you can extrapolate rough metrics with production-size populations. In other words, if you know the memory utilization of a 256MB, dual Pentium II server with 100, 200, and 300 users, you could reasonably guess its utilization with 500 or 600 users. You have to be careful how far you go, however; every server has a finite limit of how many clients it can service, and your predictions go out the window once that figure is reached.

Expend every effort in your pilot project as you would in production, and don't be afraid to make mistakes and learn from them here. The costs associated with the pilot stage are trivial compared to discovering a problem during the production rollout.

Third-Party Tools

Take this opportunity to implement a few new tools into your environment. Tasks such as security auditing, event log management, and resource reporting are well-represented by third-party tools. All these things must be done, and the reason you haven't done some of them up to now is because they're a real pain to do manually. Now you can let the tools do the grunt work for you.

Tools have been devised that make the migration path from Windows NT 4 to Windows 2000 as painless as possible. This doesn't imply that it's entirely painless—just less painful than if you attempt it manually. If you do decide that this is the right path for you, two companies can make your way easier. Mission Critical Software (MCS) and FastLane Technologies (both covered in Chapter 8, "Migrating a Windows NT 4 Network to Windows 2000") are the two leading suppliers of Windows NT domain administration and migration tools. (Personally, I wish these companies were publicly held. I consider MCS the leader in Windows NT administration products and FastLane the leader in migration products.)

Note

I was fortunate to work with and provide feedback on some of the early betas of Mission Critical Software's Enterprise Administrator product before anyone but Texaco, which MCS used as its "development site." (I have a hilarious memory of a conversation with Louis Woodhill, who with his brother Jim founded the company. I had a technical question and couldn't get in touch with Tom Bernhard, the product's system architect. Louis got the message and called me back from his cell phone while jogging around a track in Houston—we had about a half hour conversation! He's in pretty good shape.)

Mission Critical's products are very highly regarded and very popular because they fill a glaring need: that of simplified yet distributed enterprise Windows NT management. A whole parade of big companies, including Microsoft, use Enterprise Administrator to manage their Windows NT environments. Mission Critical will be happy to show you its many satisfied customers at http://www.missioncritical.com/. ◆

Politics—the Eighth OSI Model Layer

When you examine the seven-layer OSI model for network communications, keep in mind that the eighth layer—politics—rides on top of everything else and determines how a major Windows NT network plan is finally implemented. I can't overemphasize the importance of politics in Windows NT network design. Unless you work for the most autocratic of MIS departments, politics will affect every aspect of your design and deployment and can ultimately pick apart the network design if you ignore it.

> **Note**
>
> *As an example of political turf wars, consider the lowly WINS server. According to Microsoft, one WINS server should be configured for every 10,000 users. In reality, what can happen is that every major physical site, regardless of size, wants a WINS server to call its own. It's not uncommon for a Windows NT network to have three to five times the number of WINS servers actually called for in the original design.* ◆

The best way to avoid the worst of the politics is to have a clear mandate from the CIO to get Windows 2000 accomplished *together*, not as a collection of administrative fiefdoms with their own turf to protect. This assumes, of course, that all the administrative groups ultimately report to the CIO. If that's not the case, good luck—you'll need the personality of Mahatma Ghandi to bring the disparate groups together.

The next best way to keep politics to a minimum is to get all the major players involved. This means involving your stakeholders as much as possible and communicating, communicating, communicating. This is a very political area by its nature—there are always turf wars over servers—and the only way to defuse much of it is to make sure that everyone feels like their needs are being met. A nice project technique is to assign the loudest complainers the responsibility for solutions to their complaints that satisfy everyone. Work with the various teams to get a standard set of domain models and OUs hashed out.

Now is the time to begin discussions on who should run what resources in your corporate domains. Even though administrators of domains that IT doesn't own are isolated from a security viewpoint, they can easily screw up *your* domains. If they upgrade all their Windows NT 4 domain controllers to Windows 2000 and then make them domain controllers again, they've increased the replication traffic in their site. If they designate them all to be Global Catalog servers, they have affected the entire forest because they've increased the complexity of the Global Catalog replication topology across the enterprise. What if they change a user's attribute that controls email? Will the local administrators be expected to fix it, or will the call go to the corporate email group?

A ground rule is that one group (i.e., IT) should control the domain controllers for the entire company. These servers have enterprisewide effects, and (if you build them as I recommend) their only function is to perform authentication. Put it to your customer groups like this: "If you take care of the applications, we'll handle the plumbing."

Summary

When you first take responsibility for a Windows 2000 project, the natural reaction is to run off and hide. Of course, you aren't running *away*; you just need to focus on learning everything you can about the product as quickly as possible. But you should remember that the Windows 2000 project, in our own parlance, is not a single-threaded project. Multiple threads can be running at one time. While you're off learning about DNS, other team members can be working on hardware upgrades and support models, evaluating third-party tools, and meeting with the Exchange team. Lots of advance areas need to be covered before a smooth rollout, and you can't do it all. Get help—there's room for just about everyone who wants to join the Windows 2000 bandwagon.

8

Migrating a Windows NT 4 Network to Windows 2000

Devising a plan for how to migrate your existing systems from Windows NT 4 to Windows 2000 should take longer than the initial network design. It's a long process; you must do the following (in no particular order):

- Test your server applications for Windows 2000 compatibility
- Develop backout plans for everything
- Upgrade domain controllers
- Upgrade domains, in the correct order
- Choose a migration method
- Decide when to move to native mode
- Prepare your support organizations for intermediate and mixed environments
- Decide whether to perform domain restructuring
- Execute a pilot program to provide everyone (including your team) with badly needed real-world Windows 2000 experience

This is a daunting task, but there are some bright spots. For starters, you can choose how fast to proceed at almost every point. The intermediate environment of mixed Windows 2000 servers, Windows NT 4 servers, and non-Windows 2000 clients will function at every step of the migration path; whether you *should* remain at any point for long determines how complicated the support model is. Troubleshooting user infrastructure problems such as logon failure, inability to locate domain controllers, password synchronization, and so on, are extremely difficult in such complex environments because most members of the support staff don't understand the principles well enough—and especially because none have any experience with it.

Another positive feature of performing this upgrade is that (if you do a good job) the perceived user environment will change very little until you *want* it to change. If you migrate users to a new domain, they'll need to choose the new names from the domain pick list, and new features such as Dfs and RSM will not be much different. The biggest change users will see comes when they upgrade to the Windows 2000 Professional client.

The upgrade from Windows NT 4 to Windows 2000 has a very different impact than the upgrade from Windows NT 3.51 to 4. Because that upgrade was largely a user interface change, it affected clients' day-to-day work quite a bit. The way they found programs changed, and the Office suite and mail client probably upgraded as well. The Windows NT 4 to Windows 2000 upgrade, however, is more of an infrastructure upgrade; Windows NT is changing dramatically behind the scenes, but the user interface doesn't change much for the casual office user (although the magically appearing toolbar menus are a bit startling at first).

Note

A disclaimer: I make no attempt to turn this chapter into an absolute practical reference on this topic because such a reference doesn't exist yet for Windows 2000, even from Microsoft. No one has amassed enough experience in the upgrade process to truthfully state otherwise. What this chapter does is discuss the various options, raise issues you should be aware of when planning your migration, and make recommendations where appropriate. ◆

This chapter discusses migration topics in sort of a micro- to macroscopic manner, starting at the server level with individual server upgrades and ending with your systems in a Windows 2000 forest.

The Upgrade Process

The Windows 2000 upgrade process within a domain is clearly laid out in Microsoft's documentation, but most of the pitfalls aren't. What follows are strategies for upgrading the various elements of a Windows NT 4 domain to Windows 2000.

Upgrading a Domain Controller

How you decide to upgrade a domain controller depends a lot on how you configure your domain controllers and what other services you allow to run on them.

The important thing to know about domain controller upgrades is that unless you're promoting the PDC, a domain controller doesn't retain its SAM database; it's destroyed. During the PDC upgrade, after the operating system is installed, DCPROMO is automatically invoked to promote the (at this point) member server to domain controller. During this process, the Windows 2000 domain is created. If the upgrade is run against anything else, the Windows NT 4 SAM is simply removed.

This means that if your BDCs don't run other services such as DHCP, or DNS, the best upgrade isn't an upgrade at all. You should perform a fresh install of Windows 2000 and clobber the previous Windows NT 4 installation. This is a much simpler situation, ensures a clean install of Windows 2000 with no upgrade compatibility issues, and creates a potentially more reliable system.

You may be tempted initially to hedge your bets and set up a dual-boot situation on backup domain controllers that have had a fresh Windows 2000 installation. With both Windows NT 4 and Windows 2000 systems you can easily back out if there's any problem with the upgrade, right? Well, it ain't as easy as that. Assuming that you've upgraded more than one domain controller, backing one down to Windows NT 4 in such a mixed mode environment could potentially be very confusing to Active Directory (which thinks it has been upgraded and now suddenly doesn't accept its requests), Windows NT 4 (the PDC has probably disappeared from the server Windows NT 4 system thought it was on), support staff (who can't tell which server is at which level now), and the user.

If you do have services such as DHCP, WINS, or DNS installed on your domain controller (which is not recommended before the upgrade—see Chapter 7, "Preparing a Windows NT 4 Network for Windows 2000"), you must perform an upgrade. Certainly if the server is the PDC for the domain, you must perform an upgrade. The minimum required amount of free disk space is 650MB before the upgrade will even run. (Chapter 5, "Building, Maintaining, and Tuning the Box," goes into more detail on how much disk space you should have and why.)

The following are the general upgrade steps you should follow for a domain controller:

1. Perform a full backup of the system, including the Registry.

2. Before you start the upgrade, run the command

   ```
   Winnt32 /checkupgradeonly
   ```

   from the Windows 2000 source to check the hardware and software for any incompatibilities. It's by no means a foolproof check, but it's easy to run and you don't have to mess with external programs.

3. If you are upgrading a PDC or other system that can't have a fresh install, run

   ```
   Winnt32 /unattend
   ```

   to perform the upgrade without any user input. It will use the existing parameters for the upgrade and do all the reboots automatically.

3a. If you are upgrading a dedicated BDC, run

   ```
   Winnt32 /unattend :answer_file
   ```

   to perform a fresh installation in unattended Setup mode. The answer file provides your custom specifications to Setup. For more information about answer files, see the *Windows 2000 Deployment Guide*.

The Domain Controller Backout Plan

Because Windows 2000 upgrades NTFS to Version 5, a restored Windows NT 4 OS must have Service Pack 4 or better installed. The general system restoration steps are listed here:

1. Format the OS partition with FDISK or some other tool. Windows NT 4 setup will not recognize the NTFS Version 5 partition and will give an alert indicating that there's no space available.

2. Install a base Windows NT 4 OS, and back up software if your tapes aren't compatible with the NTBACKUP tape utility.

3. Restore your system from backups. This assumes that your backed-up system had SP4+ to recognize NTFS Version 5.

4. Synchronize your system with the PDC.

Upgrading a Member Server

Because they generally aren't intended to be rebuilt, member servers should be treated the same as a domain controller when they're upgraded:

1. Perform a full backup of the system, including the Registry.
2. Run

   ```
   Winnt32 /checkupgradeonly
   ```

   from the Windows 2000 source to check the hardware and software for any incompatibilities. If your servers are all standardized, you can skip this step to aid in the automation.
3. If you are upgrading a PDC or other system that can't have a fresh install, run

   ```
   Winnt32 /unattend
   ```

   to perform the upgrade without any user input. It will use the existing parameters for the upgrade and do all the reboots automatically.

The Member Server Backout Plan

The backout plan for member servers is the same as that for domain controllers, without the synchronization step. (See the previous section "The Domain Controller Backout Plan.")

Upgrading a Windows NT 4 Domain

Upgrading a Windows NT 4 domain to Windows 2000 is one of the methods to migrate from one version to the next. This method includes five major steps:

1. Setting up the backout strategy
2. Installing or upgrading your DNS infrastructure to Windows 2000
3. Upgrading the PDC
4. Rebuilding the BDCs
4a. Testing mixed mode functionality
5. Switching the domain to native mode
5a. Testing native mode functionality

Strictly speaking, there's a sixth step as well: upgrading miscellaneous member servers to Windows 2000 so that all your servers have been upgraded. Because we're focusing on core services here, we'll stick to DNS, DHCP, and WINS.

Before you start upgrading your domains, you should know that the *order* in which you upgrade is critical. Don't do anything about upgrades until you read the section "Domain Upgrade Order" later in this chapter.

Note

Note that there's a way to migrate your network to Windows 2000 without upgrading your production domains. It's covered in more detail in the section "Three Enterprise Migration Methods" later in this chapter. ◆

Setting Up the Backout Strategy

Recovery of the domain, if not of the individual servers, is straightforward if you follow these steps:

1. Perform a full synchronization of the domain. Lock out all further changes to the SAM (e.g., account or group changes). Unless you're using a sophisticated third-party account tool, this probably means to just tell your account clerks to no longer accept changes.

2. To ensure that you have a safe copy of the SAM, either take a BDC off the network or build a simple BDC out of a well-muscled PC and take it off the network. If you then promote it to a PDC, you'll avoid problems with expiring trust accounts between it and the former PDC. This is now an isolated copy of the SAM, so if you make any subsequent changes to the domain (either in Windows NT 4 or Windows 2000), you had better keep track of them to reapply to this offline server if you must recover.

Installing or Upgrading the Windows 2000 DNS Infrastructure

Before you can begin creating or upgrading Windows 2000 domains, you must have the proper DNS infrastructure in place. Indeed, if you don't have DNS working properly before attempting a DCPROMO operation to create a domain controller, the DCPROMO Wizard will install DNS on the local machine. It's obviously much better to have DNS as you want it before the domain upgrades begin.

Before you can put your Windows 2000 DNS structure in place, you must have completed the design document that explains how Windows 2000 DNS will coexist with legacy DNS in your company. As far as the actual server upgrade is concerned, this is a straightforward process as outlined in the section "Upgrading a Member Server" earlier in this chapter. The DNS and DHCP services will be automatically upgraded to their Windows 2000 versions.

When you first construct your Windows 2000 DNS infrastructure, you have no choice but to leave DNS in Standard Primary mode, using a zone file for its database, because the Active Directory doesn't exist yet. After you begin building your Windows 2000 domains, move the DNS servers into their appropriate domains and promote them to Active Directory Integrated Primary. (This is done from the General tab of the forward lookup zone's properties in the DNS Manager MMC snap-in.)

> **Note**
>
> *This chapter assumes that you've already configured your DNS and DHCP services on dedicated servers, as described in Chapter 6, "Designing Your Windows 2000 Core Services." ◆*

Upgrading the PDC

To upgrade your PDC, follow the general process outlined in the section "Upgrading a Domain Controller" earlier in this chapter. When this operation is complete, the domain will be in a functional but very mixed condition of both Windows NT 4 and Windows 2000 domain controllers. In fact, this is known as *mixed mode*. It's a complicated support and troubleshooting scenario (see the section "Dealing with a Mixed Environment" later in the chapter) that I recommend you get out of as soon as you can by completing the next step: rebuilding the BDCs to Windows 2000.

Rebuilding the BDCs

Now that you're in mixed mode, you need to get your other domain controllers up to Windows 2000. To rebuild your BDCs, follow the general process outlined in the section "Upgrading a Domain Controller" earlier in this chapter. At this point, most member servers are still at Windows NT 4.

As discussed in Chapter 6, you should not have as many domain controllers in Windows 2000 as you did in Windows NT 4. You select the appropriate number of Windows 2000 domain controllers based on hardware, domain, and physical location.

From Windows NT 4 to Native Mode

When you've completed the domain controller upgrades, the domain will still be in mixed mode. The progression of a Windows NT domain toward full Windows 2000 functionality goes like this:

1. Mixed mode: Windows 2000 and Windows NT 4 domain controllers coexist in the domain.

2. Mixed mode: All domain controllers have been upgraded to Windows 2000, but the domain hasn't switched to native mode.

3. Native mode: The native mode button is pushed, bringing the domain into full Windows 2000 functionality. No Windows NT 4 domain controllers can be part of the domain anymore, including ones that may have been active in the domain. This step is irreversible; after the domain has been switched to native mode, the only way to return is to collapse the domain by demoting all domain controllers back to member servers. This destroys the domain and all objects in it.

Testing Mixed Mode Functionality
You need to develop a Windows 2000 domain mixed mode functional test plan. Use it to confirm that all domain controllers are working as desired before you take the irreversible step to native mode. In a functional test, you should run through all the documented features a Windows 2000 mixed mode domain should support, including these:

- Inter- and intra-site replication
- Windows 2000 domain controller interaction with downlevel servers and clients
- Downlevel server and domain administration with Windows 2000 tools

Note

Note that transitive trust relationships won't work in mixed mode. ◆

Mixed Mode Backout Plan

If you've upgraded the PDC, still have Windows NT 4 BDCs, and have an offline BDC that has been off the network for a week or less, you can take the Windows 2000 domain controller (formerly the PDC) offline, bring your emergency recovery BDC online, promote it to PDC, and synchronize the domain. The Windows NT 4 domain controllers will think that the PDC (really the Windows 2000 domain controller) went off the air and was replaced by another domain controller promoted in its place. Then you can perform a clean rebuild (i.e., format the OS partition flat) of the Windows 2000 domain controller to Windows NT 4 Service Pack 3+. Note that without Service Pack 3, you won't be able to see any other NTFS partitions because they'll be running NTFS Version 5 from the Windows 2000 upgrade.

Switching the Domain to Native Mode

Mixed-mode domains are almost—but not quite—full Windows 2000 domains. They fall short of full Windows 2000 features in some areas, but the difference isn't as big as it used to be. (In earlier betas, the big difference between mixed and native mode was that native mode turned on multi-master replication.) When you've finished switching the domain to native mode, SAM is dead in the domain—long live the Active Directory!

Mixed-mode domains don't have full Windows 2000 functionality. In particular, they lack the following:

- Universal groups aren't available in mixed mode, so you can't complete that part of your group strategy without putting at least one domain in native mode. (Because I'm assuming that your root domain will have no downlevel domain controllers from the start, you can immediately move to native mode and create the groups there.)

- You can't nest groups, further cramping your group migration/upgrade strategy.

- You can't grow the domain beyond the recommended Windows NT 4 sizes, so consolidation isn't possible until you go native.

- Most importantly, no clients—Windows 2000 or otherwise—will be capable of using the Active Directory until the native mode switch is flipped.

Figure 8.1 shows the dialog box where you switch to native mode by pressing the Change Mode button. After committing to native mode, you must wait for this change to be replicated to each domain controller and then reboot it. You can only check to see whether the native mode change has been replicated to a domain controller by launching Active Directory Domains and Trusts Manager on each domain controller. Click on the domain, expand the Domain Controllers container, and look for "native mode" in the general properties.

My recommendations for native mode are listed here:

- Bring all domain controllers up to Windows 2000 as quickly as possible.

- The switch to native mode can't be reversed, so the domain will be committed to Windows 2000 after it's made. Don't move to native mode immediately after all domain controllers have been rebuilt into Windows 2000, especially early in the overall process of upgrading your domains. Wait for the dust to settle, and run a complete set of functional tests.

- Check with operations to be sure that no domain controllers are offline for maintenance or some other problem. If you switch to native mode before a domain controller is upgraded, you'll have to rebuild it straight into Windows 2000.

- Complete your tests within one week, and either move to native mode or back out. After this time, you may run into problems with your emergency BDC's domain trust account expiring.

Figure 8.1   *The Properties dialog box, where you press the Change Mode button to enter native mode.*

Testing Native Mode Functionality

Remember that the switch to native mode doesn't happen across the domain instantly—you need to allow time for the change to replicate to all domain controllers. After the switch to native mode is complete, you should test it before you proceed. As in the mixed mode plan, you need to develop a functional testing plan for Windows 2000 domain native mode. This plan must be more comprehensive than the mixed mode plan: You use it to confirm that the domain is working as desired before you continue with the domain upgrades. Test all major aspects of Active Directory functionality, and don't forget to test Windows NT 4, Windows 2000, and Windows 9x clients with the DSClient add-on. (Dsclient.exe is the directory services add-on for Windows 95 and Windows 98 clients that gives them Active Directory functionality. It's on the Windows 2000 Advanced Server CD.)

Native Mode Backout Plan

The native mode domain backout plan isn't as easy as the mixed mode plan. Except for the offline BDC, you must rebuild every domain controller in the domain.

To recover the domain, promote the emergency BDC to PDC while still offline. Then format the OS partition and rebuild each Windows 2000 domain controller with Windows NT 4 SP3 on the emergency BDC's offline network. Join them into the emergency BDC's domain. When this is complete, you will have a functioning Windows NT 4 domain from before the upgrade; you must then move the servers to the production network.

Domain Upgrade Order

Now that you have a plan for upgrading a domain, you must determine how you're going to construct the Windows 2000 domain trees you've documented in your domain namespace document. You can approach your domain upgrade order in several different ways; these methods are dictated by your existing Windows NT 4 domain architecture and your proposed Windows 2000 domain namespace.

A few unbendable rules govern the process of creating Windows 2000 domain trees, either from scratch or by upgrading a Windows NT 4 domain:

- You must create your domains in a top-down order, as shown in Figure 8.2. Create your highest-level domains, and then add on to the DNS namespace.

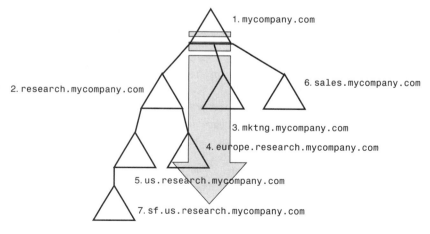

Figure 8.2 *Windows 2000 domain creation order.*

- Choose the first domain you create carefully: It will not only become the root domain for its domain tree, but it will also contain the schema and configuration information for the entire forest. It would be disastrous to delete this domain, so Windows 2000 won't let you delete it. For large enterprises, I recommend that you create your first domain as a special root domain with fault-tolerant domain controllers and no accounts or resources. For smaller enterprises, the root domain could contain corporate accounts. This domain will not change with reorganizations, so give it a generic name.

- If your enterprise will be based on a non-contiguous DNS namespace, you will create a forest (e.g., buick.com, cadillac.com, chevrolet.com). If you base your Windows 2000 architecture on a single DNS name (e.g., mycompany.com), you'll create a domain tree. (Some people will still call one domain tree a forest. Does one tree equal a forest? It sounds like a Zen koan.)

Placeholder Domains

Even though you must create domains in a top-down order, you can cheat a little. If business reasons dictate that you must upgrade a domain before its end-state parent domain is ready, you could create a placeholder domain. A *placeholder domain* is a very simple domain that exists only to reserve its place in the namespace and to handle Kerberos referrals up and down the tree. The domain can be created with one server, but if you're upgrading the child domain below with enough urgency to consider this method, you should spring for two!

In Figure 8.3, the United States research arm of MyCompany, us.research.mycompany.com, has been upgraded to Windows 2000. Its parent domain, research.mycompany.com, consists of two servers in an otherwise empty native mode domain created just so that us.research .mycompany.com could upgrade. RESEARCH01, the resource domain destined for research.mycompany.com, has a one-way trust to mycompany.com, which in this example contains all the corporate accounts.

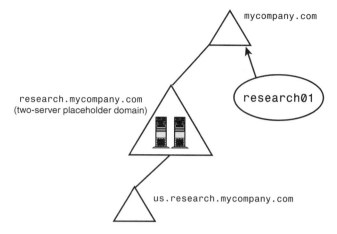

Figure 8.3   *A placeholder domain.*

When RESEARCH01 is ready to upgrade, the research.mycompany.com domain is beefed up with an adequate amount of domain controllers and Global Catalog servers to service all the resources of the RESEARCH01 resource domain. RESEARCH01 is upgraded to Windows 2000, is named staging.research.mycompany.com or something else appropriate, and is switched to native mode (see Figure 8.4).

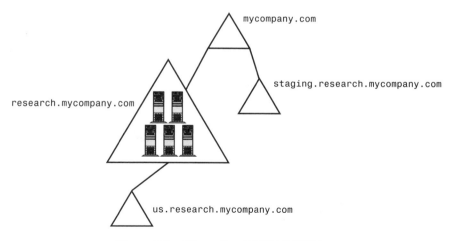

Figure 8.4   *Upgrading RESEARCH01.*

We now have `staging.research.mycompany.com` waiting to receive the resources in `research.mycompany.com`. How do we move the objects from `staging` to `research`? This operation, using more terminology related to the branch/tree/forest paradigm, is called *pruning and grafting* because you're pruning objects from one tree and grafting them to another. Unfortunately, the graphical drag-and-drop prune/graft tool we had been hoping for during the development of the product won't be part of the initial release. Until one becomes available, you can use two tools in the *Windows 2000 Resource Kit* designed to do the task: `Movetree` and `Netdom`.

`Movetree` is a command-line tool that allows you to move Active Directory objects such as OUs, users, or computers between domains in a single forest. `Netdom` moves computers from one domain to another and joins computers to domains.

For our purposes, `Netdom` syntax is simple:

```
Netdom move /d:destdomain computername
```

where

> *destdomain* is the NetBIOS or DNS name of the domain to which you're moving the workstation or member server
>
> *computername* is the NetBIOS or DNS name of the workstation or member server

The syntax for Movetree is quite a bit more complicated:

```
movetree command /s: SrcDC /d: DstDC /sdn: /ddn: [/u:{domain\user}]
➡[/p:{password¦*}]
```

where *command* can be one of the following:

> `/test`, which test-runs the command to see whether you got the syntax right and that there are no errors
>
> `/start`, which begins the `movetree` operation
>
> `/test /start`, which runs a test first and automatically begins the `movetree` operation if it returns with no errors
>
> `/continue`, which continues the `movetree` operation from where it left off after a network or domain controller error

and where

> `/s: SrcDC` is the DNS name of a domain controller in the source domain from which you want to move the objects.
>
> `/d: DstDC` is the DNS name of a domain controller in the destination domain to which you want to move the objects.
>
> `/sdn:` is the distinguished name of the object being moved. (How good are you at distinguished names?)
>
> `/ddn:` is the distinguished name of the destination to which you're moving the object.

If the command isn't being run from an account with administrative rights in both domains, the following allows you to specify a set of credentials that can be used for the command:

```
/u: domain\user /p: password *
```

This isn't terribly clear. For our example, the `movetree` syntax would be as follows:

```
Movetree /test /start
/s: dc1.staging.research.mycompany.com
/d: dc2.research.mycompany.com
/sdn: DC=staging, DC=research, DC=mycompany, DC=com
/ddn: DC=research, DC=mycompany, DC=com
```

This would move most of the objects from `staging.research.mycompany.com` to `research.mycompany.com`, pulling objects from the directory store in the DC1 domain controller in `staging` and loading them into the directory store in the DC2 domain controller in `research` (see Figure 8.5).

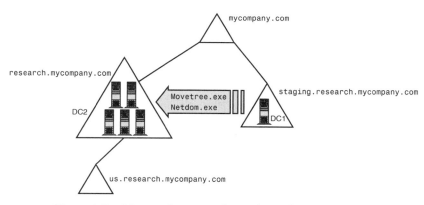

Figure 8.5 *Moving directory objects from the* `staging` *domain to* `research.mycompany.com`.

If you just wanted to move an OU named `MyOrg` from `staging` to `research` and put it in a batch file, it would look like this:

```
Movetree /test /s: dc1.staging.research.mycompany.com
/d: dc2.research.mycompany.com
/sdn:OU=MyOrg, DC=staging, DC=research, DC=mycompany, DC=com
/ddn: OU=MyOrg, DC=research, DC=mycompany, DC=com
if errorlevel 0 goto start
goto exit
:start
Movetree /start /s: dc1.staging.research.mycompany.com
/d: dc2.research.mycompany.com
/sdn:OU=MyOrg, DC=staging, DC=research, DC=mycompany, DC=com
/ddn: OU=MyOrg, DC=research, DC=mycompany, DC=com
:exit
```

> **Note**
>
> *You may have noticed that I said* most *of the objects would be moved. This is because* movetree *doesn't move everything; in particular, it doesn't move local groups, domain global groups, and computer accounts. It also doesn't move policies, profiles, and logon scripts. The computer accounts can be moved with the* netdom *tool, and the rest must be moved with scripting tools.* ◆

After you've moved all the objects out of the domain, you must "collapse" it. This is done by running DCPROMO on each of the domain controllers to demote them to member servers. When the last domain controller has been demoted, the domain will be gone (Figure 8.6).

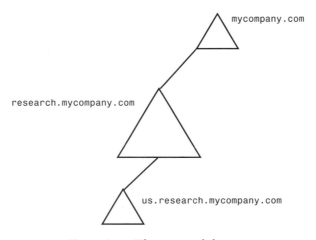

Figure 8.6   *The migrated domain*

Three Enterprise Migration Methods

You can migrate your Windows NT 4 network to Windows 2000 in three major ways. Two—upgrading domains in place, and consolidating domains and then upgrading—are variations on a similar theme; the third—migrating straight to the end state—is quite different, and, I predict, the majority of large Windows NT shops will prefer it.

Upgrading Domains in Place

Figure 8.7 shows MyCompany's Windows NT 4 architecture. MyCompany has one account domain and three resource domains. Two of the resource domains are for research, and one is for sales (they're efficient). The second research domain, RES2, exists solely because the U.S. research group insisted on managing its own domain.

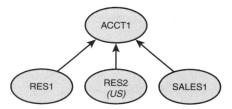

Figure 8.7 *MyCompany's Windows NT 4 architecture.*

After looking more closely at the situation and talking with the U.S. research customers, you realize that the company's needs could be met and money could be saved by an organizational unit rather than an entire domain.

Your first step (after you get your DNS house in order) is to upgrade the account domain to the Windows 2000 root domain, as shown in Figure 8.8.

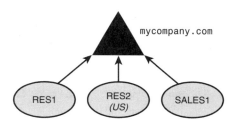

Figure 8.8 *The first domain is upgraded.*

Note that the existing resource domains continue their one-way trusts to the root domain just as though it were still a Windows NT 4 account domain. This is because one domain controller in mycompany.com is the PDC FSMO, acting as a downlevel Windows NT 4 PDC of MYCOMPANY domain for downlevel domains and workstations.

The next step is to upgrade the remaining domains to Windows 2000, as shown in Figure 8.9.

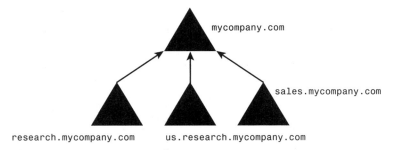

Figure 8.9 *The remaining domains are upgraded.*

Two operations must still be done: moving the objects in us.research .mycompany.com to an OU in research.mycompany.com, and collapsing us.research.mycompany.com. Moving the us.research.mycompany.com objects is done with movetree and netdom, as shown in Figure 8.10.

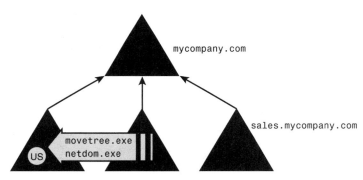

Figure 8.10 *The U.S. domain objects are moved to an OU within research.*

When all domain controllers in us.research.mycompany.com have been demoted to member servers, the final MyCompany Windows 2000 domain namespace looks as shown in Figure 8.11.

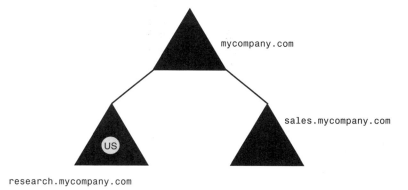

Figure 8.11   *MyCompany's Windows 2000 domain namespace.*

Windows NT 4 Trusts and Their Impact on an Upgrade in Place

This was a pretty straightforward procedure, wasn't it? Why wouldn't we want to use this migration strategy? Because this "upgrade in place" strategy doesn't scale well. If you have a small number of domains, this strategy will work. However, if you have a large enterprise—with 5 to 10 account domains and 100 or 200 resource domains—you'll run into some serious replication-related problems before you migrate your domains to an end state (if you even get to that point).

Trust relationships are a limiting factor in how large you can scale a Windows NT 4 network. You can compute the number of trusts in a multiple master domain model by using the following equation:

where

    N_t is the total number of trusts

    n_m is the number of master domains

    n_r is the number of resource domains

What really counts from a support viewpoint, however, are the secure channel trust sessions. Underlying a Windows NT 4 trust relationship between two domains are secure channel trusts between domain controllers of the domains. You can compute the number of secure channel trust sessions in a Windows NT 4 multiple master domain network by using the following equation:

$$N_{ts} = (P-1) \underbrace{\sum_{m=1}^{P} (D_{m1} + D_{m2} + \dots D_{mP})}_{MasterSessions} + (P) \underbrace{\sum_{r=1}^{S} (D_{r1} + D_{r2} + \dots D_{rS})}_{ResourceSessions}$$

where

N_{ts} is the total number of trust sessions in the trusted network

P is the total number of master domains

S is the total number of resource domains

D is the number of domain controllers in a given domain

MasterSessions is the total number of trust sessions between the master domains

ResourceSessions is the total number of trust sessions between the resource domains and the master domains

In English, it reads like this:

(total trust sessions)

=

(# master domains–1) * (# of domain controllers in all master domains)

+

(# master domains) * (# of domain controllers in all resource domains)

Why should you care about this? Any single secure channel trust that fails means that, to some portion of your user population (the ones that were authenticated by the domain controller with the failed relationship), a trust has failed and those users can't get to the accounts or resources on the other side of the trust. Keeping N_{ts} down has a direct impact on your support costs.

A little fiddling with this equation tells you that adding resource domains increases the number of secure channel trusts in a linear manner, while adding master domains increases the number of secure channels geometrically. Not only is this a reason to limit the existing number of Windows NT 4 master domains, but new Windows 2000 domains will likely be trusted by downlevel domains (both master and resource) as if they were a master domains, thus increasing the number of secure channel trusts even further.

Replication on the enterprise level is the devil here. Remember that every domain must feed its directory objects into the Global Catalog so that it has a representation of the entire forest. More domains mean more connection objects between domain controllers and Global Catalog servers across the enterprise. In a company with 10 account domains and 100 resource domains, you have 110 separate connection objects for Global Catalog population alone when they're all upgraded in place. If any one of these fails, the Global Catalog becomes out of synch with what's in the domains. If you don't have a lot of Global Catalog servers, replication between them is simpler, but the mean data path length that these many domains must take to reach a Global Catalog server is longer. Think of the troubleshooting fun!

Now let's spend a few cycles thinking about account domains—or rather, what were account domains before you upgraded them. Do any of these 10 domains span multiple sites or multiple geographic areas now? Do these geographic spans make sense from a Windows 2000 viewpoint, or were they created because a Windows NT 4 domain got too large? There are many scenarios in which a Windows NT 4 account domain would have to span multiple sites and geographic areas in Windows 2000, further complicating replication troubleshooting. Windows NT 4 account domain structures aren't necessarily the right Windows 2000 domain structures.

Every self-respecting Windows NT domain has at least two domain controllers, and it won't be any different in Windows 2000. You have the opportunity to considerably reduce your dependence on domain controllers in Windows 2000—but if you keep your existing domain count, not only will you have to keep your domain controllers, but you'll have to spend money to beef them up.

Replication to the Global Catalog servers will be very heavy during domain upgrades because they're being loaded with large numbers of new objects.

The domain upgrade process adds at least five new global and domain local groups. Multiply that by 110 domains, and you have 550 new groups across the enterprise, most of which will have to be eliminated during the domain consolidation process.

Think twice about a few non-technical reasons for doing upgrades in place. Upgrading your domains in place and then reorganizing these new Windows 2000 domains to their ultimate end state is a two-part process—and a very lengthy and tedious one. Because IT is an overhead division (i.e., it doesn't make any bottom-line profit, it only uses it up), there's a very real danger that funding for the end-state migration may dry up after the initial domain upgrade. "After all, you're running Windows 2000 aren't you? You just want to make it look nicer, and 'looking nicer' isn't something our company spends capital on." If that happens, you'll wish you never migrated in the first place.

My recommendation is that you use this upgrade-in-place approach for enterprises with no more than two or three account domains and no more than a handful of resource domains.

Consolidating Domains and Then Upgrading

The difficulty with upgrading in place comes from having so many Windows 2000 domains. What if you reduced the number of domains by consolidating them before you upgraded? Taking this approach would create a much more manageable Windows 2000 environment than a simple upgrade-in-place process. You'd end up with fewer Windows 2000 domains and less technical complexity in the underlying infrastructure.

Tradeoffs to these strategies always exist, however, and this one is no exception. Your consolidated technical infrastructure will be simpler, but your customer administration structure will probably be more difficult. Unless your Windows NT domains were originally created through inexperience (or the groups that they were originally designed for have been reorganized, divested, or otherwise made to disappear), the domains were created for a reason. If that reason still exists, so should the domains. This includes, alas, the 8th OSI layer of political reasons; they're every bit as much of a constraint as a transatlantic circuit. If you consolidate domains to make the migration to Windows 2000 easier, you'll be creating a support nightmare and a security compromise—if you're indeed allowed to do it at all.

The other factor, of course, is that Windows NT 4 domain consolidation is a very complex, tedious, and time-consuming project. Moving users around in Windows 2000 domains is much easier, but the Catch-22 is that to get to that point you must upgrade some domains and risk your replication problems. You can minimize these problems by carefully choosing your domain upgrade order. Choose two domains you intend to consolidate, upgrade them sequentially, and consolidate them into one domain before you migrate other domains. If you have a large corporation, this will be a *long* process.

If you do decide that this is the right path for you, Mission Critical Software and FastLane Technologies can make your way easier—for a price. MCS's Enterprise Domain Administrator is designed to automate the domain consolidation and migration process, and FastLane Technologies' RD/Upgrade In Place Kit does domain restructuring and reporting.

Note

Neither of these tools come cheap; the RD/Upgrade In Place Kit starts at US$40,000 for 1,000 managed user licenses. To justify their use to management, you must prove how labor-intensive a domain consolidation effort is compared to the tool's price. Don't forget to include the cost of trained personnel that will leave rather than deal with a consolidation project. (If any managers are reading this—yes, it's that ugly.) As either FastLane or Mission Critical will tell you, the most fervent believer in their software is the Windows NT administrator who has had to do a domain consolidation with no, or few, automation tools.) ♦

Migrating Straight to the End State

The third migration method is the simplest. Why not just create your end-state Windows 2000 namespace—nice and clean, with sparkling new domain controllers and no historical baggage—and migrate to it right from your production environment? You *can* do this. In the grand engineering tradition of explaining to someone how a clock works when they've only asked for the time, some background is necessary.

A security identifier (SID) identifies a security principal (user account or group) in a domain. SIDs are unique within a domain, and they can't move from domain to domain. When a process attempts to access a resource in Windows NT, the operating system compares the SID of the process attempting to access the resource to entries in the resource's access control list (ACL). If they match, the process is granted access. This is all still true in Windows 2000.

Windows 2000 adds two directory objects that make moving users between domains possible: GUIDs and SID history. The GUID, or globally unique identifier, is an evolution of the SID (I think "Son of SID" puts it eloquently). It functions like a SID in that it's a unique identifier for a security principal such as a user, group, or computer, but whereas a SID is unique within a domain, a GUID is unique within a Windows 2000 forest. GUIDs assist in moving accounts between domains because no matter where in the forest an account sits (or what it gets renamed to), no other object has its GUID.

SIDHistory is not a front man for a grunge band. It's an Active Directory user object attribute that contains the SID(s) of whatever domains the account has been in. I imagine that for most accounts, the SIDHistory attribute contains only one SID: that of the domain in which the user has always resided. If you move a user from one domain to another, however, the SID created for the user in the new domain is added to the user's SIDHistory attribute.

In Windows NT 4, the user's account SID and the SIDs of groups of which he's a member are included in the access token built during the logon process. In Windows 2000, all the SIDs in the SID history list are also included in this token.

This means that if you move to a new domain, the resources you had assigned access to your old domain's account will still work with your new account. The universal accessibility and security of the Active Directory provides a place to store not only where you are, but also where you've been. Unfortunately, this worked only for Windows 2000 domains; you couldn't "move" a user from a Windows NT 4 domain to a Windows 2000 domain and still have access to former resources.

In Beta 3 of Windows 2000, Microsoft added the capability to programmatically add to the SIDHistory attribute with the DsAddSidHistory API. It isn't a trivial programming exercise, but SIDs from Windows NT 4 domains can now be added to the user's SID history. Done badly, this is a huge security risk because a goof means exposing access to another user's resources in another domain. Lots of security has been wrapped around it, however, the least of which is that you must have administrative rights in both domains. Companies such as FastLane Technology have enhanced its DM/Manager product to take advantage of this new feature.

Here's what happens when you have the capability of adding Windows NT 4 SIDs to the SID history:

1. After being migrated over the weekend, Jim Bob logs on to his shiny new Windows 2000 user account. As part of Jim Bob's Windows 2000 account setup, administrators have added his old Windows NT 4 account SID to his Windows 2000 user account's SIDHistory attribute.

2. He begins to open his weekly progress report on a server in his old domain, just like he did last week.

3. The Windows NT 4 server that holds his weekly progress report opens Jim Bob's access token.

   Like every object on an NTFS volume, his weekly progress report has an ACL. The ACL contains a number of access control entries (ACEs), each of which has a SID (for example, the Everyone group) and an access mask (for example, Full Control).

4. The server compares every SID in Jim Bob's access token with every SID in every ACE in the ACL.

5. One of the SIDs in Jim Bob's token is his old SID, which matches the SID in his weekly's ACEs (for example, "JimBob Full Control").

6. Access is granted, just like he had last week.

Let's assume that MyCompany wants to migrate its Windows NT 4 domain architecture to a more unified environment, made possible by DsAddSidHistory.

The first step MyCompany would take is to create its end state Windows 2000 domain, as shown in Figure 8.12.

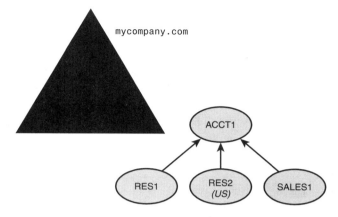

Figure 8.12   *Creating the end-state Windows 2000 domain.*

The following high-level steps would be taken for each resource domain to migrate the users to Windows 2000:

1. Account add/move/changes in the master domain ACCT1 would be frozen for members of the resource domain.

2. A one-way trust would be established from the Windows NT 4.0 resource domain to `mycompany.com`.

3. OUs would be created in `mycompany.com` to reproduce (and hopefully improve on) the Windows NT 4 administration model, shown in Figure 8.13.

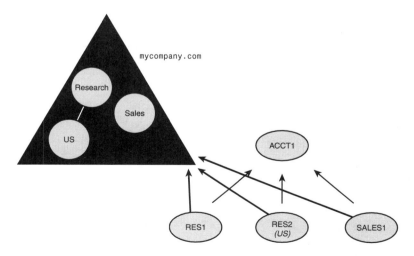

Figure 8.13   *Establishing trusts and OUs.*

4. New accounts would be created in `mycompany.com` and put in a disabled state.

5. Each user's Windows NT 4 SID would be added to his Windows 2000 account's SID history list, granting access to Windows NT 4 production domain resources from that user's Windows 2000 account.

6. The user's Windows NT 4 account would be disabled and the Windows 2000 account enabled.

7. After all users had migrated and resource access testing was complete, the account domain would be shut down.

8. Resources in the resource domains would begin to move to `mycompany.com`, beginning with user's PCs. Now would be a good time to upgrade them to Windows 2000 Professional.

9. Member servers would move to `mycompany.com`.

10. Domain controllers would move to `mycompany.com`, but not as domain controllers.

Tip

When you're in the process of collapsing a Windows NT 4.0 domain, consider this method if you have domain controllers with resources you need to move. Instead of tediously moving data and shares, upgrade the PDC (into its own forest so that it doesn't contribute to your production Global Catalog) and then upgrade each BDC that has resources you need. After a BDC has been upgraded, it becomes a Windows 2000 member server and is easily moved to your new domain. Your last act for the domain is to DCPROMO what used to be the PDC. This will demote it to a member server, and the Windows 2000 domain will be collapsed. You then can move the server into its destination domain. ◆

11. The empty resource domains are shut down, and the servers are reused.

Even though this method is far simpler than an upgrade-in-place or consolidate domains strategy, it still involves a lot of work in each Windows NT 4 domain to get the users to their final environment.

Note

To cut down on the amount of time you spend in a mixed environment, you should seriously consider Mission Critical Software's Enterprise Domain Administrator or FastLane Technology's RESOURCE DOMAIN/Incremental Upgrade Kit. I've spoken before about Enterprise Domain Administrator; the FastLane RD/Incremental Upgrade Kit is identical to its RD/Upgrade In Place Kit except that it uses the latest version (5.0) of the company's DM/Manager product. As you might suspect, DM/Manager 5.0 supports both Active Directory and Windows NT 4. ◆

FastLane's involvement in the domain migration/reconfiguration dates comes from its long (for Windows NT) history with its Final! scripting product. This is a very powerful scripting product that can be used for all kinds of administration tasks. The limitation was that FastLane mostly provided the scripting language, not any solutions built on it. Somewhere along the line, the company figured out that a lot of FastLane customers were using Final! to speed up the very ugly business of Windows NT 4. domain consolidation. They closely examined all the steps involved in this process, automated it with a general user UI and Windows NT services to handle the dirty work of re-ACLing server resources, and a badly needed product was born. As anyone who's been involved in a domain consolidation or reconfiguration can easily understand, it has been an extremely successful product. It's a logical step to carry this forward and provide a product that will take care of the dirty work in domain moves as well. FastLane has been involved with Microsoft during the final beta phases of Windows 2000 to ensure that their product integrates well with it.

Dealing with a Mixed Environment

I've defined a mixed environment as the period that begins when you begin making Windows 2000 servers part of your production environment (either through upgrades or new domain creation) and that lasts until you've upgraded your clients either to Windows 2000 Professional or installed the ADCLIENT add-on to your Windows 9x system.

> *Note*
>
> *This is a broader scope than just a mixed-mode domain. Mixed mode refers only to domain controllers in a domain; a mixed environment encompasses domain controllers, member servers, and Windows NT, Windows 2000, and Windows 9x clients.* ◆

This will be the most complicated environment to support in the process because it contains: 1) familiar Windows NT 4 networking, 2) the new, unfamiliar Windows 2000 management environment, and 3) the interaction of Windows 2000 servers with Windows NT 4 and Windows 9x clients. The best way to understand the implications is to break these down into three areas: Windows NT 4 networking, the Windows 2000 management environment, and the interaction of Windows 2000 servers with Windows NT 4.0 and Windows 9x clients.

Windows NT 4 Networking

Windows NT 4 networking is the simplest facet of the mixed environment to manage. Even this familiar area, however, isn't quite like a pure Windows NT 4 network. Viewed from the Windows NT 4.0 server's viewpoint, there are additional trusts to Windows 2000 domains to be managed. These may look like Windows NT 4 domains to the downlevel domain controllers, but system administrators need to be aware of the PDC FSMO (or Operations Master) status in the Windows 2000 domain because this controls the downlevel trust relationship. Downlevel clients are affected in a similar way; early in the migration, users will be logging on to Windows 2000 accounts from PCs that still reside in the production Windows NT 4 resource domains.

You can see and change what domain controllers the various FSMOs reside on from the Active Directory Users and Computers MMC snap-in. Right-click on the domain you're interested in, and choose Operations Masters (see Figure 8.14). You can also change them with the NTDSUTIL utility in the Windows 2000 Resource Kit.

Figure 8.14 *The PDC Operations Master.*

The Windows 2000 Management Environment

The Windows 2000 management environment is the interaction of Windows 2000 servers with other Windows 2000 servers and clients, as described in white papers, Microsoft TechNet, Microsoft TechEd presentations, the *NBC Nightly News*, and anyplace else Microsoft marketing can get some press.

The challenge here is training your support organizations early on Windows 2000 concepts, operations, and administration tools. You *must* have a core of personnel—preferably the sharpest people on each team—that gets early training by whatever method you can manage. I'll say it one more time: Windows 2000 is a huge paradigm shift in how a Windows NT network is managed. An experienced core of support team leads will both hold the boat together while everyone gains practical experience and help bring other personnel up to speed. Your key players should already be experienced in Windows NT 4 networking. To learn Windows 2000 in addition to their own jobs, they need resources such as this book or newly created Microsoft classes, Microsoft documentation, basic documentation such as Windows NT-based DNS, and so on. They also need time at work to learn it; only the most dedicated and motivated will take all this home to learn Windows 2000 on their own time.

Warning

If you don't push to get a core support team from all disciplines trained in Windows 2000 early on, guess whose door everyone will come to for answers when they need them immediately? Yours. ◆

Tip

One of the most important interactions you need to be competent with is how a Windows 2000 domain controller and how a Windows 2000 Professional client start up. Just as learning the Windows NT 4 Workstation startup sequence taught you about the details of Windows NT 4 networking, this sequence teaches you much of what can go wrong for a Windows 2000 client in a Windows 2000 network.

See Appendix C, "Windows 2000 Client Startup and Interactive Logon," for a detailed explanation of this sequence. ◆

The Interaction of Windows 2000 Servers with Windows NT 4 and Windows 9x Clients

The interaction between Windows 2000 and its downlevel clients is the aspect I've been harping on all throughout the book. It requires a deep knowledge of both Windows NT 4 and Windows 2000, the second of which is in very short supply.

We can categorize the major interactions into these groups and list the areas you need to consider:

- *Windows 2000 domain controllers and Windows NT 4 clients.* How does a Windows NT 4 client work in a Windows 2000 domain? The 4 client in a Windows 2000 domain can access resources in other Windows 2000 domains via transitive trusts, even though it doesn't itself use Kerberos authentication. How does this work? What is the authentication process? What are the interactions between a Windows 2000 "account" domain (i.e., where the user's account resides) and the user's Windows NT 4 workstation in a Windows NT 4 resource domain?

- *Windows 2000 servers and Windows 9x clients without the Directory Service Client (Dsclient.exe) installed.* The questions are similar to that of the Windows NT 4 client. What happens during startup and logon? Is it just the same as with Windows NT 4? Can it use transitive trusts to access resources in other domains, and if so, how? What are the most common error modes a user would experience that aren't usually encountered in a Windows NT 4 network?

- *Windows 2000 servers and Windows 9x clients with the Directory Service Client (Dsclient.exe) installed.* Does this client start up and interact just like Windows 2000 Professional? Or is it a little different, like the differences between Windows NT 4 Workstation and base Windows 9x? Do you still need remote BDCs like you do in Windows NT 4? What use, if any, can be made of Windows 2000's Intellimirror features?

- *Windows 2000 Professional clients and Windows NT 4 domain controllers.* Do they really start up just like Windows NT 4 workstation clients? What special requirements might they have?

Your support teams need to break down these sections and learn about them to be prepared for the situations that surely will happen.

It looks like mixed environment management will be one of MCS's OnePoint EA product's strengths. OnePoint EA is a bundling of darn near all MCS's products:

- Enterprise Directory Administrator

- Enterprise Resource Administrator

- Enterprise Domain Administrator

- Enterprise Exchange Administrator

- Enterprise Event Administrator

The first two products comprise the company's original product of Enterprise Administrator (EA). Enterprise Domain administrator is designed to automate the domain consolidation and migration process. Enterprise Exchange Administrator, well, administers Exchange; Enterprise Event Administrator manages event logs.

EA's historical benefit is that it simplifies and delegates administration of Windows NT 4 networks. With its evolution in OnePoint EA to work with the Active Directory, it can provide a unified interface to help simplify a mixed environment where you must support both types of domains.

Unified event log management has always been a tough challenge in Windows NT networks because of their size, distribution across the network on every server, and lack of native tools. I don't have personal experience with MCS's Enterprise Event Manager, but a powerful tool in this area is worth a lot of money for the early error detection and reporting it provides.

Summary

Migrating your Windows NT 4 network to Windows 2000 will be a large, long, complicated project. Unlike previous migrations from Windows NT 3.51 to 4, this migration brings major changes to all aspects of the Windows NT 4 support infrastructure—servers, domains, network services, Help Desk, Security, Account Administration, Operations, and certainly Server Engineering. You need to examine which upgrade options are the best for your environment. You then must test this upgrade in an isolated test environment with copies of the production SAMs from your account domains. Next, you must use this information to form a pilot forest so that you can test your assumptions in a real-world environment. During all this, you must remember the human aspects of this project. Who are the stakeholders? Did they have input into the design? Do you communicate with them on a regular basis so that they know exactly where the project stands? Finally, you're ready for the upgrade process itself.

Unless you're a large corporation with extremely competent individuals on your team that also happen to be code writers, I seriously suggest that you consider using tools by Mission Critical Software or FastLane Technology. You may not need their entire migration packages, but pieces of them applied at the right points of the project can save time in many areas and lessen user disruption. It won't save money at the project level, but at high corporate levels the decreased transition time, increased client uptime, reduced trouble calls, and less money spent on human resources will be worth it.

9

General Windows NT Support Fundamentals

Distributed systems such as Windows NT offer a high return on investment—you get more for your money—compared to centralized mainframe systems, but they also require more support. There are several reasons for this.

The first reason is the nature of distributed systems themselves. Unlike a mainframe system with a few complex systems closely coupled to one another, distributed Windows NT systems consist of hundreds or thousands of miniature mainframes. Each of these little mainframes has its own hardware, its own seven-layer Open Systems Interconnection (OSI) network stack, its own operating system, and its own applications. What's more, these applications are all connected together by a network that generally shares its bandwidth equally among all its citizens. Any one part of any of these components can cause a partial failure in the Windows NT network.

Also related to Windows NT's distributed nature is the difficulty of maintaining change control on hundreds or thousands of servers. The mature methodology of mainframe support requires that machines are physically secured in a single room—the "glass house"—and that change management is well-established and enforced. In contrast, distributed systems can be scattered across many rooms on many campuses about the country. Most of the support personnel for distributed systems don't have change control ingrained into their work habits. This lack of discipline, made much worse by the fact that there are many more distributed systems to manage than mainframes, is a leading factor in the unreliability of distributed systems. Enforcing strict change management practices can dramatically increase the overall availability of distributed systems. Systems under strict change management practices may not have the absolutely latest and greatest software or hardware, but at least they're available for their customers.

Another contributor to support costs in Windows NT systems is the operating system's relative immaturity. First released in August 1993, even in the hectic world of modern computing, Windows NT is a pretty new operating system (OS). As in many new products, features were deemed more important than less-glamorous support tools. (Ever tried to make sense of a Windows NT security log entry?) As a result, satisfactory tools for managing a large Windows NT network have only recently begun to enter the marketplace—and before Windows 2000, almost all of them came from third-party software vendors.

The final major factor in increased Windows NT support costs is Microsoft's tendency at the time to not follow previously established standards in favor of its own. These standards, though usually technically superior to Microsoft's own networked systems, were often incompatible with other established systems. As a result, extra support was required to manage these parallel technologies. Since the rise of the Internet, though, Microsoft is for the most part either following established RFCs (requests for comments—the specifications of Internet technologies) or is lobbying fiercely to have its own standards adopted.

This chapter discusses the general support principles and documents needed for quality support of a Windows NT network. This includes basic assumptions for different levels of support and the need for training of both quality and quantity. It also describes a structure for the support documentation of your network, from how to apply a service pack to how to manage the overall enterprise architecture of your Windows NT network.

General Support Principles

Windows NT 4 is a network operating system that can encompass thousands of servers and hundreds of thousands of user accounts—and yet have limited native tools to support it all. Windows 2000 has increased manageability but also greatly increased complexity over its predecessor. This doesn't mean you have to start using (and therefore supporting) all the new features right away!

Even though Windows 2000 is a much more complicated operating system than Windows NT 4, the vast majority of the enterprise support structure should remain unchanged, at least in the near future. All the same support requirements are still there. You still need to administer accounts, administer security, maintain and troubleshoot servers, and perform capacity planning, performance monitoring, and all the other tasks that comprise the daily care and feeding of a Windows NT network. Despite the long list of changes between Windows NT 4 and Windows 2000, a network share is still a network share, and someone needs to administer them.

What *will* change in support of Windows 2000 is that the traditional support areas will sprout new branches to accommodate the new features of the OS. The security group will need a new team and new process to handle requests for changes to the Active Directory schema. Central account administration will be able to delegate some administrative functions closer to the department or workgroup level, lessening the workload. Although some groups will have to prepare for extra support requirements immediately after deployment, most groups shouldn't change immediately.

Note

Use the same principle for your Windows 2000 support organization as you did for deploying the operating system in your enterprise: Keep it simple at first, and change as little as possible until you really know where the bugs are and what you're doing with the product. Then begin growing the support groups to handle the new functionality. Then—and only then—enable the new functions. Your entire support structure must be retrained on Windows 2000's tools just to continue their present assignments, let alone control any new features. The staff must relearn how to do their job and must learn about and understand the new features of the product they'll be working with before they're ready to fully use the new product. ◆

Support Training

Training is important for any organization, but for a group that supports distributed computing, it's absolutely necessary. The speed at which the distributed world moves has almost become cliché. As a result, the people who support the new systems need more information than the rest of the world reading about it in their morning paper—they need *training*. If a little knowledge gained through training gets a system up sooner or keeps it up longer, the training has quickly paid for itself. In this distributed world, traditional training budgets are inadequate because traditional budgets assume a stable technology over a fiscal year. Remember that in one year the Web turned the whole industry upside-down!

In the Windows NT area, training means several things:

- A base of knowledge about Windows NT 4. Ensure that everyone understands Windows NT 4 networking concepts of domains, trusts, and so on. Much of it will be changing in Windows 2000, but most of what will be taught will use Windows NT 4 as a starting point. If those concepts are unfamiliar, Windows 2000 education will be very difficult.

- Knowledge about Windows 2000. This new OS is such a paradigm shift in how Windows NT operates, and so much is new to the average Windows NT administrator that early training is critical. Much about Windows 2000 can be pulled from Microsoft's Web site. Furthermore, books such as this one are becoming available, and *Windows NT Magazine* has a continuing series of articles about Windows 2000 technology. Training classes by respected training facilities also will provide an interactive atmosphere to ask the questions that help give you a gut feel for how Windows 2000 works. Your support organization must know how to administer Windows 2000 before you can deploy it. Because Windows 2000 is such a complex and integrated operating system, the support focus must move beyond just "my backyard" to one of overall systems management. Everyone must be aware of the big picture and must be trained in the systems management discipline required to maintain their piece of it.

- Professional certification. Promote Microsoft certification in your company. This won't directly help your support groups to administer Windows 2000, but this kind of training fills in the gaps left by on-the-job experience. Professional certification is an individual's training plan goal rather than a corporate goal. Do what you can to get management to support this goal by reimbursing the training and testing fees and by providing financial incentives to employees that get certified. Microsoft certification is a first step to ensure a basic knowledge of a product or system. As with any other testing system, you'll find Microsoft-certified professionals who crammed for the tests and don't really know the subject, but in general this is useful training.

Training is a cornerstone of any successful information technology organization. Training is expensive, but it's cheaper than ignorance. Training buys you knowledge to carry out these actions:

- Support the products you have
- Implement, develop, or wisely purchase the products you need
- Understand the technology that will be part of the company's future
- Provide an intellectual change of pace to keep your top contributors happy

Many companies consider a yearly mandatory 40 hours of education across the company adequate. The truth is that an employee's educational needs vary greatly by job. A semiconductor front-end hourly employee is not going to need the same amount of education as the engineer who designs the front end using the latest technology. Forty hours of training is equivalent to one week of class; that will get you through one Windows NT Server course, one Exchange course, one SQL Server course, or one technical conference—then you've run out of training for the entire year!

For technical personnel responsible for understanding and implementing complicated, enterprise-scale technologies, a minimum of three weeks of training should be mandatory. Training beyond that amount should be justified based on project need.

Tip

Your education staff needs a technology person as the liaison between the educators and the technocrats of the company—the people who see toward what technologies the company is headed. It can take many months between discovering a need for a class and having it ready, so advance knowledge is extremely valuable.

A good analogy is that of the mail ship. Back when a mail ship was the only reliable communication between an island colony and the rest of the world, the business that got its information first had a competitive advantage. (Basic principles haven't changed much since then, have they? The cycle time has just been reduced from weeks to minutes.) The clever ones stationed sentries high up on a nearby mountain peak, armed with good telescopes. With this arrangement, they could see the mail ship—which often arrived at irregular intervals—coming before anyone else and had their couriers waiting at the dock to take advantage of the new information before their competitors.

With the help of the senior IT staff, an education technology representative can keep training in pace with where the company is going and have training ready when it's needed. ◆

Should employees attend training classes at external companies, or should you bring classes in-house? Attending outside class is faster and easier for all involved, but it's expensive. In-house training can be customized to company examples and can be cheaper, but it requires a higher minimum number of students and has more overhead. A good rule is to send students to external classes when a new technology is being looked at or designed for corporate deployment, and bring training in-house when large numbers of support personnel need to be trained.

When taking external classes, you should use certified ATECs (Authorized Training Education Centers). Your in-house trainers should be MCTs (Microsoft Certified Trainers). There are two reasons for this. Though it's debatable, the more well-known reason is for quality of education through the Microsoft certification process. Assuming that you take an official Microsoft course, the more important reason is consistency. Whether you take a Windows NT Server class in Dallas or Kuala Lumpur, it's still the same Microsoft curriculum. This ensures consistency of training throughout your enterprise. And, of course, you must actually use the skills you've acquired in class, or you'll quickly lose them.

Communication

An area that seems to always be a problem in support organizations is communication between support and the customer, and even between support groups—that is, *especially* between support groups. Support and development staff removed from direct customer contact roles tend to not be the most chatty people you've ever met; they'd rather just get the job done than sit around in meetings discussing what they're doing. As a result, one group often doesn't know what the group sitting next to them is doing on the network for the upcoming weekend and how it affects them. It's all too common for one group coming in to perform server maintenance (pulling software from a central distribution point) to discover that the network is unavailable because the network team next door has already come in to upgrade router software.

The simplest way I've come across to make sure that everyone finds out about proposed changes to the system is with a system news facility. A concept borrowed from the mainframe and UNIX world, the simplest version of system news on those platforms is ASCII text that scrolls across the screen every time a user logs on. This short eye-catcher typically lists upcoming system maintenance times, such as, "System will be unavailable Sunday 1/1 06:00–12:00 for software maintenance." More sophisticated versions are menu-driven.

A Windows NT system news utility helps in many areas. It helps change management because it can notify customers of proposed or impending changes to the network, and you can be assured that the information did at least pass before their eyes. Problem management can post up-to-the-minute system outage information and expected recovery time. The education staff can even advertise new Windows NT classes. If a system news utility is included as part of every user's logon and gets in their faces only when there's information they need to know, then everybody is kept informed—this includes the network team next door!

In today's environment, the lowest common denominator for reading information isn't ASCII text, nor is it some custom utility. It's a Web browser. A system news (SYSNEWS) utility could use the client's browser to display system information. Using a browser, it would feature the following:

- Standards-based format—All system news files are created in HTML format.

- Easy linkage to network documentation—The system news page can have links to network policies, online documentation, a network FAQ, or a local knowledge base. SYSNEWS can be the link between a user's network logon and the dynamic documents of the intranet.

- Automatic client installation—No action needs to be taken by the user.

- Small footprint—Only a few kilobytes of disk space and several registry entries on the client are required.

- "Narrowcast" notification—SYSNEWS would launch the browser to show the news home page after initial installation. After that, SYSNEWS would launch the browser only when new news has been added to the system or, optionally, if the client is part of a target group. (For example, the home directory is on a particular server or some keyword is found in their account's Description field.)

- Bookmarking—SYSNEWS would add a favorite to Microsoft Internet Explorer or would bookmark Netscape Navigator so that the client can view the system news (or, from there, link to system documentation) at any time.

- Immediate, online feedback—Proposed system changes can be posted to the System News home page, and a feedback form can be added to the bottom of the page so that customers who have a problem with the proposed maintenance can quickly and easily respond via a submitted form or email (using the MAILTO tag) to Change Management.

The biggest flaw to the SYSNEWS concept is a result of the growing popularity of Windows NT Workstation in the corporation. With all versions of Windows before Windows NT, users were trained to log off their desktop at the end of each day. This practice ensured that most users would run a logon script (and consequently a SYSNEWS utility) every business day as they logged on first thing in the morning. With Windows NT Workstation, it's not necessary to log off every day because you can simply lock the workstation with Ctrl+Alt+Del and unlock it in the morning. Windows NT Workstation users can easily go a week or more without logging off. Of course, you can lessen this practice by setting policies and procedures to encourage logoff/logon at the end of the day, such as by using the WINEXIT screen saver from the Resource Kit to force a logoff of idle desktops. In the big picture, simply setting a policy to encourage logging off at the end of the day is probably the best solution. You don't want to discourage the user of the Lock Workstation feature during the day because it's a very useful security-enhancing feature of the product.

Support Levels

Another concept necessary to set the groundwork for the following chapters is support levels. Support personnel can be divided into three general skill levels and job categories:

- Level I—Basic operational support, where the support person has a set of procedures to follow for every typical situation he may encounter. If the situation leaves the boundaries of the operational documents, support personnel are generally unable to continue working without assistance. The best example of this support level is computer operators that haven't worked with an operating system or application for long (or—let's be honest here—many operators that may have worked with the system for years). Another Level I group is the first-touch help desk personnel that field calls for potentially hundreds of systems and applications, attempt some simple solutions, and forward the call to specialists in the problem area.

- Level II—Staff that may have a set of written policies or procedures but that can read beyond them to understand the intent of the procedures. These people can act on their own initiative to solve problems. This could span a range from experienced operators to experienced troubleshooters—people who understand the concepts behind their particular area of work, but who may not understand the more complete picture outside their area of competence. An example here may be the experienced operator who has moved from basic operations to the problem management staff. Through experience, she has moved beyond basic procedures and understands the *why* well enough to creatively troubleshoot system problems.

- Level III—The experts. These people either have developed the application, have deployed the network, or are involved in setting policy and strategy for their area of expertise. They have developed the intuitive grasp of how their area functions as a complete system. Mainly involved with new development and strategy, they hopefully also have the time to pursue problems that are too complex or that take too long for Level I or II personnel to solve. When these people require help, in large corporations they contact the enterprise support staff of their product. In the case of Windows NT Server, this is usually Microsoft Premier Support, where staff work with their account's Technical

Account Manager or Enterprise Program Manager. (See Appendix A, "Working with Microsoft Support," for more information on working with Microsoft.) Outside consultants in this area will cost from $100 to $200 per hour.

Documentation

Thorough documentation is vital to the continued success of your Windows NT network. In a changing organization—especially in Windows NT, due to the demand for skilled workers—you can't afford to rely on information that lies only in the heads of your support staff. Documentation can get new hires working quickly without tying up experienced staff; it can also help the organization survive if the senior support staff gets hit by a liquid nitrogen truck on the way back from lunch (until you thaw them out). If something will be done on a repeated basis, document it.

An important step in the documentation process involves approving the document to a corporate IT standard through an approval body that spans a number of functional areas. In "young" Windows NT organizations and specialized areas where only a few content experts exist, this is often nothing more than a rubber stamp. Nonetheless, the process should be followed for several reasons. As the organization matures, more experts will be available for review and the approval meeting will be well established. The broad membership of the approving body ensures that the new document gets reviewed and questioned by a good cross-section of the technical experts in a company. Finally, when the minutes of the standards meeting are reported out to smaller team meetings and workgroups, this process helps ensure that new or revised documents get publicity to the right areas of the company.

In its first incarnation, the corporate standard will probably be a combination of what's out in production right now—good or bad—and best-known practices in emerging areas. This corporate standard will eventually encompass many different areas, such as server hardware, server software, network equipment, network cabling types and specifications—every area where standardization is desirable. Once established, the standard can be revised to new levels as technology changes and as the support staff becomes more experienced.

Where official corporate standards should be used versus best-known practices is a much-debated issue. An area such as network cabling should have one standard (e.g., Category 5) across the company so that all new construction will be able to use it without reinventing the standard. Server hardware, however, might request two or even three server types, depending on the purpose of the server. A run-of-the-mill file server doesn't require the same expensive hardware as a enterprise-scale Exchange server supporting 10,000 users. Lowering support costs by standardization often outweighs the extra hardware expenses created when the standard is too much for an application.

Once a corporate standard and the processes for maintaining it are created, there must also be a way of handling and approving exceptions to the process. These are for temporary or unusual situations, such as account migrations to a new master domain, the sudden appearance of a large non-standard environment from an acquisition or merger, or the one-time use of a product in the production environment to perform an unusual task. The key word here is *unusual*; business as usual should be handled by the corporate standard. Exceptions would go through the same review process as everything else, with the added requirement of stating when the exception will either go away or revert to the known standard.

After these corporate standard documents are written, they must be stored in a controlled-access documentation library and administered by a change management group. This ensures that a standard document set is consistent across the company. The change management people have full control, and everyone else (including the authors) have read-only access. This library can be as simple as a server share or as complex as a professional document tracking system with a Web interface. It's the only way to be sure that everyone can get the production copy of a document. The most common administration forms, such as add/move/change requests, privileged account requests, or restricted access requests, can be referenced from a common Web page that links back to this library. This makes the documents both easily accessible and version-controlled.

Version control can become complicated when documentation is tied to specific hardware or when documentation references custom-built CD-ROMs that have their own version control. When the same group producing the documentation controls the CD-ROM builds (e.g., Windows NT server builds CD and accompanying documentation), the job is easier. If a document produced by one group refers to a document or media built and controlled by another, however, it's best to simply refer to or link to the related document or build instead of explicitly stating the versions.

Figure 9.1 describes a process that could be used to create, review, and update corporate standards. Note that the document goes through two reviews. The first is by a team of individual contributors that are intimately familiar with the product and its strengths and failings. Only if the document passes this group does it move on to the higher-level corporate standards body. This ensures that the document gets an adequate technical review before it reaches too high a level.

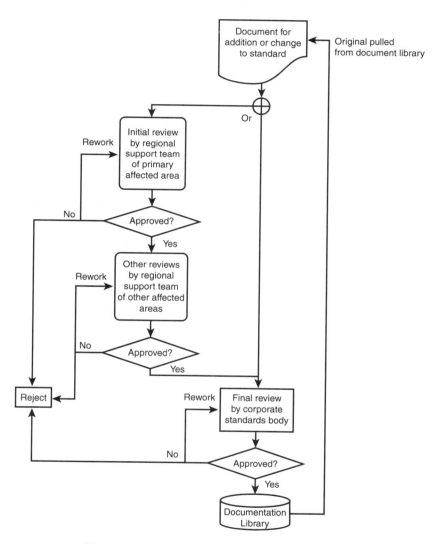

Figure 9.1   *Corporate IT standards process flow.*

The next trick is to get people to read the document, or at least know where it is when they must read it. The SYSNEWS utility can provide links to Web-based network documentation. Traditional hard copy material also works, but the key is that the documentation must be easy to find. Another idea is to store your documentation at a Web site with the URL `http://NT.<2nd-level domain if you can't avoid it>.yourcompany.com`. By using the auto-configuration features of the newest Web browsers, you can have users' startup pages point to this site, or you can add it to the Bookmark/Favorites list. An advantage of the HTML format is that it's easy to bookmark sections of a document for easy reference.

Public documentation for the Windows NT network falls into three broad categories: strategy, policy, and tactical. These documents should all have a standard set of boilerplates that, among other things, remind the reader to check for a more recent copy in the documentation library.

Strategy Documents

Strategy documents define the overall scope, design, and goals of the network. Their intent is to provide a framework from which day-to-day decisions about the network can be made. If a business organization wants to create and administer its master domain, the enterprise strategy document will show whether this is allowed. The backup strategy document will show what products are strategic for the company. If a team is formed to fix a backup-related problem—for example, how to back up mobile clients—the backup strategy describes what hardware or software can and can't be used and tells how to apply for changes to the strategy.

The Enterprise Strategy

The enterprise strategy document describes the goals of the Windows NT enterprise network—for example, one account per user across the company, high availability standards, and remote access to resources from anywhere in the company. Remember that this document often serves as an introduction to Windows NT networking in general and your Windows NT enterprise network in particular for executives and other employees unfamiliar with it. It should mainly be written to a level that doesn't require a distributed systems background, although technical detail is great if you lead up to it. A Windows NT 4 document should also include the domain model used, the number of master domains, the number of resource domains used, and other high-level features of the Windows NT enterprise network. A Windows 2000 revision would describe the enterprise's domain trees or forest, domains, organizational units and sites, and perhaps a graph that describes the special, non-Kerberos shortcut trusts between certain domains.

The Backup Strategy

The backup strategy document describes at a high level the goals and data availability of your network and tells in general how they will be achieved. This document should have information on how long a file must exist on the Windows NT enterprise network before it gets backed up, and how long it can be restored from the backup system. Disaster recovery goals and general information should be included as well.

The Security Strategy

The security strategy document outlines how standard Windows NT groups are defined in different kinds of domains, how custom administrative global groups and local groups are populated and what privileges they have, and how user rights are defined (if they differ from the standard set). It also defines the account policies in a Windows NT domain, such as password requirements, password lifetime, and lockout time after a given number of failed attempts. By extension, the document also recommends that the local groups be created on a member server because many of the domain's administrative local groups will be duplicated to ensure consistent access to both backup domain controllers and member servers in the domain. The document mainly addresses the requirements within a Windows NT domain, with the goal of quickly configuring a new Windows NT domain.

The Administration Strategy

The administration strategy document outlines what organizations administer the domains and what levels of authority they have in each domain. Exceptions for classes of individuals (such as resource domain administrators who need account operator rights in a master domain) should be noted. In Windows 2000, this can become a large document because you can delegate administration to a very finely detailed level.

Strategic Directions

Everyone needs to know where they're going, not just where they are. That's what a strategic directions document is for. Published as separate documents by subject area or as one master document with sections for each subject area, this document describes the major trends in corporate computing and tells how the company will align its direction to match that trend.

For example, Windows 2000 security has matured and expanded considerably from its NT 4 counterpart. At the same time, companies have begun to embrace the concept of the extranet—the corporate network extended beyond the company's firewall to exchange information with certain business partners. Windows 2000's security feature of public key infrastructure is a perfect complement to this expanding area of electronic commerce. How will the company take advantage of it?

The Support Strategy

A support strategy document should outline the support process from initial problem to final postmortem. The document should define the major support groups and what their responsibilities are. It should also cover problem escalation and how to handle escalations to Microsoft. Obviously, this requires far more than just a document. It's a synthesis of the organizational structure of the operations group, the various product engineering groups, and the escalation process between them.

Policy Documents

System policies don't necessarily need to each have their own document. They can be part of larger documents, such as the strategy document. Policy documents describe the rules by which the network is run. The following system policies are just a few of many policies that should be defined for your Windows NT network.

Naming Conventions

Naming conventions are very important, and a clear policy needs to be defined for these items:

- Windows NT domains (in Windows NT 4, both master and resource)
- DNS domains
- Servers
- Workstations
- Printers
- Accounts—standard, administrative, and disabled
- Global groups
- Local groups

Don't forget the physical labeling of the hardware as well. Even though it may lie outside your area of responsibility, encourage labeling of the physical infrastructure, and coordinate your labeling with that.

Other objects specific to Windows 2000 are listed here:

- Sites
- Organizational units
- Universal groups

The Account Management Policy

The account management policy is the document that outlines policies and procedures to cover most situations that the Windows NT account administrator will encounter. This document lists procedures for account additions/moves/deletions, share additions/moves/deletions, workstation machine account additions/deletions, and so on.

Scheduled Maintenance Documents

It's important that the customer population be well aware of when system maintenance is likely to occur so that business activity can be coordinated with the maintenance.

Service Level Agreements

If you have service level agreements (SLAs) with your major customer groups, they should be referenced from your system policies pages. SLAs need to be understood by the LAN administrators or the Windows NT operations staff to ensure that appropriate levels of attention are applied during multiple conflicting outages. For example, in the situation where two platforms are down, the customer with 24x7 SLA requirements may have priority over a system that is 9–5 only.

Tactical Documents

Tactical documents, also known as *operational documents*, describe how to perform certain procedures on the network, such as applying Windows NT Service Packs to servers. They're the how-to docs.

Examples of typical how-to documents would include those on server OS builds, application server builds, backup server configuration, and maintenance releases.

These documents are operational procedures to be used only once, or on rare occasions. Good examples are documents on upgrading service packs, upgrading a backup domain controller to primary, and cleaning tape heads.

Server OS Build

A server OS build document outlines all the steps necessary to build a corporate standard server, from assembling the hardware to packing it up when finished. Because the hardware build stage is a fairly manual process (no software is running to automate), it must be thorough. The software build, however, is as automated as possible, so this document will be pretty short. The test I always use for simplicity is, "Could my manager build a server with this documentation?"

Application Server Builds

Designed to be performed on top of a standard server OS build, an application server builds document customizes a server for its intended application. For example, an SQL server application build document would have SQL Server software installation and configuration in it, as well as base Windows NT configuration changes to optimize the OS for SQL Server.

Backup Software Configuration

This document details how to install and configure the corporate standard backup software, including software locations. This document may also include installation and configuration of backup hardware.

Maintenance Releases

Containing the most recent Service Pack and hot fixes, this is an integrated package to be applied to servers already in production. The contents of the maintenance release will be rolled up into the server OS build document for new server builds.

Summary

Your support strategy is one of the key components to a well-managed Windows NT network with the lowest possible cost of ownership. Effective support for a Windows NT network comes from all points of the compass, from the Help Desk trenches to management sponsorship in the executive boardroom, from the product engineering staff of other groups to vendor support of key third-party software. All these must be integrated to quickly and efficiently solve any support problem. Remember the following:

- Training is expensive, but it's cheaper than ignorance. To support a Windows NT 4 network and to be ready when you deploy Windows 2000, your support staff must be well trained. Encourage (and financially support) your staff's efforts to pursue professional certification. Pay for classes, not test-cramming software; you want your staff to have the knowledge behind the certification, not just the paper.

- Establish a liaison between your internal education group and the senior IT contributors so that the education folks have advance warning of the classes they should be developing.

- Document your processes and strategies. Get these procedures out of the heads of your staff. Keep them up to date, and store them in a central location with some kind of document control.

- Establish corporate standards for major Windows NT components such as servers, domain architecture, security structures, and account management. Store these in the central document library.

- Enforce these standards—with dismissal, if the standard warrants it.

- Start thinking about how your support/administration structure should align with the distributed administration available in Windows 2000.

After you have the overall strategy in place, you can begin thinking about the major support groups and their roles in the organization.

10

Operations, Problem Management, and Server Engineering

Operations management organizations that use the three-level support structure described in Chapter 9, "General NT Support Fundamentals," usually find that Level I maps to operations, Level II supports problem management, and Level III refers to server engineering.

If a problem goes beyond operation's procedures for dealing with it, the company creates a trouble ticket and hands it off to problem management. If the problem has that group stumped, or if it requires longer to research than PM can devote to one problem, the ticket moves upstream to server engineering. This chapter outlines some of the key characteristics of each group.

Operations

An operations group's charter varies with the size of the support organization and the number of servers it looks after, but it usually includes the regular maintenance, backup operations, monitoring, scheduled outages, and first-line troubleshooting of servers. In a controlled-access computer room environment, the operations group is also responsible for who has access to the servers.

Production Servers

An important concept in an operations environment of any scale is *production*. A production server has been verified to be of a standard configuration, follows network naming conventions, has hardware support contracts, and has whatever else is needed to keep it at a high performance and availability level. (See Chapter 11, "Configuration Management, Change Management, and Capacity Planning," for a sample checklist of production requirements.)

Only production servers get full support, and once a server is in production, no one changes its configuration, physically touches it, or reboots it without notifying operations. In larger shops, this can't be done without jumping through a number of hoops: Customer impact statements, customer communication forms, and support notification are a few of the most common checks that must be done. How many times have you called or visited some business or service, only to be told that the "computer is down" during the middle of the day and its users had no clue as to why? Except in cases of emergency, or to prevent an even longer outage, a production server or system should be left alone.

Documentation

Good operations documents are critical to the success and consistency of the group, but they're the most tiresome of all documents the Level II and III support groups must produce. You must be grindingly thorough and organized because you can't assume your Level I audience understands how to perform operations that aren't spelled out in the document. You can't say, "Check to see if this directory is shared"; you must describe how to do it, step by step. Often called *run books* or *daily operations guides*, they fall into the category of tactical documents, as described in Chapter 9. These documents are most useful only after they've been revised by operator feedback several times—after which they're often out of date!

Backups and Restores

The single most labor-intensive task in operations is system backups and restores. Especially on large systems, automating every tape operation that can be automated saves support dollars. The most common way to automate tape operations is to use a tape loader. The cost range is wide, from a few thousand dollars to hundreds of thousands of dollars. A relatively inexpensive way to automate small- and medium-size shops is to use the multitape magazines available on 4mm DAT drives. One magazine can hold up to 12 tapes, so if you plan your server disk storage and backup schedule around the magazine's capacity, you can limit human intervention to once or twice a week.

A much higher-capacity solution is the DLT loader. From just a few tapes to an automated tape library with hundreds of tapes, a DLT loader can store from a few gigabytes to many terabytes of data. If you use a tape library solution, you have to make sure that your network infrastructure is robust enough to support the throughput it's capable of. This is a much higher level of complexity, however, because it requires a high-speed dedicated backup network that contains only data being backed up from the production servers to the backup server, multiple NICs in the servers, and the resulting complications in the server's OS configurations.

Remember that none of these loaders really help with disaster recovery (DR). They're still physically very close to the server and the computer room if it floods, gets hit by a plane, suffers an earthquake, and so on. Until a tape management system is invented that carries tapes from one site to another, operators will be needed to move DR tapes out of harm's way.

Problem Tracking

For both operations and problem management, a problem tracking system can be a very worthwhile investment. System problems cost money, and once one has occurred, you don't ever want to repeat it. Certainly lots of problem causes lie beyond our control, but a problem tracking system can make sure that once a problem is encountered, the lessons it teaches us won't be forgotten. Problem tracking software offers these benefits:

- A centralized storage location for all problems.

- An organized way to record problem information systematically.

- Faster problem resolution. If a problem is encountered again, the database can be queried to see how it has been solved (or not solved!) in the past.

- Database reports. You can run reports against the database to see what kind of problems keep cropping up. For example, let's say that an unusual number of power supplies fails on the servers at one site over the course of a year. Querying the problem database shows a trend that indicates problems with the computer room power.

> **Tip**
>
> *Compare the cost of recording the problem, perhaps slowing down the resolution a bit, to the cost of relearning a solution that has already been figured out. You should never have to waste system availability and your own time to troubleshoot something twice.* ◆

The biggest drawbacks of a problem tracking system are related to operational discipline, not to the product itself. Operations and problem management must have the discipline to enter complete information into the tracking system and must have the discipline to check it before attempting problem resolution.

Problem Management

The problem management team's charter is pretty straightforward. In order of importance, the team must accomplish these tasks:

- Restore systems to full availability as quickly as possible
- Determine what caused an outage by performing a root cause analysis
- Report each problem to the group responsible for correction so that the problem won't recur

Restoring a down system in a timely manner is obviously the most important function of the problem management team, but a down system shouldn't be restored to service before two things happen: attempting a quick determination of what made the outage occur, and taking documentation. Sometimes the problem is obvious— the system partition runs out of disk space—but more often it isn't. Okay, the reason users can't access the server is because the CPU is pegged at 100%, but why is it doing that? Rebooting will fix the symptoms, but not the problem. An extra 10 minutes of troubleshooting is time well spent if it prevents another outage from occurring several hours later.

To troubleshoot or not to troubleshoot? This is a tough question. Under many circumstances, a simple reboot will solve most problems. The philosophy you choose will probably depend on staffing, time, criticality, and numerous other things. In an environment that has hundreds of Windows NT servers and a very minimal system administration staff, adopt the philosophy of collecting the necessary system data (we will cover what to collect later) and gracefully shutting down the system and rebooting. If the same problem occurs again, either on the same system or on a different system, then spend the time necessary to analyze the problem and determine a resolution.

On the other hand, it's easy to swing to the other extreme. Ex-mainframers and "trouble bulldogs" can fall into the trap of spending *too* much time trying to determine what's causing the outage; they'll lose sight of the basic goal of availability. Because of the relative immaturity of Windows NT compared to IBM's MVS, or UNIX, sometimes problems appear out of nowhere and never recur again. If this is the first time a problem has occurred, set a "drop-dead" time of about 30 minutes after someone has actively started working on the problem.

If the problem can't be determined at that point, take documentation of the system state and either reboot or rebuild. Rebooting is obvious; rebuilding is not. Ex-mainframers tend to look right past the solution of rebuilding a server's OS because it lies outside the troubleshooting paradigm they're familiar with. If you have a mainframe problem, you don't go out and reinstall the mainframe's OS! On a Windows NT server, however, it should take about 30 minutes to reinstall a basic operating system and then restore the OS partition from tape. (If you use the "backup root" technique described in Chapter 5, "Building, Maintaining, and Tuning the Box," you can cut down the recovery time to 15 minutes.) Trouble bulldogs keep pursuing the problem just because it's in their nature to seize on a problem and not let go until they get the satisfaction of figuring it out. These people are especially handy to know if you have a problem you'd like to resolve but aren't willing to spend much time on. All you have to do is get them interested in the problem, and they'll do the rest!

Following the precept that minimizing support costs is the best way to keep the overall Windows NT network costs down means "Computer, monitor thyself." Automated tools that perform remote administration, monitoring and alerting, and log collection and then take corrective action can be the most cost-effective purchases you make for a Windows NT network. This is because these tools live at the most expensive point in the human/network equation: the interface between a few support people and potentially hundreds of servers. By dropping the amount of time a human must spend on each server to as near zero as possible, automated administration tools allow just a few people to monitor many servers.

The base Windows NT Server 4 and earlier products don't have administration utilities that scale up to handle large Windows NT networks. Remote administration is absent in the base product. Monitoring the health of servers requires a third-party tool. The *Windows NT Server Resource Kit* contains a number of utilities that can help with Windows NT monitoring and administration, but in most cases quite a bit of code must be wrapped around them before they provide more value than their maintenance cost.

The following are five keys to successfully managing a Windows NT server problem:

- Backups
- Troubleshooting training
- Establishment of a troubleshooting process
- Problem analysis, resolution, and data collection
- Problem research and reporting

These keys are discussed in the following sections.

Backups

Your best tool is an up-to-date, readable backup of the entire system. This may be a tape backup, a complete clone of the primary system, or some other medium used for backing up data. If you have this, it takes an enormous amount of pressure off you. Depending on the frequency of your backups, data loss is minimal, even if you have to completely rebuild the system. With a good backup in hand, all problems can be solved, one way or the other.

Troubleshooting Training

To efficiently determine problems and then correct those problems, you need to practice. After all, practice makes perfect. Practice your troubleshooting skills by breaking Windows NT servers and recovering them. If there are multiple administrators within your organization and you have a test server (i.e., one *not* in production) to work on, take turns where one person creates a problem on the server and another must solve it. Attempt to re-create problems that you are experiencing in your environment. This will help you sharpen your skills as well as establish a repeatable problem, which makes finding a solution a lot easier. This step is essential in building your foundation of troubleshooting skills.

Establishment of a Troubleshooting Process

To act quickly when trouble occurs, you need to define a process or timeline for your troubleshooting—and then follow it. Many administrators suffer from "analysis paralysis," which is a phenomenon based largely on pride. Many administrators hate to throw in the towel. We will try one thing, then another, then another, and so on. Before you know it, several hours have gone by and the problem still exists. This is okay if it's your personal system, but when you are talking about a mission-critical server, such as a mail server, customers' patience eventually runs thin. In an effort to avoid analysis paralysis, it is essential to establish a process that includes a time-line. An example of the process is shown in Figure 10.1.

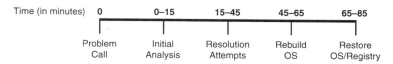

Figure 10.1   *Troubleshooting timeline.*

Problem Analysis, Problem Resolution, and Data Collection

When a problem actually hits, you must analyze it before you attempt a solution. You should always collect some kind of data for every problem you encounter, even if it's only basics about what happened, to what server, and when. If you have a problem that requires a reboot, you must collect a lot of data so that the problem can be analyzed after the server is restored to production.

Problem Analysis

When a problem arises, the first step to solving it is to collect and analyze it. Most problems encountered with Windows NT can be categorized into five areas. The following five problem types, and the native Windows NT tools typically used to resolve them, are not all the problems you'll encounter, but they will give you an idea of the steps that you need to perform in solving Windows NT-related problems. Additionally, the native Windows NT tools can be woefully inadequate for proactively managing these systems; you need to budget for helper utilities.

Spend about 15 minutes analyzing the problem to see which of the following categories it fits into:

- Connectivity problems, which can be solved with the help of these utilities:
  - Event Viewer
  - Server Manager
  - The command prompt (Net View, Net Use)
  - Remote Console (RCMD)
  - Performance Monitor
  - Domain Monitor
  - Network Monitor
  - TechNet

- Performance problems, which can be solved with the help of these utilities:
  - Performance Monitor
  - Event Viewer
  - Network Monitor
  - TechNet

- Security problems, which can be solved with the help of these utilities:
  - User Manager
  - Event Viewer
  - Server Manager
  - File Manager

- Data loss, which can be solved with the help of these utilities:
  - File Manager/Windows Explorer
  - Backup Software (such as Windows NT Backup)
  - Event Viewer (Did someone maliciously delete the data?)
  - Hardware tools (Was the data lost due to hardware error?)

- Complete system failure, which can be solved with the help of these utilities:
  - Hardware diagnostics
  - Pop-up error messages on the system console
  - The emergency repair disk
  - Solid system recovery documentation
  - TechNet
  - BlueSave (see the "Data Collection" section)

Problem Resolution
Now that you have analyzed the problem and collected information on it, it's time to try to fix the problem or problems. Examples of possible fixes for the five problem areas are listed here:

- Connectivity problems, which can be solved by attempting the following:

  - Re-establish a secure channel or trust. This task can be done through the resource kit tools Domain Monitor (DOMMON.EXE), NLTEST.EXE, or NETDOM.EXE. Another useful tool from the Resource Kit is SETPRFDC.EXE. This utility, included in Service Pack 4, allows you to supply a list of domain controllers in the order you would like them tried to establish a secure channel. This ensures that the client really does choose a domain controller that is network proximate for fastest authentication.

  - Resolve a duplicate name or IP address on the network. This will probably have to be done through WINS Administrator (WINSADM.EXE).

  - Reboot.

- Performance-related problems, which can be fixed by attempting the following:

  - Use the Performance Monitor (PERFMON.EXE) utility either remotely or locally to identify most active performance problems.

  - Kill a process that is consuming all the CPU. If you are on the console, you can use the Task Manager, Control Panel, Services to stop a service; a resource kit tool called Process Viewer (PVIEWER.EXE); or Task Killing Utility (KILL.EXE). If you are remote, you may use Server Manager (SRVMGR.EXE) to stop a service. Or you may use some type of remote console such as the resource kit tool Remote Command Service (RCMD.EXE) to remotely execute Task Killing Utility (KILL.EXE).

  - Identify a process that has a memory leak. A "memory leak" is a bit of a misnomer; it's really more accurate to say that one service is a "memory sink" because memory goes into it but never comes out again. Generally the only way to identify a memory leak is to monitor the Private Bytes counter of each service on the server over a period of time and to look for a positive trend of Private Bytes increasing. This means that memory is being allocated to a service's working set but never is being released.

- Identify system bottlenecks (memory, CPU, disk, and so on) See the section "Monitoring Performance and Tuning the Box" in Chapter 5 for details.

- Stop services that are not needed. Even if you are not using a particular service, it takes up memory. For example, if the box is not a printer server, stop the Spooler service. Other services that may not be used include Messenger, Clipbook Server, and Directory Replicator.

- Reboot—this sure fixes a lot of problems!

- Security problems, which can be fixed by attempting the following:

  - Reset passwords, using USERMGR.EXE.

  - Reset permissions. File, share, directory. Use File Manager or Explorer to view permissions.

  - If a secure channel or trust is broken, access may be affected. This task can be done through the resource kit tool DOMMON.EXE or the newer tool NLTEST.EXE.

- Data loss, which can be fixed by attempting the following to restore data from a backup.

- A dead server, which can be fixed by attempting the following:

  - Plug in the box or reset a circuit breaker.

  - Correct hardware failure. You may need to run the vendor specific hardware diagnostics.

  - Rebuild and restore the system. (Refer to the next section in this chapter.)

  - Reboot.

Conduct a Root-Cause Analysis, or Rebuild/Restore?
After about 30 to 45 minutes of analyzing and trying to recover the system, if you're unable to restore service, it's time to make a decision. Do you continue trying to fix the problem, or do you just stop, rebuild a generic operating system, and restore from a backup tape? This is not an easy

decision, and there isn't an easy answer. In my experience, most of the time when the server is experiencing a serious problem, it's better to stop, take documentation when possible, rebuild, and restore.

What's a serious problem? If the box does not provide its intended purpose or will not boot, that's considered serious. It's not easy to give up, but problem management's purpose in life is to put out the fire and restore service in a timely manner. The timeline and the processes associated with it vary according to how familiar the administrator is with using Windows NT, installing it, and using backup software.

> **Caution**
>
> *This process can work well, but you must have solid and consistent system configurations, backups, OS build procedures, data restoration procedures, and competent staff. The other important thing to remember after defining your process and troubleshooting timelines is to follow them. This can be hard, but try and force yourself; otherwise, you may encounter analysis paralysis and cause a lot longer down time than necessary.* ◆

Data Collection

To determine and resolve immediate problems, identify chronic problems, or get outside assistance, it's necessary to collect system data when a problem occurs. It's the job of the system administrator to collect the data, even if that person is not the one that analyzes it. What to collect? The more the better. It's better to collect too much than not enough, especially when you can't re-create the problem.

The following sections list commands that can be used to extract information from a Windows NT server that has a problem. These commands are in a batch file and are executed on the Windows NT server itself. Some of the commands are native to the operating system, and others are resource kit utilities. I've given examples of syntax, but refer to the online help for the exact syntax of each command.

Listing 10.1 is an example of a batch file that collects documentation. This would be run if a server was having problems, you couldn't figure out what the problem was, and you needed to reboot the server to get it back in service.

Listing 10.1. A possible batch file for data collection

```
Echo on
arp -a
net config workstation
net config server
net statistics workstation
net statistics server
ipconfig /all
netstat -e
netstat -r
net share
nbtstat -c
nbtstat -n
nbtstat -s
dumpmac
net sessions
net file
pstat
drivers
tlist /t
winmsdp /a
dumpel -l system
```

If you write a batch file to run a string of documentation commands, you should pipe its output to a log file:

```
Rundiags.bat >rundiags.log
```

This way, it can be reviewed or sent off to Microsoft for external support.

What follows is a description and sample output of the diagnostics commands in the RUNDIAGS batch stream.

Dumping the ARP Cache

As shown in Figure 10.2, arp -a displays the IP-to-physical-address translation tables used by the Address Resolution Protocol (ARP).

Figure 10.2 *An example of* arp -a *output.*

Workstation Network Configuration
As shown in Figure 10.3, net config workstation displays the current configuration of the Workstation service, which manages network connections initiated by the server (such as a net use from the server console).

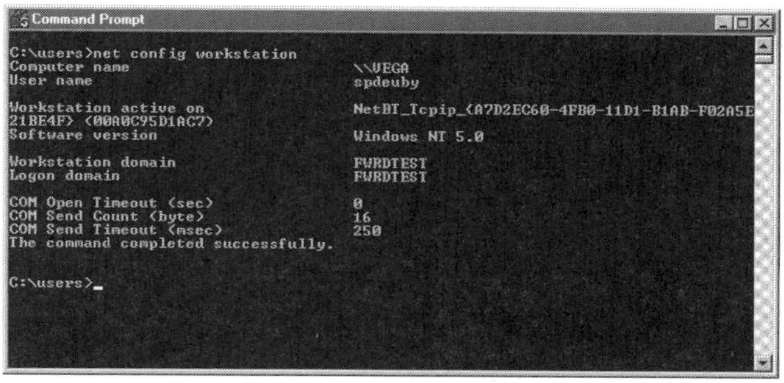

Figure 10.3   *An example of* net config workstation *output.*

Server Network Configuration
As shown in Figure 10.4, net config server displays the current configuration of the Server service, which manages network connections initiated by clients.

Figure 10.4   *An example of* net config server *output.*

Workstation Network Statistics
As shown in Figure 10.5, net statistics workstation displays performance information for the Workstation service.

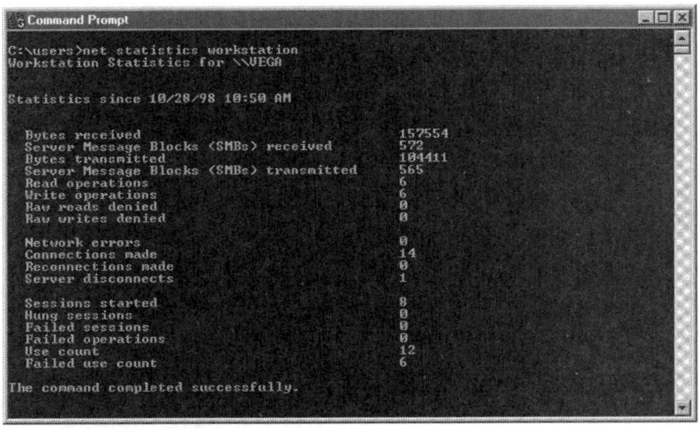

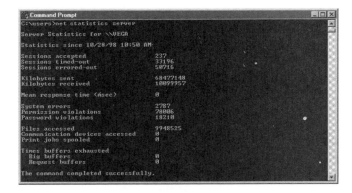

Figure 10.5   *An example of* net statistics workstation *output.*

Server Network Statistics
As shown in Figure 10.6, net statistics server displays performance
information for the Server service.

Figure 10.6   *An example of* net statistics server *output.*

Dumps of the IP Configuration
As shown in Figure 10.7, ipconfig /all displays the system's TCP/IP
configuration.

```
C:\USERS>ipconfig /all

Windows NT IP Configuration

        Host Name . . . . . . . . . : vega.fw.intel.com
        DNS Servers . . . . . . . . : 128.215.1.45
                                      128.215.1.44
        Node Type . . . . . . . . . : Hybrid
        NetBIOS Scope ID. . . . . . :
        IP Routing Enabled. . . . . : Yes
        WINS Proxy Enabled. . . . . : No
        NetBIOS Resolution Uses DNS : Yes

PPP adapter NdisWanIpIn:

        Description . . . . . . . . : NDISWAN Miniport
        Physical Address. . . . . . : 00-53-45-00-00-00
        DHCP Enabled. . . . . . . . : No
        Autoconfiguration Enabled . : No
        IP Address. . . . . . . . . : 0.0.0.0
        Subnet Mask . . . . . . . . : 0.0.0.0
        Default Gateway . . . . . . :

PPP adapter NdisWanIpOut<A7D2EC6F-4FB0-11D1-B1AB-F02A5E21BE4F>:

        Description . . . . . . . . : NDISWAN Miniport
        Physical Address. . . . . . : 00-53-45-00-00-00
        DHCP Enabled. . . . . . . . : No
        Autoconfiguration Enabled . : No
        IP Address. . . . . . . . . : 0.0.0.0
        Subnet Mask . . . . . . . . : 0.0.0.0
        Default Gateway . . . . . . :

Ethernet adapter <A7D2EC60-4FB0-11D1-B1AB-F02A5E21BE4F>:

        Description . . . . . . . . : Intel 82557-based Ethernet PCI Adapter

        Physical Address. . . . . . : 00-A0-C9-5D-1A-C7
        DHCP Enabled. . . . . . . . : No
        Autoconfiguration Enabled . : No
        IP Address. . . . . . . . . : 172.17.11.35
        Subnet Mask . . . . . . . . : 255.255.255.0
        Default Gateway . . . . . . : 172.17.11.251
        Primary WINS Server . . . . : 172.17.12.102
        Secondary WINS Server . . . : 128.215.1.71

C:\USERS>_
```

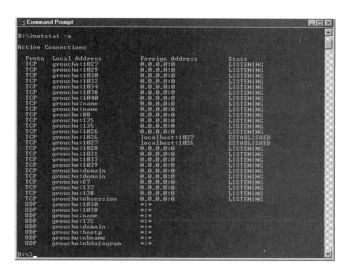

Figure 10.7 *An example of* `ipconfig /all` *output.*

Dumps of the Protocol Statistics and Current TCP/IP Network Connections
As shown in Figure 10.8, `netstat -a` lists all connections and listening ports.

```
D:\>netstat -a

Active Connections

  Proto  Local Address          Foreign Address        State
  TCP    groucho:1027           0.0.0.0:0              LISTENING
  TCP    groucho:1029           0.0.0.0:0              LISTENING
  TCP    groucho:1030           0.0.0.0:0              LISTENING
  TCP    groucho:1032           0.0.0.0:0              LISTENING
  TCP    groucho:1034           0.0.0.0:0              LISTENING
  TCP    groucho:1038           0.0.0.0:0              LISTENING
  TCP    groucho:1040           0.0.0.0:0              LISTENING
  TCP    groucho:name           0.0.0.0:0              LISTENING
  TCP    groucho:name           0.0.0.0:0              LISTENING
  TCP    groucho:80             0.0.0.0:0              LISTENING
  TCP    groucho:135            0.0.0.0:0              LISTENING
  TCP    groucho:135            0.0.0.0:0              LISTENING
  TCP    groucho:1026           0.0.0.0:0              LISTENING
  TCP    groucho:1026           localhost:1027         ESTABLISHED
  TCP    groucho:1027           localhost:1026         ESTABLISHED
  TCP    groucho:1028           0.0.0.0:0              LISTENING
  TCP    groucho:1031           0.0.0.0:0              LISTENING
  TCP    groucho:1033           0.0.0.0:0              LISTENING
  TCP    groucho:1039           0.0.0.0:0              LISTENING
  TCP    groucho:domain         0.0.0.0:0              LISTENING
  TCP    groucho:domain         0.0.0.0:0              LISTENING
  TCP    groucho:67             0.0.0.0:0              LISTENING
  TCP    groucho:137            0.0.0.0:0              LISTENING
  TCP    groucho:138            0.0.0.0:0              LISTENING
  TCP    groucho:nbsession      0.0.0.0:0              LISTENING
  UDP    groucho:1030           *:*
  UDP    groucho:1038           *:*
  UDP    groucho:name           *:*
  UDP    groucho:135            *:*
  UDP    groucho:domain         *:*
  UDP    groucho:bootp          *:*
  UDP    groucho:nbname         *:*
  UDP    groucho:nbdatagram     *:*

D:\>_
```

Figure 10.8 *Some of the output from* `netstat -a`.

Ethernet Statistics

As shown in Figure 10.9, `netstat -e` displays Ethernet statistics.

Figure 10.9   `netstat -e` *output.*

Routing Table Contents

As shown in Figure 10.10, `netstat -r` displays the contents of the routing table.

```
Command Prompt

C:\USERS>netstat -r

Route Table

Active Routes:

  Network Address          Netmask  Gateway Address        Interface  Metric
        0.0.0.0          0.0.0.0    172.17.11.251      172.17.11.35       1
      127.0.0.0        255.0.0.0        127.0.0.1          127.0.0.1       1
    172.17.11.0    255.255.255.0    172.17.11.35      172.17.11.35       1
   172.17.11.35  255.255.255.255        127.0.0.1          127.0.0.1       1
172.17.255.255  255.255.255.255    172.17.11.35      172.17.11.35       1
      224.0.0.0        224.0.0.0    172.17.11.35      172.17.11.35       1
255.255.255.255  255.255.255.255    172.17.11.35      172.17.11.35       1

Active Connections

  Proto  Local Address        Foreign Address       State
  TCP    vega:nbsession       DEUBY:1263            ESTABLISHED
  TCP    vega:389             VEGA:1098             ESTABLISHED
  TCP    vega:389             VEGA:1099             ESTABLISHED
  TCP    vega:389             VEGA:1103             ESTABLISHED
  TCP    vega:389             VEGA:kpop             ESTABLISHED
  TCP    vega:389             VEGA:1115             ESTABLISHED
  TCP    vega:389             VEGA:1116             ESTABLISHED
  TCP    vega:389             VEGA:1120             ESTABLISHED
  TCP    vega:389             VEGA:1125             ESTABLISHED
  TCP    vega:389             VEGA:1139             ESTABLISHED
  TCP    vega:389             VEGA:1144             ESTABLISHED
  TCP    vega:389             VEGA:1658             ESTABLISHED
  TCP    vega:1092            VEGA:389              CLOSE_WAIT
  TCP    vega:1098            VEGA:389              ESTABLISHED
  TCP    vega:1099            VEGA:389              ESTABLISHED
  TCP    vega:1103            VEGA:389              ESTABLISHED
  TCP    vega:kpop            VEGA:389              ESTABLISHED
  TCP    vega:1115            VEGA:389              ESTABLISHED
  TCP    vega:1116            VEGA:389              ESTABLISHED
  TCP    vega:1120            VEGA:389              ESTABLISHED
  TCP    vega:1125            VEGA:389              ESTABLISHED
  TCP    vega:1139            VEGA:389              ESTABLISHED
  TCP    vega:1144            VEGA:389              ESTABLISHED
  TCP    vega:1658            VEGA:389              ESTABLISHED
  TCP    vega:1944            DEUBY:nbsession       ESTABLISHED

C:\USERS>
```

Figure 10.10   *Some of the output from* `netstat -r`.

Share Information

As shown in Figure 10.11, `net share` displays shared network resources.

```
C:\USERS>net share

Share name   Resource                        Remark

-------------------------------------------------------------------------------
ADMIN$       C:\WINNT                        Remote Admin
D$           D:\                             Default share
C$           C:\                             Default share
IPC$                                         Remote IPC
Altosu       D:\Users\Altosu
CD           E:\
CKyan        D:\Users\CKyan
Clients      E:\clients                      Network Client Distribution Share
CMotobu      D:\Users\CMotobu
DEBUG        C:\WINNT\debug                  Logon server share
Dfs          D:\DfsRoot
EShimabukuro D:\Users\EShimabukuro
GFunakoshi   D:\Users\GFunakoshi
KMiyahira    D:\Users\KMiyahira
KToyama      D:\Users\KToyama
MOyama       D:\Users\CChibana
NETLOGON     C:\WINNT\sysvol\SCRIPTS         Logon server share
Public       D:\Public
SIha         D:\Users\SIha
SNakazato    D:\Users\SNakazato
SYSVOL       C:\WINNT\sysvol                 Logon server share.
TYamashita   D:\Users\TYamashita
wwwroot      D:\InetPub\wwwroot
The command completed successfully.

C:\USERS>
```

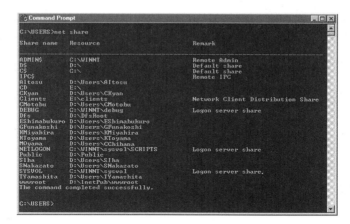

Figure 10.11 *An example of* `net share` *output.*

Protocol Statistics and Current TCP/IP Connections

As shown in Figure 10.12, `nbtstat -c` lists the remote name cache including the IP addresses.

```
C:\USERS>nbtstat -c
Node IpAddress: [172.17.11.35] Scope Id: []

                  NetBIOS Remote Cache Name Table

      Name              Type       Host Address     Life [sec]
    ----------------------------------------------------------
TCULBERT-DESK  <00>  UNIQUE      143.181.63.138       540
CWW            <00>  UNIQUE      143.183.202.162      60
ALMINT02       <00>  UNIQUE      143.184.33.98        120
Node IpAddress: [0.0.0.0] Scope Id: []

                  NetBIOS Remote Cache Name Table

      Name              Type       Host Address     Life [sec]
    ----------------------------------------------------------
TCULBERT-DESK  <00>  UNIQUE      143.181.63.138       540
CWW            <00>  UNIQUE      143.183.202.162      60
ALMINT02       <00>  UNIQUE      143.184.33.98        120
Node IpAddress: [0.0.0.0] Scope Id: []

                  NetBIOS Remote Cache Name Table

      Name              Type       Host Address     Life [sec]
    ----------------------------------------------------------
TCULBERT-DESK  <00>  UNIQUE      143.181.63.138       540
CWW            <00>  UNIQUE      143.183.202.162      60
ALMINT02       <00>  UNIQUE      143.184.33.98        120
Node IpAddress: [0.0.0.0] Scope Id: []

                  NetBIOS Remote Cache Name Table

      Name              Type       Host Address     Life [sec]
    ----------------------------------------------------------
TCULBERT-DESK  <00>  UNIQUE      143.181.63.138       540
CWW            <00>  UNIQUE      143.183.202.162      60
ALMINT02       <00>  UNIQUE      143.184.33.98        120

C:\USERS>
```

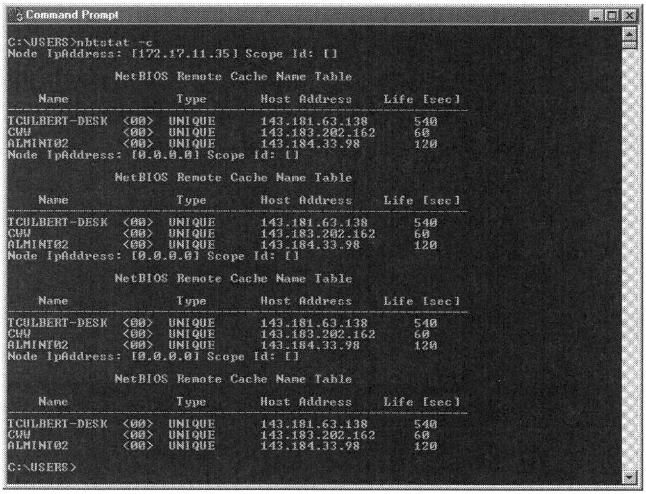

Figure 10.12 *An example of* `nbtstat -c` *output.*

Local NetBIOS Names

As shown in Figure 10.13, `nbtstat -n` lists the local machine's NetBIOS names.

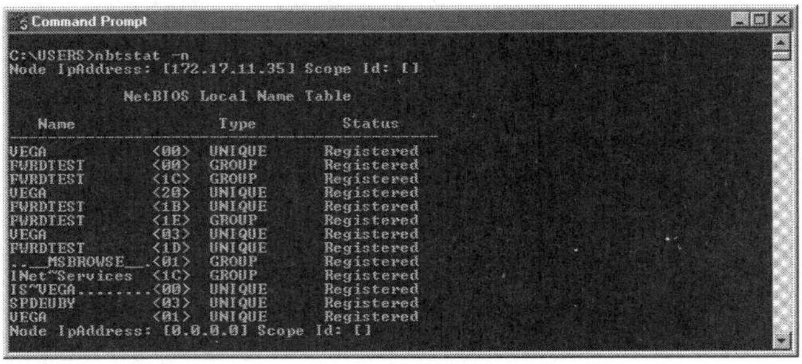

```
Command Prompt
C:\USERS>nbtstat -n
Node IpAddress: [172.17.11.35] Scope Id: []

                NetBIOS Local Name Table

   Name               Type         Status
---------------------------------------------
VEGA           <00>  UNIQUE      Registered
FWRDTEST       <00>  GROUP       Registered
FWRDTEST       <1C>  GROUP       Registered
VEGA           <20>  UNIQUE      Registered
FWRDTEST       <1B>  UNIQUE      Registered
FWRDTEST       <1E>  GROUP       Registered
VEGA           <03>  UNIQUE      Registered
FWRDTEST       <1D>  UNIQUE      Registered
..__MSBROWSE__.<01>  GROUP       Registered
INet~Services  <1C>  GROUP       Registered
IS~VEGA........<00>  UNIQUE      Registered
SPDEUBY        <03>  UNIQUE      Registered
VEGA           <01>  UNIQUE      Registered
Node IpAddress: [0.0.0.0] Scope Id: []
```

Figure 10.13 *An example of* `nbtstat -n` *output.*

Host Names Resolved from Destination IP Addresses

The `nbtstat -s` (note the lowercase "s") feature displays both client and server sessions. It uses the HOSTS file, if present, to convert the remote computer's IP address to a name (see Figure 10.14).

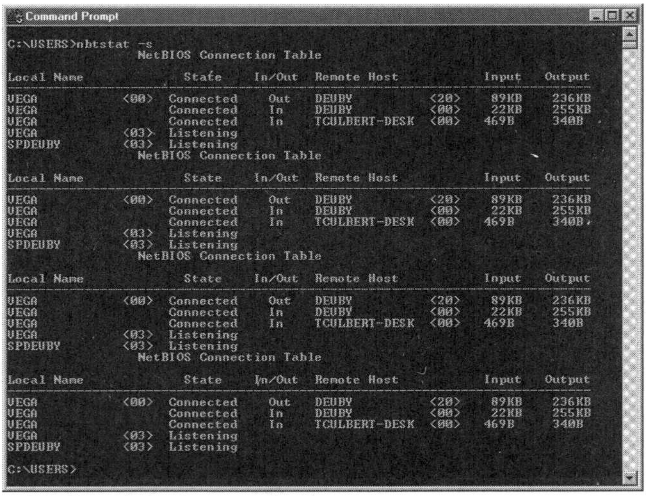

```
Command Prompt
C:\USERS>nbtstat -s
                NetBIOS Connection Table

Local Name          State      In/Out  Remote Host           Input   Output
----------------------------------------------------------------------------
VEGA           <00>  Connected   Out   DEUBY           <20>   89KB    236KB
VEGA                 Connected   In    DEUBY           <00>   22KB    255KB
VEGA                 Connected   In    TCULBERT-DESK   <00>   469B    340B
VEGA           <03>  Listening
SPDEUBY        <03>  Listening
                NetBIOS Connection Table

Local Name          State      In/Out  Remote Host           Input   Output
----------------------------------------------------------------------------
VEGA           <00>  Connected   Out   DEUBY           <20>   89KB    236KB
VEGA                 Connected   In    DEUBY           <00>   22KB    255KB
VEGA                 Connected   In    TCULBERT-DESK   <00>   469B    340B
VEGA           <03>  Listening
SPDEUBY        <03>  Listening
                NetBIOS Connection Table

Local Name          State      In/Out  Remote Host           Input   Output
----------------------------------------------------------------------------
VEGA           <00>  Connected   Out   DEUBY           <20>   89KB    236KB
VEGA                 Connected   In    DEUBY           <00>   22KB    255KB
VEGA                 Connected   In    TCULBERT-DESK   <00>   469B    340B
VEGA           <03>  Listening
SPDEUBY        <03>  Listening
                NetBIOS Connection Table

Local Name          State      In/Out  Remote Host           Input   Output
----------------------------------------------------------------------------
VEGA           <00>  Connected   Out   DEUBY           <20>   89KB    236KB
VEGA                 Connected   In    DEUBY           <00>   22KB    255KB
VEGA                 Connected   In    TCULBERT-DESK   <00>   469B    340B
VEGA           <03>  Listening
SPDEUBY        <03>  Listening

C:\USERS>
```

Figure 10.14 *Some of the output from* `nbtstat -s`.

The Current MAC Address

As shown in Figure 10.15, `getmac` is a windows NT Resource Kit utility that displays the MAC (Ethernet) layer address and binding order for all network cards on the computer.

Figure 10.15   *An example of* `getmac` *output.*

The Session Table

As shown in Figure 10.16, `net sessions` lists sessions between the computer and other computers on the network.

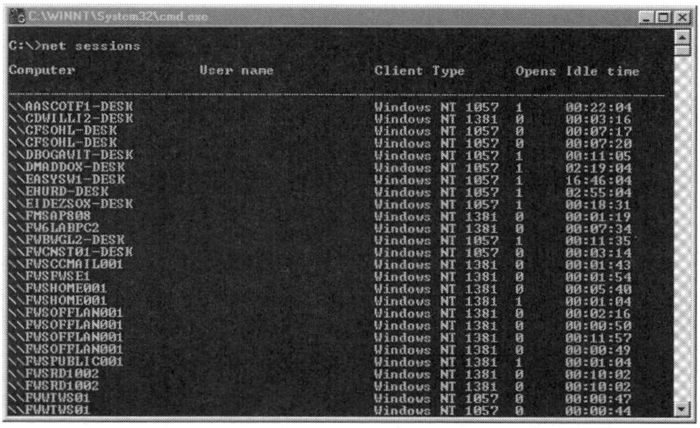

Figure 10.16   *An example of* `net sessions` *output.*

The File Table

As shown in Figure 10.17, `net file` lists the open files on a server.

```
Command Prompt
D:>net file

ID          Path                                    User name         # Locks
-------------------------------------------------------------------------------
18          F:\Documentation                        A0176108          0
20          F:\Documentation\DSKS70prod             A0176108          0
22          F:\Documentation\DSKS70prod\NTDocs      A0176108          0
24          F:\Documentation\...\NTDocs\General     A0176108          0
36          D:\netlogon                             A0176108          0
44          F:\Software                             A0176108          0
73          F:\Software\ServicePacks                A0176108          0
75          F:\Software\ServicePacks\nt40sp3        A0176108          0
85          F:                                      A0176108          0
87          F:\temp                                 A0176108          0
The command completed successfully.

D:\>_
```

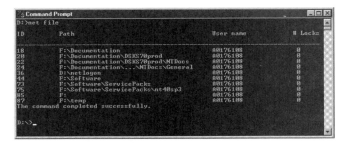

Figure 10.17 *An example of* `net file` *output.*

Process Information

As shown in Figure 10.18, `pstat` is a Windows NT Resource Kit utility that lists all running processes and threads and then displays their status. It produces a lot of output, some of which is shown here.

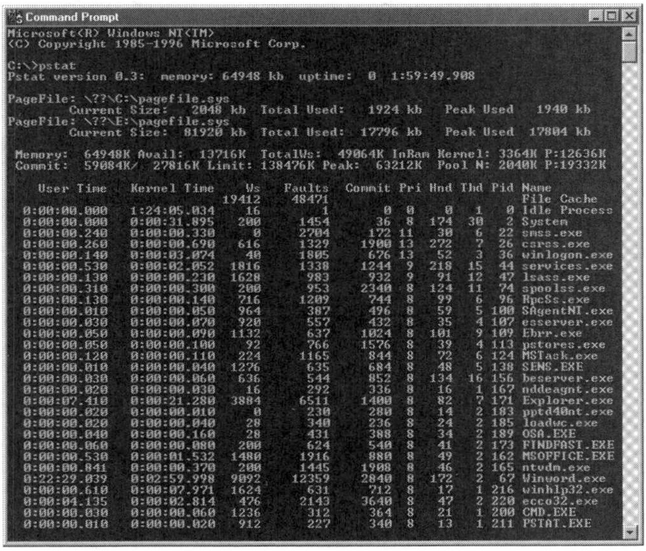

```
Command Prompt
Microsoft(R) Windows NT(TM)
(C) Copyright 1985-1996 Microsoft Corp.

C:\>pstat
Pstat version 0.3:  memory: 64948 kb  uptime:  0  1:59:49.908

PageFile: \??\C:\pagefile.sys
        Current Size:   2048 kb  Total Used:   1924 kb   Peak Used   1940 kb
PageFile: \??\E:\pagefile.sys
        Current Size:  81920 kb  Total Used:  17796 kb   Peak Used  17804 kb

 Memory:  64948K Avail:  13716K  TotalWs:  49064K InRam Kernel: 3364K P:12636K
 Commit:  59084K/  27816K Limit: 138476K Peak:  63212K  Pool N: 2040K P:19332K

    User Time   Kernel Time    Ws   Faults  Commit Pri Hnd Thd Pid Name
                             19412   48471                         File Cache
  0:00:00.000  1:24:05.034    16       1       0  0    0   1   0 Idle Process
  0:00:00.000  0:00:31.895   200    1454      36  8  174  30   2 System
  0:00:00.240  0:00:00.330     0    2704     172 11   30   6  22 smss.exe
  0:00:00.260  0:00:00.690   616    1329    1900 13  272   7  26 csrss.exe
  0:00:00.140  0:00:03.074    40    1805     676 13   52   3  36 winlogon.exe
  0:00:00.530  0:00:02.052  1816    1338    1244  9  218  15  44 services.exe
  0:00:00.130  0:00:00.230  1628     983     932  9   91  12  47 lsass.exe
  0:00:00.310  0:00:00.300   200     953    2340  8  124  11  74 spoolss.exe
  0:00:00.130  0:00:00.140   716    1209     744  8   99   6  96 RpcSs.exe
  0:00:00.010  0:00:00.050   964     387     496  8   59   5 100 SAgentNT.exe
  0:00:00.030  0:00:00.070   920     557     432  8   35   4 107 esserver.exe
  0:00:00.050  0:00:00.090  1132     637    1024  8  101   9 109 Ebrr.exe
  0:00:00.050  0:00:00.100    92     766    1576  8   39   4 113 pstores.exe
  0:00:00.120  0:00:00.110   224    1165     844  8   72   6 124 MSTask.exe
  0:00:00.010  0:00:00.040  1276     635     684  8   48   5 138 SENS.EXE
  0:00:00.030  0:00:00.060   636     544     852  8  134  16 156 beserver.exe
  0:00:00.020  0:00:00.030    16     292     336  8   16   1 167 nddeagnt.exe
  0:00:07.410  0:00:21.280  3884    6511    1400  8   82   7 171 Explorer.exe
  0:00:00.020  0:00:00.010     0     230     280  8   14   2 183 pptd40nt.exe
  0:00:00.020  0:00:00.040    28     340     236  8   24   2 185 loadwc.exe
  0:00:00.040  0:00:00.160    28     431     388  8   34   2 189 OSA.EXE
  0:00:00.060  0:00:00.080   200     624     540  8   41   2 173 FINDFAST.EXE
  0:00:00.530  0:00:01.532  1480    1916     880  8   49   2 162 MSOFFICE.EXE
  0:00:00.841  0:00:00.370   200    1445    1908  8   46   2 165 ntvdm.exe
  0:22:29.039  0:02:59.998  9092   12359    2840  8  172   2  67 Winword.exe
  0:00:00.610  0:00:07.971  1624     631     712  8   17   1 216 winhlp32.exe
  0:00:04.135  0:00:02.814   476    2143    3640  8   47   2 220 ecco32.exe
  0:00:00.030  0:00:00.060  1236     312     364  8   21   1 200 CMD.EXE
  0:00:00.010  0:00:00.020   912     227     340  8   13   1 211 PSTAT.EXE
```

Figure 10.18 *Some of the output from* `pstat`.

Dumps for All Device Driver Information
As shown in Figure 10.19, drivers is a Windows NT Resource Kit utility
that lists loaded drivers and displays character-based information about the
installed device drivers.

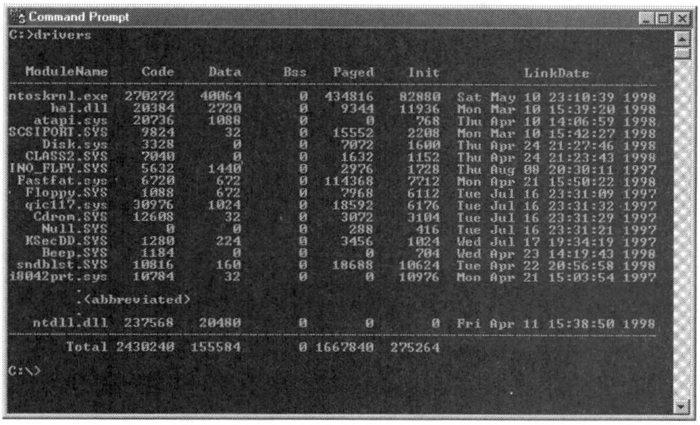

Figure 10.19 *Some of the output from* drivers.

Dumps for All Processes
As shown in Figure 10.20, tlist is a Windows NT Resource Kit utility that
displays a list of tasks, or processes, currently running. For each process, it
shows the process ID number and process name. The -t flag prints a task
tree that shows what processes are dependent on one another.

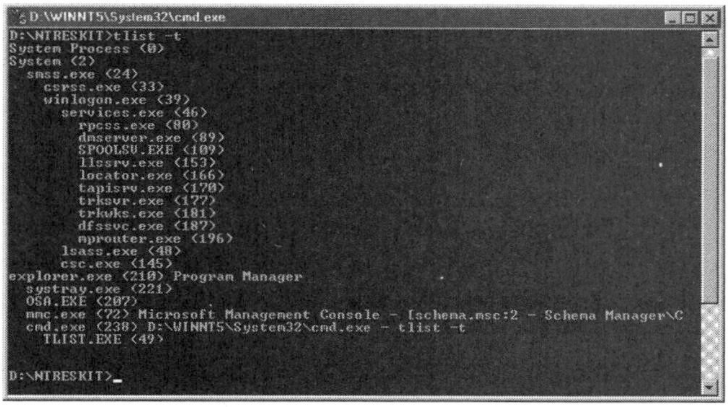

Figure 10.20 *Some of the output from* tlist -t.

System Diagnostic Report

The Windows NT Resource Kit utility `winmsdp` is based on the WINMSD graphical diagnostic utility that provides information about your system configuration and status. It generates a thorough text report named `msdrpt.txt`. The `/a` indicates all settings.

Dumps for the System Event Log

The Windows NT Resource Kit utility `dumpel` dumps an event log for a local or remote system into a tab-separated text file. The -f parameter indicates the output (default is `stdout`, usually the screen), and `-s` must be `system`, `security`, or `application`. Usage is shown here:

```
dumpel -f systemlog.txt -l system
```

Problem Research and Reporting

If you're in a position where you can submit an SR to Microsoft, for quickest problem resolution make sure you've done your homework first. When you encounter a new problem, check the following resources to see if the problem has already been encountered and a solution or workaround has already been devised:

- The online Microsoft Knowledge Base: `http://support.microsoft.com/`. This is the company's database of support information, some of which is restricted to premium customers.

- TechNet: `http://www.microsoft.com/technet/`. This is the place to go to learn about all things Microsoft. Historically a subscription-only CD, much of its content is now on the Web.

- The Microsoft Developer's Network (MSDN)): `http://msdn.microsoft.com/developer/`. This is the software and hardware developer's home.

- `http://www.sysinternals.com`: This Web site offers a number of unique tools for exploring the internals of Windows NT and solving some problems no one else has been able to do (See Appendix B, "Windows 2000-Related Web Sites," for more details). One very useful tool for data collection is BlueSave, a tool that saves Windows NT BSODs (blue screen of death) to a text file. Another is ERD Commander, a tool that lets you boot off a set of standard Windows NT setup disks into a command interpreter that's almost identical to the command prompt. From there you can access drives on the system and perform standard file-related commands! Pretty cool, eh?

- Public Microsoft news groups. Found on the news server `msnews.microsoft.com`, or hopefully available from your Internet service provider, these groups generally are not nearly as helpful as TechNet and Support Online.

If this search doesn't turn up anything and you still want to pursue the issue, gather all the documentation you can on the problem. This may include the following:

- Problem data.

- Network Monitor traces.

- Performance Monitor logs.

- Event logs.

- Condensed system dump files. Because all your servers will have the Write Debugging Information To check box checked (that's a hint!), thus taking a memory dump if they bluescreen, you need to process this data into a condensed report. If Microsoft needs the full dump, they'll request it, but this report contains most of the pertinent data and is only a few kilobytes in size, versus up to 128MB for a full dump. (See Chapter 5 for more details on reducing a dump.) The section "Data Collection," later in this chapter, provides a simple utility that collects a lot of data. If you do have to send a full dump to Microsoft, it'll probably require a tape of some kind. Be sure to keep track of the tape's whereabouts; it's your company data.

The more work you do up front, the faster a result Microsoft can give you. From years of working with Microsoft support, I get the impression that most people don't do much research at all before submitting a ticket. Indeed, your company develops a reputation with the local support staff. They know whether you're likely to give them tough questions that require them to be on the ball, or simple ones that the junior person on the team can answer.

Server Engineering

The server engineering group's mission is to be the leaders in new Windows NT technology, crafting it to best suit corporate business needs. Their objective is to provide their customers with timely implementations of Windows NT solutions that either solve existing problems, provide better ways to help achieve business goals, or save money. At the same time—and this is often a conflicting requirement—they must keep the enterprise Windows NT network manageable, usually through standardization. This unfortunately often means that new technology must be tabled because it's unmanageable on a large scale. Server engineering's customer base may be very large because the scope of this group in a central IS department can encompass the entire company. This also unfortunately brings more political dimensions to the workplace because it can be almost impossible to devise technology solutions that completely satisfy the different needs of different divisions.

In addition to needing good Windows NT engineers, then, it's important to have a team that communicates well. Their charter is to specifically be responsible for the design of the Windows NT Server network, to create the process for deploying the network, to participate in at least the initial deployment, to provide Level III support of the network, and to be the focal point of Windows NT network strategy.

It's worth mentioning again that the scope of the server engineering group can be the entire company. In this case, the group must implement solutions that are best for the whole company—not just for who shouts the loudest. For this to have any hope of succeeding, the group's management must have control over the network, whether it's budgetary or technical control. Without a big stick, uniform network designs and standards can't be enforced, which means that the group has responsibility without authority. In the absence of this authority, you can use cross-business teams to make decisions that span the company.

People in the server engineering group should love to learn and should deal quickly with change. Distributed computing is a very fast-moving business in general, and Windows NT engineering competes with Web and telecommunications for the title of "fastest moving technology." This group should also have a high percentage of MCSEs because a broad knowledge of all types of Microsoft network knowledge is required.

The senior engineers in this group should be on the Microsoft Premier contract. If they spend more than a few hours working on a problem, it's more cost-effective to spend the money to open a Premier SR ticket and speed resolution than spend hours digging and digging.

Summary

Operations, problem management, and server engineering are where the company's support organization meets the server infrastructure. It's these staff members' responsibility to keep this tangle of servers available and working as designed. All three groups have different charters. Operations' is the care and feeding of servers, problem management's is speedy problem resolution and root cause analysis, and server engineering's is design of the Windows NT network in the first place. In a successful large IT shop, however, all share two common traits—skill in problem solving and discipline to follow established processes rather than the "just do it" approach.

11

Configuration Management, Change Management, and Capacity Planning

Managing change in a distributed environment is a really challenging task, and a few specialized disciplines have developed to cope with it. *Configuration management* is the task of knowing the configuration of a system (in this case, the Windows NT network) and all its components (the servers, the operating systems, and the applications). *Change management* is the process of deploying changes within that system in a controlled manner and passing the changes to the configuration management team to update its information. *Capacity planning* is the process of forecasting future hardware needs based on the current system's performance and capacity from collected monitoring data.

Configuration Management

The vision of the configuration management team is to know (or have in a database) the configuration of every significant hardware and software component of a Windows NT network. The reality is a little less grandiose. The task of configuration management, well-defined in the mainframe world, is complicated in the Windows NT network by the same factors that tangle up other areas of the support staff. Every Windows NT server in production could easily have 20 different areas whose configuration is important to the server's continued good health. If you have 100 servers in production, that's 2,000 configuration items to track.

An aphorism that's been around as long as systems have had administrators is, "Any configuration database is useless if the data in it isn't always current and accurate." This means that either a human must diligently stay on top of things or the configuration database update process should be automated. Microsoft Systems Management Server (SMS) is a good example of a tool that automatically collects hardware and software configuration information.

Inventory collection is usually the first SMS function that's implemented. An SMS agent runs on every Windows NT server and desktop in the enterprise, collecting information on hundreds of variables that's stored in an SQL database. A query interface allows an administrator to quickly create lists of servers fitting any criteria they can dream up. For example, an SMS query to find out how many servers are on Windows NT Server 4, Service Pack 5 can be built and executed in a few minutes. Without utilities like SMS, keeping a reasonably accurate configuration database for a medium- to large-size company is prohibitively expensive.

Most of the change/configuration management team's time seems to be taken up with the change management role, however. Let's discuss what happens to change management in the real world.

Change Management

Change management people don't get no respect. In an industry where new software releases come out every full moon, desperate fixes to that too-quickly released software tend to come out two weeks later, and anything that's six months old is obsolete. Even the term *change management* is barely accurate. Perhaps a better name in the distributed computing arena would be *change survival*. To make life more difficult for the change management folks, there's no history of change management for distributed computing as there is for mainframes. As a result, many of the people who work in it are unclear on the concept.

Another problem common to the whole distributed network arena also surfaces here: Everyone's an expert. Because they have a PC on their desk and are familiar with the ins and outs of their desktop, some users think that servers are little different. "Why is it taking you two months to deploy Windows NT x.x on our network? It only took me a half-hour to put it on my workstation!"

Strategies

All this is trivial compared to the fact that someone has to *make* all these changes to the servers. Obviously, performing all these tasks individually, with no automation, would be a monumental task. Several basic CM strategies make this task easier—some obvious and some not so obvious:

- It's a good idea to group products at a certain release level that are known to work together into a suite. Freeze the configuration of this suite of products into a "baseline," and distribute this package to all production servers. An OS baseline might contain server hardware (RAID configuration, partitioning) ROM BIOS level, OEM support software, an operating system release level, a service pack, hot fixes, and third-party system software such as backup software, defragmentation utilities, and virus scanners. When an OS baseline is applied to a server, all this software will be verified or upgraded to that level. The CD format is perfect for this because it groups the changes together and freezes them in a read-only medium. It's still possible to break the changes apart, but it's definitely more trouble to tamper with.

- Have the operations staff perform the changes, based on CM documents, at remote sites. A drawback to this method is that most changes require full administrator rights, so more administrators are added to the domain. In a perfect world, administrator rights could be granted to operators for just the change period; this adds more complexity to the upgrade process, especially when multiple upgrades are being performed at different sites. The upgrade document would have to include mandatory pre- and post-implementation steps to grant and revoke the rights.

In the perfect Windows NT network, changes would be made only by authorized personnel as the result of change management process or, in emergencies, by problem management staff. In this perfect Windows NT network, the problem management team would always report the smallest change to the configuration management team so that the state of the network could be updated and remain accurate.

Hah! If you don't have a tightly controlled administration group, changes are made by problem management, capacity planning, operations, systems engineering, and anyone else in the administrators group that thinks there's a need. Oh yes, and that includes change management.

Process is all-important in the change management world. When a change needs to be made to a Windows NT system, a very clear process should begin that ensures that the change is well thought out, that the impact of this change is well known, that it's scheduled to cause minimum impact to the network's customers, and that both customers and (often forgotten) the rest of the support staff know about it.

The following sections describe some steps that should be used when implementing a change management process for a Windows NT network of any size. How thorough the process is depends on the size of the network and how much effort will be put into the change management process. A five-server Windows NT network probably won't need a formal results evaluation but will want to include a customer notification.

The Change Submission Procedure

You must have a written *change submission procedure* so that proposed changes to the Windows NT network can be documented and tracked. This procedure may include the following:

- Three types of requests usually seen in change management: *normal*, for changes to be made without immediate time urgency; *urgent*, such as for a system that is not fully functional but that can last until off-hours; and *emergency*, which indicates that immediate action is to be taken.
- A *change checklist* that clearly lays out the kind of impact this change will have on the server, the network, the users, and the support staff. The following checklist is pretty thorough; you should use as much of it as applies to your situation.
- A place to list these dependencies.
- Documentation that the change has been tested. If it has been tested, how? (Make 'em prove it!)

A Sample Change Checklist

☐   Describe the change as succinctly as possible.

☐   Determine why you are making the change.

☐   Determine the consequences of doing nothing.

☐   Contact asset management to order hardware and/or software.

☐   Obtain necessary software licenses.

☐   Built in automation to the management of this product, if possible.

☐   Talked to the automation group about this process.

☐   Determine the class or category of service into which this technology falls.

    ☐   Manufacturing

    ☐   Commercial

    ☐   Workgroup

- ☐ Determine where there is a monitoring tool in place to detect outages.
- ☐ Determine whether the outage statistics for this product will be collected. If so, where?
- ☐ Establish a system administrator for this.
- ☐ Locate a defined vendor report card for the vendor, if one exists.
- ☐ Ensure that enough disk space exists to run the product.
- ☐ Determine whether the product produces capacity information, such as log records, trace data, monitors, and so on.
- ☐ Determine whether any benchmark data has been produced, and briefly describe this data.
- ☐ Notify change management of this project.
- ☐ Determine whether training is required for change management.
- ☐ Identify any expected impact to the customers or production environment.
- ☐ Determine whether customers or the environment will be affected if the installation is postponed or backed out.
- ☐ Advise change management of installation tests and beta tests.
- ☐ Determine whether the product is intended for use on all servers and sites.
- ☐ Identify prerequisites and co-requisites.
- ☐ Submit the change management request form.
- ☐ Ensure that network engineering has verified this product's impact on the network.
- ☐ Complete customer acceptance testing and collect customer sign-off messages.
- ☐ Determine at what site the machine will reside.
- ☐ Notify the help desk of the installation.
- ☐ Determine who is to be notified of problems with the product and what that person or group's contact information is.
- ☐ Assess the customer's expectations of performance.
- ☐ Gather defined vendor support and escalation procedures.
- ☐ Gather the technical training documentation for the following:
    - ☐ Problem management
    - ☐ Operations
    - ☐ Help desk

continues ▶

▶ *continued*

☐   Identify the recovery/restoration process.

☐   Determine whether training will be required for customers.

☐   If so, ensure that customers have been notified that they need training.

☐   Determine whether this change will affect more than one site.

☐   Determine whether the change has been approved by the appropriate local and corporate review boards.

☐   Ensure that the change is Year 2000-compatible.

☐   Ensure that the change has been tested. Attach the test plan or include the URL.

☐   Identify dependencies with this change. In other words, do other changes depend on this one, or does this one depend on other changes being made? Does this change need to be made as part of a group (i.e., at the same time as other changes), or can it stand apart?

☐   Update the documentation for the changing system to reflect the changes.

☐   Obtain a tested back-out plan with full instructions. Attach the test plan or include the URL.

☐   Ensure that the operational execution document has been written and reviewed.

Figure 11.1 is an example of a form that collects key information for a proposed change to a Windows NT network.

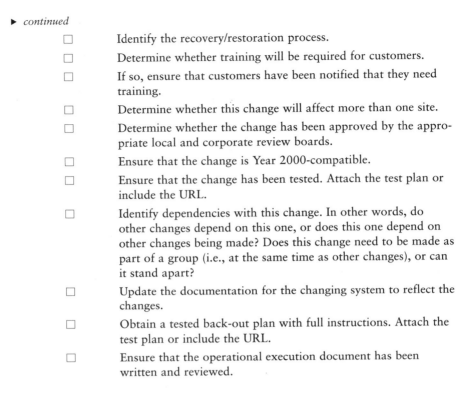

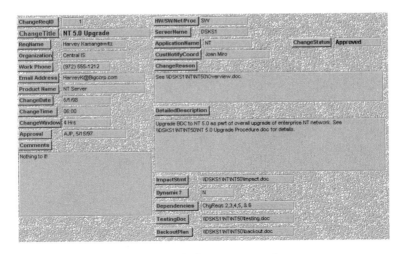

Figure 11.1   *A change request form.*

This change request must be signed off by the appropriate review board or emergency change manager before any work can proceed. No authorization means no change. This implies that emergency change management authorization must have a clear escalation process so that someone with signature authority can always be reached.

User Notification

Another vital task that's part of any change to the production environment is notifying the user community of the proposed change. Remember the users? They're the ones paying for all of this. Besides simply letting the community know when the system is unavailable, a good user notification process gets the users involved in the review of the change requests. Any conflicts with the user's schedules, such as month-end close, should be avoided or at least negotiated. A process should exist for resolving conflict between the user's needs and the system maintenance needs. The goal is to have no surprises for the users—sometimes a difficult task because the average network users see so much information that it's difficult to get their attention.

A list of key users should be compiled for each major component of the network. For example, one or more key contacts should be identified for the server ZEPPO. If ZEPPO has SQL Server, a key contact should be on file for each database.

Key users (group managers and power users in the areas) should be notified of proposed changes to the systems that they use. Another method is to hold change review meetings on a regular basis to review all proposed changes to the network. Both key users and support personnel are invited to attend to ensure that their groups' requirements are represented. Users should be notified if the proposed change will affect them, if it will affect other systems they might use, or if the status changes (e.g., the change gets cancelled).

A good way to notify the user community of proposed or impending changes is via a system news utility, as described in Chapter 9, "General NT Support Fundamentals."

The Review Process

A review process is important both before and after the system changes. An example of a prechange review is described earlier in this chapter. Postchange reviews are equally important and harder to implement because everyone wants to move on to the next problem. The postchange review is really a results evaluation. What worked is as important as what didn't work. Life in the distributed arena, however, moves at such a fast pace that postchange reviews are conducted only if something goes seriously wrong. This review has been given in many companies the somewhat macabre name *post mortem* ("after death") review.

Capacity Planning

The capacity planning team's charter is to be able to predict the trends of server usage so that users won't run out of capacity. Conversely, capacity planning involves knowing how to redeploy systems if utilization is on a downward trend. This might almost be called *capacity control* in an attempt to manage the rampant disk space consumption that always happens when no quota management or space chargeback is done.

You must do capacity planning, or you're driving into the night without any headlights. That armadillo that just went *bump* under your car is one of your servers that has run out of disk capacity. Your users are calling for relief, you don't have the time to clean up the file system for free space, and you can't buy a new drive array fast enough.

Capacity Planning Methodology

The major steps involved in capacity planning are listed here:

1. Gather data on your existing systems.
2. Track the growth of these systems.
3. Using the data, predict future growth or decline of your systems so that you can make hardware purchases at the right time, and in the right amounts.

Chapter 5, "Building, Maintaining, and Tuning the Box," goes into detail on what kind of data to gather and how to do it. Managing all this data is quite a challenge, second only to audit logs in amount of disk space consumed. This is another area in which automation is sorely needed. The most important counters you should set are as follows:

- Disk utilization - Disk space utilization, Avg. Disk Queue Length, % Disk Time
- % Processor Time
- Memory utilization - Pages / sec, Available Bytes
- Network Interface - Bytes Total / sec

You can record the data from these counters on your servers using the DATALOG utility, a service from the Windows NT Resource Kit. Now that you're collecting this data, however, what arises is a classic example of the difficulties of supporting a Windows NT network: The native Windows NT tools are inadequate for the task of automated gathering, managing, and analyzing performance data on multiple systems. You must either roll your own system or look for a third-party solution. The home-grown solutions I've seen use a combination of available tools: DATALOG, batch scripts, uploads to mainframes for SAS analysis, and downloads to Web pages. A number of applications such as Demand Technology Software's NTSMF, Hewlett-Packard's PerfView for Windows NT, and products from BMC and Landmark Systems are available that will collect performance data on multiple servers. Index sites for Windows NT applications, such as `http://www.winntsolutions.com/`, `http://www.bhs.com/` and `http://www.microsoft.com/industry/directory/` (for Microsoft registered solution providers), can help you quickly review what's available.

Analyzing the data for a few systems can be done with Excel and the FORECAST function, but for medium- to large-size networks, you must have a more industrial-strength solution. With the above counters, their suggested thresholds (listed in Chapter 5), and proper analysis tools, you can predict about when a system will run out of a resource (disk space, processor power, memory, network bandwidth) and then can forecast your purchasing accordingly.

The area of most rampant system usage growth is disk space. Without management, disk space use will grow unchecked. There's a universe of interesting things to download from the Internet, and when the Windows Explorer on your user's workstation indicates 2.3GB free on the network home directory, why not save it there? Why not back up the C: drive there while they're at it? Quota management, restricting users to a limited amount of disk space, is one solution. Several quota management products are available, but all have drawbacks largely related to the issues of quota management. Windows 2000 has quota management built in; because it handles only the most basic functions, however, expect to see the major players in this area: Argent Software and NTP Software, enhanced versions for Windows 2000.

Summary

Managing change isn't a glamorous profession, but it's as critical a component to high availability in a big business as good technical support. Predicting growth is also a hidden vocation. It's like—stay with me on this—a French horn player in a symphony orchestra. In much of the horn player's repertoire (especially Mozart and Beethoven), the player is called on to just sit there and let his lips get cold while the strings play. Occasionally he must just drop in a note to add a little more fullness to the orchestral sound. If he does his job right, the listener isn't really aware that the horn is playing. But if the player flubs an entrance, every person in the concert hall knows it. It's the same with the capacity planner: If these people they do their job right, the end user isn't even aware of their presence. Woe be to the planner that underestimates, however; then everyone knows his name and office location!

12

Security and Account Management

As Windows NT has grown dramatically in popularity, security on Windows NT systems has become a hot topic. Mainly focused on Internet attacks on corporate networks and small office/home office (SOHO) users through Internet service providers, every new release of a Microsoft network-related product is shortly followed by a series of security bug fixes. (Despite this, Microsoft's Internet Explorer 4 Web browser was downloaded more than a million times in the product's first two weeks of availability.)

This chapter focuses on the basics of a secure Windows NT network inside a corporation—in particular, auditing policies, audit log guidelines, system policies, account policies, and password policies. Corporate networks, especially when talking about Web services, are often referred to as an *intranet*. Intranets are separated from the Internet by a corporate *firewall*, a network gateway that stops many kinds of insecure network traffic and filters other traffic to protect the company against unauthorized access attempts.

At every level of security in a Windows NT network comes an either/or proposition: Either you have very high security, or you have a Windows NT network with a relatively low cost of ownership—not both. In the real world, you must judge how secure to make your network. You must decide which security enhancements go too far and give you a highly secure system that can't be managed with the headcount you have.

If you manage a small network not attached to the Internet, you probably don't have as high a security risk as the Central Intelligence Agency. You *could* enforce strong password support, requiring your users to have 14-digit alphanumeric passwords that include extended characters to slow down password-cracking programs—but the crackers could simply get the password from the large sticky note on the monitor because *no one* can remember such a password. There's a whole spectrum of steps you can take to secure your Windows NT network, from single-checkbox steps to complicated procedures that must be run on every server and PC on your network. Somewhere in between is the compromise that fits your situation.

Another problem is that these cracking utilities have been getting more user-friendly. Utilities such as the L0phtCrack password cracker and the Back Orifice remote administrator are very easy to use, encouraging neophyte crackers to try their hand.

As professional administrators, it's easy to forget that Windows NT is sold as a shrink-wrapped piece of software at the local computer store. It's designed to be easy to use out of the box, so it's not especially secure. We as administrators have to do the work of learning and configuring the system as it comes, keep up with Service Packs for both their hot fixes and new capabilities, and pay attention to new attacks as they arise. As in other administration areas, the corporation must have a goal or strategy that you can look to when you need to make day-to-day tactical security decisions.

Auditing Policies

The three audit logs—System, Security, and Application—are the heart of auditing a Windows NT system. All auditable events in Windows NT go into one of these three logs.

Unfortunately, the auditing design in Windows NT 4 is unwieldy and doesn't scale well. Event Viewer, the tool that the system or security administrator uses to view the audit logs, has limited flexibility and can be very slow on large logs. The logs aren't centrally stored for the domain; each server and workstation has its own set of logs. When you compound the problem by repeating this discrete three-log system on hundreds of servers across a Windows NT network, it's unmanageable without sophisticated automation and data storage tools. Many of the log entries themselves are just about useless if you aren't the Microsoft developer. Figure 12.1 shows a security log entry of a user (spdeuby) that resulted from reading a file marked for auditing. Other than the username, it's just about impossible to discern what happened.

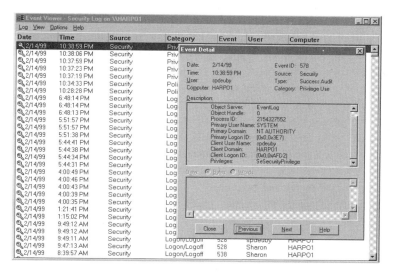

Figure 12.1   *A Windows NT 4 security log entry of audited file access.*

For example, let's say someone is trying to crack into your Windows NT domain. Assuming that you have auditing turned on correctly (which is not as common as you might think), the Security log is recording these attempts on the domain controller that responded first to the authentication request. You don't know which one that is; depending on the remote access design, there may be 20 different domain controllers the cracker has touched. The log settings are most likely set to wrap so that they overwrite from the beginning when full, so if you don't have some kind of automated log file archiving your break-in, data will be clobbered after an unknown period. If you're looking for a pattern of attacks, you must analyze the Security logs of all 20 machines over a period of several days or weeks, with full auditing turned on. This calls for some heavy-duty log consolidation and analysis tools.

Note

You need a third-party or an independent software vendor (ISV) tool to help manage your logs, such as Mission Critical Software's SeNTry or Aelita's EventAdmin. ◆

In Windows 2000, auditing is both better and worse than in Windows NT 4. On the plus side, administrators can view audit information on Active Directory objects in one location, using the Microsoft Management Console (MMC), regardless of where they are on the network.

This location independence occurs because the domain controller log itself is an Active Directory object. (Member servers use the Windows NT 4 access method.) As a result, it's replicated to every domain controller along with the other Active Directory objects. Another benefit of being an Active Directory object is that access to the log is very finely configurable, and the permissions to view the log can be delegated.

On the minus side, the amount of traffic generated by new security and the Active Directory can dramatically increase the amount of log entries generated if you aren't selective about what you audit. The average user will be constantly accessing Active Directory objects during the course of the day, so there's a great potential for high event log activity.

The audit logs can be reached several ways. The simplest is the same way you access audit logs in Windows NT 4: Select Start, Programs, Administrative Tools, Event Viewer. It looks a bit different now—it has changed into an MMC snap-in with scope and detail panes. As you can see in Figure 12.2, this revision allows other services, such as DNS, to also include their logs.

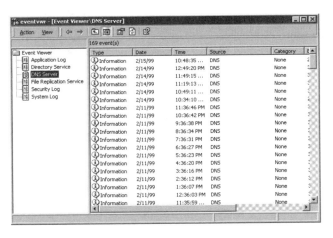

Figure 12.2   *The Windows 2000 Event Viewer snap-in.*

There's another tradeoff for going from isolated event logs on Windows NT 4 servers to Windows 2000 distributed logs for Active Directory objects. To keep the data consistent around the network, you must pass the information around the domain controllers—and that causes network traffic you didn't have before. As you increase the amount you audit, you also increase the Active Directory replication traffic, in volume if not in frequency. And the amount of traffic isn't proportional because each increase in object audit increases the traffic on every domain controller in the domain.

Audit Log Guidelines

The following are general guidelines for creating and maintaining your audit log:

- Turn on auditing. It won't do you any good if you don't use it. A surprising number of companies don't turn auditing on because they don't have a way to manage it. Even if you configure the event logs to overwrite events as needed and to allocate large log sizes so that they probably won't overwrite (for a while, at least), you've set up some kind of rudimentary audit trail that doesn't have to be maintained.

- Choose what you audit carefully. The audit log will generate megs and megs of data until you turn it off. If you want to maintain an audit trail that's several months long, you'll have to archive this data somewhere. The moral is to start simply, and then increase auditing while monitoring system performance.

- In Windows NT 4, auditing takes up two major system resources: disk space and processor utilization. In Windows 2000, you must be aware of increased Active Directory replication traffic. You must strike a balance between auditing in enough detail and bogging down your server's processors while burying them in data. (This typically makes for exciting meetings between the information security team and systems administrators.)

- Work closely with your Information Security group and check with your legal department to determine how long to keep the audit logs. Don't arbitrarily decide yourself. There are legal reasons, every bit as important as technical reasons, and statutes of limitations that determine how long system logs should be kept.

- Review your audit logs. I know it's a pain, but at least scan through the logs to look for glaring event errors that leap out at you. This is made much easier with an event log management tool.

- If you really want to keep track of the events on your network, get an audit log tool such as the ones mentioned previously. (Are you getting the idea that I think they're worthwhile?)

The following are guidelines for creating and maintaining your Windows NT 4 audit log:

- When you enable SAM (Security Accounts Manager) auditing, remember to also turn on NTFS auditing on your servers.

- Change the log settings (found in Event Viewer) to enable log wrapping, which overwrites the oldest entries and continues logging when the log reaches the maximum size specified. This means that overwritten data will be lost, but if you don't have some kind of log management software installed, you'll otherwise run into log full conditions.

- Increase the log settings from their default of 512KB. This is an inadequate setting even for systems that don't have auditing turned on. Figure 12.3 shows the adjusted log settings for a Windows NT 4 system, each of which is reached individually from the Log, Log Settings menu items in Event Viewer. Figure 12.4 shows the default Windows 2000 System Log setting, reached by right-clicking the log and choosing Properties from the Event Viewer snap-in. Starting with 5MB, increase the log size in increments until you can determine what size holds the log data for your desired number of weeks.

Figure 12.3   *Windows NT 4 Event Viewer log settings.*

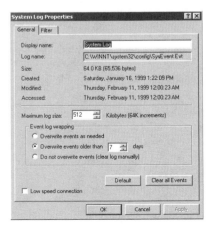

Figure 12.4   *Windows 2000 Event Viewer log settings.*

- Use the DUMPEL utility from the Resource Kit to dump the log files to a plain text file regularly.

The following are guidelines for creating and maintaining your Word 2000 audit log:

- Start with the default audit settings until you can see their impact and how they suit your needs.
- There's a great deal of flexibility in auditing Active Directory objects. You can audit certain key objects, such as the schema for any kind of change by the Everyone group, ensuring that nothing happens to the structure of the Active Directory without it being noted in the Security log. Conversely, you can set auditing on an individual user or group and then follow someone's every move in accessing Active Directory objects. As I've said, this flexibility comes at the price of increased system overhead because more auditing takes more resources. Try to keep your auditing as narrowly focused as possible to minimize the impact on the log size and system performance. On the other hand, don't get carried away with the most arcane audit settings at first. Start with the simplest audit settings before you drill down into the deep security dialogs; the Active Directory security settings are among the most complicated dialogs in all of Windows 2000.
- Use the Security Configuration Editor to set and apply security policies across the servers and domains.

System Policies

The following are some basic security measures you should incorporate into your system security policy:

- Keep SAM safe. If unauthorized users can access your servers, they can get access to SAM-stored passwords in any number of ways. This means keeping the servers locked up and disabling the Everyone group from being able to remotely access the registry.
- Audit the administrators. Keep track of who's in the administrators group (both directly and indirectly, through global group membership) and audit their actions. An administrator can clear a log to cover their tracks, but the action of clearing the log is itself logged. So, if nothing else, the rogue administrator may be caught if he keeps clearing the log again and again!

- Trust in few. Especially limit trusts in which one of your corporate domains trusts a domain that you have no control over. If security on that domain is compromised, the intruder may then be able to gain access to your domains as well.

- Forbid trespassing. Display a legal notice upon logon that says "Unauthorized use of this resource is prohibited." This gives you legal ground because all logged-on users must acknowledge by pressing the OK button. This legal notice can be found here:

```
HKEY_LOCAL_MACHINE
    \Software
        \Microsoft
            \Windows NT
                \CurrentVersion
                    \Winlogon
                        \LegalNoticeText
```

- Lock it up. Teach users how to use the Lock workstation feature of Windows NT Workstation and set the screen saver to lock up with a password. For particularly secure environments, you could use the WINEXIT screen saver in the Resource Kit to automatically log the user off after a certain amount of inactivity.

- Allow no Guests. If no one outside the trusted Windows NT network must have access to resources in the network, disable the Guest account, rename it, and assign it a random password. If you must have a Guest account, limit its access by removing it from Domain Users, set logon hours, and rename the account. By default, it's disabled. A drawback of having the Guest account disabled is that users from untrusted domains will not be able to access any resources in the trusted network, including public shares. This can be a pain when your company has a lot of standalone domains on your corporate network.

- Identify the culprit. Your information security department is usually responsible for tracking security violations, but it's not unusual for them to seek an experienced administrator's help in specialized Windows NT topics. For example, it's possible to track the user who changed the Administrator (or whatever you renamed it to) password. See Microsoft Support Online (http://support.microsoft.com) and search for article Q173939.

- Allow locals only. Consider disabling network access to the registry. This can be done by creating the following key:

```
HKEY_LOCAL_MACHINE
    \CurrentcontrolSet
        \Control
            \SecurePipeServers
                \winreg
```

The security setting on this key determines who has network access to the registry.

- Allow the administrator to lock out. The PASSPROP utility from the Resource Kit will enable account lockout for remote logons that use the administrator account. This will make the administrator (or whatever you've renamed it to) subject to system lockout policies in situations other than interactive logons.

- Stay current. Keep up with current news on Windows NT security enhancements and fixes. http://www.microsoft.com/security and http://www.winntmag.com are good places to stay on top of security announcements. For example, Windows NT 4 Service Pack 3 incorporates a number of security enhancements that might be missed from a cursory inspection of its contents. Service Pack 4 is very large and has a lot of security hot fixes rolled into it.

Windows NT Account Policies

Before you begin deploying Windows NT, you must have well-defined processes for granting, auditing, and revoking administrative rights. If you don't, coming back after deployment and cleaning up the administrative structure is a prohibitively costly exercise.

In Windows NT 4's security model, the domain is the smallest administrative unit. You either have rights in the entire domain, or you don't. The various administrative local groups—administrators, account operators, server operators, backup operators, and print operators—are the keys to the kingdom that must be managed. Unfortunately, Windows NT doesn't come with any tools to tightly monitor these groups and what their members are up to.

If administrative rights processes aren't in place, you can usually find the fallout in the Administrators local group because that's typically the area where most of the abuse takes place. It takes knowledge of the Windows NT administrative local groups—and a bit of self-restraint—to determine the exact needs of someone asking for administrative access; usually, the person is just added to Administrators. Compounding the problem is the fact that the Domain Admins global group is automatically part of the Administrators local group. This global group is included by default into the Administrators local group of all Windows NT workstations registered in the domain. This gives anyone in the Domain Admins the ability to do just about anything to hundreds or thousands of workstations in your domain.

The account operator local group runs a close second in the abuse department because distributed account management is one of the areas where Windows NT 4 is the least flexible. Windows NT 4 account management is also domain-based; you either have no rights to manage accounts, or you can alter accounts at your rights level and below for the entire domain.

Note

Unless you have a tightly controlled, centralized account management group, Account operator rights must be granted to a wide range of individuals throughout the enterprise. Therefore, account security will not be as tight as it should be. ◆

Third-party products such as Mission Critical Software's Enterprise Administrator are required to sidestep this lack of flexibility. Enterprise Administrator does this by simply revoking all account operator rights and most administrator rights from everyone. Account operators then perform adds/changes/deletes through an Enterprise Administrator GUI, which passes them to its own engine. There the actions are logged and verified against a detailed and flexible table of rights. The engine performs the actual account work, so it's the only account that shows up in the system log. All the detail of who, what, when, and where is in Enterprise Administrator's logs.

A typical area of contention over who gets account operator rights comes about with resource domain administrators. By definition, a resource domain has its server resources (file shares, printers, and son on) in one Windows NT domain, while the resource domain's users accounts are in another master account domain. A one-way trust to the account domain allows the accounts from the master domain access to the resource domain's shares and printers. Because of this setup, administrators of the resource domain can control the resources but typically not the accounts. They can reboot their servers, alter their system configurations, and do whatever they want to the hardware in their domain—but if their boss in the office next door forgets his password and needs it to be reset, they're helpless. This doesn't sit well with the boss next door.

The inability to reset your boss's password is annoying, but other situations can be more critical to business. A popular model in sales force automation is to have your company's salespeople always on the go with their information packed along—road warriors with notebooks, modems, and cell phones. Occasionally, they stop moving between sales calls long enough to check their email and download the latest parts information and sales news from a central database. If they have a problem with their password when they alight at a pay phone with an RJ11 jack, they need to make a support call and have it fixed immediately. Unlike a typical knowledge worker, they can't wait at their desk for a callback from their problem ticket; Flight 1158 to Little Rock is in final boarding. To support this person, an account administrator must be able to immediately correct the problem. This can be solved two ways: Your central administration number must be able to deliver a guaranteed turnaround time of one hour or less, or distribute the ability to manage accounts to local help desks where operators can closely support smaller groups of users.

So how do you manage administrative groups in a Windows NT domain? First, implement a grant process that must be followed for every administrative account. Second, make every account that's currently in the administrative groups go through the process. Third, buy or build a monitoring tool that tracks the membership of the administrative groups. If you purchase a third-party security management tool, you must still go through the first two steps. No Windows NT security tool will build your request process for you.

The Grant Process for Administrators

The user or manager must write a message to security that requests administrative rights for a user. This message must include the following points:

- What resources they need to access (*not* what administrative rights they need). For example, a user might request the ability to add Windows NT Workstations to a domain. He should not request administrator access. Security will determine the level of administrative rights required (in this case, the "Add a Workstation" user right only).

- Justification based on job need: "Why I need to be able to perform this function."

- Information security will review all requests, with assistance from the Windows NT engineering team if extra expertise is needed. Upon approval, put the approved requests into a database. Include the date of approval so that a query can be run regularly that creates a list of accounts due for regular review.

Monitoring and Reviewing Administrative Rights

The now-clean administrative groups should be regularly reviewed at two levels. First, a simple program should be run daily or hourly that monitors the group membership of key administrator groups such as administrators, domain administrators, account operators, backup operators, and server operators. If an account or a group has been added to any of these groups, an email is generated to the information security staff for investigation. Obviously, this method won't catch a quick addition-deletion of group membership, but it will catch the more casual "sure, give him rights" situation.

Second, every six months all administration accounts should be reviewed again to see whether their owners still require administrative rights:

- The senior Windows NT security team members should be MCSEs because security touches all aspects of the operating system and the network. A systems engineer certification helps ensure that these people can look at the Windows NT network as a whole, from Windows 95 workstations to multiprocessor Windows NT servers.

- "Securing NT Installations," at http://www.microsoft.com/security/, is a good document that covers security requirements at different security levels, including recommended group rights and audit settings.

Password Policies

Every domain should adopt some very basic password policies to slow down any potential crackers:

- It's too hard to type anyway—rename the administrator account. Although it doesn't stop some attacks, such as RedButton, it does prevent brute-force attacks that attempt to logon as an administrator and guess the password.

- Protect your Emergency Recovery Disk (ERD). The ERD contains a copy of all your Registry files, including SAM accounts database. If it's stolen, a cracker can run security attacks against it without any audit warnings to you. I recommend keeping two ERDs in a sleeve inside the front cover of your servers in their physically secured environment.

- Three strikes, and you're out. Use the account lockout feature of the account security policy to lockout after three bad logon attempts. This will prevent someone from attempting a brute-force login by trying endless variations of passwords. Don't set the reset count number too low, either; it should be at least 15 minutes.

- Be strong. Use strong password support, or at least some of it. Windows NT 4 Service Pack 3, for instance, incorporates strong password support. This means that a new DLL, PASSFILT.DLL, is installed that lets you enforce stronger password requirements for users. If you don't actually install the support, you can still incorporate some of its principles into your network's user policies. Strong password support means a minimum password length of six characters, and passwords must contain characters from at least three of the following four formats: uppercase English, lowercase English, Arabic numerals (0,1,2,3, and so on), and special characters such as punctuation symbols. I might also add—no spouses', kids', or dogs' names for passwords! As an IBM VM administrator, I was able to see user passwords, and I was astounded by how many people did that.

- Don't recycle. Set account rights to remember the last five passwords.
- Know it to change it. Check the checkbox that says users must logon to change their password.

Account Management

On the surface, Windows NT account management would seem to be a simple duty of order entry. In reality, the area of Windows NT account management is vitally important to the organized growth, structures, and security of a Windows NT network. Unfortunately, it's also a responsibility that tends to be overlooked because it isn't as sexy as other areas.

> **Note**
>
> *A solid, well-trained account management team is critical to the continued success of a large Windows NT network.* ◆

Account management is the entry point for a user into a Windows NT network. It's here that the initial user account, local groups, global groups, home server, and home directory are set up. If these are being set up incorrectly, the least problem is the consistency of the account conventions; at the worst, the integrity of the Windows NT network may be at risk. Many problems and inadequacies exist with Windows NT account management. Without automating large portions of the job, it's not possible to anticipate and create procedures for every problem an account management staffer may encounter. Good account management staff must be able to understand the intent of the procedures so that they're empowered to do some of their own problem solving. That's one reason it's so important for these people to be of Level II support quality or to have at least one Level II type person on the team that others can go to for help.

The following sections list major and minor issues in account management beyond such basic tasks as account adds/changes/deletes. Some of these are obvious, but some are the result of not considering them until too late. Some of these issues can be resolved by devising the right policies and procedures, some by training, some by intergroup communication, some by third-party utilities—and some just plain can't be easily solved in Windows NT 4.

Resource Ownership

All network resources must be identified and an owner associated with them. How can you manage resources if you don't know who owns them? In Windows NT 4, there's no clear-cut way to make this association, so you must come up with a creative solution. In Windows 2000, the Active Directory will have fields for every kind of information about a resource you'll ever want. You won't be required to fill them in at migration time, but this kind of centralized directory service can be so useful that you'll *want* to fill them in.

A possible solution would be a separate database that maps Windows NT resources such as servers, shares, printers, and so on to owner information. This would allow great flexibility in the information tracked and how easily it can be queried. However, this would be a separate database that must be scrupulously kept in synchronization with the contents of the SAM and general network configuration—a full-time job.

A simpler solution would be to use Description fields. Every Windows NT resource (servers, printers, shares, and so on) has a Description field that can be diced up to contain both human-friendly information and ownership information. The advantages of this approach are that it's simple, it's centrally located, and it's easy to access programmatically through existing WIN32 APIs. In addition, the information can easily be viewed through standard administrative tools such as User Manager for Domains, Server Manager for Domains, Print Manager, and simply NET VIEW. This database can't get lost or accidentally erased, either. Disadvantages, however, are that the field size is limited to 48 characters, and it adds to the SAM size and therefore the amount of memory required in a server.

Identifying and Tracking Resource Locations

Account management must involve determining what drive (logical partition) a user or group share resides on. When any maintenance is to be done on the share, the account clerk must connect to each logical drive in turn and search through hundreds or thousands of shares to find the target share. This can be a very time-consuming job, especially for servers with three or four logical drives. Logical drive information would be well worth 2 bytes (drive letter + delimiter) in the Description field. In Windows 2000, this can be stored in a property in the Active Directory.

Secondary Resource Contacts

You need a reliable contact for a resource when the person documented is no longer with the group. The simplest solution for this problem is to put a higher-level manager's employee number in the Description field after the owner's employee number. In Windows 2000, this should be stored in the manager attribute of the user object in the Active Directory.

Enterprise Group Naming Standards

You must have a consistent policy for naming local and global groups within a domain and between domains. Most importantly, the name of a local group should map to the name of its related global group so that one can be logically derived from the other. One way of doing this is to name both the local group and the global group the same in the beginning, but use a suffix for the local group so that they show up next to each other in User Manager for Domains. For example, a multiple master domain Windows NT network has the global group MTS_Admins in every master domain. The local group MTS_Admins_LG would contain only the MTS Admins global groups. Site-specific global or local groups should also have their site code in the description.

Group naming conventions are important to nail down from the beginning because it's so difficult to rename Windows NT groups after they've been created. Native Windows NT utilities will not allow you to rename Windows NT 4 groups, but at least one third-party utility (Mission Critical Software's Enterprise Administrator) provides this function. This is as important in Windows 2000 as it is in previous versions.

The Process for Group Access

You need a standard request process for adding users to existing group shares or global groups/local groups. For the purposes of these requests, share security can be broken down into three categories:

- *Level 1, or low*—Add a new user on request, and don't ask the owner for permission
- *Level 2, or medium*—Ask for permission from the owner of record
- *Level 3, or high*—Only accept addition requests from the owner, and notify the owner if someone requests access

The category should be determined with the owner when the share is created.

Machine Accounts

Keep workstation machine accounts current. Machine accounts (server and especially workstation accounts) tend to be created and never deleted. Each account occupies 512 bytes in the Registry. Whenever a Windows NT machine is removed from service or reinstalled with a different NetBIOS name, the original machine account remains orphaned in the domain. The other most common cause of inactive machine accounts is from computers with multiple Windows NT configurations because each configuration requires a machine account in the domain to fully participate in Windows NT networking. These multiboot configurations complicate the process of weeding out inactive accounts because there's no way to distinguish between a multiboot computer and an orphan machine account.

One way to keep track of dead machine accounts in a domain with multiboot computers is to remove all inactive accounts. When multiboot owners complain, re-create their machine account and add the comment `"multiboot"` in the workstation's Description field. The owners will cooperate because if that comment isn't in the field, the next time they boot to another operating system, they're going to lose their machine account again. The problem of old, unused machine accounts will continue to be a problem in Windows 2000.

Acronym Management

Provide information on what acronyms in groups and shares stand for. Every industry suffers from acronym overload, but the technology business must be the worst. To compound the problem, many people assume that whoever they talk to understands the jargon they use in their own project. With acronym definitions, the account management team can more easily identify a resource or track ownership of the resource.

The Web—or, more specifically, the company's intranet—is a perfect collaborative medium to quickly build a corporate acronym database. All you need is a page with A-to-Z links to bookmarks lower on the page, a starting list you can compile yourself or steal from Appendix D, "Glossary," and a mailto: tag at the top of the page. (A catchy URL helps, too.) Advertise this and encourage new submissions every time someone comes across a new acronym. You'll be amazed at how quickly the list can grow—and the bigger a list, the more useful it is.

Nonstandard Account Management

Establish nonstandard user account policies. Two major types of these accounts are contractor accounts and service accounts:

- In addition to their user information, contractor accounts should have the name of their sponsor or project on which they're working. Because sponsors tend to be hired and released on a frequent basis, these accounts should be often updated for accuracy.

- Service accounts are used for application services, such as backup utilities or scheduling software, that can't use the built-in System account. These accounts present a whole set of problems of their own. They shouldn't change passwords frequently because every service that uses the account on every machine must then be updated from Control Panel, Services, Startup, Logon As. These services can't use user accounts because production services then depend upon a user not changing a password—if this happens, the service will fail.

Terminating Accounts

Delete disabled user accounts after six months. It's a hassle to re-create access to a user's data once the account has been removed. The simplest technique is often to log onto the account and look for connected network drives and the like. Make sure that the disabled account's manager has been notified several times. Wait until the account has been backed up by a full backup, and then remove the account.

Moving Accounts

In a multiple-master-domain environment, moving an account between master domains is a tedious process that involves a lot of manual labor. Most of the work involves determining what to do with the user's data from the old group. Though it's doubtful it will make the initial release, Windows 2000 will eventually have a utility to seamlessly move users from one Windows 2000 domain to another (*prune & graft*, stretching the Windows 2000 tree analogy still further).

New Accounts

A very important first step in the new account process is most often over-looked. In a multiple-master-domain network, ideally you have only one account per employee across all domains. Before creating a new Windows NT account, the account clerk must search to see whether an account exists in any other master domain on the trusted network. If this isn't done, duplicate accounts will be created. In Windows 2000, the user ID has to be unique only within a domain, but there's no question that having a unique ID across the network will make working in the thousands of non-Active Directory-enabled applications easier.

Multidomain Access Issues

If you have independent groups administering their own master domains, these groups must have a smooth way of passing customer requests between them so that the customer doesn't suffer. Some possible solutions are listed here:

- Direct access "back door" phone lines between administrators, bypassing queues
- Special ticket queues
- Some other kind of rights granted for each administrative group in the other master domains

The basic tenet of managing users among several administrative groups is simple: If administrators in Domain A don't have rights in Domain B, they must have immediate access to people who do have administrative rights in B. This problem will get much worse in Windows 2000 because security can be delegated to many administrative groups instead of just a few. A user in one organizational unit managed by a few local administrators may have problems accessing a server administered by another small group. Unlike the larger administrative bodies working with Windows NT 4 domains, these two groups may not have any well-established back doors or ticket queues to get the user's problem quickly resolved.

There are conflicting needs in how to populate an ACL in the Windows NT file system. On one hand, it's smart administrative policy to require that only groups, not user accounts, are put directly in ACLs. Doing this ensures that looking at an account will list all the resources to which an account has access. Otherwise, if an account must move for some reason (job change, domain migration, and so on), there's no way to know what resources it accesses. The only way to tell is to move it and see what breaks. This approach is impossible when high security is required because anyone with account operator rights can alter the membership of a group and thereby allow access to the resource.

The Employee Termination Process

Quickly and correctly dealing with the computer accounts of terminated employees is an important security issue, but it's one that's often performed haphazardly. Here's a possible process to handle the Windows NT account(s) of a terminated employee:

1. A daily feed of terminated employees is received from a corporate database. It's programmatically compared with the accounts in the Windows NT enterprise network (all account domains), so notification doesn't depend on someone calling from Human Resources.

2. Locate the employee's account(s), and disable it.

3. Promptly change the password of any administration accounts to which the employee may have had access. Locate the user's personal share, if applicable, and rename the on-disk directory to DISABLED_<account name>.

   Keep the share name the same so that the ex-employee's manager can review and move the data. It's easy for administrators to see, but it doesn't affect access of the person cleaning up the share. You will have to re-share the directory after renaming it.

4. Contact the ex-employee's manager. Get from this person the account(s) authorized to review the account, and add them to the access permissions. Assign a drop-dead date: one month from the date of termination. After one month, remove the share (hopefully prodding old coworkers to action when the data is "gone"). After two months, back up the data to a special "terminated employees" backup that's kept for one year.

5. After one year, delete the account, share, and directory.

A solid process for dealing with terminated employees is a critical part of your system security. I know of employees who have left a company and have been able to access important systems for months afterward. A good process here is especially important because of the circumstances under which the employee might have left.

Summary

Security and account management is an area that demands careful attention to system settings, that benefits tremendously from automated tools, and that must have well-defined processes surrounding all aspects of account management. The basic system as it comes out of the box isn't secure enough for the corporate environment, so you must tighten the screws on the network and monitor the event logs to stay aware of the server's state.

Finally, you must build up a solid foundation of management processes, based on security and account strategies, to hold together a large Windows NT network. It's very often overlooked because process work doesn't offer any buttons to push or GUIs to manipulate. System and IT policies must take over where this still-maturing operating system leaves off.

Part **V**

Appendixes

Working with Microsoft Support

Microsoft isn't the only company that supports its own products—it's just the best-known. It's also debatable whether this company is the best at it. Hewlett-Packard, Compaq (the Digital part, at least), and others have large and well-respected Microsoft support groups. There's no arguing, however, that Microsoft has the highest visibility for supporting its stuff. After all, isn't it logical to go to the source?

When Microsoft first dipped into networking software, the company marketed a product co-developed with IBM called LAN Manager (a.k.a. LANMAN). In those days, Microsoft was mainly a company that sold shrink-wrapped desktop software through retail channels. LANMAN was not a significant source of revenue for the company. At that time, dealing with Microsoft on enterprise issues was like the old television commercial where a finger pushed the Pillsbury Doughboy in the belly: It had an immediate effect, but as soon as you removed your finger, you couldn't tell that anything had happened.

Since then, Microsoft has been bending over backward to prove to the large-scale computing community that it can indeed support the big corporate customers in the manner they demand. They aren't there yet, but they've improved a lot since the LANMAN days. Their support model continues to improve, but the basic Microsoft culture of "we're the best" hinders their customer responsiveness. And as with many U.S.-based companies, change and improvements made in the United States can take a long time to trickle down to the international offices.

Microsoft's Premier support is the most common method by which the large corporate customer gets Microsoft product support. Depending on how many products you put on Premier support and how many contacts are authorized, it can get very expensive—up to seven figures in large corporations with many products and contacts. In most cases, only a few contacts are given, usually in the centralized IT organization. If you aren't in that IT organization and would like to be able to submit a service request (SR), you need to find out how to work through that organization. Often there isn't any policy on how to do this because of the expense and time associated with an SR.

Problem Resolution

The SR is the method by which you submit problems to Microsoft for resolution. You can submit one by phone or the Web. Submitting SRs by the Web has the advantage of a documented track by both parties of the problem's life cycle. SRs by telephone are often faster than the Web and therefore are more appropriate for time-critical problems.

Most Premier contracts allow a limited number of SRs to be submitted in a year under the cost of a contract; beyond this number of SRs, an addition charge is levied. Even under the cost of a five-figure Premier account, each submitted SR costs between $100 and $200. (If Microsoft determines it's a bug in its product, though, they don't charge you.) Obviously, in an enterprise environment, if a senior support person must spend more than a day looking at a problem, it's cost-effective to submit an SR. If you aren't a member of the group that has the Premier contacts, you must work through that group to get an SR submitted.

After you find out who has a Premier account number, getting that person or group to submit an SR for you is still not an easy task. The "keepers of the SRs" are often reluctant to spend an SR—as well as their time to submit it and manage it—on *you* unless you provide a very convincing case. If your organizational structure is set up so that you can easily forward problems to be submitted as SRs, consider yourself lucky because you're in the minority! This is the best way to take advantage of a Premier account; but to keep the numbers down, potential SRs should go through some kind of review process or board to determine whether they should be submitted.

The Technical Account Manager and the Customer Service Manager

Each Premier account has a technical account manager (TAM) and a customer service manager (CSM). A TAM is the main go-between for your company and Microsoft. The TAM is the person who handles all technical issues between your company and Microsoft that aren't specifically entered as SRs. The TAM also monitors the status of open SRs to ensure that they're being handled quickly enough. A TAM needs to be well-connected and respected; without this, his usefulness is limited. My experience with six TAMs over several years has been less than stellar. I've had only one TAM I considered outstanding, and we lost him after several months when he was promoted to manage other TAMs. A TAM is a difficult job; while your customers demand instant response and the inside track from them, in Microsoft's meritocracy they're considered pests because their job is to bug people to get things done quicker, to get inside information, to complain for the customer's behalf, and so on. This partly explains the rapid turnover of the position.

Tip

Try to find out how good your TAM is from someone else in the Microsoft support organization who will tell you the truth. Generally, the support techies in the trenches that work with your SRs will give it to you straight if you get one that works in the same support center as your TAM. A dedicated, onsite TAM might be worth the expense if you have one or more high-availability projects that are very expensive or high risk (say, $25K per day). A good example would be a Web server used for electronic order processing.

Have regularly scheduled meetings with your TAM to discuss open SRs, work in progress, and any other issues before they grow large. You must build a working relationship with the TAM to really get the most out of one.

The biggest mistake most accounts make is to not put the appropriate customer service manager in charge of the Premier account or carefully chosen senior, reliable, and methodical SR contacts. Submitting an SR means a lot of work on your side as well as Microsoft's. You must do your own "due diligence" on the problem before you submit it, and be prepared to be available to work on the problem when you get a callback.

If a company has more than 5,000 client PCs and is running mission-critical software on Microsoft platforms, consider paying for an Enterprise Program Manager (EPM). This may save much more in the long run than it costs. The EPM will help architect solutions correctly based on experience with a number of other large companies, which will save you money by doing it right the first time. ◆

The CSM is supposed to be the main contact for all non-technical issues between your company and Microsoft. This includes Premier contract issues, licensing questions, purchasing questions, and the general state of communication between Microsoft and your company. The technical contributor generally has very little communication with the CSM, but it's always good to have this person's name and number in your contacts list just in case.

Supportability Review

If you have a Premier support contract with Microsoft, one service that's offered is the supportability review. A supportability review is a technical assessment of or a recommendation for your designs and plans to deploy or upgrade Microsoft products. Each Premier account is entitled to one supportability review per year. Your TAM and a team of Microsoft consultants who specialize in supportability reviews perform the review. The supportability review report typically includes the following steps:

1. Orientation meeting—This two-hour telephone meeting with your TAM and other representatives who will work with the Premier support team on the review addresses the objectives, scope, and documentation to be shared, as well as the format of the final report.

2. Technical information review—During this phase, the review team gathers the information it requires to perform the review. They may also conduct additional interviews with members of your staff.

3. Plan analysis—After reviewing your plan and gathering additional information, the supportability review team evaluates potential problems in the plan. Team members use their experience with Microsoft products and their knowledge of many kinds of customer environments to recommend actions.

4. Supportability report—The supportability review team summarizes its research results. Further assistance with specific supportability issues is available by telephone.

5. Report presentation—The report contents are discussed during a teleconference. Your TAM will also follow up within 30 days to determine whether you have any remaining questions.

Each supportability review report includes the following sections:

- Review goals—The areas of analysis covered by the review.
- Summary of results and recommendations—The conclusions of the report, with specific steps the company should take.

- Project objectives—Agreed upon by you and your TAM for this review.
- Review of technical information—Your support plan, completed information template, and other relevant data.
- Detailed results and recommendations—To increase the supportability of the products' deployment, in order of priority. A recommendation marked as high priority will realize the greatest returns, while medium- and low-priority items will realize less tangible gains.
- Customer survey—Included with every supportability review report to help Microsoft gather feedback on the deliverables and the process.

Microsoft Consulting Services

Companies that have large Microsoft technology environments often contract with Microsoft Consulting Services (MCS) for technical expertise. After all, as the rationale goes, who better to consult with than the company itself? MCS's charter is to consult on Microsoft products for businesses of all sizes. Microsoft consultants provide businesses, government agencies, and other large organizations with assistance in planning, building, and managing distributed computing environments using Microsoft technology. By working onsite with the client's staff, they transfer their knowledge of Microsoft technology and how it functions in the client's computing environment.

Technical staff of a client contracting with MCS mainly encounter two types of consultants: consultants and senior consultants. Senior staff and senior management of the client also interact with principal consultants, managing consultants, and enterprise program managers.

MCS Consultants

Reporting to a managing consultant, the consultant's purpose is to assist MCS clients in building mission-critical systems to run on networks of workstations and servers. The consultant's responsibilities include interviewing MCS clients, capturing specific client requirements in concise format, designing and writing code for small systems, maintaining advanced knowledge of a relevant programming language (for example Microsoft C or C++), building relationships with client technical and project management personnel, assisting in building strong relationships with client management, and working together with field sales personnel to support account strategy and control objectives.

MCS Senior Consultants

Like a consultant, the senior consultant also reports to a managing consultant. The senior consultant's purpose is the same as the consultant's; the difference lies in the senior consultant's experience and expertise because this person takes responsibility for larger systems and works with higher management of the client.

The senior consultant's responsibilities include designing large information systems according to client needs; implementing an entire system with all its implications (for example, testing, documenting, and meeting user expectations), and forging relationships with Microsoft technical groups, client groups, and mid-level client management while maintaining a productive interaction. These consultants manage the entire client relationship for small to medium-size accounts under direction of a managing consultant. They also assist the managing consultant with sales of additional service to assigned accounts, maintain advanced knowledge of a relevant programming language, direct day-to-day activities of other consultants, and mentor client and Microsoft personnel in area of expertise.

MCS Principal Consultants

The principal consultant's role is a juggling act of serving as a technical leader to the client, leading other MCS consultants, and managing whole relationships between Microsoft technical groups and upper-level client management. These consultants spend most of their time in boardrooms, not cubicles.

Principal consultants conceive architectural designs for major information subsystems that provide feasible solutions to technical or business problems and opportunities. They provide leadership and advice to support the implementation of large systems, including methodology, design approaches, and architectural and engineering considerations. They maintain advanced knowledge in an area of technological expertise, such as LANs, DBMS, Windows, CASE Tools, and so forth. They develop and deliver presentations in the designated expertise area that can be used for both selling and training. They provide feedback, including suggestions for product improvements, to product groups. They manage the entire relationship with Microsoft technical groups, client groups, and upper-level client management. They assist with sales of professional services to new and existing accounts. They develop medium-term technical plans with other consultants working on a project, providing solid technical leadership. And in their spare time, they direct day-to-day technical activities of other consultants and act as mentors to client and Microsoft personnel in their area of expertise. The MCS Principal Consultant I know works about 70 hours a week.

MCS Managing Consultants

Managing consultants manage three main areas: large projects, a profit and loss statement, and the people of MCS. They are also responsible for selling MCS consulting services to businesses at the upper-management level. Principal and managing consultants are rare; this job is limited to no more than 3% of Microsoft employees.

Enterprise Program Managers

You should consider using an enterprise program manager (EPM) if your investment in Microsoft products is more than $3 million per year. An EPM is a senior-level consultant from Microsoft Consulting Services who works with you in designing and implementing Microsoft products. This onsite consultant combines high-level architecture expertise with a long-term commitment (for which you're paying dearly) and in-depth knowledge of your business, tailoring specific guidance to the way your organization uses technology to achieve its business goals. A key point is that this senior consultant will be around your business long enough to truly understand how it works and how the management personalities and political realities of your business combine to define what's possible and what isn't. A good EPM combines the usefulness of a TAM with heavyweight technical expertise: If this person can't answer a question, he should be able to ask a developer who can.

B

Windows 2000-Related Web Sites

This appendix is a short list of the Windows NT-related Web sites that I refer to on a regular basis. Keep in mind that, as with all Web sites, these might get moved around. Whenever possible, I've tried to stick with the URL that's the most centralized and the least likely to change.

General Sites

- http://www.winntmag.com/. A great starting point, this is the home page of *Windows NT Magazine,* the leading Windows NT-related magazine. This site includes daily news, archived magazine articles, online user communities and forums, Web-only articles, and comprehensive user group listings. It's a very busy home page; they opt for utility over aesthetics.

- http://www.winntsolutions.com/. This is *Windows NT Magazine*'s directory of Windows NT-based solutions. It's searchable and contains thousands of applications.

- http://www.sans.org/. The SANS Institute is a research and education organization of more than 62,000 system administrators, security professionals, and network administrators who help find solutions for challenges they face. This site contains good information, especially related to security.

- http://www.sunbelt-software.com. This is a very good site with all kinds of Windows NT-related information.

- http://www.ntfaq.com/. This is John Savill's FAQ on various Windows NT topics.

Microsoft Support Sites

- http://windowsupdate.microsoft.com/nt5help/Server/en/nt_frame.htm. This is the complete help documentation set for Windows 2000 Server on the Web. It's a fantastic Windows 2000 resource, but not well known. Work your way through this comprehensive documentation, and you'll have a great feel for the scope of this product.

- http://www.microsoft.com/ntserver/. Microsoft's home for Windows NT Server tells you about the latest companies to be assimilated into the Windows NT Collective and tells why you should be running Windows NT on your clock radio. If you keep digging, you'll find documents on Windows 2000 and links to support-related downloads, such as the latest Service Packs and hotfixes.

- http://support.microsoft.com/. The Microsoft Knowledge Base is the database of all support-related information on their products.

- http://technet.microsoft.com/. The Microsoft Technical Network was recently expanded to hold a lot more content on the Web. In addition to its CD-based subscription service, it's the basic technical subscription to which all Windows NT support personnel should have access. It's free with registration and contains tons of documentation—far more than you'll find on the better-known Windows NT Server home.

- http://www.microsoft.com/security/. This security home page for Microsoft products lists all the latest security alerts and fixes.

- http://www.microsoft.com/security/services/bulletin.asp/. The Microsoft product security notification service is a mailing list that sends you a security bulletin (and usually a fix, too) every time a major security alert has been posted.

- ftp://ftp.microsoft.com/bussys/winnt/winnt-public/fixes/usa/. This is Microsoft's FTP site for Windows NT Service Packs and hotfixes.

- http://www.microsoft.com/msj/. This monthly publication, *Microsoft Systems Journal*, talks about technology related to Microsoft products. It's generally geared toward developers, but it also contains good articles for administrators.

Third-Party Vendors

- http://www.sysinternals.com/. This is a collection of unique, remarkable Windows NT tools such as NTFSDOS, BlueSave, ERD Commander, and FAT32 for Windows NT 4 by Mark Russinovich and Bryce Cogswell. Mark is considered by the senior Windows NT community to be the most knowledgeable Windows NT internals consultant outside of Microsoft. Both Mark and Bryce have PhDs in computer engineering from Carnegie-Mellon University.

- http://www.aelita.net/. Aelita Software Group's Web site covers for the event log manager EventAdmin.

- http://www.missioncritical.com/. This is Mission Critical's Web site for its enterprise management tools.

- http://www.ntpsoftware.com. New Technology Partners, the maker of Quota Manager, maintains this site.

- http://www.veritas.com/. This site is maintained by a storage management vendor whose Volume Manager product is the basis for Windows 2000's Disk Manager.

Technology Sites

- http://www.microsoft.com/management/mmc/. Microsoft maintains this MMC (Microsoft Management Console) Web page.

- http://www.microsoft.com/win32dev/base/pnp.htm. This is Microsoft's Plug and Play Web site.

- http://www.microsoft.com/hwdev/ONNOW.HTM. This is Microsoft's OnNow Web site.

- http://www.teleport.com/~acpi/. This is the ACPI (Advanced Configuration and Power Interface) Web page.

- http://www.microsoft.com/hwdev/desinit/WDMview.HTM. Microsoft maintains this WDM (Windows Driver Model) Web page.

- http://developer.intel.com/design/usb/index.htm. Intel's USB (Universal Serial Bus) Web site contains good descriptions of how the product works.

- http://developer.intel.com/technology/1394/index.htm. This is Intel's IEEE 1394 (FireWire) Web page.

- http://www.microsoft.com/hwdev/1394/. Microsoft maintains this IEEE 1394 (FireWire) Web page.

- http://www.i2osig.org/. This is the I_2O (Intelligent I/O) Web page.
- http://www.microsoft.com/hwdev/manageability/default.htm#papers. This is the WMI (Windows Management Instrumentation) Web page.

Windows 2000 Client Startup and Interactive Logon

Understanding what happens when a Windows 2000 client is powered on in a Windows 2000 server-based network, and then what happens when a user logs on from that client, is very important to understand when you're putting together the architecture. When you understand the startup sequence, you can use it to analyze and troubleshoot the various network services that will be servicing the client. You should also apply the Windows NT 4 and Windows 9x startup sequences to your design because you'll probably be living in a mixed environment of Windows 2000 servers and these clients for quite a while The startup sequence for downlevel clients (like NT 4 Workstation) acts exactly as it does for NT 4 Server, because Windows 2000 domain controllers masquerade as NT 4 domain controllers.

Before Startup

Upon powering on, a Windows 2000 domain controller registers itself in DNS with SRV and A records and registers its NetBIOS name with WINS. The A record is registered in DNS so that downlevel clients that don't recognize the SRV record can still look up the domain controller with a standard DNS query. The server is also automatically registered in a Windows 2000 site, although it can be manually changed by the Active Directory sites and Services Manager.

Client Startup

Here's the startup sequence, including some important steps by the domain controller:

1. The client boots and goes through its DHCP D–O–R–A (discover, offer, request, acknowledgement) sequence to receive its IP address, subnet mask, default gateway, and other options. In particular, the client receives the IP addresses of its DNS servers as part of the DHCP configuration.

2. The very first time a Windows 2000 client is booted (i.e., right after it's built or upgraded), it has no idea what site it's in. It issues a DNS query to enumerate the SRV records for _ldap._tcp.*domain.name*.com records in the DNS database, where *domain.name* is the domain it's registered in.

   In English, this means, "give me a list of domain controllers that are in my domain."

3. The client issues a string of CLDAP (connectionless LDAP) pings to all the servers in the list DNS returns, and waits for a reply. (The API that does this—DSGetDCName—has a few options that allow you to specify whether you want a writeable domain controller, any domain controller, or perhaps the domain controller that's masquerading as an NT 4 PDC for the downlevel servers in its domain.)

4. The Netlogon service of the client, which is handling much of this location process, passes along information from the first responding domain controller to the client services. (Using information from the quickest domain controller increases the possibility that, in a very large site, the client sets up a session with a "nearby" domain controller.)

5. The domain controller returns three items to the client:

   - The site the domain controller is in
   - The site the client is in
   - The *closest bit*

   The domain controller determines which site the client is in by comparing the client's subnet (dervied from its IP address and subnet mask) with the contents of the Subnets container (under the Sites container in the Active Directory Sites & Services Manager), and then sends the site name to the client. The closest bit value is 1 if the domain controller is the most network-proximate domain controller, 0 otherwise.

6. If the domain controller has returned a closest bit with a value of 1 to the client, authentication continues. Also, if the client has already tried to find a domain controller in the site in which the domain controller claims the client is located, the client uses this domain controller regardless of how the closest bit is set.

7. If the domain controller has returned a closest bit with a value of 0 ("I'm not the closest domain controller"), the client queries DNS again for a more appropriate domain controller. This time the client knows what site it's in, so it can be more specific. It asks DNS to enumerate the SRV records for `_ldap._tcp.`*`sitename`*`._sites.dc._msdcs.`*`domain`* *`.name`*`.com` records in the DNS database, where *sitename* is the client's site and *domain.name* is the domain he's registered in. The client's last used site is stored in its local registry at `HKLM\SYSTEM\CCS\Services` `\Netlogon\Parameters\DynamicSiteName`.

In English, this means, "Give me a list of domain controllers that are both in my domain and in my site." Unlike the WINS 1C list of domain controllers in Windows NT 4, this ensures (assuming that you've got your sites configured correctly) that only domain controllers that are network-proximate to the client will be queried.

(You can see the list of servers DNS will return from the DNS Manager by looking in the DNS server's forward lookup zone. Drill down into *`domain.name`*, `_msdcs`, `dc`, `_sites`, *`sitename`*, `_tcp`, and double-click on each `_ldap` object.)

8. Once the client has selected a domain controller that's in the same site or the closest that can be found (and obviously in the same domain as the client), authentication will proceed.

Notes

- If the client has changed sites (a traveling laptop user, for example), like the initial startup, it will only query DNS for the domain controllers in its domain. Like the initial startup procedure, the domain controller to respond first to the client's query will return a closest bit value of 0 or 1; the domain controller's site, the client's site, and the selection procedure continue as in Step 7.

- If the DNS server doesn't respond, it's rotated to the bottom of the client's list of DNS servers. (DNS round-robins the SRV records that are returned to the client so that the first server registered with an SRV isn't always the first to be queried by a client.)

- If by some chance there is no domain controller in the client's site, a process known as *site coverage* takes place. (A site might not have a local domain controller because it doesn't have one to begin with (not a smart idea) because it's a small site and it has only one that's crashed, or because there are several domains onsite and not all have domain controllers. When a site has no domain controller, a a domain controller that determnes it's the most network proximate to a client will insert itself into DNS as a domain controller for that client's site. The Netlogon service ensures there's always a domain controller for a site by adding a domain controller that's physically closest ti the site's configuration. This allows the rest of the startup/authentication process to continue as if there really is a domain controller onsite. The consequence is that there's the possibility a server can be registered in more than one site. Another important side effect is that if your subnets aren't close to one another (e.g., 192.168.121.1 is in the same city as 192.168.122.1), site coverage will assign a domain controller that might be on the other side of the world.

Interactive User Logon

After the client has started up in the domain, the Windows 2000 network has another valid portal by which users can access its resources. Before this can happen, though, there's still the small matter of the interactive user logon using Kerberos:

1. The user sits down at his Windows 2000 Professional workstation and hits Ctrl–Alt–Del, the Secure Attention Sequence (SAS).

2. The Winlogon service brings up the Graphical Identification and Authentication (GINA) dynamic link library.

3. The user enters his user ID, or user principal name (UPN), and selects his account domain from the pick list that GINA presents to him.

4. GINA collects the user's account and password and sends them to LSASS, the Local Security Authority Subsystem.

5. LSASS runs the user's password through a one-way hash operation to convert the clear-text password into a secret key. It saves the result in a credentials cache so that the password can be retrieved as needed.

6. LSASS takes the UPN (user principal name, such as JimBob @mycompany.com), the user's account domain, and Windows NT-specific security information known as pre-authentication data, and bundles it (now called the session key) into what's called an *AS* (authentication service) *request*. The pre-authentication data has been encrypted with the secret key derived from the user's password.

7. LSASS works through the Kerberos Security Support Provider (SSP) on the client to send the AS request to the Key Distribution Center on the preferred domain controller.

8. The KDC authenticates the user's logon attempt by comparing the encrypted pre-authentication data to what it develops from its own hashed copy of the user key. Even though it doesn't have the actual password the user typed in at the workstation's console, the KDC does

have the same one-way hashing algorithm. If the two data compare, this means that the user supplied the right password.

9. The KDC builds the user's security token to be included in a ticket-granting ticket (TGT) that will be sent back to the workstation. The TGT contains both a session key (which has been encrypted with the secret key derived from the user's password), and Windows NT-specific authorization data (the user's SID, the SIDs for security groups in the user's account domain in which he's a member, and SIDs for universal groups that include either the user or one of his domain groups).

9a. Of particular interest, universal groups are stored only on Global Catalog servers. This means that the authenticating domain controller must query DNS for a Global Catalog server, which it then contacts to discover the universal groups to which the client may belong. To complete client logon, a Global Catalog server must be available to the authenticating domain controller. Remember that the authenticating domain controller may itself be a Global Catalog server, but that's unlikely because there will be many more domain controllers than Global Catalog servers.

10. The KDC sends the TGT to the client. This ticket-getting ticket is used by the client to get service tickets (used to access server resources) in the user's domain.

11. The first service ticket the client requests on the user's behalf is to access his own workstation. The client sends a session ticket request to the KDC, which includes among other things the user's TGT and an authenticator that has been encrypted with the session key (refer back to Step 6) that the user shares with the KDC.

12. The KDC responds to the request. The response contains two parts: a session key for the user to share with his own workstation (encrypted with the session key he shares with the KDC), and the user's session ticket to his workstation (encrypted with the secret key his workstation shares with the KDC). The session ticket includes both a session key for the workstation to share with the user and authorization data copied from the user's TGT.

13. LSASS decrypts the user's session ticket with the computer's secret key and extracts his authorization data. It then queries the local SAM database to discover whether the user is a member of any security groups local to the computer and whether he has been given any special privileges on the local machine. The LSASS adds any SIDs returned by this query to the list taken from the ticket's authorization data. The entire list is then used to build an access token, and a handle to the token is returned to the Winlogon service, along with an identifier for the user's logon session and confirmation that his logon information was valid.

14. Winlogon creates a window station and several desktop objects for the user, attaches the access token, and starts the shell process the user will use to interact with the computer. The user's access token is subsequently inherited by any application process started during the logon session.

The user is now logged onto the Windows 2000 network—and, believe it or not, it's faster than a Windows NT 4 NTLM logon.

After Client Startup

The client retains its list of domain controllers in its domain. It refreshes its cache on a regular basis by going through the startup sequence again, which guarantees a reasonably dynamic list of local domain controllers.

Glossary

Sometimes we're loath to admit it, but humor columnist Dave Barry skewers the situation squarely: "The computer world has a language all its own, just like Hungary, the difference being that if you hang around with Hungarians long enough, you eventually start to understand what they're talking about; whereas the language used in the computer world is specifically designed to prevent this from happening." (*Dave Barry In Cyberspace*, Crown, 1996)

This appendix is an attempt to stay ahead of the flood of new acronyms arriving with Windows 2000 and to reacquaint you with some old ones. Use it as a handy reference when you're blindsided by a furtive little acronym in the Microsoft documentation. Many of the entries have some kind of explanation; those that don't either are considered very basic or would require too long-winded an explanation.

A   Address record. A DNS resource record that maps a fully qualified domain name to an IP address.

ACE   Access control entry. The basic unit of NTFS security that is associated with an NTFS object and that contains a SID and an access level.

ACL   Access control list. The Windows NT File System element that contains a list of access control entries.

ACPI   Advanced configuration and power interface.

ADSI   Active Directory Service Interfaces. A programming interface to simplify accessing Active Directory objects.

adversary   Generic term in the security field for an individual(s) attempting to crack a system.

Alpha   A RISC microprocessor made by Compaq Computer Corporation.

API   Application programming interface. The documented pathways that programs use to ask the operating system to perform some function.

ATM   Asynchronous Transfer Mode. A high-speed network technology capable of transferring data at rates of 25Mbps to 622Mbps.

attribute   A characteristic of an object. In Windows 2000—especially when replication is discussed—it's often called a *property*.

basic disk   Any disk that has been initialized with a utility such as FDISK that existed before Disk Management in Windows 2000.

BIOS   Basic Input/Output System.

Blue Screen of Death   The blue screen displaying system information when the operating system fatally crashes. Officially known in Microsoft as a STOP error (old OS/2 term) or a bugcheck.

CA   Certificate Authority. A service such as Microsoft Certificate Server that issues digital certificates.

CDFS   Compact Disc File System. The file system used on CD-ROMs (ISO 9660).

child domain   A Windows 2000 domain whose DNS name is subordinate to another. For example, `research.mycompany.com` is a child domain of `mycompany.com`.

CIFS   Common Internet File Sharing.

ciphertext   Encrypted data.

CLDAP   Connectionless LDAP.

cluster   Individual computers connected to act as a single whole computer.

Connection object   A unidirectional replication path between two domain controllers. Two connection objects are required for the bidirectional ring used in Active Directory replication.

container   Holds groups of objects and other containers.

crack   An attack, either externally or internally, on a system's security to gain unauthorized access.

cryptography   Protecting data by changing it into an unreadable format (encryption). Returning the data to a readable format is decryption.

CSP   Cryptographic service provider.

CSRSS   Client/server runtime subsystem. The Windows NT/Windows 2000 Win32 subsystem.

DCDEMO   A colloquialism for executing the DCPROMO operation that demotes a domain controller. The command doesn't really exist; it's just an easier way to describe the act of demoting a domain controller.

DCPROMO   The wizard that promotes a Windows 2000 member or standalone server to a domain controller. Running this program on a domain controller demotes it back to a member or standalone server.

DDNS   Dynamic DNS. DNS records are updated dynamically by DHCP and Windows 2000 clients instead of the traditional method of manually adding them to (static) DNS.

delegation   The ability of a higher administrative authority to grant specific rights to groups and individuals.

Dfs   Distributed file system.

DHCP   Dynamic Host Configuration Protocol.

digital certificate   An attachment to a data stream that confirms the identity of the sender or encrypts the data.

DN   Distinguished name. A unique description of the object and its path in the Active Directory. For example,
`/O=Internet/DC=COM/DC=Intel/CN=Users/CN=Sean Deuby`.

DNS   Domain Name System. The IP-address-to-name-resolution system of the Internet.

domain tree   A hierarchy of Windows 2000 domains, connected by transitive trusts, that form a contiguous namespace.

DORA   A mnemonic for client-DHCP lease assignment:
D = discovery
O = offer
R = request
A = acknowledgment

downlevel   Any object at an earlier release level than the target object. For example, Windows NT 4 systems are downlevel systems compared to Windows 2000.

downlevel trust   A trust explicitly established between a Windows 2000 domain and a Windows NT 4 domain.

DSA   Directory System Agent. The process that manages the Active Directory's physical storage.

DSCLIENT   Directory Service Client. The Win9x add-on to make these operating systems Active Directory aware.

dynamic disk   A disk that supports volume sets after you use Windows 2000's Disk Management utility to convert it from basic to dynamic storage.

EFS   Encrypting File System.

EISA   Extended Industry Standard Architecture. The successor to ISA and the predecessor to the PCI bus architecture.

EMA   Enterprise Memory Architecture. A Windows 2000 improvement that allows applications to address up to 64GB of virtual memory.

encryption   The process of taking readable text (plaintext) and rendering it unreadable (ciphertext) by applying an encryption algorithm.

explicit trust   A trust manually established between two Windows 2000 domains (in addition to their built-in transitive trusts with one another, if they're in the same forest).

extranet   A corporate intranet that can be accessed by authorized users outside the corporation.

FAT   File Allocation Table. Microsoft's original file system for MS-DOS, still used today.

FAT32   The successor to the File Allocation Table file system.

first-layer domain   A Windows 2000 domain whose parent domain is the root domain (or domains, in a forest).

folder   A directory (or what may appear to be a directory).

forest   A set of one or more domain trees that don't form a contiguous namespace.

FQDN   Fully Qualified Domain Name. A DNS term that describes a host name plus the full path, listing all domain memberships from left to right. For example, res-server1.research.mycompany.com.

FSMO   Flexible single master object. The master copy for certain internal Active Directory functions, such as schema changes and PDCs for downlevel Windows NT 4 clients. The term is being phased out in favor of *operations master*.

FTP   File Transfer Protocol.

GINA   Graphical Identification and Authentication. The subsystem that handles the logon presentation to the user.

Global Catalog   An index containing every Active Directory object, but only a few attributes. Used for quickly locating an object outside the local domain.

GPO   Group policy object.

GUI   Graphical user interface. *See* UI.

GUID   Global unique identifier. Pronounced "gwid." A 128-bit number guaranteed to be unique and used to uniquely identify any object in the Active Directory. Can be thought of as Son of SID.

hack   Verb: To access a system's functions in a nonstandard manner. For example, "I hacked the registry with a '1' in the ShutdownWithoutLogon" key, so now I can shut down right after Ctrl+Alt+Del." Noun: A person or program that can access a system's functions in a nonstandard manner. For example, "There's a registry hack in the Resource Kit that will let you do that." *Compare with* crack.

HAL   Hardware Abstraction Layer. The software in the Windows NT kernel that maps a specific server's hardware to the operating system.

HDD   Hard disk drive.

HSM   Hierarchical storage management. A data storage system that automatically moves data between high-cost and low-cost media, based on parameters the administrator sets.

HTML   Hypertext Markup Language.

HTTP   Hypertext Transfer Protocol.

IA   Intel Architecture. PCs that are descendants of the original IBM PC architecture (in contrast to Alpha or Sparc architecture).

IETF   Internet Engineering Task Force.

inheritance   The capability of a child object to automatically acquire specific rights from a parent object.

Internet   The worldwide network of computer networks.

intranet   A corporate internal network. Usually referred to in the context of Web services, with an implied firewall between the corporation and the Internet.

IPsec   IP-level security for authentication and encryption.

ISA   Industry Standard Architecture. The original PC bus architecture.

ISD   Independent software developer.

IT   Information technology. Usually used to describe the group charged with the enterprise's computing infrastructure.

KCC   Knowledge Consistency Checker. An Active Directory function that monitors and dynamically configures replication connectors between domain controllers.

KDC   Key Distribution Center. A Kerberos function, running on every domain controller, that controls the issue of keys and tickets.

Kerberos   An authentication protocol, defined by the IETF in RFC 1510.

key   A password, usually encrypted. It may or may not be publicly available.

key pair   Public key infrastructure. A key pair consists of a public key and a private key, used together to encrypt and decrypt data.

LAN   Local area network.

LDAP   Lightweight Directory Access Protocol. A small and fast protocol, based on X.500's Directory Access Protocol, that is the core protocol used for communication with the Active Directory.

MAC address   Media Access Control address. A hardware address, encoded into every NIC, that uniquely identifies each node of a network.

MAN   Metropolitan area network. A network most often used to connect different business campuses that are separated by distances larger than a LAN can support, but not so great as to require a WAN.

MCSE   Microsoft Certified Systems Engineer.

MDHCP   Multicast DHCP.

MDI   Multiple document interface. Specifically refers to the MMC.

MFT   Master file table. The relational database at the heart of the NTFS volume structure that contains all information about files on that volume.

MIS   Management of Information Systems, or Microsoft Indexing Service.

MMC   Microsoft Management Console. The UI framework to which you add snap-ins to perform management tasks.

MPR   Multiprotocol routing.

MSCS   Microsoft Clustering Service.

multihomed   A server that has two or more NICs and therefore multiple network connections.

mutual authentication   A feature of authentication protocols such as Kerberos. Both client and server must prove their identity before authentication proceeds.

namespace   Any bounded area in which a name can be resolved. In the case of the Active Directory, a namespace is equal to a directory tree, within which names are resolved by DNS.

NBT   NetBIOS over TCP/IP.

NC   Naming context.

NetBEUI   NetBIOS Enhanced User Interface. A small, fast protocol for use in unrouted networks.

NetBIOS   Network Basic Input/Output System.

NIC   Network interface card.

NOS   Network operating system.

NSS   Native Structured Storage. A Windows 2000 feature for storing ActiveX documents.

NTFS   Windows NT File System.

NTLM   Windows NT LanMan authentication protocol. The primary Windows NT 4 security protocol.

object   A collection of attributes or characteristics that represents something.

OEM   Original equipment manufacturer, such as Compaq, Dell, or IBM.

OID   Object identifier.

OS   Operating system.

OSI   Open System Interconnection. A networking framework for implementing network protocols between computers in seven layers.

parent domain   A Windows 2000 domain that has another domain subordinate to it in the DNS namespace. `mycompany.com` is a parent domain of `research.mycompany.com`.

PCI   Peripheral Component Interconnect. A current bus architecture.

PKI   Public key infrastructure.

plaintext   Unencrypted data.

POTS   Plain old telephone system.

private key   One-half of a key pair, used to decrypt data that was encrypted with the same user's public key.

property   A characteristic of an object. Often used interchangeably with *attribute*.

PSE36   Page Size Extension 36-bit. A Windows NT device driver that's used to take advantage of physical memory greater than 4GB on Intel Pentium II Xeon processors.

PTR   Pointer record. A DNS resource record that maps an IP address to a (fully qualified domain) name. Often referred to as a *reverse lookup record*.

public key   One-half of PKI that is used to encrypt data.

RAID   Redundant Array of Independent Disks.

RAS   Remote Access Service.

replication topology   The configuration of the replication schema between domain controllers.

RFC   Request for comments. The basic Internet documentation standard.

RID   Relative identifier. A component of the SID.

RISC   Reduced instruction set computer. The counterpart of the IA architecture whose best-known examples are Compaq's Alpha and Sun's Sparc.

root domain   The top-level domain in a Windows 2000 domain tree. Also the top-level DNS domain in the Internet.

RR   Resource record. A DNS zone file entry.

RRAS   Routing and Remote Access Service.

RSA   A well-known public key algorithm, invented by Rivest, Shamir, and Adleman.

RSS   Remote storage service. HSM for Windows 2000.

SAM   Security accounts manager.

SAS   Secure attention sequence. Otherwise known as the three-finger salute: Ctrl+Alt+Del.

Schema   The definition of all the object types that can be stored in the Active Directory.

SCSI   Small computer serial interface. Pronounced "scuzzy."

shortcut trust   An explicit trust established for the purpose of circumventing the trust referral process up and down the directory tree.

SID   Security identifier. A unique number by which a user is identified in a Windows NT domain.

signed data   Data with a digital certificate attached as proof of origin or authenticity.

site   A collection of domain controllers that have high-speed connections. They are defined by the subnets the domain controllers are in.

site connector   The link (usually TCP/IP) over which replication between two sites occurs.

site link   A means of weighting the relative cost of replication between sites.

SMP   Symmetric multiprocessing.

snap-in   A management object that is added to the MMC to handle tasks such as Active Directory management and disk defragmentation.

SNMP   Simple Network Management Protocol.

SOA RR   Start of authority resource record.

Sparc   RISC microprocessor made by Sun Microsystems.

sparse file   A large file that has been preallocated but is mostly empty, such as a database log file.

SSP   Security support provider.

SSPI   Security support provider interface.

T1   A permanently connected telecom line that supports data rates of 1.544Mbps. It's most often used for interconnecting businesses over WANs.

T3   A permanently connected telecom line that supports data rates of 43Mbps. It's most often used for interconnecting businesses over WANs.

TCO   Total cost of ownership.

TCP/IP   Transmission Control Protocol/Internet Protocol.

ticket   A Kerberos object that contains user information, access rights, an expiration time, and more information. Like an electronic driver's license for the user.

TLD   Top-level domain.

transitive trust   A trust established between Windows 2000 domains that allows referrals from one domain to another.

UDF   Universal Disk Format. The successor to CDFS.

UDP   User Datagram Protocol.

UI   User interface. Also called *graphical user interface*, but the "G" tends to be dropped because just about all user interfaces are graphic these days.

UNC   Universal naming convention. A "universal" convention that is used only in Microsoft networks, with the syntax `\\server\share\directory\file.ext`.

UPN   User principal name. A "friendly" name used to reference a user in the Active Directory. For example, `sean.deuby@intel.com`.

URL   Uniform resource locator. The addressing method of the Internet whose syntax is `protocol//server-DNS-name/directory/file`.

USB   Universal serial bus.

USN   Update sequence number. A 64-bit unique number used to track updates to Active Directory properties. Integral to the replication scheme.

VAR   Value-added reseller. For example, Fry's, CompUSA.

VLM   Very large memory. Superseded by EMA.

WAN   Wide area network.

WBEM   Web-based enterprise management.

WINS   Windows Internet Naming Service.

WMI   Windows Management Instrumentation.

X.500   A directory information model. Very complete, but very cumbersome. Many current directories are derived from X.500 but are not fully X.500–compliant because there's too much overhead. The Active Directory is X.500–derived.

X.509   A digital certificate standard.

The following Web-based glossaries provide further information:

- Microsoft's Windows 2000 glossary:
  `http://windowsupdate.microsoft.com/nt5help/Server/en/glossary_srv.htm`

- Microsoft's own glossary, at least for hardware:
  `http://www.microsoft.com/hwdev/glossary.htm`

- PC Webopaedia. A very useful, fun place to just browse. Many of the definitions list sites that discuss the acronym's topic:
  `http://www.webopaedia.com/`

Index

C

O

dedicated, compared to multiple
   applications, 154-155
DHCP servers
   authorizing, 105-106
   rogue server detection, 105
disk I/O, tuning, 202-204
domain controllers, startup, 409
expandability, 156
fault tolerance, 129-130
   disk controllers, 130-131
   PCI Hot Plug, 130
   RAID, 131-139
   recommendations, 139-142
file servers, 149
firewall servers, 151
fragmentation, 186-187
hardware, 111
   *homogeneous versus
      heterogeneous hardware
      environments, 149-153*
   I/O subsystem, 121-127
   memory, 117-120
   *NICs (network interface
      cards), 128*
   processors, 112-116
infrastructure servers, 150-151
member servers, upgrading, 291
memory, tuning, 197-201
naming conventions, 164-165
network configuration,
   displaying, 351
network I/O, tuning, 204-207
network operating system
   environments, 153-154
network statistics, displaying, 352
OEM support, 156
OS build (tactical documents), 335
partitions, 159-161
   FAT versus NTFS, 161-162
   OS partition, 160-161

   recommendations, 163-164
   system partition, 159
preparations for upgrading to
   Windows 2000, 272
print servers, 150
problem-solving, dead servers,
   348-349
processors, tuning, 195-197
production servers (operations
   group), 340
rebuilding, 348
reliability, 156
scalability, 129
security roles
   changes in Windows 2000, 71
   domain controller, 71
   multimaster replication, 71
sessions, displaying, 356
software
   hotfixes, 187-188
   *maintenance recommendations,
      191-192*
   Service Packs, 188-189
   system dump files, 189-191
viruses, 185-186
WINS servers
   configuration, 257-258
   recommendations, 258-259
service accounts, 391
**service level agreements (SLAs),
   policy documents, 335**
Service Packs, 188-189
service requests (SRs), 398
session setups (Kerberos), 85-88
sessions, displaying, 357
shared disk clusters, 144
**shared networks, displaying
   information, 355**
**shared nothing model
   (clustering), 144**

X-Z

New Riders Professional Library

Michael Masterson, Herman Kneif, Scott Vinick, and Eric Roul:
Windows NT DNS
(ISBN: 1-56205-943-2)

Sandra Osborne:
Windows NT Registry
(ISBN: 1-56205-941-6)

Mark Edmead and Paul Hinsburg:
Windows NT Performance Monitoring, Benchmarking, and Tuning
(ISBN: 1-56205-942-4)

Karanjit Siyan:
Windows NT TCP/IP
(ISBN: 1-56205-887-8)

Ted Harwood:
Windows NT Terminal Server and Citrix MetaFrame
(ISBN: 1-56205-944-0)

Anil Desai:
Windows NT Network Management: Reducing Total Cost of Ownership
(ISBN: 1-56205-946-7)

Eric K. Cone, Jon Boggs, and Sergio Perez:
Planning for Windows 2000
(ISBN: 0-7357-0048-6)

Doug Hauger, Marywynne Leon, and William C. Wade III:
Implementing Exchange Server
(ISBN: 1-56205-931-9)

Janice Rice Howd:
Exchange System Administration
(ISBN: 0-7357-0081-8)

Sean Baird and Chris Miller:
SQL Server Administration
(ISBN: 1-56205-955-6)